The Adaptation of Long-Term Gas Sale Agreements by Arbitrators

International Arbitration Law Library

VOLUME 41

Editor

Professor Julian D.M. Lew QC has been involved with international arbitration for more than 40 years as counsel, as arbitrator and as an academic. He has held the position of Professor and Head of the School on International Arbitration, Centre for Commercial Law studies, Queen Mary University of London since its creation in 1985. He is now an independent arbitrator at 20 Essex Street, London.

Introduction

Since its first volume published in 1993, this authoritative practitioner-oriented series has published in-depth and analytical works on niche aspects of international arbitration, authored by specialists in the field.

Objective

This authoritative and established series covering in-depth analyses of niche areas appeals to both practitioners and academics.

Frequency

A volume is published whenever an interesting topic presents itself.

The titles published in this series are listed at the end of this volume.

The Adaptation of Long-Term Gas Sale Agreements by Arbitrators

Pietro Ferrario

Published by:
Kluwer Law International B.V.
PO Box 316
2400 AH Alphen aan den Rijn
The Netherlands
Website: www.wolterskluwerlr.com

Sold and distributed in North, Central and South America by:
Wolters Kluwer Legal & Regulatory U.S.
7201 McKinney Circle
Frederick, MD 21704
United States of America
Email: customer.service@wolterskluwer.com

Sold and distributed in all other countries:
Quadrant
Rockwood House
Haywards Heath
West Sussex
RH16 3DH
United Kingdom
Email: international-customerservice@wolterskluwer.com

MIX
FSC® C103993

Printed on acid-free paper.

ISBN 978-90-411-8232-6

e-Book: ISBN 978-90-411-8616-4
web-PDF: ISBN 978-90-411-8617-1

© 2017 Kluwer Law International BV, The Netherlands

All rights reserved. No part of this publication may be reproduced, stored in a retrieval system, or transmitted in any form or by any means, electronic, mechanical, photocopying, recording, or otherwise, without written permission from the publisher.

Permission to use this content must be obtained from the copyright owner. Please apply to: Permissions Department, Wolters Kluwer Legal & Regulatory U.S., 76 Ninth Avenue, 7th Floor, New York, NY 10011-5201, USA. Website: www.wolterskluwerlr.com

Printed in the United Kingdom.

To my grandfather, Italo

About the Author

Pietro Ferrario was born in Milan (Italy) on 7 June 1980. He graduated in law in 2003 at Bocconi University of Milan and passed the bar exam in 2006. In 2008, he received an LLM in International Business Law (with focus on International Commercial Arbitration) from Queen Mary University of London and in 2015, he received a Ph.D. degree (research field in International Arbitration) from Bocconi University of Milan.

Since April 2010, he has been working in the litigation and commercial law department of 'Perani Pozzi Associati' in Milan. Previously, he worked from more than four years for the law firm 'Rucellai&Raffaelli', always based in Milan and, between 2009–2010, he got a six months internship in the international arbitration group at Wilmer Hale LLP in London.

He published the following articles in arbitration:

'*The Group of Companies doctrine in International Commercial Arbitration: is there any reason for this doctrine to exist?*', Journal of International Arbitration, 2009;

'*Challenge to Arbitrators: Where a Counsel and an Arbitrator Share the Same Office - The Italian Perspective*' Journal of International Arbitration, 2010;

'*The Role of Arbitration in Company Law Disputes - The Italian Perspective*' Young Arbitration Review, 2011.

Table of Contents

About the Author		vii
Preface		xiii

CHAPTER 1
The Gas Market and the Relevant Agreements   1
§1.01   Introduction   1
§1.02   The Gas Market and Sale Agreements   2
       [A]   The Evolution of the Dutch Market and Relevant Gas Sale Contracts   4
       [B]   The Evolution of the UK Market and Relevant Gas Sale Contracts   8
       [C]   The Evolution of the Norwegian Market and Relevant Gas Sale Contracts   11
       [D]   The Evolution of the US Market and Relevant Gas Sale Contracts   13
       [E]   The Evolution of the Russian Market and Relevant Gas Sale Contracts   17
       [F]   The Evolution of the Algerian Market and Relevant Gas Sale Contracts   20
§1.03   The Development of Gas Spot Markets   21
§1.04   The 2009 Crisis   27
§1.05   Conclusions   28

CHAPTER 2
Take or Pay Clauses   31
§2.01   Introduction   31
§2.02   Main Characteristics   32
§2.03   The Nature of Take or Pay Clauses   35
       [A]   The Common Law Approach   36

		[1]	English Law	36
			[a] The Distinction Between Penalties and Liquidated Damages	36
			[b] The Distinction Between Debts and Damages	42
			[c] Take or Pay Clauses as Penalties	48
			[d] Take or Pay Clauses as Main Obligations	53
		[2]	US Law	54
			[a] Take or Pay Clauses as Main Obligations	54
			[b] Take or Pay Clauses as Penalties	59
		[3]	Australian Law	61
	[B]	The Civil Law Approach		62
§2.04	Conclusions			65

CHAPTER 3
The Adaptation of Long-Term Gas Sale Agreements by Arbitrators
Contracts Without an Adaptation Clause — 71

§3.01 Introduction — 71
§3.02 Price Review and Hardship Clauses — 79
§3.03 The Procedural Applicable Law Perspective — 84
  [A] Conservative Legal Systems — 88
    [1] The French Legal System — 88
    [2] The Belgian Legal System — 94
    [3] The Swiss Legal System — 99
    [4] The Common Law — 102
  [B] Semi-conservative Legal Systems – The Italian Legal System — 114
  [C] Non-conservative Legal Systems — 121
    [1] The German Legal System — 121
    [2] The Dutch Legal System — 125
    [3] The Swedish Legal System — 130
  [D] Conclusions on the Procedural Law Perspective — 133
  [E] Arbitration Rules — 137
§3.04 The International Arbitration Perspective — 138
§3.05 The Scope of the Arbitration Agreement and Arbitrability — 144
§3.06 Conclusions — 149

CHAPTER 4
The Adaptation of Long-Term Gas Sale Agreements by Arbitrators
Contracts with an Adaptation Clause — 167

§4.01 Introduction — 167
§4.02 ICC Case n. 10351/2001 — 169
§4.03 The *Atlantic* Case — 172
§4.04 ICC Cases n. 9812/1999 and n. 13504/2007 — 177
  [A] ICC Case n. 9812/1999 — 178
  [B] ICC Case n. 13504/2007 — 182

§4.05	The *Quintette* Case	185
§4.06	The *Esso* Case	189
§4.07	Conclusions	191

Bibliography	195
Table of Cases	205
Index	213

Preface

This book deals with the issue of the adaptation of long-term gas sale agreements by arbitrators upon the occurrence of unforeseen events altering their balance. The power of courts and arbitrators to adjust contracts is, in general, a controversial and discussed matter that assumes a particular importance in relation to long-term gas sale agreements due to their specific features and scope as well as to the recent renegotiation processes and arbitration proceedings regarding the modification of the price formula and of the minimum purchase volume obligations therein provided. With regard to the characteristics, gas sale agreements usually have a long duration and require relevant investments. Moreover, they include a price formula, normally linking the gas price to that of oil products, and the so called 'take or pay clauses', i.e., clauses providing, on the one hand, for the buyer's obligation to take and pay for a minimum quantity of gas every year or just to pay for it (and take it later) and, on the other, for the seller's obligation to supply such quantity. In this way, the seller is granted a stable flux of money necessary to recover the investments made, while the buyer is granted a stable flux of gas in order to cope with the demand in the market in which it operates. It is clear that, in order to reach such purpose, the parties aim to preserve their relationship for the entire duration agreed. However, in this lapse of time, the original market conditions may change and alter the contractual *equilibrium* originally found by the parties. Therefore, in such case, it is necessary to adapt the agreement in order to rebalance it and, consequently, to keep it alive. For this reason, the parties often, but not always, provide for adjustment clauses – and, in particular, with regard to the price and the minimum purchase volume obligations – establishing the duty to renegotiate the contract's terms upon the occurrence of unforeseen events. Moreover, even in case such provisions are included in the agreement, not always the renegotiation process is successful and, consequently, the parties submit the matter to arbitration (due to their international nature, gas sale contracts usually provide for an arbitration clause). In this situation, therefore, the issue of the power of arbitrators to intervene on the agreement becomes crucial.

    This book aims to provide an analysis of such matter under a procedural law and arbitrability perspective by considering both contracts without an adaptation clause and contracts including it, as well as to find out whether it is possible to determine a

Preface

principle of law justifying the aforementioned power with regard to both these categories of agreements. In order to carry out such analysis, this book is organised in four chapters.

The first chapter provides for a definition of long-term gas agreements and for an overview of the evolution of some of the main European and extra-European gas markets as well as of the relevant contracts in order to better understand the problem of their adaptation. Moreover, the effects produced on such contracts – and, in particular, on the relevant mechanism for the gas price calculation and on their structure – by the development of spot markets and the occurrence of the 2009 crisis affecting the gas sector will be considered.

The second chapter focuses on the analysis of take or pay clauses by considering their key characteristics and scope as well as the main issues they can give rise to with particular regard to their nature and the consequences that the different qualifications of such provisions can have on the arbitrators' adaptation power.

The third and fourth chapters, besides providing for an analysis of adaptation clauses (and, in particular, of price review and hardship provisions), deal with the issue of the arbitrators' power to adjust long-term gas sale agreements by considering both the case in which such contracts do not provide for an adaptation clause and the case in which, instead, they include it. This analysis, aiming to determine whether it is possible to find a justification for the aforementioned authority, is carried out under a procedural law and arbitrability perspective and provides an overview of some of the most relevant European legal system as well as of the US one. Moreover, the approach adopted by arbitration tribunals in relation to the aforementioned issue is examined. In this regard, it has to be noted that, due to the few published awards in the gas field, the analysis will also consider courts decisions issued in setting aside or enforcement proceedings of commercial arbitration awards handed down in energy disputes.

Furthermore, I carried out some interviews with lawyers and arbitrators (and, namely, Professor Ana Stanic, Ms Lisa Beisteiner, Ms Courtney Lotfi, Mr Steven Finizio, Mr Craig Tevendale, Mr Aadne Haga, Dr Johannes Willheim, Marco Lorefice) experts in the field and involved in some of the most recent arbitration proceedings regarding the adaptation of long-term gas sale agreements. In this regard, it has to be underlined that no-confidential information was provided by the persons interviewed.

Finally, I would like to record my sincere thanks to the above-mentioned experts that I interviewed and to Professor Maxi Scherer of Queen Mary University of London for the help and support provided to me.

CHAPTER 1
The Gas Market and the Relevant Agreements

§1.01 INTRODUCTION

The expression "long-term gas sale agreements" is used in this book to identify, in general, international commercial contracts concluded among producers, wholesalers and distributors for the sale of gas. The common feature of these agreements is to be characterised by a long duration (usually twenty or more years) and by relevant investments. During such lapse of time, the original market conditions – representing the basis on which the agreement was negotiated and concluded – may change due to the occurrence of unforeseen events affecting the contract's balance. Therefore, it is necessary to review the contractual terms and conditions, especially those regarding the price and the minimum purchase volumes established by take or pay clauses (i.e., clauses providing for the obligation of the buyer to purchase a minimum fixed volume of gas every year and to pay for it even in case the buyer does not actually take it), in order to adapt them to the actual market situation. For this reason, parties often (although not always) include in their contract specific clauses providing for the adaptation/adjustment of the latter terms and conditions. According to such provisions, usually the first step is the parties' renegotiation and, in case of its failure, the second step is the submission of the matter to arbitration or, more rarely, to courts (indeed, due to their international nature, gas sale agreements normally include an arbitration clause). In this situation, arbitrators (and courts) have to carry out the difficult task of the determination of their powers with regard to the adjustment of gas sale contracts. In order to do that, they have to interpret and analyse the contract's provisions (and, in particular, the adaptation, if any, and the arbitration clause) and the applicable procedural law. As seen more in detail below, such double analysis is necessary since, on the one hand, the arbitration tribunal's jurisdiction and authority find their source in the parties' will (i.e., in the contract and, in particular, in the arbitration clause) and, on the other, the issue of the arbitrators' adaptation power has a procedural nature.[1] It is, therefore, clear that the above-mentioned task is more complicated in case the procedural applicable law does not provide arbitrators with the adaptation power and/or the contract does not provide for an adjustment clause. In the latter situation, it will be necessary to determine whether the adaptation process can be carried out on the basis of the general arbitration clause. Furthermore, a problem can arise with regard to the extent of the arbitration tribunal's authority in particular if the contract does not contain any specific definition and indication of the arbitrators' adaptation powers.

The issue of the adjustment of long-term gas sale agreements by arbitration tribunals, on which this work is mainly focused, has assumed even more relevance due to the recent renegotiation and adaptation processes, as well as arbitration proceedings, that involved such agreements, especially in relation to the price and the minimum purchase volume obligations therein provided. The origin of such processes and proceedings can be mostly identified in the crisis that in 2009 affected the gas market and in the emergence and development of spot or traded gas markets, i.e., 'markets in which commodities are bought and sold for immediate or very near-term delivery, usually within a period of thirty days or fewer. The transaction does not imply a continuing arrangement between the buyer and the seller. A spot market is more likely to develop at a location with numerous pipeline interconnections, thus allowing for a large number of buyers and sellers'.[2] As to the price, it has to be underlined that such issue is particularly relevant for gas sale contracts since it has given rise to a debate in relation to which mechanism has to be applied for its determination. In this regard, it is possible to identify two main different methods for the price calculation: the oil price indexation, consisting in determining the gas price by linking it to that applied to oil products (this is the most common method in continental Europe) or the spot/traded markets price indexation, consisting in applying to the sale of gas at the price determined in spot markets (this is the method mainly used in the United States (US) and United Kingdom (UK)).

In order to better address the problem of the adaptation of long-term gas sale agreements, as above identified, it is important to analyse first their key characteristics and the context in which they developed. For this purpose, this chapter will provide a brief analysis and overview of the evolution of some of the main European and extra-European gas markets as well as of the relevant contracts.

§1.02 THE GAS MARKET AND SALE AGREEMENTS

In the international scenario, Europe represents a key area for the gas trade, especially for that of natural gas. As said before, an issue particularly hot and relevant in this market is the method of determination of the gas price. In Europe, it was developed (and it is still the most used in continental European countries) the mechanism of the so called "oil indexation" by which the gas price is determined by referring it to that

---

1. *See* Ch. 3.
2. American Petroleum Institute, *Understanding Natural Gas Markets*, www.api.org, 32 (2014).

applied to oil products. This mechanism, that was also exported to Asia, is the opposite to that developed in the US where the price of gas provided in sale agreements is that determined in spot markets. However, it has to be noted that also in Europe the latter method of price calculation has begun to spread and to be used in contractual relationships (in particular, in the UK).

The importance of the European scene was recently underlined by Professor Melling who stated that:

> Today, Europe is witnessing an unprecedented collision between these two pricing mechanisms and gas industry cultures. According to the International Energy Agency, one of the most essential questions related to global energy supplies and security is whether the traditional link between oil and gas prices will survive. While Europe is currently the battleground, the implications stretch beyond Europe's borders because once-isolated regional markets are now interconnected through the rising trade in liquefied natural gas. If the spot market model gains the upper hand in Europe, Asia will be the last remaining stronghold of oil-indexed pricing, possibly making it unsustainable. Alternatively, if oil indexation re-exerts its predominance, there is the prospect that spot prices in North America will be influenced by this model.[3]

It is commonly recognised that the growth of natural gas market in Europe began in the 1960s, in particular, as a consequence of the discovery of natural gas fields in the Netherlands (and, in particular, of the Groningen field) and in the North Sea. Indeed, due to such discoveries, the Netherlands and Norway could begin to export their gas to other European countries and the UK gas market could develop. Moreover, the importations of Russian and Algerian gas also contributed to the growth of the gas trade in Europe.[4]

It is possible to identify seven European main gas markets developed during the period between 1960 and 1990: the Netherlands, UK, Norway, France, Germany, Italy and Belgium. In particular, the first three countries played a key role in the creation and growth of the gas trade in Europe. For other European countries, that lacked local resources and that were far from the major suppliers, it was, instead, difficult to develop a specific gas market especially because of the high costs linked to the pipelines transportation of gas.[5]

As already mentioned, it is important to note that the main feature of the developing gas market was the use of long-term gas sale contracts providing for oil-indexed price. The price of natural gas was, therefore, linked to prices of other competing fuels and, first of all, to that of oil products. Within the described context, it is interesting to provide a brief overview and analysis of the evolution of the three most important European gas markets (the Dutch, UK and Norwegian markets), as well as of other relevant international experiences connected to the European scenario (the US,

---

3. A.J. Melling, *Natural Gas Pricing and Its Future*, http://carnegieendowment.org, 7–8 (2010). For a general overview of the gas markets, *see* DNV KEMA Energy & Sustainability in collaboration with COWI Belgium, *Study on LT-ST Markets in Gas*, www.ec.europa.eu (2013).
4. Melling, *id.*, at 9 et seq.; J.P. Stern, *European Gas Markets*, 2 et seq. (The Royal Institute of International Affairs 1990).
5. Stern, *id.*

Russian and Algerian markets), with particular attention to the development and main characteristic of the relevant sale contracts.

[A] The Evolution of the Dutch Market and Relevant Gas Sale Contracts

As said above, the discovery of the Slochteren Groningen field in 1959 was crucial for the development of the European gas trade.[6] Indeed, this discovery made possible for the Netherlands not only to cope with its domestic market demand but also to export the gas towards other European countries and, in particular, to Germany, France and Belgium (exportations were also facilitated by the proximity of the Groningen field to the main urban areas of these countries). For several years, the Groningen field was the exclusive source for the production of Dutch gas. Only after the oil crisis of 1973–1974, other marginal fields were exploited in order to preserve the reserves of the Groningen field.[7]

Before its discovery, the Dutch gas market was characterised by the government's monopoly of the wholesale of natural gas. In particular, according to the law in force at that time, the company established for the exploration and development of the hydrocarbons discovered in the Netherlands – *Nederlandse Aardolie Maatschappij BV* (NAM) whose shareholders were Shell and Exxon – had the obligation to sell for a twenty-year period any gas surplus to the State Gas Board (SGB), a state-owned entity, which, in return, was required to pay for any quantity of gas offered by NAM. Upon the discovery of the Groningen field, the Dutch government decided to change strategy and to end the monopoly of the gas supply held by SGB without, however, completely losing the control of such resource. Therefore, it was decided to involve in the exploitation and marketing process another state-owned entity, Dutch State Mines (DSM), that was the main producer and distributor of solid fuels and coke-oven gas in the Netherlands. Thanks to this decision, it was also possible for DSM not to be negatively affected by the discovery and supply of the Groningen gas since the latter was in competition with the products sold by DSM. Moreover, it was established the direct involvement of Shell and Exxon also in the gas marketing phase (which, until that moment, was an exclusive prerogative of the State) in addition to the role already played in the production process. Furthermore, other two entities were set up: the *Maatschap*, by which the State controlled the production's costs and profits, and the *N.V. Nederlandse Gasunie* (Gasunie) – that in 2005 was split into GasTerra (a gas trading company) and Gasunie (a gas transportation company) – involved in the transportation and marketing of gas and whose shareholders were for 50% Shell and Exxon (with 25% of shares each one) and for the remaining 50% DSM and the State. It was also decided that NAM, through a specific separate division (NAM-Gas Export),

---

6. *See*, in general, Melling, *supra* n. 3, at 16–19; A.F. Correljé & P.R. Odell, *Four Decades of Groningen Production and Pricing Policies and a View to the Future*, 28 Energy Policy 19 (2000); Stern, *supra* n. 4, at 42 et seq.; M.V.H. Peebles, *Evolution of the Gas Industry*, 113 et seq. (Macmillan Press Ltd. 1980).
7. M. van der Hoeven, M. Kraven & B. van de Leemput, *The Netherlands: The Energy Hub of Europe*, Oil & Gas Financial Journal, 1 (2010).

would have been in charge of the gas exportations for Gasunie (after 1975 Gasunie started to directly export the Groningen gas).

As explained by Professors Correljé and Odell, in 1963 the structure of the Dutch gas sector was the following:

> i) The holder of the Groningen concession, the *Nederlandse Aardolie Maatschappij BV* (NAM), a 50/50 joint venture of Shell and Exxon, was exclusively to undertake the production activities. ii) The state, via the Staatsmijnen (later Dutch State Mines or DSM), was to participate in the costs of exploiting gas from the Groningen field and in the flow of revenues through a financing partnership, known as the *Maatschap* (40% DSM, 60% NAM). iii) Gasunie was established as a joint venture owned by the Dutch State Mines (DSM) (40%), the Dutch State directly (10%) and Exxon (25%) and Shell (25%). Gasunie was given the exclusive responsibility to co-ordinate the commercialization of the Dutch natural gas resources on behalf of the Sate and the concession-holder, NAM. NAM Gas Export was to be responsible for the sales of gas abroad.[8]

It is clear that, through the above-mentioned structure of the gas market, the Dutch government, although not directly involved in the production and exploitation process of the gas, had a key role and relevant control in all the decisions regarding the Groningen field (from the prices to the production and trade volumes). Thus, what was created and implemented was a de facto monopoly. More specifically, the Dutch government had the following powers:

> the right of approval of the transfer price between the 'Maatschap' and Gasunie; the right of approval of the gas sales plan; the right of approval of conditions and tariffs for the delivery of gas by Gasunie to public distribution companies in the Netherlands, as well as the right to approve the price level for other customer categories; the right of approval for the construction of transmission lines and other equipment for the transportation and storage of gas; the right of approval of the Dutch border prices for export sales; and the right to have limited quantity of gas supplied by and for the account of Gasunie at prices and conditions as stipulated by him after consultation with Gasunie to customers to be designated by him, if he should consider the desirable to promote industrial development in certain parts of the country.[9]

Moreover, with regard to the demand of gas, 'the conditions for market developments were equally propitious. Groningen was located close to the centre of one of the world's most energy intensive using regions, within which the two most important suppliers of hydrocarbons were the two companies, viz. Shell and Exxon, which had discovered the fields. Under these conditions, the creation of a set of national or regional monopolistic transporters and another set of monopsonistic distributors and marketers of the potential gas supply from Groningen was axiomatic. Monopoly plus monopsony was thus imposed and implemented on the emerging European natural gas industry'.[10]

---

8. Correljé & Odell, *supra* n. 6, at 20.
9. Peebles, *supra* n. 6, at 128–129.
10. Correljé & Odell, *supra* n. 6, at 21.

As to the sale contracts employed for exportations of the Dutch gas, it is important to underline the method for calculating the relevant price. This method was based on the so called "market-value" or "netback-value" principle, that was established by the Dutch Minister of the Economic Affairs at that time (Jan Willem de Pous) in the *Nota inzake het aardgas* of 1961–1962. It should be distinguished from the so called "cost-plus" principle, that was the prevailing method used until that time for the calculation of the town gas price (i.e., a kind of manufactured gas deriving from the distillation of coal, that was the most common type of gas used before the discovery and development of natural gas). In particular, the netback price is calculated by identifying the market value of natural gas in a specific market sector. This process requires, first, to take into account the other competing fuels sold in the same sector (the gas price is, therefore, linked to other fuels' price and, in particular, to that of gasoil, for small customers, and of heavy fuel oil, for large customers) and, then, to deduct from such value the relevant costs (such as, transportation and storage costs), general expenses, taxes and profits. Through this method, it is possible to determine the value of the gas at the moment of the sale. A clear explanation of such principle is provided by the International Energy Agency, according to which:

> the price paid by the gas company to the foreign or domestic gas producer at the border or the beach is negotiated on the basis of the weighted average value of the gas in competition with other fuels adjusted to allow for transportation and storage costs from the beach or the border and any taxes on gas. There are in principle three different average netback market values. These correspond to existing gas users, new gas users (such as Greenfield industrial plants) and to existing oil users with no dual firing capability (the market value of the latter being the lowest because of the high capital cost of fuel switching). The beach/border base price that is ultimately negotiated will correspond to a level between the highest and the lowest of the three values, weighted across the different end-user customer categories. The base price is usually indexed to oil product prices (usually heating oil and/or heavy fuel oil) or simply to crude oil (on the implicit assumption that the ratio of crude to product prices will remain broadly constant). This is to ensure that effective prices over the life of the contract remain broadly in line with market values.[11]

On the contrary, according to the cost-plus method, the sale price is calculated as the sum of production and transportation costs, general expenses and profits. It is, therefore, clear that the price based on the netback-value principle is more competitive and attractive for customers that are incentivised to buy natural gas instead of other fuels. Thus, such price was the one used for the exportation of the Groningen gas in order to enter into new markets and, in particular, into the German one where the prevailing type of gas consumed until that moment was the town gas. It follows that it was necessary to practise prices appealing for the customers in comparison to other fuels. Provided that, the application of the market-value principle, in any case, permitted to the Dutch government and producers to earn high revenues since, on the one hand, the Groningen gas price was linked to that of alternative fuels which at that time were high-priced (there was no cheapest gas available in the market) and, on the

---

11. International Energy Agency (IEA), *Natural Gas Pricing in Competitive Markets*, 32 (IEA 1998).

other, the production and transportation costs were low. On the contrary, consumers would have been more advantageous (and, consequently, less convenient for the State and the producers) if the gas sale price had been referred to the production costs of the Groningen gas that, as said, were low. In this regard, it was noted that:

> At the time of gas' extensive introduction to the markets, Europe consisted of a set of relatively high-priced energy markets arising from the combination of highly protected indigenous coal and a less than fully competitive supply of oil products. Thus, the netback value of the Groningen gas marketed could be a multiple of the very low long-run supply price of the commodity; leading to consequential super-normal profits for the producers and generous revenues for the state. Energy consumers were, of course, the losers; but this was largely unrecognized by them in the context of the ordered system imposed. They were, in any case, ... very used to high-energy prices, so that gas could, in effect, be offered on a take-it or leave-it basis as a so-called premium fuel at so-called 'competitive' prices, in a market in which no gas at lower prices was available. Monopoly power was effectively exercised.[12]

The same price mechanism was applied by Dutch exporters to Belgian and French buyers. Due to the fact that the netback price was different from country to country, since the market value of the gas and the transportation costs varied on the basis of the place of destination, the Dutch gas sale contracts included the so called "destination clauses" in order to match a specific price with a specific destination. Another characteristic of the above-mentioned contracts (i.e., common to gas sale agreements in general) was the long duration (usually around 20–25 years). For this reason and the possible variation of the netback value of the gas (and, therefore, of the sale price) over such a long period of time, such contracts also provided for the possibility to review the price by means of the so called "price review" or "price re-opener" clauses allowing the parties to periodically adjust the price on the basis of unforeseeable changes incurred in the relevant market that affected the gas price.

Other features of Dutch gas sale contracts were, on the one hand, the flexibility with regard to the daily and annual volume of gas that the buyers were obliged to take according to take or pay clauses and, on the other, the application of an additional charge (so called "capacity charge") to be paid independent of the gas consumed in order to compensate the aforementioned flexibility. As shown below, the exportation gas contracts employed by other countries were not characterised by the same degree of flexibility as Dutch contracts. This was mainly due to the following factors. First, the long distance existing between suppliers and buyers that implied high transportation costs through pipeline systems (often dedicated to a single buyer), involving, as a consequence, relevant investments by the seller. The latter, therefore, required the buyer to pay for an agreed minimum annual quantity, usually ranging from 80% to 90% of the so called "Annual Contract Quantity (ACQ)" of the gas to be supplied pursuant to the sale agreement. Such payment obligation was due even in case the gas was not actually taken by the buyer (this is a peculiarity of take or pay clauses). In this way, the seller was sure to recover the capital costs borne for the gas transportation.

---

12. Correljé & Odell, *supra* n. 6, at 21.

The second reason was represented by the particularly low production costs in the Groningen field that, consequently, made Dutch gas sale contracts more competitive (in terms of flexibility) than the others.

The above-mentioned characteristics can also be found in the ongoing gas sale agreements. However, it has to be noted that, due to the liberalisation, the development of spot markets and the crisis, some of the most recent contracts for the exportation of Dutch gas have a duration of one or two years and the relevant price is determined on the basis of spot markets.

[B] The Evolution of the UK Market and Relevant Gas Sale Contracts

The other most important European gas market considered in our analysis is the one developed in the UK.[13] Even in this case the trigger event was the discovery of new gas fields and, in particular, of those located in the North Sea during the years 1965–1966. Before such discoveries, the most common type of gas used in the UK was the town gas[14] and the market players were small private companies and county councils. In 1948, with the enactment of the Gas Bill, the UK gas industry was nationalised and twelve autonomous Area Boards were established with the task to organise their supplies and the relevant financial aspects. In particular, 'they were permitted to fix their own prices, insofar as this was compatible with the general direction that "every Area Board shall reduce, so far as practicable, the price of gas and coke, and avoid undue preference in the supply of gas and coke". At the same time, the Area Boards were required "to secure that the revenues of the Board are not less than sufficient to meet their outgoings properly chargeable to revenue account, taking one year with another"'.[15] In order to better coordinate these activities among the Boards, it was decided to set up a central body, the Gas Council, gathering the twelve Area Boards chairmen and dealing with some matters of general interests. In particular, this central organisation had the following tasks: '(a) to advise the Minister in questions affecting the gas industry and matters relating thereto; and (b) to promote and assist the efficient exercise ad performance by Area Boards of their functions'.[16]

Moreover, from October 1964, the UK started to import liquefied natural gas (LNG) from Algeria pursuant to a fifteen-year contract, concluded by the Gas Council on behalf of eight Area Boards, at a fixed price. Almost in the same period of time (and, precisely, from September 1964), the British government, according to the Continental Shelf Act of 1964, authorised the oil main companies to explore the UK area of the

---

13. *See*, in general, Melling, *supra* n. 3, at 22–23, 97–100; C. Webber, *The Evolution of the Gas Industry in the UK*, International Gas Union Magazine 198 (2010); A. Juris, *Market Development in the United Kingdom's Natural Gas Industry*, 3 et seq. (The World Bank, Private Sector Development Department, Private Participation in Infrastructure Division 1998); Stern, *supra* n. 4, at 2 et seq.; T.I. Williams, *A History of the British Gas Industry* (Oxford University Press 1981); M.V.H. Peebles, *supra* n. 6, at 21 et seq.
14. As defined in the previous paragraph.
15. Williams, *supra* n. 13, at 116.
16. Gas Act, s. 22 (1948).

North Sea in order to discover gas fields. The first was the West Sole gas field that was discovered by the British Petroleum in 1965.

With regard to the supply phase, the Continental Shelf Act provided that:

> (2) The holder of the licence shall not without the consent of the Minister of Power use the gas in Great Britain and no person shall without that consent supply the gas to any other person at premises in Great Britain. (3) The Minister of Power shall not give his consent under this section to the supply of gas at any premises unless satisfied - (a) that the supply is for industrial purposes and that the Area Board in whose area the premises are situated has been given an opportunity of purchasing the gas at a reasonable price.[17]

Thus, by means of such provision, the Gas Council (and, therefore, the government) was granted the monopoly of supply of gas in the UK taking also into account that the Gas Council could avail itself of a distribution system covering the national territory.

In 1973, following the enactment of the Gas Act of 1972, the Gas Council was replaced by the British Gas Corporation (British Gas) which had the duties 'to develop and maintain an efficient, co-ordinated and economical system of gas supply for Great Britain, and to satisfy, so far as it is economical to do so, all reasonable demands for gas in Great Britain'.[18] The decision to replace the Gas Council was based on the consideration that after the discovery of the North Sea fields it was necessary to have just one central entity taking all the decisions regarding the acquisition and distribution of natural gas in the UK instead of having twelve autonomous Boards coordinated by a central organisation only for some matters. In this way, the State's monopoly of the gas supply was reinforced. In particular, British Gas held the monopoly of the gas supply in the UK until 1986, when, as a consequence of the enactment of a new Gas Act, it was privatised and its shares were quoted on the London Stock Exchange. Moreover, a new regulation authority, the Office of Gas and Electricity Markets (OFGEM), was set up by the government and it started a process of market liberalisation. Such process led, on the one hand, to changes in the British Gas structure – that, firstly, was reorganised into five new divisions and in 1994 was split into British Gas plc and Centrica plc (whose assets included British Gas Energy Supply, Services, Energy Centres, Accord Energy and HRL, the gas production business of the North and South Morecambe gas fields)[19] – and, on the other, to the introduction of competition in the gas market. One of the first steps in this direction was, for example, the possibility for third parties to conclude specific contracts for the transportation of their gas in the UK (the so called "Third Party Access Agreements"). In this way, they could get direct access to the pipeline system without passing by British Gas that, until the 1990s, had the monopoly of the onshore transportation system. The competition process allowed new players to enter into the market, bypassing British Gas and selling gas directly to customers.

---

17. Continental Shelf Act, Ch. 29, §9 (15 April 1964), www.legislation.gov.uk.
18. British Gas Act, Ch. 60, §2 (9 August 1972), www.legislation.gov.uk.
19. *See* www.centrica.com.

In the above-mentioned scenario, it is interesting to analyse the main characteristics of the contracts concluded between the gas sellers and the Gas Council/British Gas. Like the most part of the contracts used in the gas field, they were depletion contract (i.e., contract by which the producer commit all the gas quantity located in a specific field to a particular buyer until the reserves are depleted) characterised by a long duration (usually 20–25 years) and by take or pay provisions. Moreover, with regard to the buyer's minimum volume purchase obligation established by such clauses, it was provided for a mechanism according to which, in case the minimum annual quantity of gas agreed was not taken, but paid for, the buyer was allowed to take such amount in a later moment free of charge (so called "make-up clauses"). In case, instead, the buyer took more gas than the minimum volume agreed, it was granted a discount on the quantity in excess.

As underlined by Professor Williams:

> contracts were usually subject to the following general provisions: (1) An annual contract quantity (ACQ) was agreed. This was the amount of gas the industry agreed to pay for each year whether or not it was actually taken. (2) Up to an agreed limit the industry may purchase further gas (called 'valley' gas, after the summer dip in the load curve) at a lower price. (3) The producers undertake to supply relatively more gas in the high-demand winter months. This would commonly be about 167 per cent of the ACQ expressed as average daily quantity (ADQ) over the year.[20]

After the 1970s, sale contracts were modified by providing, in particular, for more flexibility in relation to the quantity of gas to be taken by the Gas Council/British Gas.

As to the price mechanism of the first UK gas sale contracts, it has to be noted that disputes arose between gas producers and the Gas Council/British Gas around the meaning of the expression "reasonable price" (provided by the Continental Shelf Act of 1964) at which the gas from the North Sea had to be offered to the Gas Council/British Gas. In particular, the latter required the application of a price calculated on the basis of the "cost-plus" principle and the inclusion of inflation as a one of the elements for the price determination. On the other side, the producers would have preferred an oil-indexed price in order to gain more profit taking into account the relevant risk they were incurring due to the fact that no one could foresee the result of the future explorations of the North Sea fields. At the end, the reasons of the Gas Council/British Gas prevailed since it had the monopoly of the gas market in the UK and, moreover, according to the Continental Shelf Act, producers were required to sell the gas of the North Sea to it. In particular, the price formula included, as calculation factors, the inflation (based on the UK Producer Price Index) and the prices applied to UK final industrial customers for the purchase of gasoil and heavy fuel oil (other contracts also referred to the prices of coal and electricity). From 1986, due to the fact that oil prices fell down, the gas price was mainly linked to and calculated on the basis of the oil products' price. Furthermore, it seems that, in general, the contracts provided for an automatic price adjustment on the basis of the main price indices regarding oil

---

20. Williams, *supra* n. 13, at 208.

products, for periodic renegotiations and for arbitration.[21] One of the reasons that led to the renegotiation of the existing gas contracts was the development from 1995 of spot markets that made inconvenient the application of oil-indexed prices to gas sale contracts. Therefore, in 1997 such agreements (that in 1996 were transferred by British Gas to Centrica) were renegotiated in order to obtain from gas producers more competitive prices (those paid by British Gas/Centrica until that moment were almost twice of spot market prices). In general, it can be said that, although the oil indexation mechanism is sometimes still used in gas sale contracts, with the development of spot markets this method has gradually become less common with the consequent increase of the price calculation based on traded markets. Nowadays, it can be dais that the UK is the European country where the spot markets indexation is more spread and used in contrast to continental Europe where the oil indexation mechanism is still prevailing.

From the analysis carried out so far, it is possible to underline four main differences between the Dutch and UK market:

> i) the UK fields were offshore, which made them more expensive to develop and required relatively high load factors, or higher prices ii) the UK fields were developed (until the late 1990s) purely for the domestic market iii) the UK fields were much smaller than the Groningen field ad not of sufficient size to sign long-term supply contracts of the same order as the Dutch contracts. (West Sole, the first UK gas field development, had reserves equivalent to 2 percent of the size of Groningen) iv) the lack of obvious low-cost means to provide seasonal and daily swing on natural gas in the UK.[22]

The smaller dimension of the UK gas fields was probably the main reason why the UK became a natural gas exporter only in the 1990s. Other reasons that favoured the exportation were, on the one hand, the market liberalisation and the end of the monopoly of British Gas – that until that moment was the sole purchaser of gas coming from the North Sea and was the only supplier in the UK – and, on the other, the discoveries of undeveloped gas fields. In this regard, it has also to be noted that in 1998, the UK-Belgium Interconnector was commissioned and the exportations of UK gas towards Belgium started in 1999. At the same time, gas sale contracts were concluded with Dutch and German customers providing for oil-indexed prices.

[C] The Evolution of the Norwegian Market and Relevant Gas Sale Contracts

The other European gas market analysed is the Norwegian one that mainly developed, thanks to the several fields discovered from 1970 onwards in the North, Norwegian and

---

21. Williams, *id.*, at 209; Peebles, *supra* n. 6, at 32. However, it was affirmed that: '[c]ompared with Continental Europe the adjustment of prices to changed market circumstances remains relatively slow. Prices paid to producers are usually adjusted once a year with a reference period of one year ... It is also worth noting that UKCS [UK Continental Shelf] contracts do not contain "reopener" or "renegotiation" clauses. Certain elements of the old Southern Basin contracts have been renegotiated, but the decision to act in this way was in itself a negotiated trade-off between the buyer and the producers' (Stern, *supra* n. 4, at 18).
22. Melling, *supra* n. 3, at 22.

Barents seas.[23] The first discoveries were the Balder, Ekofisk, Frigg and Statfjord fields, while the most important was the Troll field since it represented the largest European gas discovery after the Groningen one. Due to such discoveries, the Norwegian gas was exported towards both in the UK and continental Europe (and, in particular, to Germany).

With regard to the main characteristics of the contracts employed for the sale of Norwegian gas, it has to be noted that the first agreements were depletion contracts[24] providing for take or pay obligations and for a price indexed to oil products (in particular, the price fixed in the Statfjord, Heimdal, Gullfaks contracts was linked to crude oil). Such contracts did not include price renegotiation clauses at all or provided for very limited possibilities of renegotiation. With the discovery of the Troll field, the contractual structure used until then for the exportation of Norwegian gas changed. Indeed, due to the large size of such field, it was possible to adopt a more stable and durable type of agreement than the depletion one. The new gas sale contracts were, therefore, long-term supply contracts (providing for contractual extensions and renewals at the expiration date) with take or pay clauses, that usually established a minimum annual quantity to be purchased ranging from 85% to 90% of the Annual Contract Quantity agreed. Furthermore, these contracts gave the buyer the possibility to take gas in excess of such minimum volume within the limit of 110%–115% of the Annual Contract Quantity. Although at the beginning, Norwegian sellers claimed for the application of a sale price higher than in the past (due to the relevant production costs and to the strategic importance of the Troll field for the European market), at the end, such price was calculated on the basis of the netback principle and, consequently, it was linked to that of other competing fuels and, in particular, oil products (such as, gasoil and heavy fuel oil). In this way, buyers could sell, on its turn, the Norwegian gas at a competitive price to their customers. In this regard, it is also important to note that the price used in the so called "Troll contracts" became a reference price for the European gas market and, therefore, such agreements were used as a model in the renegotiation of the previous gas agreements concluded in the 1970s.

The long-term oil-indexed contract is still the most common type of gas sale agreement used. However, some contracts have been recently renegotiated by reducing the minimum volume commitments and introducing the reference to spot market prices in the formula. Other kinds of contracts, instead, did not provide for oil-indexed prices but for spot markets' prices. In this regard, it was underlined that in some cases '[b]uyers have successfully argued that their end-user alternative fuel is spot market gas. As a result, the sellers have made concessions whereby a percentage of the contract volumes are sold at market prices. Spot percentages were further increased

---

23. *See*, in general Melling, *supra* n. 3, at 84 et seq.; T. Hylleberg & M.A. Pedersen, *Overview of the Norwegian Oil and Gas Industry*, www.offshorecenter.dk, 14 (2009),; Stern, *supra* n. 4, at 38 et seq.; J. Estrada, H.O. Bergesen, A. Moe & A.K. Sydnes, *Natural Gas in Europe*, 212 et seq. (Pinter Publishers Limited, 1988); G. Hognestad, *The Role of the Norwegian Government When Selling Natural Gas*, in *Natural Gas Markets and Contracts*, 173 et seq. (R. Golombek, M. Hoel & J. Vislie, Elsevier Science Publishers B.V. 1987).
24. As defined in the previous paragraph.

during recent price renegotiation - as announced by Statoil in the first quarter of 2010'.[25]

A further point to be addressed in relation to Norwegian gas sale agreements is the role played by the Norwegian government in the contractual negotiation. In particular, the earlier contracts 'were negotiated mainly by the international companies which owned the gas through concessions. The government did not intervene in these commercial negotiations, but rather reviewed the results when they were presented as part of the application for approval of the development and landing of the gas abroad. Furthermore, the government stipulated conditions before giving its approval. Some of the conditions were of a general nature and some related to deliveries of gas to Norway'.[26] Moreover, Statoil, the Norwegian State oil company created in 1972, was in charge of the negotiations of sale contracts with the supervision of a special committee. Later, negotiations were, instead, led by a committee of three companies: Statoil, Norsk Hydro (that in 2007 merged with Statoil) and Saga Petroleum. In any case, even for contracts concluded after the 1972, the policy of the government was always the same: it did not directly conduct negotiations, but it just gave the final approval of the contracts.

[D] The Evolution of the US Market and Relevant Gas Sale Contracts

With regard to non-European markets, it is worth to analyse, first of all, the US gas experience where spot markets have developed since 1980s with consequences on the duration of gas sale agreements (i.e., the increase of medium and short-term contracts instead of long-term ones) and on the relevant price calculation mechanism (i.e., from the oil to spot market indexation).[27,28]

Until the middle of the twentieth century, the most common type of gas used in the US (from illumination to heating and cooking) was the manufactured gas (i.e., gas deriving from the manufacturing, through different processes, of oil, coal and coke). From the 1930s, natural gas started to appear on the market scene, although the manufactured gas industry tried to slow down such process in order not to lose their market's shares. One of the fundamental steps in this direction was the enactment in 1938 of the Natural Gas Act that empowered the Federal Power Commission (established in June 1920) of the regulation of the gas sale and transportation system between states (the so called "interstate market"), leaving the regulation of the distribution system within a state territory to the relevant local authorities. The aim of the Act was

---

25. Melling, *supra* n. 3, at 86.
26. Hognestad, *supra* n. 23, at 177.
27. *See*, in general, A. Juris, *Development of Natural Gas and Pipeline Capacity Markets in the United States*, 4 et seq. (The World Bank, Private Sector Development Department, Private Participation in Infrastructure Division 1998); Peebles, *supra* n. 6, 51 et seq. *See also* DNV KEMA Energy & Sustainability, *supra* n. 3, at 65 et seq.
28. Such process has been recently strengthened by the increase of the production of shale gas, i.e., natural gas that is trapped within fine-grained sedimentary rock formations (American Petroleum Institute, *supra* n. 2, at 15 and 22). As it was underlined by the US Energy Information Administration in its 2014 Report (available on www.eia.gov), such increase will have consequences not only on the domestic market but also in relation to the exportations of the US gas.

mainly to protect the end-users' interests and to provide for a mechanism to settle disputes between companies involved in the gas market: producers, transportation companies and distribution companies. As to the latter, it has to be noted that many producers of manufactured gas converted their activity and became distributors of natural gas. In particular, the new law provided that:

> The provisions of this Act shall apply to the transportation of natural gas in interstate commerce, to the sale in interstate commerce of natural gas for resale for ultimate public consumption for domestic, commercial, industrial, or any other use, and to natural gas companies engaged in such transportation or sale, but shall not apply to any other transportation or sale of natural gas or to the local distribution of natural gas or to the facilities used for such distribution or to the production or gathering of natural gas.[29]

Furthermore the Act established that:

> All rates and charges made, demanded, or received by any natural-gas company for or in connection with the transportation or sale of natural gas subject to the jurisdiction of the Commission, and all rules and regulations affecting or pertaining to such rates or charges, shall be just and reasonable, and any such rate or charge that is not just and reasonable is hereby declared to be unlawful.[30]

The power to regulate the gas price in the interstate market, attributed to the Federal Power Commission by the legislation, was also affirmed by the case law and, in particular, by the landmark decision of the Supreme Court of 7 June 1954 in the *Philips Petroleum Company v. Wisconsin Public Services Commission* case in which it was held that:

> We believe that the legislative history indicates a congressional intent to give the Commission jurisdiction over the rates of all wholesales of natural gas in interstate commerce, whether by a pipeline company or not and whether occurring before, during, or after transmission by an interstate pipeline company. There can be no dispute that the overriding congressional purpose was to plug the "gap" in regulation of natural gas companies resulting from judicial decisions prohibiting, on federal constitutional grounds, state regulation of many of the interstate commerce aspects of the natural gas business.[31]

The method followed by the Federal Power Commission in the price regulation process, at the beginning, was based on a case-by-case system and, later, on the so called "area approach" by which a specific gas price was set for any major producing area. Therefore, within the same area all the producers had to apply the same maximum price established by the Federal Power Commission. Moreover, different prices were set for new and old gas: the first was higher than that applied to the second in order to favour the exploration of new fields. However, both of the above-mentioned approaches encountered some difficulties in their application and, consequently, the

---

29. Natural Gas Act, Ch. 556, §1(b) (21 June 1938), http://legcounsel.house.gov.
30. *Ibid.*, at §4.
31. *Phillips Petroleum v. Wisconsin*, 347 U.S. 672, 683 (U.S. 7 June 1954).

Chapter 1: The Gas Market and the Relevant Agreements §1.02[D]

Federal Power Commission decided to provide for just one national gas price (the first was established in June 1974).

On 4 August 1977, with the enactment of the Department of Energy Organization Act, the Federal Power Commission was replaced by two new bodies: the Federal Energy Regulatory Commission (that carried out almost all the functions previously assigned to the Federal Power Commission, including the price regulation) and the Economic Regulatory Administration (that mainly dealt with gas importations). Furthermore, on 1 December 1978, the Natural Gas Policy Act entered into force with the aim to create one national natural gas market and to balance the supply and demand of gas. In particular, the Act set maximum prices for the sale of gas on the interstate and intrastate markets. According to the new legislation, the Federal Energy Regulatory Commission had the control of the gas sales also on the latter market. The situation changed with the enactment of the Natural Gas Wellhead Decontrol Act on 3 January 1989 that provided for the deregulation of the price applicable to the first sales of natural gas (i.e., the sales of gas to pipelines, local distributors, consumers – as well as any preceding sales – and those that the Federal Energy Regulatory Commission established to be first sales) in order to favour the competition between producers and sellers. In this regard, it has to be noted that few years before the enactment of such statute, the Federal Energy Regulatory Commission had adopted another measure fostering the competition and, namely, the Order n. 436 of 1985[32] that introduced the possibility to have open access to the interstate pipeline transportation system and entitled the local distributors to withdraw the contracts entered into with pipeline companies (including take or pay obligations) and to buy the gas directly from the producers. On the contrary, the long-term contracts concluded between pipeline companies and gas producers, including the relevant take or pay clauses, remained in force. It is, therefore, clear that, due to the huge decrease of customers, the obligations deriving from such provisions became more and more burdensome for pipeline companies. However, the situation improved when the Federal Energy Regulatory Commission issued the Order n. 500 of 1987 by which pipeline companies could recover part of the costs deriving from the above-mentioned take or pay provisions from both producers and their customers.[33]

After the Gas Wellhead Decontrol Act entered into force, the deregulation process took another fundamental step with the enactment of the Order n. 636 of 1992.[34] By means of such measure, the Federal Energy Regulatory Commission significantly modified the structure of the gas industry and opened the market to competition. The main provision of such order regarded the obligation of pipeline companies to separate the gas sale from the transportation phase. In particular, the Commission, first, clarified which was the main purpose pursued with the enactment of this measure, stating that:

> [its] primary aim in adopting the instant regulations is to improve the competitive structure of the natural gas industry and at the same time maintain an adequate

---

32. Federal Energy Regulatory Commission, Order n. 436/1985, www.ferc.gov.
33. Federal Energy Regulatory Commission, Order n. 500/1987, www.ferc.gov. *See* also Juris, *supra* n. 13, at 12.
34. Federal Energy Regulatory Commission, Order n. 636/1992, www.ferc.gov.

and reliable service. The Commission will do this by regulating pipelines as merchants and as open access transporters in a manner that accomplishes two fundamental goals. The first goal is to ensure that all shippers have meaningful access to the pipeline transportation grid so that willing buyers and sellers can meet in a competitive, national market to transact the most efficient deals possible. The Commission's second fundamental goal is to accomplish the first goal in a way that continues to ensure consumers "access to an adequate supply of gas at a reasonable price." The Commission will act in a way that harmonizes both goals and thereby promotes competition and protects gas consumers [...] The Commission believes that to accomplish those objectives it is vital to give all gas purchasers (LDCs and end users, such as industrials and gas-fired electric generators) the ability to make market-driven choices about the price of gas as a commodity and about the cost of delivering the gas. Simply put, efficiency in the now national gas market can be realized only when the purchasers of a commodity know, in a timely manner, the prices of the distinct elements associated with the full range of services needed to purchase and then deliver gas from the wellhead to the burnertip. Only then will gas purchasers be able to purchase, based upon their needs, the exact services they want with full recognition of the prices that they would have to pay. And only then will the Commission be assured that all gas is transported to the market place on fair terms. What best serves the interests of gas purchasers – the ability to make informed choices – is also important for gas sellers. Nonpipeline sellers also need to know the prices of the distinct elements of pipeline services in order to price their product and to decide the exact pipeline services needed to bring their gas to market. This rule provides both gas purchasers and gas sellers with the ability to make the necessary informed choices.[35]

Then, the Commission affirmed that, in order to achieve the above-mentioned purpose, it was necessary to require 'pipelines to unbundle (i.e., separate) their sales services from their transportation services at an upstream point near the production area and to provide all transportation services on a basis that is equal in quality for all gas supplies whether purchased from the pipeline or from any other gas supplier. This rule issues blanket sales certificates to pipelines so that they can offer unbundled firm and interruptible sales services at market-based rates. In addition, pipelines will be required to provide a variety of transportation services to their shippers'.[36]

As above mentioned, the deregulation and competition process of the gas market also affected the structure of the contracts employed between the different market players: producers – transportation companies; transportation companies – distributors; distributors – end-users. In particular, before 1985 (when the deregulation process began) the contracts used in all the three main gas industry levels (production, transportation, distribution) were long-term contracts including take or pay provisions and whose prices, upon the development of spot markets, were often determined by having them as reference. After the 1985, as said, local distributors were allowed to purchase gas directly from producers bypassing pipeline companies and withdrawing the long-term contracts entered into with them. At the same time, some large end-users directly accessed to the pipeline system in order to bypass local distributors and to directly enter into the wholesale market. In this way, they could benefit of a lower price

---

35. *Ibid.*, at 7 et seq.
36. *Ibid.*

than that paid by small customers still depending on local distributors. On the other side, pipeline companies remained bound by the long-term contracts concluded with the producers. The performance of the take or pay obligations included in such agreements became burdensome due to the loss of clients (and, in particular, local distributors) that, as mentioned, were allowed to withdraw the long-term contracts signed with pipeline companies and to buy gas directly from producers. Therefore, with the deregulation of the gas market, the operators began to use medium and short-term contracts negotiated on a bilateral basis. Such agreements gave the contracting parties the opportunity to better face market changes affecting the contractual terms and conditions, and, in particular, the price and, consequently, altering their balance. Often one of the contracting parties was a gas marketing company negotiating on behalf of other market players and, in particular, of consumers or small customers that did not have the necessary skills and information to conclude a contract economically advantageous.

As to the main characteristics of these new kinds of agreements, it can be pointed out that medium-term contracts had an average duration of one year and provided for a monthly or daily minimum quantity of gas (with relevant allowed variations) and for a price determined on the basis of spot markets. While short-term contracts usually had a duration of one month and were negotiated on spot markets. Therefore, the relevant price was fixed and determined on the basis of that mainly practised on such markets at the time of conclusion of the agreement. Due to the increase of the number of contracts and gas transactions occurred in spot markets, the Gas Industry Standard Board has developed a standard model of gas sale short-term contract. This allowed the contracting parties to have uniform and accepted terms and conditions to which they can refer when negotiating without the need to determine every time the content of any single agreement. Furthermore, the standardisation process had the advantage to facilitate short-term transactions by saving time and money.[37]

Nowadays, short-term contracts are the prevailing kinds of agreements used in the domestic market, and the prices are usually spot prices (even in case long-term agreements are employed). As to the exportations, the contracts are both short and long term, and the price is usually based on spot markets. Moreover, it has to be noted that the US are foreseen to become a major exporter of natural gas in the future especially due to the growth of the production of shale gas.[38]

[E] The Evolution of the Russian Market and Relevant Gas Sale Contracts

In our brief analysis of the evolution of the main gas markets and of the characteristics of the relevant sale contracts, other two extra-European experiences are worth to be considered: the Russian and the Algerian gas markets.[39]

---

37. Juris, *supra* n. 13, at 12.
38. American Petroleum Institute, *supra* n. 2, at 15 et seq.; the US Energy Information Administration's 2014 Report, *supra* n. 28; DNV KEMA Energy & Sustainability, *supra* n. 3.
39. *See*, in general, J. Henderson, *Evolution of the Russian Gas Market – The Competition for Customers*, https://www.oxfordenergy.org/wpcms/wp-content/uploads/2013/01/NG_73.pdf,

With regard to the first, it has to be mentioned, *in primis*, that in Russia are located the largest resources of natural gas in the world. This makes it one of the main exporters of natural gas to Europe. In particular, the state-owned company, Gazprom, has the monopoly of the domestic and international gas market. As it was noted, 'Gazprom is considered a monopolist because it owns all of the high pressure interregional pipeline network as well as nearly seventy-five percent of low pressure distribution networks. It owns about half of Russia's proved reserves of natural gas and all the main gas processing facilities, as well as a legal export monopoly. Private companies do own reserves, but because domestic price is regulated by the state, and export is forbidden, their participation in the industry is comparatively small'.[40]

However, some competitors have recently appeared to the scene. According to a study carried out for the Oxford Institute for Energy Studies, 'significant change is occurring in the Russian gas sector, catalysed both by the political decision to increase gas prices and by the consequent reaction of a set of Non-Gazprom Producers (NGPs) who are now starting to exploit the opportunity to sell their product at negotiated prices and contract terms directly to Russian consumers who are increasingly keen to find alternative sources of supply'.[41] Some of Gazprom's competitors are Novatek, Itera, Rosneft, Lukoil, TNK-BP and Surgutneftegas. One of the factors that favoured competition in the domestic gas market was the increase of regulated prices established by the Federal Tariff Service. In fact, until recently these prices were kept at a low level discouraging competition making impossible for Gazprom's potential competitors to gain any profit by selling their gas (even Gazprom, that is required to sell gas at the regulated price, for many years did not make any profit from its domestic sales but only from the international ones). Thus, inevitably, they had to apply a higher price and, consequently, the only market sector they could pierce was that represented by consumers which needed more gas than the quantity provided by Gazprom at the regulated price.

Another measure adopted in order to favour competition in the Russian gas market was the enactment in 1997 of the government resolution n. 858 providing for the possibility for gas companies to access to the Unified Gas Transportation System (so called "Third Party Access" or "TPA"). Until 1997, Gazprom also had the monopoly of the pipeline and transportation system through its subsidiary Transgaz. However, as it was noted, 'with no effective body to enforce this, implementation of this provision was left to the goodwill of Gazprom management'.[42] Moreover, it was underlined that:

> Although Third Party Access regulation was enacted in Russia as early as 1997, Gazprom has retained a large measure of *de facto* control over access to the UGS [Unified Gas Transportation System] through its monopolization of data on

---

1 (2013); Melling, *supra* n. 3, at 77 et seq.; Y. Grigoryev, *The Russian Gas Industry, Its Legal Structure, and Its Influence on World Markets*, in 28 Energy L.J., 125 (2007); J.P. Stern, *The Future of Russian Gas and Gazprom* (Oxford University Press, 2005); *Id.*, *supra* n. 4, at 51 et seq.; Estrada, Bergesen, Moe & Sydnes, *supra* n. 23, at 169 et seq.; Peebles, *supra* n. 6, at 147 et seq.
40. Grigoryev, *id.*, at 125-126. As underlined by the Author, the reference to the ownership of gas reserves by companies means the right to exploit them since the State is their actual owner.
41. Henderson, *supra* n. 39, at 1-2.
42. Grigoryev, *supra* n. 39, at 125-126.

capacity utilisation in the system, which has allowed it to argue that requested capacity is not always readily available or that the most direct route to consumers cannot always be used (thus increasing the cost to independent suppliers). It has also to date been reluctant to agree long-term access for NGP [Non-Gazprom Producers] producers, restricting contracts to a maximum of three years, which has not been enough to encourage producers to develop new fields or to satisfy consumers about long-term security of supply.[43]

As pointed out in the above-mentioned study, competition is mainly developing in the domestic market, while exportations, especially towards Europe, are still dominated by Gazprom through its subsidiary Gazpromexport (Gazexport). However, even in this sector, changes have been occurred and it is possible to see some signals of competition. One example of this phenomenon is the long-term supply agreement concluded in 2012 between Novatek and the German company EnBW. It is interesting to note that this contract, contrary to Gazprom's sale agreements, does provide for prices determined with reference to European spot markets and not to oil products.

With regard to the characteristics of contracts concluded with European buyers, it has to be noted that, as already seen for other countries, they are long-term supply agreements, including take or pay clauses, since '[t]he European communities realize that their growing needs, the bulk of which are met with Russian gas, can only be adequately supplied if Russia is able to invest in new gas fields and pipeline construction. They understand that if gas is supplied exclusively through spot deals, gas suppliers, Gazprom included, will not be willing to shoulder the risks associated with multi-billion dollar investments with long payback periods and high quantity risk. Thus European importers are committed to their long-term agreements with Gazprom'.[44] Moreover, such contracts provide for a price linked to oil products and, in particular, to gasoil and heavy fuel oil. In this regard, it has to be noted that some agreements, especially those regarding the German market, contain specific clauses, providing, for instance, an indexation mechanism, alternative to inflation, by which a percentage of the oil product – used as reference for the determination of the gas price (for Germany the heavy fuel oil) – is kept (capped) at a low level.

As a consequence of the 2009 crisis, that in 2009 affected the gas market and the relevant sale contracts, Gazprom, in spite of being in favour of oil-indexation mechanism and long-term contracts (especially in light of large infrastructure projects already initiated and in progress), started negotiations with its leading customers and contracts were amended in order to face the European gas oversupply. In particular, '[b]enchmark deals were struck with pivotal customers including E.On and ENI who jointly purchase around 40 percent of Gazprom's exports to Europe. These deals serve as models for later deals, some already completed and others either in progress or awaiting the scheduled dates for price renegotiation discussions'.[45]

---

43. Henderson, *supra* n. 39, at 15.
44. Grigoryev, *supra* n. 39, at 134–135.
45. Melling, *supra* n. 3, at 83–84; DNV KEMA Energy & Sustainability, *supra* n. 3, at 25 et seq. Moreover, in some cases, due to the failure of renegotiations, Gazprom had to face arbitration (*see* Ch. 4).

[F] The Evolution of the Algerian Market and Relevant Gas Sale Contracts

Algeria is one of the major suppliers of natural gas to the European market.[46] The first gas discoveries are dated in 1956, when the country was still a French colonial. After Algeria had reached the independence in 1962, the government created the state-owned company *Société Nationale pour le Transport et la Commercialisation des Hydrocarbures* ("Sonatrach") in order to operate in the oil and gas sector and by 1971, it nationalised the whole hydrocarbons industry. Sonatrach has the monopoly of the production and transmission of gas. In particular, Algerian gas is exported both as pipeline gas and as liquefied natural gas (LNG) representing around 40% of the overall exportations (Algeria was the first country to build in 1964 a liquefaction gas plant).[47] The first type of gas is transported by means of two pipeline systems: (i) the Transmed pipeline (also called "Enrico Mattei Pipeline system") that brings Algerian gas to Italy under the Mediterranean sea (the Ente Nazionale Idrocarburi (ENI) – is the most important customer of Sonatrach); (ii) the Gaz Maghreb Europe pipeline (also called "Pedro Duran Farrel Pipeline") that brings Algerian gas to Spain under the Mediterranean sea. The relevant sale contracts are long-term supply agreements with take or pay obligations.

As to the LNG, the first exportations were towards the UK, France and US. The relevant contracts were signed between Sonatrach and, namely, British Gas Corporation in 1964, Gaz de France in 1965 and El Paso Natural Gas Company in 1969. They were long-term agreements providing for fixed quantities of gas to be supplied and for a price determined on the basis of capital and operating costs with inflation as an indexation element. In this regards, it was noted that:

> more than 80 per cent of the base price reflected the cost of capital and was fixed for the entire duration of the contracts. The other portion of the price reflected the operating cost and was, in the context of declining prices of oil products in the 1960s, indexed to inflationary parameters measured by the evolution of steel product prices and wages in the UK and US economies. Basically, these price arrangements were geared towards securing adequate returns on the capital invested. In addition, price indexation, which reflected solely the macroeconomic and industrial environment of importing countries, was completely divorced from the evolution of energy markets.[48]

Furthermore, the above-mentioned contracts did not contain any price review provision allowing to modify the price to changed circumstances in the market.

The first changes in the contractual structure of gas sale contracts were registered in the 1970s after the nationalisation of the gas industry. In particular, prices were linked to oil products traded in the buyers' market and take or pay clauses as well as

---

46. *See, in general,* Melling, *id.*, at 88 et seq.; M. H. Hayes, *Algerian Gas to Europe: The Transmed Pipeline and Early Spanish Gas Import Projects,* http://www.africanews.it (May 2004); A. Aissaoui, *The Political Economy of Oil and Gas,* 166 et seq.(Oxford University Press 2001); Stern, *supra* n. 4, at 46 et seq.; Estrada, Bergesen, Moe & Sydnes, *supra* n. 23, at 188 et seq.
47. Melling, *id.*, at 88.
48. Aissaoui, *supra* n. 46, at 191.

price re-opener provisions (by which the price could be reviewed periodically or in case important changes occurred in the relevant market) were introduced. However, due to the oil price increase as a result of the Iranian revolution in 1979, Algerian government (and, therefore, Sonatrach) decided to amend the price formula previously established by linking the price not to the oil products traded in the buyer's market but to the international price of crude oil. This choice had positive consequences in the short term since it allowed Sonatrach to benefit more of the oil price increase occurred in 1979, but it came out to be a negative decision in the long term since the Algerian gas price was too high and became, therefore, non-competitive. As a result, Sonatrach lost its market's share in the US, Canada and Western Europe favouring, in particular, Norwegian and Russian exportations.

In 1986, with the collapse of the oil price, Sonatrach started to renegotiate its contracts in light of the new market situation. In the renegotiation process, two main factors were considered: 'Firstly, the company was no longer in a position to transfer market risk to its clients. Indeed, buyers unsure of their future market share could not shoulder 'take-or-pay' commitments, requiring instead greater flexibility in contracted volumes over shorter time spans. Secondly, the development of spot markets [...] facilitated price discovery for prompt deliveries and for future spot gas supplies. As a result, market-based prices replaced the old indexation formula where gas prices had been linked to those of crude or oil products'.[49] In addition, it was provided for more flexibility in relation to buyers' off-take obligations and for a so called "pass-through indexation formula", according to which any change in the price of competitive fuels in the market was reflected in the gas price.

Another renegotiation process of the Sonatrach's contracts followed the crisis that invested the gas market in 2009 also affected Algerian gas exportations, and, especially, those of pipeline gas that decreased of almost 10%. In particular, Sonatrach's customers (and, mainly, ENI and Gas Natural) represented that they had difficulties in complying with their take or pay obligations. As a consequence, in the re-negotiation process, Sonatrach had to make some concessions in this regard. However, not always the renegotiation process worked out and, consequently, the matter was submitted to arbitration.[50] Furthermore, it seems that '[i]n response to the drop in global demand for natural gas and the problems of negotiating long-term oil-indexed contracts in the current environment, Sonatrach has recently stated its intention to offer customers short-term gas contracts'.[51]

§1.03 THE DEVELOPMENT OF GAS SPOT MARKETS

The development of spot or traded gas markets has been affected and modified the traditional contractual structure of gas sale contracts (i.e., long-term agreements providing for take or pay obligations and for oil-indexed prices) by introducing the use

---

49. *Ibid.*, at 193.
50. *See*, Ch. 4.
51. Melling, *supra* n. 3, at 92.

of more flexible short and medium-term contracts and a new mechanism for the determination of the gas price different from that based on oil products indexation.[52]

The emergence of spot markets is mainly due to the enhancing of competition and liberalisation in the market and, in particular, to the introduction, on the one hand, of the obligation for gas producers to unbundle the supply and transportation services and, on the other, of the so called "Third Party Access" (i.e., the possibility for third parties, that do not own any transportation infrastructure, to create a connection with the pipeline system to buy gas directly from the producers bypassing other intermediate levels of the sale chain and, in particular, distribution companies). This process, first, occurred in the US (during the 1980s) and in the UK (during the 1990s). In such countries, indeed, it is possible to register the existence of already developed traded gas markets and, namely, the Henry Hub and the National Balancing Point (NBP).

In continental Europe, instead, the liberalisation process was slower and, consequently, affected the growth of national-traded markets and frustrated the idea to integrate the latter by creating a single internal gas market. In particular, the first step of the European Community towards the development of a competitive integrated market was the enactment of the Gas Transit Directive in 1991, which provided for the above-mentioned Third Party Access. However, this measure was not sufficiently effective and was not properly enacted by the Member States. Therefore, additional interventions were necessary in order to achieve the goal of creating a competitive European gas market. As a consequence, three other directives were enacted in this direction: 98/30/EC; 2003/55/EC; 2009/73/EC.

In particular, the last one (so called "Third Energy Package") provides that:

> With a view to creating an internal market in natural gas, Member States should foster the integration of their national markets and the cooperation of system operators at Community and regional level, also incorporating the isolated systems forming gas islands that persist in the Community [and] shall cooperate ... to: (a) foster the creation of operational arrangements in order to enable an optimal management of the network, promote joint gas exchanges and the allocation of cross-border capacity, and to enable an adequate level of interconnection capacity, including through new interconnections, within the region and between regions to allow for development of effective competition and improvement of security of supply without discriminating between supply undertakings in different Member

---

52. On the development of spot markets and on the relevant impact on long-term gas sale agreements and on the oil-indexation mechanism, *see* P. Heather, *Continental European Gas Hubs: Are They Fit for Purpose?* https://www.oxfordenergy.org/wpcms/wp-content/uploads/2012/06/NG-63.pdf, 1 (2012); J.P. Stern, *The Transition to Hub-Based Gas Pricing in Continental Europe* https://www.oxfordenergy.org/wpcms/wp-content/uploads/2011/03/NG49.pdf, 1 (2011); Melling, *supra* n. 3, at 40 et seq.; J.P. Stern, *Continental European Long-Term Gas Contracts: Is a Transition Away from Oil Product-Linked Pricing Inevitable and Imminent?*, https://www.oxfordenergy.org/wpcms/wpcontent/uploads/2010/11/NG34ContinentalEuropeanLongTermGasContractsIsATransitionAwayFromOilProductLinkedPricingInevitableandImminentJonathanStern2009.pdf, 1 (2009); J.P. Stern, *Is There a Rationale for the Continuing Link to Oil Product Prices in Continental European Long-Term Gas Contracts*, https://www.oxfordenergy.org/wpcms/wpcontent/uploads/2010/11/NG19IsThereARationaleFortheContinuingLinkToOilProductPricesinContinentalEuropeanLongTermGasContracts-JonathanStern-2007.pdf, 1 (2007).

Chapter 1: The Gas Market and the Relevant Agreements §1.03

States; (b) coordinate the development of all network codes for the relevant transmission system operators and other market actors.[53]

Furthermore, such directive 'establishes common rules for the transmission, distribution, supply and storage of natural gas. It lays down the rules relating to the organisation and functioning of the natural gas sector, access to the market, the criteria and procedures applicable to the granting of authorisations for transmission, distribution, supply and storage of natural gas and the operation of systems'.[54] It also created a specific body, the Agency for the Cooperation of Energy Regulators (ACER), with the objective to favour the creation of the internal European energy market and that cooperates with the CEER.

Following the above-mentioned provisions, the Council of European Energy Regulators (CEER) – a non-profit association (through which national regulators cooperate and exchange best practice) whose main scope is to facilitate the creation of a single, competitive, efficient and sustainable European internal energy market that works in the public interest – organised the European Gas Regulatory Forum in Madrid on September 2010. In view of that event, it invited the European Commission and regulators to explore, in close cooperation with system operators and other stakeholders, the interaction and interdependence of all relevant areas for network codes and to initiate a process establishing a gas target model (so called "GTM"), i.e., the structure of the future integrated European gas market.

An additional measure enacted by the European Union in order to achieve the creation of European gas-traded market is the Regulation n. 1227/2011 (so called "REMIT") that establishes rules prohibiting abusive practices affecting wholesale energy markets with the scope to improve and promote transparency on traded markets. However, as it was noted, '[t]here is still a long way to go, in defining the rules and regulations that will permit such a unified market, in ironing out capacity bottlenecks to allow a market mechanism to work properly, and in writing and implementing coordinated Network Codes across the EU and, not least, getting the approval of all the Member states. However, much has already been achieved and it now looks as though the overriding goal as set out in the 3rd Package may be achieved'.[55]

As mentioned above, with the development of spot markets the traditional structure of gas sale contracts has changed since such markets provide buyers and sellers with the possibility to conclude short-term transactions and, therefore, to join more flexibility and to diversify their portfolio. In particular, buyers have the possibility to sign contracts with different gas producers without being bound by long-term agreements and the relevant take or pay obligations, that often can become burdensome. Thus, it can be said that the growth of traded markets, and the consequent use of short-term sale agreements, seems to be more advantageous for buyers than for producers and wholesalers that could not rely anymore on the long-term commitment of their customers (and on the relevant "guarantee" deriving from take or pay

---

53. Directive 2009/73/EC, whereas (56) and Art. 42, §2 (13 July 2009), http://eur-lex.europa.eu.
54. *Ibid.*, Art. 1.
55. Heather, *supra* n. 52, at 22.

obligations), that allows them to recover the investments made for the exploration and production of gas.

Moreover, sport markets imply the creation of hubs, i.e., physical or virtual points where gas is traded. In order for a hub to properly work, two main conditions are necessary: sufficient liquidity and transparency. The first condition is measured by the so called "churn *ratio*" that can be defined as 'the ratio between the total volume of trades and the physical volume of gas consumed in the area served by the hub'.[56] Usually a market can be deemed liquid and mature when the churn *ratio* is above the value of ten. As to the second condition, transparency means that prices are public and not manipulated by the main market players.

As to the types of hubs, it is possible to identify three main categories: Trading Hubs; Transit Hubs; Transition Hubs that were defined as follows:

> Trading Hubs as those which have reached a certain level of maturity and which are already being used for the financial risk management of gas portfolio. They are based on virtual trading points, have open and easy access to trade to a variety and number of participants, have good transparency and reporting and have proven to be reliable markets. The second category of Transit Hubs includes those hubs that are actual transit locations, or physical points, at which market participants can choose to trade gas; however, their primary role is to facilitate the transit of large quantities of gas for onward transportation. The final category is that of Transition Hubs by which I mean hubs that are based on a virtual trading point but have not yet reached a mature level. They are for the most part (but not all) attracting more volumes year on year and are showing signs of progress towards a becoming 'market price' for their respective national markets. Indeed, they are (again, for the most part) already being used as 'balancing markets' for shippers delivering or taking gas in those grids.[57]

As already mentioned, the US and UK have developed in the last decades mature spot markets (namely, the Henry Hub and the NBP). On the contrary, the emergence and development of spot markets in continental Europe has been slower. However, it is possible to identify some relevant hubs that have been lately seen a significant growth: the Dutch Title Transfer Facility (TTF), that together with the Henry Hub and the NBP can be considered as a Trading Hub (i.e., a mature market); the Belgian *Zeebrugge* (ZEE) and the Austrian Central European Gas Hub (CEGH) that can be defined Transit Hubs; the German Gaspool (GPL) and NetConnect (NCG), the French *Points d'Echange de Gaz* (PEGs), the Italian *Punto di Scambio Virtuale* (PSV) that can be considered as Transition Hubs.

The second main consequence that the development of spot markets determined on gas sale contracts (in addition to the duration) was the introduction of a new mechanism for the determination of the price: the market or hub-pricing method instead of the oil indexation, traditionally used in long-term contracts. This new method, by which the gas price is determined in light of the gas market and not of other

---

56. EU Energy Sector, *2007 Inquiry*, §70, n. 52, www.ec.europa.eu.
57. Heather, *supra* n. 52, at 5.

energy sources' market, has become prevailing in the US and UK where, as said, spot markets are already developed and mature, while in continental Europe oil-indexed prices are still prevailing in gas sale contracts. In particular, in order for the new mechanism to spread and become used, it is necessary for trading hubs to be enough liquid and transparent; characteristics that have still to be developed in many of the continental European hubs. In this regard, it was noted that '[t]he problem with Continental European hubs is threefold: lack of trading volume, insufficient liquidity, and risk of price manipulation by dominant national players'.[58] The issue of a possible transition in long-term gas sale contracts from oil-indexed prices to market-based prices has given rise in the last years to a huge debate. As above stressed, this problem mainly involves continental Europe. In this regard, it can be underlined that the debate concerned the main question whether the reference to the price of oil products for the determination of the gas price is still justified. The relevant analysis carried out have examined the arguments claimed by those supporting the mechanism based on the oil price indexation. In particular, the original justification brought by supporters of oil-indexed prices is that their customers could decide to return to use oil instead of gas in case the price of the first is more convenient. However, this argument was criticised since, for economic and efficiency reasons, it is rare that customers build plants or buy equipment that can burn either gas or oil and, therefore, that can easily switch from the first to the latter. In this regard, it was noted that:

> a combination of: the virtual elimination of oil products from many stationary energy sectors in these markets; the cost and inconvenience of maintaining oil-burning equipment and substantial stocks of oil products; the emergence of modern gas-burning equipment in which the use of oil products means a substantial loss of efficiency; tightening environmental standards in relation to emission, particularly sulphur content and nitrogen oxide; rendered the original rationale increasingly dubious, particularly in North West Europe. There is no commercial scenario in which users installing *new* fuels-burning equipment will choose to use oil products rather gas in stationary uses, unless they have no access to a gas supply.[59]

Additional main arguments brought in favour of maintaining the oil-indexation mechanism were: the lack of liquidity of European hubs, the price volatility and the risk of manipulation by market players.

As to the first, we have already underlined that, although progresses have been made, the continental European hubs' lack of sufficient liquidity to be considered as mature markets. The only exception is represented by the Dutch TTF that, as seen above, can be included in the category of Trading Hubs.

With regard to the volatility of hub prices (compared to oil-indexed prices), it was highlighted – on the basis of the data collected by the ICIS-Heren (one the main providers of information on the petrochemical market) – that:

---

58. Stern, *Is There a Rationale for the Continuing Link to Oil Product Prices in Continental European Long-Term Gas Contracts*, supra n. 52, at 17.
59. Id., *The Transition to Hub-Based Gas Pricing in Continental Europe*, supra n. 52, at 2.

the degree of hub price volatility is evident ... increased price volatility is an inevitable consequence of the need to balance the market in the short term. However, small and medium sized customers will not be exposed to daily or monthly changes, since companies supplying the residential and small industrial and commercial sectors will use a variety of trading strategies to manage volatility and pass through a smoother price pattern to smaller customers. Larger industrial customers and power generators will often have in-house trading capabilities to optimise their own portfolios.[60]

The concerns about the risk of hubs manipulation by major market players are mainly due to the fact that European continental gas markets are characterised by the presence of few buyers and sellers (they are de facto oligopolies). This market structure can potentially be a fertile ground for manipulation. Therefore, the possible transition from oil indexation to a market-based price mechanism in long-term contracts passes through the general development and growth of continental European spot markets (and, in particular, of their liquidity). Only in this way, such markets can become mature and constitute a benchmark for the determination of the gas price.

The development of spot markets and the consequent introduction of a different mechanism for the determination of the gas price could also have an impact on the existing long-term agreements since the price review process, usually provided in such contracts, could be triggered. Price review provisions can be included in the category of the so called "adaptation clauses" since they give the parties the possibility to renegotiate the elements of the formula used for the determination of the price in case unforeseen events change the conditions of the relevant market and, consequently, such formula does not reflect anymore the actual market situation and makes the contract unbalanced. Therefore, in case spot prices result to be lower than oil-indexed prices, buyers could claim the application of the price review mechanism. As it will be shown below,[61] when the renegotiation between parties fails usually an arbitration proceeding is started. One of the difficulties faced by arbitrators in performing their task is the interpretation of the above-mentioned clauses and, especially, the interpretation of the meaning of the expression "unforeseen events". In particular, arbitration tribunals have to determine whether the formation of a different price in spot markets for the same product (gas) can be considered as an unforeseen events beyond the control of the parties. This decision requires a preliminary step represented by the determination of whether spot markets prices can be recognised as benchmark prices for the sale of gas. Moreover, even in the affirmative case, another problem to be resolved is whether the arbitration tribunal can modify the original formula by replacing the reference to oil prices with that to spot markets price. However, before answering such questions, a preliminary issue has to be addressed, i.e., whether arbitrators have the power to adapt the contract on the basis of the latter's provisions and the procedural applicable law, that is the main focus of this book.

---

60. *Ibid.*, at 15–16.
61. *See* Chs 3 and 4.

§1.04 THE 2009 CRISIS

The other main event affecting long-term gas sale contracts was the crisis that in 2009 invested the European gas market causing a decrease and a contraction of consumptions and demands.[62]

The origin of this crisis can be found not only in the global economic recession started in 2008 but also in the following reasons: the competition and liberalisation process; the oversupply of gas; the uncertain gas demand; the entrance into the market of new players.[63]

We have already mentioned the competition and liberalisation process that involved the gas market. As said, it started before in the US and UK, where mature spot markets developed, and more recently in continental Europe, where, although the path is still long, some progresses and improvements have been made. Such process favoured the access of new players to the market. In particular, the new players (so called "second-tier players") can be mainly identified in those entities that previously were the customers of incumbent wholesalers (such as, local distributors, industrial customers, etc.). Furthermore, in some cases, they were the same wholesalers that expanded their business in other markets where 'they have joined the ranks of the second-tier players'.[64] The second-tier players – that in some countries (like, the Netherlands and Germany) could even withdraw their long-term contracts with wholesalers – gained a great benefit from the development of spot markets and from the consequent use of short and medium-term agreements. Indeed, due to liberalisation, they could deal directly with the producers and diversify their gas portfolio without being bound by long-term commitments and take or pay obligations. On the contrary, this situation was, instead, negative for wholesalers since they started losing clients and remained bound by their take or pay obligations included in the sale long-term contracts signed with the producers and still in force. In many cases, in order to comply with these obligations, they had to resell the gas purchased under such long-term agreements to second-tier players, or other end-customers, on the basis of short-term contracts.[65]

As to the second reason of the crisis, (i.e., the oversupply of gas), it was noted that:

> In the years leading up to the financial crisis of 2008, four factors may have contributed to over-contracting by key players in Europe for the current period: Bullish forecasts of gas demand in Europe; the defensive strategy of over-purchasing in order to prove to regulatory authorities that there was no room in the marketplace for competitive supplies; Optimistic estimates of market shares by

---

62. Heather, *supra* n. 52, at 1 et seq.; Melling, *supra* n. 3, at 40 et seq.
63. Melling, *id.*, at 45.
64. *Ibid.*, at 53.
65. *Ibid.*, at 68–70. In particular, according to the Author, the 'clearest beneficiaries of the collision between spot and oil-indexed gas on the continent are second-tier buyers, local distribution companies and industrials, and new market entrants that source gas under shorter-term contracts, and who have seized the moment, capitalizing on liberalized infrastructure access to source and move cheaper gas and grow their market share'.

individual players, contributing to aggregate purchases in excess of market size; Alleged corrupt practices by the representatives of national gas companies.[66]

In particular, the decrease of the gas demand experienced in 2009 on the market (that determined the oversupply) was so relevant that could not be faced through the normal contractual flexibility remedy provided in long-term contracts. It was reported that in 2009 the gas demand was equal to 523 billion cubic metres (bcm) – in 2008 it was equal to 563 bcm – while usually in the European market it ranges from 580 bcm to 620 bcm per year. If we consider that the downward quantity flexibility provided in long-term contracts is about 48 bcm per year, it is clear that it was not possible to face with normal flexibility the decrease of the gas demand in 2009.[67] An additional cause of the gas oversupply can be found in the exportations of LNG gas from the US sold in spot markets.

With regard to the uncertainty of the gas demand, it has to be noted that a key role was played by power generators which preferred to conclude short-term contracts on traded markets and to avoid take or pay obligations provided by long-term oil-indexed contracts. The main reason behind this choice was that '[t]he developer can rarely guarantee that electricity prices will be sufficient to cover the cost of gas, and Take-or-Pay commitments can potentially result in the necessity to purchase out-of-the-money gas year after year. In short, oil-indexed contracts are incompatible with traded electricity markets and can provide a significant barrier to investment in CCGTs [Combined Cycle Gas Turbines]'.[68]

§1.05 CONCLUSIONS

Our brief analysis and overview of the gas market has shown that gas (pipeline and LNG) producers and wholesalers are still using long-term agreements (with a duration of around 20–25 years) with oil-indexed prices and take or pay clauses (usually providing for a minimum volume commitment ranging from 80% to 90% of the Annual Contract Quantity agreed between the parties). However, due to the development of traded markets, shorter kinds of contracts and spot prices have become more common and used for the sale of gas (e.g., in the US and UK). Furthermore, the emergence and growth of spot markets together with the global recession (and the consequent decrease of the gas demand), the gas oversupply and the access into the market of new competitors made necessary the renegotiation of long-term contracts between producers and wholesalers. Such process concerns not only the price clauses (by, for instance, providing for price indexed to spot market instead of oil indexation) but also take or pay provisions. Indeed, the original minimum volume commitment (and the relevant amount of money to be paid even in case the minimum quantity of gas agreed is not taken) can become not sustainable anymore for wholesalers due to the change of the economic situation and market structure. In case of failure of the renegotiation, the

---

66. *Ibid.*, at 50.
67. *Ibid.*, at 48–50.
68. *Ibid.*, at 52.

parties usually submit the matter to arbitration and arbitrators have to face the problem of the interpretation and adaptation of the existing contracts. In some cases, the review of contracts has already been started or completed by the parties. For example, Gazprom, Statoil and GasTerra renegotiated with their most important customers some of the contractual terms included in their sale agreements by reducing prices and minimum volume commitments, as well as by introducing spot markets-elements in the price formula (in particular, by linking part of the gas volume to the price based on traded markets instead to oil products' price).[69] In other cases, as seen more in detail in the fourth chapter, the renegotiation process failed and parties started arbitration proceedings. Some of them have been recently concluded and determined the modification by arbitrators of the relevant price formula in order to adapt the contract to the new market circumstances.

---

69. *Ibid.*, at 123 et seq.; DNV KEMA Energy & Sustainability, *supra* n. 3, at 25 et seq.

CHAPTER 2
Take or Pay Clauses

§2.01 INTRODUCTION

Long-term contracts are still the most common types of gas sale agreements at least in continental Europe, while in the US and UK, where spot markets are more developed, short and medium-term contracts have, instead, become the prevailing form used.[70] The two main kinds of gas sale contracts are depletion and supply agreements.[71] The first provides for the sale of all – or of a determined quantity – of the gas located in a specific field to a specific buyer (usually the field, or part of it, is dedicated to such buyer). Therefore, the contract ends when the field's reserves are depleted. The other kind of agreement, that is the most used for the sale of gas, is the supply contract. Pursuant to such agreement, the seller supplies a determined volume (daily and annual) of gas to the buyer for the entire contractual duration. The supply of gas is not linked to the resources of a specific field. Indeed, the seller is free to choose from which field or source (even third parties) to take the gas to be provided. This type of agreement can be spot or long term. Our analysis will mainly focus on the latter that is characterised by an average duration of around 20–25 years and by the provision of an oil-indexed price, i.e., a price determined with reference to that of oil products (in particular, gasoil and heavy fuel oil).[72]

In consideration of the long duration of gas sale agreements, it is unlikely that the relevant contractual terms (and, in particular, the price and the minimum volume commitments) are able to reflect the actual market conditions for such a period of time. This is mainly due to unforeseen events that may change the economic conditions of the relevant market existing at the time of the stipulation of the contract altering its

---

70. *See* Ch. 1.
71. D. Beggs & D.W. Sapte, *Gas Sales and Supply Contracts, Natural Gas Agreements*, 149–168 (M.R. David, Sweet & Maxwell 2002).
72. The oil indexation mechanism is still the most common in continental Europe, while in the US and UK the price is mainly determined with reference to spot markets (*see* Ch. 1).

balance. For this reason, it is necessary for the parties to review or renegotiate the contractual terms periodically or when relevant changes in the market occur. Thus, long-term gas sale contracts usually (although not always) include review or adaptation provisions with particular reference to the price (so called "price re-opener clauses" or "price review clauses"). Moreover, they normally provide for take or pay clauses establishing the buyer's obligation to pay for a minimum volume of gas even in case it is not actually taken. In this chapter, we mainly focus on the characteristics of such provisions and on the main issues that they can give rise to, with particular reference to the problem of their nature and the consequences that the different interpretations in this regard can have on the arbitrators' power to adjust long-term gas sale agreements. The analysis of such power and of the adaptation clauses (and, in particular, price review and hardship provisions) will be dealt with in the third and fourth chapters.

§2.02 MAIN CHARACTERISTICS

Long-term gas sale contracts usually provide for an overall annual volume of gas that the buyer can purchase, the so called "Annual Contract Quantity" (ACQ). Moreover, it is often a fixed daily volume of gas that can be supplied, the so called "Daily Contract Quantity" (DCQ), normally calculated by dividing the ACQ for 365 days.[73] The seller's obligation to deliver the gas will rise upon the buyer's request of the amount of gas to be provided within the ACQ (so called "nomination"). For this reason, gas sale agreements are also defined as "nominated contracts". Furthermore, gas sale contracts usually grant the buyer a certain degree of flexibility (both upwards and downwards) in relation to the ACQ and DCQ. As to the upwards flexibility, they set a maximum annual quantity (often equal to 110 or 115% of the ACQ) that the buyer can purchase and, normally, they also provide for a relevant maximum daily quantity calculated by dividing the maximum annual quantity for 365 days. With regard to the downwards flexibility, contracts generally establish a minimum annual quantity (so called "Annual Take or Pay Quantity" or "Minimum Bill Quantity", usually equal to 85%–90% of the ACQ) that the buyer has the obligation to purchase and that represents the key element of take or pay obligations. Sometimes, the contract also specifies a minimum daily quantity to be bought, for example, in case gas infrastructures need a minimum production volume in order to properly work.

In particular, the mechanism provided by a take or pay clause, on the one hand, establishes the obligation of the buyer to take (and pay for) the Minimum Bill Quantity or, in any case, to pay for such quantity, even if the gas is not actually taken (all or in

---

73. *See*, in general, P. Roberts, *Petroleum Contracts - English Law and Practice*, 178 et seq. (Oxford University Press 2013); G. Leonardo, *L'obbligo di take or pay: Qualificazione e gestione delle sopravvenienze*, I Contratti, 605 (2013); Melling, *supra* n. 3; Y. Osikilo, *How Are the Problems of Buyer in Long-Term Take or Pay Contracts in the Gas Industry Mitigated?*, 9 CEPMLP Annual Review, 1 (2005); Beggs & Sapte, *supra* n. 71; L. Parola, *Contratti di somministrazione di gas naturale "Take or Pay" e project financing*, I Contratti, 192 (2002); B. Phillips, *Examining the Future of Long-Term Take or Pay Contracts*, 3 O.G.L.T.R., 73 (1997); H. Davey, *"Take or Pay" and "Send or Pay": A Legal Review and Long-Term Prognosis*, 11 O.G.L.T.R., 419 (1997).

part). It follows that the buyer's failure to withdraw the Minimum Bill Quantity will not exempt it from the duty to pay the relevant price. On the other hand, such mechanism provides for the corresponding obligation of the seller to supply the aforementioned minimum quantity. Therefore, take or pay clauses accomplish double functions. First, they provide the seller with a fixed and constant flux of money by the buyer independent of the fluctuations and variations of the actual demand of gas in the market where the latter operates. In this way, the seller can at least recover the investments made in view of the performance of the contract (for instance, for the infrastructures) that, especially in the gas field, are particularly relevant. Moreover, the seller can fulfil its payment obligations deriving from any loan agreements entered into with banks to finance such investments. Second, take or pay clauses provide the buyer with a regular and steady supply of gas in order to meet the relevant demand in the market (without the need to negotiate every time with the seller the conditions for the supply of gas).[74] As seen more in detail in the third chapter, this double function is fundamental since it represents the essential scope characterising long-term gas sale agreements. In particular, in order to reach such scope, and, consequently, to fulfil the parties' will, the contract has to be maintained for the entire duration originally agreed. It follows that, in case its *equilibrium* is altered upon the occurrence of unforeseen events, it is necessary to adjust it in order to re-establish its balance. On the contrary, the termination or maintenance of the agreement without adaptation to the new market conditions are not the best solution for long-term gas sale agreements (and for long-term contracts in general) since they do not consent the achievement of the above-mentioned purpose and the consequent satisfaction of the parties' will.

As to the determination of the Annual Take or Pay Quantity, it has to be noted that it is subject to some adjustment mechanisms in case events beyond the buyer's control occur. In particular, such quantity (and, consequently, the buyer's take or pay obligation) has to be determined considering the following circumstances: the seller's failure to deliver the quantity of gas duly nominated by the buyer; force majeure events that prevent the buyer taking the quantities of the gas ordered or events making its performance extremely burdensome;[75] the lack of conformity of the gas delivered to the quality or standards agreed in the contract. In order to establish whether or not the buyer has actually breached its take or pay obligation it will, therefore, be necessary to verify if some of the above-mentioned circumstances happened. In the affirmative case, the relevant volumes of gas not taken by the buyer have to be deducted from the Minimum Bill Quantity. In case after this operation a difference between such quantity and the gas actually taken still remains, the buyer has to pay for such difference. Furthermore, other adjustment mechanisms to be considered in the determination of

---

74. Melling, *id.*; Osikilo, *id.*
75. *See International Minerals and Chemical v. Llano*, 770 F.2d, 879 (10th Cir. 9 August 1985) in which the Court affirmed that the entrance into force of a new environmental regulation, requiring the buyer to change its production process, was a circumstance making its performance impracticable (i.e., extremely burdensome). As a consequence, the Court held that the buyer was not completely excused from paying the Minimum Bill Quantity but it was entitled to a reduction of the latter.

the Annual Take or Pay Quantity are represented by the following contractual provisions: make-up; carry-forward and make-good clauses.

According to the first type of provision, the buyer has still the obligation to pay for the Minimum Bill Quantity but it is entitled to take such amount of gas in a later moment (usually in a subsequent contractual year). The volumes of gas paid but not simultaneously taken by the buyer are called "Make-Up Volumes" or "Annual Deficiencies". Such mechanism, on the one hand, consents the buyer to benefit from a certain degree of flexibility with regard to the actual withdrawal of the gas purchased and, on the other, does not interrupt the flow of payments towards the seller. However, make-up provisions present some critical issues. In particular, the most relevant problem with these clauses concerns the difficulty for gas producers to efficiently plan the transportation phase since there will be moments in which the transportation system risks to be overloaded and others in which, on the contrary, there will be a low flux of gas. Sellers, instead, generally prefer to have a stream of gas as constant and regular as possible in order to be able to efficiently program the transport operations. For this reason, usually gas sale contracts provide for some limitations of both the amount of Make-Up Volumes (i.e., generally equal to 15% of the ACQ) and the application of the aforementioned clauses.

The second kind of provision is the carry-forward clause that sets a compensation mechanism by which the buyer, in case in a specific contractual period it took and paid for gas in excess of the Minimum Bill Quantity, is entitled to use such surplus in a subsequent period of time in which it will not be able to comply with its take or pay obligation. In this way, it can compensate for the withdrawal of a quantity of gas lower than the minimum volume agreed. It has also to be noted that often the quantity of gas used as a benchmark for the determination of the possible surplus is the ACQ and not the Annual Take or Pay Quantity. In this regard, it was underlined that:

> In some cases, the threshold amount is the minimum bill quantity, but more commonly the threshold is reached when the customer has taken and paid for the ACQ. Therefore any payments for volumes in excess of the ACQ will be carried forward and can be offset against the ACQ for a subsequent year. Where the threshold for Carry Forward is based on the Minimum Bill Quantity, make-up rights often elapse on a "first in, first out" basis after a negotiated period of, for example, three to five years, sometimes ten years. The expiration periods used in European contracts are usually of the same duration as those set for make-up rights. Where the threshold is based on the ACQ, Carry Forward may be unlimited and any unused volumes will simply lapse at the termination of the contract. Maximum Carry Forward volumes that can be used in any contract year will generally be limited to a percentage of ACQ, typically 10 or 15 percent.[76]

Like make-up clauses, carry-forward provisions can give rise to problems in relation to the transportation phase since they provide the buyer with a certain degree of flexibility that can cause an inconstant and unsteady demand/flux of gas and, consequently, an irregular use of the transportation system.

---

76. Melling, *supra* n. 3, at 131–132.

A compensation mechanism is also provided by the so called "make-good clauses". According to such provisions, the buyer is entitled, in a specific contractual period, to take an amount of gas lower than the Annual Take or Pay Quantity and to offset such purchase against future withdrawals of gas in excess of such minimum volume. The lower gas off-take does not trigger the buyer's obligation to pay, in any case, for the Minimum Bill Quantity. Like for make-up and carry-forward provisions, contracts usually set specific limits for the application of this type of clause.

§2.03   THE NATURE OF TAKE OR PAY CLAUSES

The nature and qualification of take or pay clauses has given rise to a debate among scholars and case law that will be examined more in detail in the next paragraphs through the analysis of the approaches adopted in the common and civil law systems. In particular, it seems possible to identify two main interpretations. The first considers take or pay clauses as penalties, i.e., clauses providing for a sum to be paid by a party in case of a breach of contract and, namely, the failure to take or request the minimum quantity of products or services agreed.[77] Therefore, such money represents an advanced liquidation of damages. This qualification of take or pay clauses has relevant consequences on their enforceability since in some legal systems (and, in particular, within the common law area) penalties are usually not recoverable unless the sum therein specified represents a genuine, reasonable and commercially justifiable pre-estimate of damages. In this case such sum is not considered as a penalty anymore but as liquidated damages that are, instead, recoverable.[78] In civil law systems, instead, penalty clauses are generally considered valid and enforceable save for the power of courts and arbitrators to reduce the amount herein provided if it results to be excessive and unreasonable.[79]

On the contrary, according to the second interpretation, take or pay clauses are not considered penalties but clauses providing for two alternative ways to perform the contract for the buyer. In particular, with regard to gas sale agreements, the latter can choose whether to take and pay for the Minimum Bill Quantity or whether to just pay for such amount of gas and take it later. In both cases, the buyer complies with its main obligation in return for the main performance of the seller, that is to supply and make available the Minimum Bill Quantity agreed in the contract. Therefore, the buyer's obligation to pay for the Minimum Bill Quantity, even when it does not actually take such amount of gas, does not derive from a breach of contract (i.e., the failure to

---

77. See *E-Nik v. Department for Communities and Local Government*, http://www.bailii.org/ew/cases/EWHC/Comm/2012/3027.html (EWHC (QB) 2 November 2012); Order n. VAS-6632/09 (Supreme Commercial Court of the Russian Federation 28 May 2009), as cited in M. Polkinghorne, *Take-or-pay Conditions in Gas Supply Agreements*, http://www.whitecase.com/sites/whitecase/files/files/download/publications/paris-energy-series-no7_2016.pdf (2013); *M&J Polymers v. Imerys Minerals*, http://www.bailii.org/ew/cases/EWHC/Comm/2008/344.html (EWHC (QB) 29 February 2008); *Lake River v. Carborundum*, 769 F.2d, 1284 (7th Cir. 9 August 1985).
78. See §2.03[A][1].
79. See §2.03[B].

withdraw all or part of the Minimum Bill Quantity), that is, instead, a necessary condition for a penalty clause to become effective. As a consequence, the sum due by the buyer to the seller under a take or pay clause when the gas is not taken is a debt (since it represents one of its alternative main obligations due in return for the main performance of the seller) and not damages.[80]

[A] The Common Law Approach

[1] English Law

As it will be shown by the analysis carried out below, it seems that the most recent English courts' decisions, that addressed the issue of the nature of take or pay clauses, adopted an approach in favour of the application of the law of penalties to such provisions. However, even if the remedy against penalties is the non-enforcement, we will see that English courts tend to save them if, on the basis of the facts of the case, they can be considered reasonable and justifiable on the basis of the facts of the case. Before examining the aforementioned case law, it is necessary to briefly analyse the distinction between penalties and damages and between debts and damages since these concepts are referred to by courts with regard to take or pay clauses. Moreover, we have seen that the distinction between penalties and damages is particularly relevant since, in common law, the formers are not enforceable.

[a] The Distinction Between Penalties and Liquidated Damages

The landmark authority on penalty clauses is the *Dunlop Pneumatic Tyre v. New Garage and Motor* decision.[81] In such case, the parties entered into a contract for the supply of motor-tyre covers and tubes that provided for the obligation of New Garage and Motor ("New Garage") to pay for a specific sum to Dunlop Pneumatic Tyre ("Dunlop") 'for each and every tyre, cover or tube sold or offered in breach of this agreement; as and by way of liquidated-damages, and not as a penalty'.[82] Once Dunlop had discovered that New Garage had sold covers and tubes in breach of the contract, it started a lawsuit claiming for the relevant damages. In the first grade, it was held that

---

80. *See*, in general, M. Iynedjian, *Gas Sale and Purchase Agreements under Swiss Law*, 4 ASA Bulletin, 746 (2012); Roberts, *supra* n. 73, at 183 et seq.; *id.*, *Gas Sales and Gas Transportation Agreements*, 195 et seq. (Sweet & Maxwell 2011); B. Holland & P. Ashley, *Enforceability of Take-or-Pay Provisions in English Law Contracts*, 26 J.E.R.L., 610 (2008); Beggs & Sapte, *supra* n. 71; A. Oladotun, *M&J Polymers Ltd. v. Imerys Mineral Limited: Can Take or Pay Clause in Gas Contract Be Considered a Contractual Penalty?*, 14 CEPMLP Annual Review, 1 (2005); H. Davey, *supra* n. 73, at 420 et seq. As to the case law, *see Styrpac v. Gaz de France* (Court of Appeal of Angers n. 04/01783 15 June 2005), as cited in M. Polkinghorne, *supra* n. 77, at 4; *Roye Realty & Developing v. Arkla*, 863 P.2d, 1150 (Okla. 13 July 1993); *Colorado Interstate Gas v. Chemco*, 854 P.2d 1232 (Colo. 14 June 1993); *Coneco v. Foxboro Great Britain*, LEXIS (EWCA Civ 24 February 1992); *Prenalta v. Colorado Interstate Gas*, 944 F.2d, 677 (10 4 September 1991); *Universal Resources v. Panhandle Eastern Pipe Line*, 813 F.2d, 77 (5 31 March 1987).
81. *Dunlop Pneumatic Tyre v. New Garage and Motor*, 1915 AC, 79 (UKHL 1 July 1914).
82. *Ibid.*, at 85.

a breach of contract occurred and that the sum claimed by Dunlop had to be qualified not as a penalty but as liquidated damages and, therefore, it was recoverable. However, in the appeal judgment, the Court reversed such decision and qualified the amount in dispute as a penalty. Upon the Dunlop's appeal, the House of Lords held that:

> It is just, therefore, one of those cases where it seems quite reasonable for parties to contract that they should estimate that damage at a certain figure, and provided that figure is not extravagant there would seem no reason to suspect that it is not truly a bargain to assess damages, but rather a penalty to be held in terrorem.[83]

In reaching such conclusion, the House of Lords fixed a set of criteria and rules to be followed when courts face the question whether a contractual provision, that contains an advanced liquidation of damages in case of breach of contract, can be qualified as a penalty. In this regard, it was stated that such issue is a matter of construction of contractual terms and interpretation of the specific circumstances of the case that have to be analysed at the moment of the conclusion of the contract and not when the breach occurred. Furthermore, the House of Lords provided a series of indications to be used in carrying out such construction and interpretation process. In particular, it was affirmed that:

> 1. Though the parties to a contract who use the words "penalty" or "liquidated damages" may prima facie be supposed to mean what they say, yet the expression used is not conclusive. The Court must find out whether the payment stipulated is in truth a penalty or liquidated damages. This doctrine may be said to be found passim in nearly every case. 2. The essence of a penalty is a payment of money stipulated as in terrorem of the offending party; the essence of liquidated damages is a genuine covenanted pre-estimate of damage ... 3. The question whether a sum stipulated is penalty or liquidated damages is a question of construction to be decided upon the terms and inherent circumstances of each particular contract, judged of as at the time of the making of the contract, not as at the time of the breach ... 4. To assist this task of construction various tests have been suggested, which if applicable to the case under consideration may prove helpful, or even conclusive. Such are (a) It will be held to be penalty if, the sum stipulated for is extravagant and unconscionable in amount in comparison with the greatest loss that could conceivably be proved to have followed from the breach. ... (b) It will be held to be a penalty if the breach consists only in not paying a sum of money, and the sum stipulated is a sum greater than the sum which ought to have been paid ... (c) There is a presumption (but no more) that it is penalty when "a single lump sum is made payable by way of compensation, on the occurrence of one or more or all of several events, some of which may occasion serious and others but trifling damage" ... On the other hand (d) It is no obstacle to the sum stipulated being a genuine pre-estimate of damage, that the consequences of the breach are such as to make precise pre-estimation almost an impossibility. On the contrary, that is just the situation when it is probable that pre-estimated damage was the true bargain between the parties.[84]

---

83. *Ibid.*, at 88.
84. *Ibid.*, at 86–88.

The principles stated in the *Dunlop* case were reaffirmed also in more recent decisions. For example, in *Philips Hong Kong v. Attorney General of Hong Kong*,[85] the Privy Council considered that the sum to be paid by Philips Hong Kong, in case of delay in carrying out the works provided in the contract, was not a penalty. In particular, it was held that that:

> Except possibly in the case of situations where one of the parties to the contract is able to dominate the other as to the choice of the terms of a contract, it will normally be insufficient to establish that a provision is objectionably penal to identify situations where the application of the provision could result in a larger sum being recovered by the injured party than his actual loss. Even in such situations so long as the sum payable in the event of non-compliance with the contract is not extravagant, having regard to the range of losses that it could reasonably be anticipated it would have to cover at the time the contract was made, it can still be a genuine pre-estimate of the loss that would be suffered and so a perfectly valid liquidated damage provision. The use in argument of unlikely illustrations should therefore not assist a party to defeat a provision as to liquidated damages.[86]

The same conclusions were reached in *Murray v. Leisureplay*.[87] In this case, the Court considered that the clause of the service agreement providing for 'the payment of a year's gross salary in the event of termination of Mr Murray's employment without one year's notice is unenforceable as a penalty' was not a penalty.[88]

---

85. *Philips Hong Kong v. Attorney General of Hong Kong*, 61 BLR 49 (JCPC 9 February 1993).
86. *Ibid.*, at 58–59. *See also* the Australian case *AMEV-UDC Finance v. Austin* (mentioned in the *Philips* case, in which it was stated that '[t]he test to be applied in drawing that distinction is one of degree and will depend on a number of circumstances, including (1) the degree of disproportion between the stipulated sum and the loss likely to be suffered by the plaintiff, a factor relevant to the oppressiveness of the term to the defendant, and (2) the nature of the relationship between the contracting parties, a factor relevant to the unconscionability of the plaintiff's conduct in seeking to enforce the term. The courts should not, however, be too ready to find the requisite degree of disproportion lest they impinge on the parties' freedom to settle for themselves the rights and liabilities following a breach of contract. The doctrine of penalties answers, in situations of the present kind, an important aspect of the criticism often levelled against unqualified freedom of contract, namely the possible inequality of bargaining power. In this way the courts strike a balance between the competing interests of freedom of contract and protection of weak contracting parties' (162 CLR 170, 193 (HCA 4 November 1986)).
87. *Murray v. Leisureplay*, http://www.bailii.org/ew/cases/EWCA/Civ/2005/963.html (EWCA Civ 28 July 2005).
88. *Ibid.*, at para. 1. In the same sense, *Azimut-Benetti v. Healey*, http://www.bailii.org/ew/cases/EWHC/Comm/2010/2234.html, para. 29 (EWHC (QB) 3 September 2010), in which the Court, that referred to the principles stated in *Murray v. Leisureplay* case, considered a sum equal to 20% of the contract price – to be paid by the defendant (a purchaser of a luxury yacht) upon its breach of contract (namely, the lack of payment of the first instalment to the builder) – not as a penalty but as a genuine pre-estimate of damages. In particular, it was held that '[i]n my judgment, the evidence clearly shows that the purpose of the clause was not deterrent, and that it was commercially justifiable as providing a balance between the parties upon lawful termination by the builder. I do not accept the defendant's submission that the court has to form a view as to the maximum possible loss that the parties would have expected to flow from any determination of the contract and the extent to which the stipulated figure for liquidated damages exceeded that maximum possible loss, and that since it cannot do so without extensive disclosure, and factual and expert evidence, the defendant must be permitted to defend the claim. This was a contract for the construction and sale of a very expensive yacht, aptly

It is interesting to note that the Court, in reaching its decision, underlined that the principles of parties autonomy and *pacta sunt servanda* are well established in the English contract law and that, therefore, English courts tend not to modify or re-write contractual terms. However, the Court also pointed out that an exception to such rules regards penalty clauses since it would be against public policy to allow a party to recover an unjustifiable and not proportionate sum as a consequence of a breach of contract. In this situation, therefore, courts have to verify whether, in light of the facts of the case and of the content of the agreement, the penalty clause can be considered a genuine pre-estimate of damages and, as such, it is enforceable. In particular, the Court observed that:

> [t]he penalty issue is one of considerable jurisprudential interest. English law is well-known for the respect which it gives to the sanctity of contact. The question which the law of penalties poses is this: to what extent does English contract law allow parties to a contract to specify for their own remedies in damages in the event of breach? The answer is that English law does not in this particular field take the same *laissez-faire* approach that it takes to (for example) the question whether parties can agree to time limits for the performance of obligations which they subsequently find difficulty in meeting. So far as that is concerned, *pacta sunt servanda*. So far as pre-determined damages clauses are concerned, English contract law recognises that, if the parties agree that a party in breach of contract shall pay an unjustifiable amount in the event of a breach of contract, their agreement is to that extent unenforceable. The reasons for this exception may be pragmatic rather principled.[89]

What emerges from the analysis of the case law carried out above is that the relevant criterion to determine if a clause is a not enforceable penalty is to ascertain whether it amounts to a genuine pre-estimate of damages and, therefore, if:

- it is proportionate to the loss suffered by the non-breaching party and it is not extravagant;

---

described in the evidence as a "super-yacht". Both parties had the benefit of expert representation in the conclusion of the contract. The terms, including the liquidated damages clause, were freely entered into. As the authorities referred to above show, in a commercial contract of this kind, what the parties have agreed should normally be upheld. In my view, the clause in question is not even arguably a penalty, and is enforceable in its terms'. See also, *General Trading Company (Holdings) v. Richmond*, 2 Lloyd's Rep., 475 (EWHC (QB) 3 July 2008); *Tullett Prebon Group v. Ghaleb El-Hajjali*, http://www.bailii.org/ew/cases/EWHC/QB/2008/1924.html (EWHC 31 July 2008).

89. *Murray v. Leisureplay, id.,* at para. 29. The Court also referred to *Robophone Facilities v. Blank* in which it was held that '[i] make no attempt, where so many others have failed, to rationalise this common law rule. It seems to be sui generis. The court has no general jurisdiction to re-form terms of a contract because it thinks them unduly onerous on one of the parties - otherwise we should not be so hard put to find tortuous constructions for exemption clauses, which are penalty clauses in reverse; we could simply refuse to enforce them ... But however anomalous it may be, the rule of public policy that the court will not enforce a "penalty clause" so as to permit a party to a contract to recover in an action a sum greater than the measure of damages to which he would be entitled at common law is well established, and in these days when so often one party cannot satisfy his contractual hunger a la carte but only at the table d'hote of a standard printed contract, it has certainly not outlived its usefulness' (1 WLR 1428, 1446–1447 (EWCA Civ 1 January 1966)).

– its function is not to punish or "terrorise" the other party (in this regard, a factor to be considered is whether such clause was negotiated between the parties and whether they have an equal bargaining power).

However, it has to be noted that in a recent decision, the English Supreme Court seems to have followed a different criterion.[90] Indeed, the Court affirmed that, in order to determine whether a clause is a penalty or not, it is not relevant if such clause amounts to a genuine pre-estimate of damages or if it is *in terrorem* of the other party but 'whether the impugned provision is a secondary obligation which imposes a detriment on the contract-breaker out of all proportion to any legitimate interest of the innocent party in the enforcement of the primary obligation'.[91] Therefore, according to the Supreme Court, what is relevant in carrying out the analysis of the contract is to determine whether the clause assists a legitimate interest of the party in whose favour such clause was provided and, in the affirmative case, if it is extravagant with regard to this interest.[92]

Before concluding our analysis on the distinction between penalties and liquidated damages, it is worth mentioning the case *Jobson v. Johnson*[93] in which the Court adopted different approach and principles with regard to penalties. In such case, the parties entered into an agreement for the sale of shares in a football club from Mr Jobson (Claimant) to Mr Johnson (Defendant) at the price of GBP 40,000 plus an additional sum of GBP 311,688 divided into six equal half-yearly instalments of GBP 51,948 each one (such amount was then reduced by the parties to GBP 300,000). Furthermore, the contract (at clause six, letter b) provided that, in case of lack of payment by the Defendant of such instalment, the latter had to transfer the shares back to the Claimant at the price of GBP 40,000. The Defendant paid the initial sum of GBP 40,000 (and, as provided by the agreement, it received the shares) and just GBP 100,000 of the GBP 300,000 agreed. As a consequence, the Claimant started a lawsuit asking for the re-transfer of the shares, while the Defendant rebutted that the above-mentioned clause amounted to an unenforceable penalty. The trial judge found in favour of the Claimant and, consequently, ordered the Defendant the specific performance of the agreement, i.e., the re-transfer of the shares. The latter appealed such decision. The Court of Appeal affirmed the general principle that, in case of a penalty clause (as it was considered the above-mentioned provision), the latter has not

---

90. *Cavendish Square Holding BV v. Talal El Makdessi and ParkingEye Limited v. Beavis*, https://www.supremecourt.uk/cases/uksc-2013-0280.html (UKSC 4 November 2015). The Supreme Court decided two appeals in conjunction.
91. *Ibid.*, at para. 32.
92. The Court based its statement on the fact that a penal and a pre-estimate of loss 'are not natural opposites or mutually exclusive categories. A damages clause may be neither or both. The fact that the clause is not a pre-estimate of loss does not therefore, at any rate without more, mean that it is penal. To describe it as a deterrent (or, to use the Latin equivalent, in terrorem) does not add anything. A deterrent provision in a contract is simply one species of provision designed to influence the conduct of the party potentially affected [...] The question whether it is enforceable should depend on whether the means by which the contracting party's conduct is to be influenced are "unconscionable" or (which will usually amount to the same thing) "extravagant" by reference to some norm' (*ibid.*, at para. 31).
93. *Jobson v. Johnson*, 1 Weekly Law Reports, 1026 (EWCA Civ 25 May 1988).

to be struck down but it has to be enforced only for the amount corresponding to the actual loss suffered by the non-breaching party. In particular, it was held that:

> An obligation to make a money payment stipulated in terrorem will not be enforced beyond the sum which represents the actual loss of the party seeking payment, namely, principal, interest and, if appropriate, costs, in those cases where ... the primary obligation is to pay money, or where the primary obligation is to perform some other obligation, beyond the sum recoverable as damages for breach of that obligation ... Accordingly, once a court becomes aware that the amount claimed by the plaintiff is a penalty arising on default of payment of a specific sum of money the legal consequence which follows ... is that the amount claimed will be scaled down by the court to the sum equal to the unpaid principal, with interests and costs.[94]

Thus, in such case, the Court departed from the approach usually adopted by English case law with regard to penalty clauses, i.e., the non-enforcement of the latter. Indeed, by maintaining such provision and de facto reducing the amount of the penalty exceeding the actual loss suffered by the claimant, it adopted an approach that is typical of civil law courts.[95]

However, the Court also noted that it would be more difficult to exercise such power (i.e., the scaling-down of the penalty), in case the obligation provided by the latter for the breach of contract does not consist in the payment of money but in a different obligation (such as the transfer of property) like in the present case. In particular, the Court underlined that such problem arises, especially, in situations where 'the value of the property agreed to be transferred exceeds the actual loss of the innocent party'.[96] Moreover, in this case, it was considered not 'right to order a specific performance of cl. 6(b) in part only, namely in respect of the reduced number of shares whose value does not exceed the actual loss of the plaintiff. That, indeed, would be to make a new bargain for the parties'.[97] At the same time, the Court did not consider right either the order to re-transfer of all the shares, since their actual value could have exceeded the loss of the Claimant, or the decision not to grant any specific relief. Indeed, in both cases, one of the parties would have suffered an unjust prejudice. Thus, the Court concluded that, in this situation, the proper remedy was to provide the Claimant with two alternatives: (1) the sale of the shares and the consequent payment to the Claimant of the instalments still due plus interests; or (2) the determination of the shares' value and, in case it did not exceed the Claimant's actual loss (i.e., the not paid

---

94. *Ibid.*, at 1040. See also *Beckham v. Drake*, 2 Cl.&F. 579, 622 (UKHL 11 July 1849). In such case (that concerned an employment contract providing for a penalty of GBP 500 to be paid by the breaching party to the other) the Court held that: '[t]he clause by which, in the event that has happened, the master agreed to pay the servant 500l., is certainly in its terms an agreement to pay money, and though the construction which the law requires to be put upon it prevents the whole sum from being payable when it would be more than a reasonable compensation for a failure of performance, it is not thereby rendered wholly inoperative, but it retains the effect of binding the failing party to pay such part of the sum as may be reasonable in respect of the failure'.
95. See §2.03[B].
96. *Jobson v. Johnson*, supra n. 93, at 1040.
97. *Ibid.*

instalments plus interests) more than GBP 40,000 (i.e., the price to be paid by the Claimant for the re-transfer), the latter could obtain the re-transfer.

[b] The Distinction Between Debts and Damages

The second important distinction to be drawn is the one between debts and damages.[98] In general, a debt is considered 'a definite sum of money fixed by the agreement of the parties as payable by one party in return for the performance of a specified obligation by the other party or upon the occurrence of some specified event or condition [other than a breach of contract]'.[99] In other words, a debt represents the main obligation of one party and not a secondary obligation that becomes effective when a breach of contract occurred.

---

98. *See*, in general, Roberts, *supra* n. 73, at 26 et seq.; J. Chitty, *Chitty on Contracts* vol. 1, 1202-1203 (Sweet & Maxwell 2015); R. E. Cerchia, *Quando il vincolo contrattuale si scioglie*, 96 et seq. (Giuffrè 2012); G. H. Treitel, who underlines that '[t]he distinction is sometimes overlooked because there is a tendency to describe any claim for money as one for damages, even when it is actually a claim for the enforcement of a primary obligation to pay an greed sum' (*The Law of Contract*, 861 (Sweet & Maxwell 2011)). *See also* A. Burrows who identifies three main types of agreed sum: (1) the agreed price or remuneration (i.e., due in return for the main performance carried out by a party); (2) the agreed sum payable on breach of contract (that amounts to liquidated damages/penalties); (3) the agreed sum different from the agreed price/remuneration and payable upon the occurrence of an event other than a breach. The Author affirms that the latter category 'occupies a position between an agreed price and an agreed sum payable on breach. Traditionally it is treated like an agreed price, so that once the event has occurred the sum can be recovered without any type of liquidated damages/penalty analysis. However, the main controversy is whether it is always sensible so to distinguish these agreed sums from those payable on breach' (*Remedies of Torts and Breach of Contract*, 451-452 (Oxford University Press 2009)). As to the case law, *see Re Park Air Services v. Bairstow*, 1 All ER 673, para. 79 (UKHL 4 February 1999), in which it was held that: '[t]here is a critical distinction between contracts which have been fully performed by the creditor and contracts which remain executory on his part. The creditor who has lent money which has not been repaid or supplied goods or services which have not been paid for sues or proves in respect of a debt ... The creditor who has contracted for payment for goods or services still to be supplied by him, however, is not and may never become entitled to payment. He cannot sue or prove in respect of a debt ... But if the creditor is entitled to treat the contract as discharged by breach or the office-holder disclaims the contract, the creditor is entitled to compensation. He may quantify his loss and prove for it, giving credit for the cost of the goods or services which he is no longer bound to supply'.
99. Chitty, *id. See* always Chitty, *Chitty on Contracts* vol. 2, 1253-1254 (Sweet & Maxwell 2015). *See also* Roberts, *id.*, at 26, who affirms that '[a] debt arises in its own right and is not necessarily dependent upon any breach of contract or other wrong having been committed against a contracting party ... the accepted wisdom is that an action for the recovery of a debt which has fallen due is distinct from the recovery of damages payable as compensation for a breach of contract (or for the commission of a tort). This is so notwithstanding that both damages and debt reflect pecuniary satisfaction which is recoverable by success in an action to enforce a right'; J. Beatson, A. Burrows & J. Cartwrigth that underlines that '[w]here, for example, it is agreed to sell goods for a certain price, the seller may seek payment of the agreed price. The claim, a liquidated claim for the precise sum, is for the payment of a debt ... The law of contract also draws a clear distinction between a claim for the agreed sum and a claim for damages for breach of contract' (*Anson's Law of Contract*, 573 (Oxford University Press 2010)); P. Davenport who affirms that '[t]he essence of the claim in debt is that a benefit has actually been conferred. There is not a mere breach of a promise to provide a benefit' (*Construction Claims*, 8 (The Federation Press 1995)).

On the contrary, damages have the function to compensate the innocent party for the breach committed by the other. Indeed, 'damages may be claimed from a party who has broken his contractual obligation in some way other than a failure to pay such a debt (it is also possible that, in addition to a claim for a debt, there may be a claim for damages in respect of consequential loss caused by the failure to pay such a debt at the due date)'.[100] The payment of damages, therefore, represents a secondary obligation of the breaching party that does not find its justification in the other party's performance of a specific primary obligation. Furthermore, damages can be liquidated or unliquidated. The first are agreed and fixed in advance by the parties (or in some cases by statute) upon the occurrence of a specific breach of contract, while the second are determined by courts or arbitrators. Although liquidated damages represent an agreed and a definite sum of money (leaving aside for a moment the question whether they amount to a not enforceable penalty or to a genuine pre-estimate of damages), it is clear that they are, in any case, different from debts since they still represent a secondary obligation becoming effective upon a breach of contract and they are not due in return for the main performance of a specific obligation carried out by the other's party.

An explanation of the distinction between debts and liquidated damages was provided by the House of Lords in *President of India v. Lips Maritime Corporation*.[101] Such decision dealt with a dispute that arose out of the payment of demurrage by a charterer under a charterparty establishing that 'if the ship should be detained beyond the lay days demurrage should be paid at the rate of U.S. $6,00 per day and pro rata'.[102] The House of Lords pointed out the above-mentioned difference by analysing the legal nature of demurrage. In particular, it holds that:

> It is not money payable by a charterer as the consideration for the exercise by him of a right to detain a chartered ship beyond the stipulated lay days. If demurrage were that, it would be a liability surrounding in debt ... It is a liability in damages to which the charterer becomes subject because by detaining the chartered ship beyond the stipulated lay days he is in breach of his contract. Most, if not all, voyage charters contain a demurrage clause, which prescribes a daily rate at which the damages for such detention are to be quantified. The effect of such a clause is to liquidate the damages payable: it does not alter the nature of the charterer's liability, which is and remains a liability for damages, albeit liquidated damages ... Once it is recognized that a claim for demurrage sounds in damages rather than in debt, it becomes apparent that the two concepts, first, of a contractual date for the payment of such damages, and, secondly, of a claim for damages for breach of contract in not paying them by such date, have no basis in law. As I said earlier an owner's cause of action for demurrage, being one for damages, albeit liquidated damages, accrues de die in diem from the moment when the ship is detained beyond the stipulated lay days. There is no such thing as a cause of action in damages for late payment of damages. The only remedy which the law affords for delay in paying damages is the discretionary award of interest pursuant to statute.[103]

---

100. Chitty, *id. See also* Beatson, Burrows & Cartwrigth, *ibid.*, at 573.
101. *President of India v. Lips Maritime Corporation*, AC, 395 (UKHL 29 July 1987).
102. *Ibid.*, at 409.
103. *Ibid.*, at 412–413.

The above-mentioned distinction between damages and debts has also relevant consequences on the applicable discipline. Indeed, for instance, in case of a claim in debt the burden of proof is less onerous for the claimant since it has just to prove that it performed the contract (or that the event/condition, other than the breach of contract, occurred) and not the loss suffered because of the other party's failure to pay the debt.[104] Moreover, the claimant usually does not have any duty to mitigate the above-mentioned loss (at least this seems to be the prevailing view in English law)[105] and the law of penalties does not apply since, as said before, no breach of contract occurred.[106] With regard to the latter point, the non-applicability of the law of penalties in case of a claim in debt was stated, for instance, by the House of Lords in *White & Carter (Councils) v. McGregor*.[107] In such case, the claimants were advertising contractors that concluded an agreement by which they undertook to display advertisements for the defendant's garage for a period of time of three years. On the same day of the conclusion of the agreement, the defendant repudiated it alleging that the sale manager, who signed the contract, did not have the necessary authority to conclude it. However, the claimants refused such repudiation and performed the agreement. Upon the defendant's refusal to pay the relevant price, they started a lawsuit claiming for the payment of the entire amount provided in the contract. As said before, the Court upheld the claim affirming that the relevant payment request was a claim in debt and not in damages since such money was due in return for the performance of their main obligation. For this reason, it was not necessary to consider whether the sum in dispute amounted or not to a penalty. In particular, it was stated that:

> It is, however, unnecessary in view of the opinion I have expressed to consider the question whether the sum claimed is recoverable as a genuine pre-estimate of

---

104. Chitty, *supra* n. 98, at 1201 et seq.; Beatson, Burrows & Cartwrigth, *supra* n. 99, at 573. See also *Hyundai Heavy Industries v. Papadopoulos*, 2 All ER, 29 (EWCA Civ 1980).
105. Treitel, *supra* n. 98, at 1096–1097, who, however, points out that 'it is submitted that the policy of the mitigation rules (which is to prevent needless waste) should make those rules applicable, even in an action for the agreed sum, where at the time of repudiation the claimant has not yet done all that is required of him to make that action available'. In support of this statement, the Author mentions the *Attica Sea Carriers v. Ferrostaal Poseidon Bulk Reederei, The Puerto Buitrago* case 1 Lloyd's Rep., 250 (EWCA Civ 1 January 1976). The mitigation duty, in cases not concerning claims in damages, can also consist in just requiring the innocent party to act reasonably, as it was held in *Gator Shipping v. Trans-Asiatic Oil, The Odenfeld*, 2 Lloyd's Rep. 357, 374 (UKHL 1 January 1978), in which the Court affirmed that 'any fetter on the innocent party's right of election whether or not to accept a repudiation will only be applied in extreme cases, viz. where damage would be an adequate remedy and where an election to keep the contract alive would be wholly unreasonable'. With regard to the non-applicability of the duty of mitigation to cases concerning claims for an agreed sums and not damages *see also* Beatson, Burrows & Cartwrigth, *id.*; K. Scott, *Contract-Repudiation-Performance by Innocent Party*, 1 C.L.J. 12, 14 (1962). In particular, the Author, with reference to *White & Carter (Councils) v. McGregor* decision (AC, 413 (UKHL 6 December 1961)), affirms that 'since the claim was in debt, the question of mitigation of loss, whether an attempt to relet the advertising space ought to have been made, does not arise. That is only relevant in a case involving a claim for damages'.
106. For a detailed analysis of the case law on this issue, *see* Chitty, *supra* n. 98, at 1257 et seq.
107. *White & Carter, supra* n. 105, at 413 et seq.

probable or possible interest in the due performance of the contract or is irrecoverable as a penalty.[108]

Although it goes beyond the scope of the present analysis, it has to be noted that the *White & Carter* case gave rise to a debate in common law on whether a party, upon the repudiation of the contract by the counterparty, has the right to refuse it and, consequently, to perform its obligations and ask for the relevant payment, instead of accepting the repudiation and suing the other party for damages.[109] The critics moved towards the *White & Carter* decision were mainly based on the fact that the above-mentioned option granted to the innocent party could favour 'wasteful performance, as being inconsistent with the mitigation rule (which it is said should apply to actions for an agreed sum) and as giving what amounts to indirect specific performance of contracts which are not specifically enforceable'.[110] However, it has to be underlined that in *White & Carter* case the court, even if it held in favour of the above-mentioned right, specified that the non-repudiating party can choose to keep the contract in force only if it can perform the latter without needing the cooperation of the other party and 'if it can be shown that a person has no legitimate interest, financial or otherwise, in performing the contract rather than claiming damages'.[111] Moreover, it was affirmed that, in case the breach of contract is the failure to pay an agreed sum of money due in return of the main performance of the other party (i.e., a claim in debt), 'a court of common law could compel the obligor to perform it. Historically this was the only remedy which the court would grant at common law when an obligor failed to perform this kind of obligation. The remedy of damages for non-performance of the obligation

---

108. *Ibid.*, at 427.
109. Burrows, *supra* n. 98, at 435 et seq., observing that, in this case, the duty to mitigate applies.
110. Beatson, Burrows & Cartwrigth, *supra* n. 99, at 575. The Authors also underline that the position adopted in *White & Carter* case was not followed in other common law jurisdictions (for instance, in the US. In this regard, *see Clark v. Marsiglia*, 1 Denio 317 (Supreme Court of Judicator New York July 1845). *See also* s. 253 of the Restatement (Second) of Contracts, providing that '[w]here an obligor repudiates a duty before he has committed a breach by non-performance and before he has received all of the agreed exchange for it, his repudiation alone gives rise to a claim for damages for total breach', and s. 2–709.1.b UCC, providing that 'the seller can recover the price for goods identified to the contract if the seller unable after reasonable effort to resell them at a reasonable price or the circumstances reasonably indicate that such effort will be unavailing').
111. *White & Carter*, *supra* n. 105, at 413. The same principle was also stated, for instance, in *Reichman v. Beveridge*, http://www.bailii.org/ew/cases/EWCA/Civ/2006/1659.html, para. 17 (EWCA Civ 13 December 2006), in which it was held that '[t]here is, therefore, a very limited category of cases in which, although the innocent party to a contract has not accepted a repudiation by the other party, and although the innocent party is able to continue to perform all his obligations under the contract despite the absence of cooperation from the other party, nevertheless the court will not allow the innocent party to enforce his full contractual right to maintain the contract in force and sue for the contract price. The characteristics of such cases are that an election to keep the contract alive would be wholly unreasonable and that damages would be an adequate remedy'. *See also Hounslow London Borough Council v. Twickenham Garden Developments*, Ch, 233 (UKHL 1 January 1971). In such decision, the Court affirmed that also passive cooperation had to be included in the concept of cooperation expressed in *White & Carter* case. Therefore the Court limited the cases in which the innocent party can opt for the maintenance of the contract instead of repudiation upon the counterparty breach.

was not available as an alternative'.[112] The same conclusion of *White & Carter* case on the non-applicability of the law of penalties to a claim in debt was reached in cases in which the claim for the agreed sum was due upon the occurrence of a specific event different from a breach of contract (as above mentioned, also these sums are considered debts). For instance, such principle was affirmed in *Export Credits Guarantee Department v. Universal Oil Products* decision – regarding a clause providing for the reimbursement of the amount paid by the guarantor to third parties – in which it was held that:

> one purpose, perhaps the main purpose, of the law relating to penalty clauses is to prevent a plaintiff recovering a sum of money in respect of a breach of contract committed by a defendant which bears little or no relationship to the loss actually suffered by the plaintiff as a result of the breach by the defendant. But it is not and never has been for the courts to relieve a party from the consequence of what may in the event prove to be an onerous or possibly even a commercially imprudent bargain. The defendants could only secure the finance from Kleinworts if the ECGD [Export Credits Guarantee Department] were prepared to give Kleinworts the guarantee which Kleinworts required ... on the terms of the premium agreement ... The defendants accepted those terms which provided for the right of recourse to arise on the happening of a specified event, and that specified event has now happened ... The clause was not a penalty clause because it provided for payment of money upon the happening of a specified event other than a breach of a contractual duty owed by the contemplated payer to the contemplated payee.[113]

---

112. *Moschi v. LEP Air Services*, 3 All ER 393, 400 (UKHL 26 April 1972). However, the Court affirmed that in that case the obligation of the guarantor towards the creditor, upon the debtor's failure to pay the latter a sum of money, was not a claim in debt but a claim in damages. *See also* Chitty, *supra* n. 98, at 1281 et seq., who underlines that '[t]he common law did not specifically enforce contractual obligations except those to pay money'; *Id. supra* n. 99, at 1249 et seq. *See also* the Sale of Goods Act, ss 49 and 52 (6 December 1979).
113. *Export Credits Guarantee Department v. Universal Oil Products*, 2 All ER 205, 224 (UKHL 1983). With regard to this case, it was noted that '[a]lthough the case concerned a guarantee in a complex commercial arrangement and the plaintiff was claiming only the sum it had actually lost, their Lordships' limitation on the scope on the law of penalties was expressed in such wide terms that it would prevent many other clauses from being subject to that law' (Chitty, *supra* n. 98, at 1258). In the same sense of the *Export Credits* case, *see also Alder v. Moore*, 2 QB, 57 (EWCA Civ 18 November 1960). In this case, a football player ("Defendant") and the Association Football Players' and Trainers' Union ("Claimant") signed a policy insurance by which the Defendant received from the latter a sum of money after an injury to his right eye (that was considered as a permanent total disablement preventing him from playing football) and undertook not to play as a professional in the future. The agreement also provided that, in the opposite case, he would have had to pay back the money received by the Claimant. After six months, the Defendant was engaged by a professional team and, consequently, the Claimant asked the money back. The Defendant contended that such payment amounted to a penalty and, therefore, was not enforceable. A dispute arose between the parties and the Court, notwithstanding in the agreement it was used the word "penalty", decided in favour of the Claimant holding that the repayment of a sum of money upon the occurrence of a specific event (in this case, the fact that the defendant was able to re-start playing again notwithstanding the injury) was not a penalty and, therefore, it was recoverable. In particular, it was stated that '[d]espite the unsuitability of the words and phrasing, the sense of the obligation the defendant entered into is that if he played professional football again he would refund the sum he had received on the basis that he could not so do' (*id.*, at 60). It, therefore, seems that the Court considered that the Defendant's obligation to repay the money received was 'a true alternative mode of performing the contract' (*see* G. C., Cheshire, C.H.S. Fifoot & M.P. Furmston, *Cheshire,*

However, it is interesting to note that in *Workers Trust & Merchant Bank v. Dojap Investments*,[114] the Privy Council considered the payment of a deposit as a penalty and, therefore, not enforceable. This case concerned a contract for the sale of land providing for the payment of a deposit equal to the 25% of the contract price. In particular, according to clause 13 of the agreement, in case the purchaser failed to pay the remaining sum of money the seller would be entitled to forfeit the above-mentioned deposit. The Privy Council had to resolve 'the question whether a deposit in excess of 10% paid under a contract for the sale of land can be lawfully forfeited by the vendor in the event of a failure by the purchaser to complete on the due date'.[115] In other words, 'whether or not the deposit of 25% in this case was reasonable as being in line with the traditional concept of earnest money or was in truth a penalty intended to act in terrorem'.[116] In this regard, it was held that:

> Since a true deposit may take effect as a penalty, albeit one permitted by law, it is hard to draw a line between a reasonable, permissible amount of penalty and an unreasonable, impermissible penalty. In their Lordships' view the correct approach is to start from the position that, without logic but by long continued usage both in the United Kingdom and formerly in Jamaica, the customary deposit has been 10%. A vendor who seeks to obtain a larger amount by way of forfeitable deposit must show special circumstances which justify such a deposit ... Their Lordships agree with the Court of Appeal that this evidence falls far short of showing that it was reasonable to stipulate for a forfeitable deposit of 25% of the purchase price or indeed any deposit in excess of 10% ... In the view of their Lordships, since the 25% deposit was not a true deposit by way of earnest, the provision for its forfeiture was a plain penalty. There is clear authority that in a case of a sum paid by one party to another under the contract as security for the performance of that contract, a provision for its forfeiture in the event of non-performance is a penalty from which the court will give relief by ordering repayment of the sum so paid, less any damage actually proved to have been suffered as a result of non-completion ... If a deposit of 25% constitutes an

---

Fifoot & Furmston's Law of Contract, 569 (Oxford University Press 2007)). Furthermore, the Court held that, even if the sum should be considered as damages it would not be unreasonable '[i]f the sum claimed is to be regarded as damages it is, in effect, an agreed and fair pre-estimate of the loss which the underwriters have suffered. However, that way of putting it does not seem to me to be quite appropriate' (*id.*, at 60). A similar decision was reached by the Court of Appeal in *Campbell Discount v. Bridge*, 2 All ER, 97 (EWCA Civ 1 March 1961) in which the parties concluded a hire-purchase agreement for a motor car providing for the faculty of the hirer to terminate the contract and, in this case, for his obligation to pay an agreed sum for the depreciation of the vehicle. Upon the termination of the contract by the hirer, a dispute arose between the parties regarding the above-mentioned payment. The Court decided in favour of the owner of the vehicle affirming that the agreed sum did not constitute a penalty since it was not payable upon a breach of contract but on the exercising by the hirer of its option to terminate the contract. However, in the following judgment, the House of Lords held that a breach of contract occurred and, therefore, the owner was not entitled to recover the agreed sum provided by such agreement for the depreciation of the vehicle but only the damages actually suffered (1 All ER, 385 (UKHL 25 January 1962)). The same claim was, therefore, qualified in two opposite ways: as a claim in debt by the Court of Appeal and as a claim in damages by the House of Lords.

114. *Workers Trust & Merchant Bank v. Dojap Investments*, 2 All ER, 370 (JCPC 22 February 1993).
115. *Ibid.*, at 372.
116. *Ibid.*, at 373.

unreasonable sum and is not therefore a true deposit, it must be repaid as a whole.[117]

The Privy Council also stated that 'it appears that the bank may have suffered some damage as a result of Dojap's failure to complete. If so, the bank is entitled to deduct the amount of such damages from the 'deposit' of 25%'.[118]

The law of penalties was also applied to the interest rate provided by the contract in case of late payment of invoices. In *Jeancharm v. Barnet Football Club*,[119] the Court of Appeal qualified the interest of 5% per week (equal to an annual rate of 260%) as a penalty and, as such, considered it not enforceable. In particular, it was held that '260% is an extraordinarily large amount to have to pay for the suggested administrative costs, even if the sums involved were relatively small … I think this is a penalty clause in the Dunlop sense and unenforceable'.[120]

[c]   Take or Pay Clauses as Penalties

The *M&J* Case

The most important English case in which the issue of the interpretation of take or pay clauses was addressed is the *M&J Polymers v. Imerys Minerals* decision.[121] Such decision did not deal with a gas sale agreement but with a contract for the sale of chemical products by which M&J Polymers ("M&J" or "Claimant") supplied dispersants, containing acrylic acid, to Imerys Minerals ("Imerys" or "Defendant"). The commercial relationship between the parties had been going on since 1991 when Imerys was still known as English China Clays (that was acquired by the Imerys Group in 1999). On 26 January 2005, the parties entered into a new sale contract of the minimum duration of three years by which '[t]he Buyers want to ensure a regular and reliable supply of the Products and the Supplier agrees to guarantee such supply under the terms and conditions of this Agreement'.[122] In particular, Article 5.3 provided for the obligation of Imerys to order a specific minimum quantity of products and Article 5.5 included a take or pay clause so reciting: 'the Buyers collectively will pay for the minimum quantities of Products as indicated in this Article at 5.3 … even if they together have not ordered the indicated quantities during the relevant monthly period'.[123]

In May 2006, Imerys terminated the contract claiming that the dispersant supplied by M&J were defective and not complying with the quality standards specified in the agreement. Therefore, it did not take nor pay for the minimum quantities of products provided by the above-mentioned Article 5.3 of the contract. M&J rejected

---

117. *Ibid.*, at 373–375.
118. *Ibid.*, at 375.
119. *Jeancharm v. Barnet Football Club*, 92 Con LR, 26 (EWCA Civ 16 January 2003).
120. *Ibid.*, at paras 17–18. The same conclusion was reached by the other two judges forming the Court's panel.
121. *See supra* n. 77.
122. *Ibid.*, at para. 3.
123. *Ibid.*, at para. 4.

such arguments and, consequently, started a lawsuit in order to recover the sums due by the Defendant in relation to the minimum quantities of dispersants pursuant to the take or pay clause. In this context, one of the issues addressed by the Court was '[w]hether the sums due to be paid by the Defendant to the Claimant in respect of the period prior to what is now accepted to have been the repudiatory breach by the Defendant in May 2006 are recoverable in debt, in respect of the price of the minimum quantities of dispersants pursuant to the "take or pay" clause set out in paragraph 4 above, or by way of damages (the "penalty issue")'.[124] The Court, after having stated that the products were conforming to the contract, concluded its analysis on the above-mentioned issue by holding in favour of the second interpretation. In particular, it was held that:

> I do not see how a payment obligation can arise under Article 5.5 in a case other than where there has been a breach of the obligation to order under Clause 5.3. If the goods are in fact ordered, then they will be delivered, and the price will be due quite irrespective of Article 5.3 or 5.5 ... I am satisfied therefore that, as a matter of principle, the rule against penalties may apply ... it is certainly not the ordinary candidate for such rule, such as where, for example, a sum is specified which is found not to be a "*genuine pre-estimate of damage*" or a sum is stipulated as "*in terrorem*" of the offending party.[125]

In this regard, it has to be underlined that the Court reached such conclusion although it had qualified the M&J's claim as in debt[126] and not in damages notwithstanding, according to prevailing view, the law of penalties does not apply to the first. Indeed, we have seen that a debt is a sum of money due in return for the main performance and not for a breach of contract, as instead damages and penalties are.[127] It follows that the qualification of the minimum payment request pursuant a take or pay clause as a claim in debt implies the interpretation of such provision as establishing two main alternative obligations (i.e., take and pay for the minimum products agreed or just pay for it). Indeed, if the aforementioned request is considered a claim in debt, it means that it does not derive from the buyer's failure to take the minimum quantity of products provided in the take or pay clause, but that it is due as a consequence of the execution of the seller's main obligation (i.e., to make available such quantity for the buyer). Therefore, the buyer's minimum payment obligation is necessarily a main obligation and not a secondary one triggered by a breach of contract, as instead it occurs for penalties. In light of the above, the Court, on the basis of the qualification made of the M&J's claim (i.e., a claim in debt), should have not considered the take or pay clause included in the contract as a penalty, but as providing for main alternative obligations. On the contrary, the Court, by concluding for the application of the law of penalties to such provision, de facto considered the M&J's claim as in damages.

Apart from the aforementioned contradiction between the interpretation of the M&J's claim and that of take or pay clauses provided by the Court, the latter's decision was criticised by those who, in general, reject the view that such provisions are

---

124. *Ibid.*, at para. 6.
125. *Ibid.*, at paras 41–44.
126. Notwithstanding the contract was terminated by the parties.
127. *See* §2.03[A][1][b]. The Court in the *M&J* case expressly disagreed with such position.

penalties and consider a 'sum due to a seller under take or pay provisions has the essential hallmarks of a debt. Namely, the payments are a definite sum of money fixed by the agreement of the parties as a payment by one party in return for the performance of a specified obligation by the other party'.[128] In particular, 'to take and pay and/or to pay is an option for the buyer, i.e., to take and pay or just pay; and since there is no obligation on the buyer to take, take or pay is nor a payment made as a result of a breach of an obligation, so cannot be a penalty'.[129] The buyer's payment obligation is, therefore, 'an independent (alternative) undertaking which can be enforced by the seller when the buyer opts not to perform its obligation to take delivery of, and pay for, the minimum quantity of gas'[130] and, as a consequence, such obligation is in debt and not in damages.

As said above, the qualification of take or pay clauses as penalties has relevant consequences since in common law only liquidated damages (i.e., a genuine, reasonable and commercially justifiable pre-estimate of damages) can be recoverable and not penalties, although courts tend to be cautious before striking down a penalty clause as not a genuine pre-estimation of damages.[131] Such approach was also adopted in the *M&J* decision. In this regard, the Court affirmed that, although in principle the law of penalties was applicable to the case, the take or pay clause included in the contract between M&J and Imerys was enforceable since it was reasonable, justifiable and was negotiated by the parties. In particular, it was held that:

> On the facts of this case, I am entirely satisfied that the take or pay clause was *commercially justifiable*, did not amount to *oppression*, was negotiated and freely entered into between *parties of comparable bargaining power*, and did not have the *predominant purpose of deterring a breach of contract* nor amount to a provision *"in terrorem"*. The evidence was wholly clear. The negotiations took place between extremely well-qualified, able and savvy commercial men against a very significant commercial background, including a background of previous dealings ... the take or pay provision does not offend against the rule against penalties and that the Claimant is entitled to recover the price of the shortfall pursuant to Article 5.5.[132]

In reaching its decision, the Court referred to some of the cases analysed above[133] that dealt with the issue of penalty clauses in general since 'there is no direct authority on the impact of the law of penalties on a take or pay clauses'.[134]

---

128. Holland & Ashley, *supra* n. 80, at 615. The Authors also underline that if 'M&J Polymers had argued that the sum was due because M&J Polymers had performed "a specified obligation" (the seller making the chemicals available for order) it is conceivable that Burton J may have found differently' (*ibid.*). For a critic to the *M&J* decision, *see* Roberts, *supra* n. 73, at 183–184; Oladotun, *supra* n. 80, at 14 et seq. In general, in favour of the interpretation of take or pay clauses as main alternative obligations and not penalties, *see* §2.03.
129. Beggs & Sapte, *supra* n. 80, at 152.
130. Iynedjian, *supra* n. 80, at 750.
131. *See* §2.03[A][1][a].
132. *M&J* case, *supra* n. 77, at paras 46 and 48.
133. *See* §2.03[A][1][a].
134. *M&J* case, *supra* n. 77, at para. 45. In this regard, it has to be noted that the issue of the qualification of take or pay clauses had already addressed in *Coneco v. Foxboro Great Britain*, *supra* n. 80 (*see* §2.03[A][1][d]).

The E-Nik Case

Five years later the *M&J* decision, English Courts had to address again the issue whether take or pay clauses can be qualified as penalties in the *E-Nik v. Department for Communities and Local Government* case.[135] Such decision concerned an IT contract concluded in 2009 between E-Nik ("E-Nik" or "Claimant") and the Department for Communities and Local Government ("Department" or "Defendant") that included a provision (Article 2.1) by which the latter undertakes to purchase a minimum quantity of days of consultancy from E-Nik per year. A dispute arose between the parties in relation to some unpaid invoices by the Defendant equal to GBP 760,920. It has to be noted that the contract was never terminated by the parties.

Of the eight issues addressed by the Court in order to reach its decision those that are relevant for our analysis are the following three: (1) whether the Defendant was obliged to buy for the minimum days of consultancy per year provided in the contract independent of its project requirement; (2) whether the claim of E-Nik was in debt or in damages; (3) whether the amount claimed by E-Nik was a penalty and, therefore, was not enforceable. Before analysing such issues, it has to be underlined that the above-mentioned clause requiring the buyer to order for a minimum number of days, although not expressly defined in the contract as a take or pay provision, was considered as such by the Court.

As to the first question, the latter (upholding the Claimant's argument) stated that the contract provided for a minimum purchasing obligation on the Defendant indepent of its project requirement since the reference, included in clause 2.1 of the agreement, to latter was just 'explanatory, showing how the minimum ... days has been arrived at, i.e. by calculating what the Defendant considers it (minimum) project requirements will be ... so that the availability of the Claimant to supply that minimum will be secured. It does not mean, nor say, "**subject to** *project requirements*", in the sense that some arbitrary decision can reduce that obligation possibly to nil'.[136]

With regard to the second issue (i.e., whether the E-Nik's claim was in debt or damages), the Court again upheld the Claimant's arguments by which the Defendant's obligation to purchase the minimum quantity of days of services agreed in the contract was not linked to a specific order to be issued every time. More specifically, according to the Court, Article 2.1 of the agreement provided for the obligation of E-Nik to be ready and available to supply its services at any time for the entire duration of the contract for at least the minimum number of days per year therein established independent of a specific order by the Defendant. Thus, the money claimed by E-Nik was not due because of a breach of contract (i.e., the failure of the Department to actually order such minimum quantity) but in return for the performance of the Claimant's main obligation (i.e., to keep the services available for the minimum number of days agreed). For this reason, the Court considered the sum requested by E-Nik not as a compensation for damages but as a debt. As said with regard to the *M&J* case, such qualification implies the interpretation of the take or pay clause in question

---

135. *See supra* n. 77 (the judge was the same as in the *M&J* case).
136. *Ibid.*, at para. 14.

not as a penalty but as providing for two main alternative obligations: to request and pay for the minimum number of days of services agreed or just pay for it even if the latter was not actually ordered. The Department's payment was in any case justified by the Claimant's execution of the aforementioned main obligation. The Court, in reaching its decision, rejected the Defendant's arguments by which it did not have a minimum payment obligation towards E-Nik that was not linked to specific orders. On the basis of such assertion, the Defendant alleged that, if any liability could be deemed to exist upon it, that would be for the failure to provide E-Nik with the relevant orders and, consequently, it would only be for damages. In this regard, the Court held that:

> It is plain on the evidence that the Claimant continued to keep services available ... neither party terminated the Contract, either in accordance with its terms (Clause 8.1) or even, in the part of the Defendant, by unilateral attempted repudiation; and that if there was a repudiatory failure by the Defendant to call off/request the minimum ... days' services ... the Claimant did not accept such repudiation, as it was on the facts fully entitled not to do so.[137]

As to the third question (i.e., whether the amount claimed by E-Nik was a penalty and, therefore, was not enforceable), the Court reached the same conclusion as in the *M&J* decision (to which it referred)[138] holding that the E-Nik's payment claim, pursuant to the take or pay clause, could be qualified as a penalty. However, it was enforceable since it was 'commercially justifiable, did not amount to oppression, [was] negotiated and freely entered into between parties of comparable bargaining power and did not amount to a provision *in terrorem*'.[139] Like in the *M&J* case, although the Court qualified the E-Nik's claim as in debt and not in damages (and, therefore, implied the interpretation of take or pay clauses as providing for main alternative obligations),[140] it held that the law of penalties was, in theory, applicable to this case. Due to the substantial difference between debts and damages,[141] the Court should have, instead, excluded *in toto* the application of the law of penalties since in case of a claim in debt (as the one of E-Nik was qualified) the sum requested is not due on the basis of a breach of contract (in this case the Department's failure to request the minimum days of services agreed in the contract) but in return for the main performance carried out by the claimant (that, in the *E-Nik* case, was represented by the fact that the Claimant kept its services, and the relevant necessary resources, available to the Defendant for the minimum number of days agreed). The breach of contract is, instead, a necessary condition for a penalty provision to become effective, provided that it is a genuine liquidation of damages.[142] Therefore, also in this case, the qualification of the E-Nik's claim as in debt and not in damages provided by the Court was in contradiction with

---

137. *Ibid.*, at para. 22.
138. The Court, like in the *M&J* decision, also referred to the *White & Carter* case that (as seen at §2.03[A][1][b]), in case of breach of contract by a party, the other can decide not to accept the repudiation and, consequently, keep the agreement alive, perform it and claim for the money due in return of execution of its obligations.
139. *E-Nik* case, *supra* n. 77, at para. 25.
140. The contract was not considered as repudiated.
141. *See* §2.03[A][1][b].
142. *See* §2.03[A][1][a].

the latter's conclusion on the applicability of the law of penalties to the take or pay clause included in the contract (although, at the end, it was considered to be enforceable).

[d]   *Take or Pay Clauses as Main Obligations*

The *Coneco* Case

As mentioned above, the approach adopted by the most recent English case law that addressed the issue of the nature of take or pay clauses is to consider them as penalties. According to such view, the sum that the buyer has to pay, pursuant to these provisions, is not due in return for the performance of the counterparty but it derives from its breach of contract (and, namely, the failure to take or order the minimum quantity of products/services agreed). We have also seen that, although the remedy against a penalty is the non-enforcement, English courts tend to save such clause if it can be considered, on the basis of the facts of the case, reasonable and justifiable. Even if the cases above analysed did not deal with gas sale agreements, the same principle also applies to such contracts. Thus, according to this interpretation, the sum to be paid by the buyer when it does not take the Minimum Bill Quantity would be considered a penalty deriving from a breach of contract (i.e., the lack of withdrawal of the gas).

However, it has to be noted that a different interpretation of take or pay clauses was adopted by less recent case law. In particular, in *Coneco v. Foxboro Great Britain*[143] such provisions were deemed to establish two alternative methods of performing the contract independent of the occurrence of a breach. This case concerned a contract by which Coneco ("Claimant"), provided Foxboro ("Defendant"), with some engineering services (such as, planning, project design, procurement, installation, etc.). The agreement also fixed a minimum sum, equal to GBP 1,750,000, to be paid by the Claimant for the first year ("Minimum Sum") and contained a take or pay clause providing that, in case the overall invoices issued by the Claimant during such period of time would have been less than the Minimum Sum, the Defendant should have paid for the difference between the latter and the sum invoiced. The main issue of the dispute was whether the above-mentioned take or pay provision amounted to an unenforceable penalty clause (as alleged by the Defendant) or whether it just provided for a payment obligation independent of a breach of contract (in other words, whether it was a main obligation). The Court embraced the second interpretation holding that, despite the wording of the agreement, the latter did not provide for the Defendant's obligation to place orders corresponding to the Minimum Sum and, therefore, the payment of the difference between the latter and the amount actually corresponded by the Defendant to the Claimant was not due as a consequence of a breach of contract (and, namely, the failure to place orders).

---

143. *See supra* n. 80.

In particular, it was stated that:

> Taking the clause as a whole, however, it seems to me that the parties have been very careful to draft it so as not to impose an obligation on the defendant to place orders up to the total annual value of GBP 1,750,000 in the first year. It is not in doubt that, by appropriate drafting, the pitfall of penalty can often be avoided ... In my view, what we have here is not a penalty clause in the sense that there is an obligation on the defendant to place orders of a minimum value.[144]

Moreover the Court reaffirmed the principle by which the application of the law of penalties should be limited only to cases in which the obligation to pay an agreed amount of money is linked to the occurrence of a breach of contract and not to the happening of a different specific event.

[2] US Law

The interpretation of take or pay clauses, included in gas sale agreements, as providing for main alternative obligations seems to be the one embraced by the prevailing US case law. According to such view, the minimum sum to be paid by the buyer is not the liquidation of damages deriving from the failure to take (all or in part) the Minimum Bill Quantity but it represents one of the two alternative ways for the buyer to perform the contract (take and pay for the Minimum Bill Quantity or just pay for it and take it later). Despite that, in some cases, courts considered such amount as the measure of the damages due to the seller upon the buyer's breach of its obligations provided by the take or pay clause. In others, instead, they awarded damages on the basis of section 2-708 of the Uniform Commercial Code (UCC).[145]

[a] Take or Pay Clauses as Main Obligations

The *Prenalta* Case

The first approach was adopted in the *Prenalta v. Colorado Interstate Gas* decision.[146] In such case, the parties entered into six gas sale and purchase long-term agreements. The dispute arose out of contracts 422 and 516 that contained a take or pay provision according to which Colorado Interstate Gas Company ("CIG"), undertook to take and pay for the Minimum Bill Quantity (defined in the agreements as "Contract Quantity")

---

144. *Ibid.*, at 2–3.
145. Section 2-708 provides that: '(1) the measure of damages for non-acceptance or repudiation by the buyer is the difference between the market price at the time and place for tender and the unpaid contract price together with any incidental damages provided in this Article (Section 2-710), but less expenses saved in consequence of the buyer's breach. (2) If the measure of damages provided in subsection (1) is inadequate to put the seller in as good a position as performance would have done than the measure of damages is the profit ... which the seller would have made from full performance by the buyer, together with any incidental damages provided in this Article ....'
146. *See, supra* n. 80. In the same sense, *see Colorado Interstate Gas* case, *supra* n. 80.

or just to pay for it and take it later (and, more specifically, during the following five years). In particular, the contracts provided that:

> If during any one year period, commencing with the 1st day of the month in which initial delivery is made from each well, Buyer shall fail to take the Contract Quantity of gas from such well, then Buyer shall pay Seller on or before the 20th day of the 2nd month of the next following year for that quantity of gas which is equal to the difference between the Contract Quantity and Buyer's actual takes during such period.[147]

The reason originating the dispute was the decision of CIG to stop making payments pursuant to the above-mentioned take or pay clause in consideration of the changes occurred in the market and, in particular, in light of the passage from regulated to deregulated prices as of January 1985 as a consequence of the enactment of the Natural Gas Policy Act of 1978. Due to such circumstances, the conditions included in the ongoing long-term contracts became excessively onerous for CIG. Indeed, the deregulation determined an unexpected relevant increase of natural gas prices that favoured the search of new gas fields resulting in the oversupply of gas. In light of such market changes, the parties entered into contracts' renegotiations without success. For this reason, Prenalta sued CIG for the failure to comply with its minimum payment obligation pursuant to the take or pay clause. In this regard, it has to be noted that the claimant did not repudiate the contract and asked the Court to be granted damages that it quantified in the difference between the Contract Quantity and that actually taken (and paid for) by CIG (according to the contract the latter was entitled to withdraw the gas not taken but paid for in a later moment). CIG resisted to such claim and, in addition, counterclaimed the reimbursement of the overpayments made to Prenalta since it alleged that the price applied by the latter was not the correct one according to the contract. The District Court held in favour of CIG. In particular, with regard to the measure of damages claimed by Prenalta, it affirmed that, since the gas could not be considered as identified goods, section 2-709 of the UCC was not applicable (providing for the possibility for the seller to recover the price in case it is not able to resell the goods after reasonable efforts and at a reasonable price) but section 2–708.

Prenalta appealed such decision and its appeal was upheld. In particular, one of the issues addressed by the Court of Appeal was the qualification of the take or pay provisions included in the contracts in dispute. In this regard, Prenalta alleged that such clauses provided for 'the contract remedy for breach, and that the measure of damages under the provision is the value of the "quantity of gas which is equal to the difference between the Contract Quantity and Buyer's actual takes" for each year CIG has been in breach of the Contracts'.[148] On the other side, CIG argued that the aforementioned clauses provided, instead, for an alternative method of performing the contract and not for damages in case of breach of the latter. Moreover, it alleged that,

---

147. *Prenalta* case, *id.*, at 687.
148. *Ibid.*

in case the second interpretation prevailed, such clauses would amount to unenforceable penalties. On the one hand, the Court confirmed the CIG's qualification of take or pay provisions, holding that:

> CIG could elect either to purchase the contract quantity or to pay for the value of the contract quantity (the "minimum bill") in exchange for Prenalta's tender of the contract quantity of gas or any make-up gas due CIG for past deficiencies. This is clearly an alternative contract which allows CIG to perform either alternative, to "take" or "pay" for the gas, in exchange for Prenalta's return performance, rather than a contract which requires CIG to "take" the contract quantity of gas with a triggering liquidated damages provision if CIG fails to do so.[149]

On the other hand, the Court upheld the Prenalta's damages claim. In particular, it, first, noted that, after one year from the initial delivery of gas without CIG taking the minimum quantity agreed, it remained upon the latter only the "payment" obligation according to the take or pay clause. Therefore, after the expiration of such period of time, the contract was not alternative anymore ('[t]his type of alternative contract eliminates the availability of one alternative with the passage of time').[150] Then, the Court referred to section 2-719 of the UCC[151] and considered that the damages suffered by Prenalta were 'measured by CIG's obligation to pay – the value of which is the contract price in effect at the time such deficiency occurred multiplied by the difference between the contract quantity and the actual quantity of gas purchased for any year CIG was in breach of Contract 422 and/or Contract 516'.[152]

In other words, the Court considered that the parties, by means of the take or pay clause, provided for a specific remedy in case of breach of contract by CIG (different from the general one established by the above-mentioned section 2-708 of the UCC) that consisted in 'requiring CIG to pay the value of the shortfall – the contract price multiplied by the difference between the contract quantity and the amount of gas actually taken during each one year period'.[153]

It emerges from the above that such decision is in contradiction with the qualification that the Court provided with regard to the buyer's minimum payment obligation pursuant to take or pay clauses, i.e., that it represents one of the two alternative ways to perform the contract. The Court, notwithstanding that, de facto treated such amount as a liquidation of damages according to what alleged by Prenalta.[154] Furthermore, it has to be noted that such contradiction is even more evident if we consider that the Court clearly distinguished a take *or* pay from a take *and* pay provision. The latter, that also characterises gas sale agreements (also some contracts concluded between Prenalta and CIG included such clause), provides for only

---

149. *Ibid.*, at 689.
150. *Ibid.*
151. Section 2-719 provides that: 'the agreement may provide for remedies in addition to or in substitution for those provided in this Article and may limit or alter the measure of damages recoverable under this Article …'.
152. *Prenalta case*, at 689.
153. *Ibid.*, at 688.
154. For a critic to such approach, *see also* Roberts, *supra* n. 73, at 183.

one obligation of the buyer, i.e., take the gas delivered and pay for it, and, consequently, in this case the failure to take the Minimum Bill Quantity is a breach and the relevant payment represents the relevant damages. Thus, it is clear that, if we interpret a take *or* pay clause as providing for a penalty in case the buyer fails to take the Minimum Bill Quantity, we would actually treat it as a take *and* pay provision. As said, the Court, in conformity with the definition of take *or* pay clauses it provided (i.e., main alternative obligations), highlighted the aforementioned distinction affirming that, upon the buyer's failure, 'to take the quantity of gas specified in a "take-or-pay" contract, Buyer is required to pay for the specified quantity of gas [since it is one of two alternative obligations provided by take or pay clauses]. In the event of failure of Buyer to take the quantity of gas specified in a "take-and-pay" contract, the contract measure of damages is applicable'.[155] Notwithstanding such distinction, the Court, in its decision, de facto equalised the two above-mentioned provisions.

Moreover, in light of the qualification of take or pay clauses made by the Court, the latter's claim (i.e., the payment of the Minimum Bill Quantity), should have not been considered as in damages but in debt. Indeed, according to such view, the minimum sum to be paid by the buyer when it does not take the gas is due in return for the seller's main performance (i.e., the supply of the gas) and, as such, it is a debt. In other words, although qualified as damages, the remedy claimed by Prenalta was actually the specific performance of the contract, as also confirmed by the fact that it did not repudiate the contract, and, in practice, that was what the Court granted. In the event, instead, of repudiation of the contract, the Prenalta's claim would have been in damages but the relevant measure should have not been determined on the basis of the take or pay clause unless the latter had been differently qualified, i.e., not as a provision establishing for alternative main obligations (as affirmed by the Court) but as a liquidation of damages for the buyer's failure to take the gas.

Provided the above, a final consideration has to be made with regard to the calculation of damages carried out by the Court. The latter, in support of its decision, also referred to Professor Corbin who affirmed, in relation to the measure of damages in case of alternative contracts, that:

> An alternative contract may be so drawn as to limit the power of the promisor to discharge his contractual duty by performing one of the alternatives to a definite period of time, after the expiration of which only the other alternative is available to him. After the expiration of the specified period, the obligation of the promisor becomes single and is no longer an alternative contract. In cases like this, *the promise must always estimate his damages on the basis of the second alternative* ... Usually the alternative that is eliminated by the expiration of the period of time is the performance of service or the transfer of property, while the second alternative is the payment of a named sum of money.[156]

However, the Court did not consider – as, instead, occurred in *Roye Realty* case below – the part of the treatise of Professor Corbin (section 1081) in which it is

---

155. *Prenalta* case, *supra* n. 80, at 689–690.
156. A.L. Corbin, *Corbin on Contracts* vol. 5, §1085, 469–471 (West Publishing Co. 1964), as mentioned in *Prenalta* case, *id.*, at 689.

specified that in case the second alternative obligation is the payment of money the damages should be calculated on the basis of the less valuable of the two alternative obligations.

The *Roye Realty* Case

The issue of the nature of take or pay clauses was also faced by the Supreme Court of Oklahoma in the *Roye Realty & Developing v. Arkla* case.[157] In such decision, the qualification provided by the Court was the same as that of the *Prenalta* case (i.e., take or pay clauses as main alternative obligations), but the method of assessment of damages in favour of the seller of gas upon the buyer's breach was different since it was based on section 2-708 of the UCC and not on the minimum payment obligation established in the take or pay provision.

In this case, Arkla concluded a fifteen-year gas sale agreement with an oil corporation ("Seller"), providing for a take or pay clause. In particular, according to the latter, the Minimum Bill Quantity was calculated on the basis of so called "deliverability tests". Later, the Seller transferred its contractual rights to Roye Realty & Developing ("Roye Realty"). Upon Arkla's refusal to take the Minimum Bill Quantity, Roye Realty claimed that the latter repudiated the contract and asked for the damages that it determined as being equal to the minimum payment obligation for the remaining duration of the contract. A dispute arose between the parties over the measure of damages. In this regard, it has to be noted that the Court was not asked to ascertain whether or not Arkla, by failing to comply with its take or pay obligations, had repudiated the contract but only to assess the damages 'if Roye Realty establishes at trial that Arkla repudiated the take-or-pay gas purchase contract'.[158] First of all, the Court qualified the take or pay contract as one providing for two main alternative obligations for the buyer and, consequently, the minimum payment obligation did not constitute a liquidation of damages for the failure to take the gas. In particular, it was held that:

> First the deficiency payment obligation [i.e., the payment for the minimum quantity of gas agreed in case the latter is not taken] is neither a *remedy* for breach of the first alternative performance nor a clause which *alters or limits* the measure of damages ... the deficiency payment is not a liquidated damages provision which sets the amount of damages when Arkla breaches its obligation to take and pay for gas ... Because there is a second alternative available for Arkla to perform, failure to take and pay for gas merely constitutes a decision not to perform the first alternative obligation and *is not a repudiation of the contract. Repudiation of the contract does not occur until Arkla also refuses to make the required deficiency payments*. Hence, the deficiency payment obligation is not a provision designed to provide the measure of damages when Arkla fails to take and pay for gas under the contract. Rather, it is a portion of the overall obligation which Roye Realty alleges Arkla anticipatory repudiated.[159]

---

157. See *supra* n. 80.
158. *Ibid.*, at 1153.
159. *Ibid.*, at 1157-1158.

Therefore, the Court, in determining the damages for Arkla's repudiation, correctly did not refer to the minimum payment obligation provided in the take or pay clause – as, instead, occurred in the previous judgment (and in *Prenalta* case) – but applied section 2-708(1) of the UCC holding that:

> Because the provisions of the UCC apply to gas purchase contracts, we hold that the measure of damages for anticipatory repudiation of both the take and the pay obligations in a take or pay gas purchase contract is the difference between the market price at the time when the aggrieved party learned of the repudiation and the unpaid contract price ... the more appropriate measure of damages should be in accordance with the less valuable of the two alternatives which is usually the market value of the specific alternative.[160]

In reaching its decision, the Court, like in *Prenalta* case, referred to Professor Corbin. However, in this case, the judges also considered the part of the treatise in which the latter pointed out that, if the second alternative obligation is the payment of a sum of money, the damages should be assessed not on the basis of such amount but 'in accordance with the less valuable of the two alternatives promised'.[161]

In light of the above, it can be concluded that the decision adopted in *Roye Realty* case is conforming to the qualification of take or pay clauses as main alternative obligation that seems to be the main view adopted by the US case law.[162]

[b]   Take or Pay Clauses as Penalties

The *Lake River* Case

An exception to the main position adopted by US Courts with regard to the nature of take or pay provisions is the *Lake River v. Carborundum* decision[163] in which such clauses were, instead, considered as penalties (or, in case of gas sale agreements, as

---

160. *Ibid.*, at 1154. Section 2-708(1) provides that 'the measure of damages for non-acceptance or repudiation by the buyer is the difference between the market price at the time and place for tender and the unpaid contract price together with any incidental damages provided in this Article (Section 2-710), but less expenses saved in consequence of the buyer's breach'.
161. Corbin, *supra* n. 156, §1081, at 461–462, as mentioned in *Roye Realty* case, *id.*, at 1158.
162. The same correct approach was adopted in *Universal Resources* case, *supra* n. 80. However, in such case the remedy requested by Universal ("Seller") was not the liquidation of damages upon the repudiation of the contract but the specific performance of such agreement by Panhandle ("Buyer") and, namely, of the second alternative obligation provided by the take or pay clause, i.e., the payment for the Minimum Bill Quantity that was tendered to the Buyer. In other words, the claim of the Seller was a claim in debt. The dispute arose when upon the Buyer's failure to take the entire amount of gas offered by the Seller and refused to pay for the difference between the Minimum Bill Quantity and the gas actually withdrawn, as provided by the take or pay clause. The Court, upholding the previous judgment of the district court, first of all, qualified the take or pay provision included in the contract not as a penalty or liquidation of damages but as providing for main alternative obligations. Second, according to such definition, it granted (although not for the entire period of time requested by the Seller) the remedy claimed by the Seller (that, as such, was a claim in debt). Therefore, like in *Roye Realty* case, the decision of the Court was conform to the definition of take or pay clauses that it provided.
163. *See supra* n. 77.

liquidated damages). In this case, the parties concluded a contract by which Lake River provided Carborundum with distribution services (receipt, bagging and shipping) in its warehouse in relation to the latter's product (an abrasive powder used in the preparation of steel). The agreement included a clause that, although not qualified as a take or pay provision, had similar nature and effects. Indeed, it established that, if at the end of the initial term of the agreement (three years) Carborundum had not shipped to Lake River the minimum quantity of products fixed by the parties (equal to 22,500 tonnes), it should have in any case paid Lake River the difference between such minimum quantity and that actually shipped and bagged. Due to the decrease of the steel demand, Carborundum failed to send Lake River the minimum quantity agreed and, once the latter asked for the payment provided by the above-mentioned clause, Carborundum rejected such request alleging that the latter amounted to a penalty. Therefore, a dispute arose between the parties and the Court had to decide whether the aforesaid provision represented a not enforceable penalty or recoverable liquidated damages. The Court, after having underlined the already known distinction between them, affirmed that:

> The damage formula in this case is a penalty and not a liquidation of damages, because it is designed always to assure Lake River more than its actual damages. The formula – full contract price minus the amount already invoiced to Carborundum – is invariant to the gravity of the breach ... As a result, at whatever point in the life of the contract a breach occurs, the damage formula gives Lake River more than its lost profits from the breach – dramatically more if the breach occurs at the beginning of the contract.[164]

The Court, after having qualified the provision in dispute as an unenforceable penalty, held that the claimant was in any case 'entitled to his common law damages ... the unpaid contract price of $ 241,000 minus the costs that Lake River saved by not having complete the contract (the variable costs on the other 45 per cent of the Ferro Carbo that I never had to bag)'[165] and remanded the case to the district judge to determine such damages.

Provided the above, it is interesting to note that the Court has also specified that the decision would have been different if the dispute had arisen out of a gas sale agreement including a take or pay clause. In this regard, the Court stated that, in this case, such provision is usually considered valid and enforceable since it represents a genuine liquidation of damages (and not a penalty) that compensates the seller for the costs incurred. In particular, the Court held that:

> We do not mean by this discussion to cast a cloud of doubt over the "take or pay" clauses that are a common feature of contracts between natural gas pipeline companies and their customers. Such clauses require the customer, in consideration of the pipeline's extending its line to his premises, to take a certain amount of a gas at a specified price – and if he fails to take it to pay the full price anyway. The resemblance to the minimum-guarantee clause in the present case is obvious, but perhaps quite superficial. Neither party has mentioned take-or-pay clauses,

---

164. *Ibid.*, at 1290.
165. *Ibid.*, at 1293.

and we can find no case where such a clause was even challenged as a penalty clause ... If, as appears not to be the case here but would often be the case in supplying natural gas, a supplier's fixed costs were a very large fraction of his total costs, a take-or-pay clause might well be a reasonable liquidation of damages. In the limit, if *all* the supplier's costs were incurred before he began supplying the customer, the contract revenues would be an excellent measure of the damages from breach.[166]

Two considerations can be made in light of the above. First, the different interpretation of the nature of take or pay clauses included in gas sale agreements (i.e., penalties) from that usually adopted by US case law (i.e., main alternative obligations). Second, according to the Court, with regard to such contracts (unlike for different kinds of contracts) take or pay clauses, although qualified as penalties, are normally enforceable since they represent a reasonable liquidation of damages.

[3] Australian Law

Within the common law system, a final consideration has to be made with regard to two recent Australian decisions that dealt with the problem of the application of the law of penalties.

The first is the *Andrews and Others v. Australia and New Zealand Banking Group* case[167] in which the scope of the application of the doctrine of penalties was extended also to cases where no breach of contract has occurred. In such case, a group of customers of Australia and the New Zealand Banking Group ("ANZ") started a representative action claiming that the fees charged by ANZ on the basis of their contracts amounted to penalties and, consequently, were not enforceable.

The Federal Court stated that only some of these fees could be considered as penalties since the others were not payable upon a breach of contract. In reaching this conclusion the Court, therefore, reaffirmed the principle that a clause can be deemed to amount to a penalty only in case the relevant payment depends on the occurrence of a breach of contract.

Such decision was appealed before the High Court which, in rejecting the conclusion reached in the previous judgment, held that:

> The upshot is that the restrictions upon the penalty doctrine urged by the Court of Appeal in *Interstar* [i.e., that it is limited to cases of breach of contract] should not be accepted. The primary judge erred in concluding, in effect, that in the absence of contractual breach or an obligation or responsibility on the customer to avoid the occurrence of an event upon which the relevant fees were charged, no question arose as to whether the fees were capable of characterisation as penalties.[168]

---

166. *Ibid.*
167. *Andrews and Others v. Australia and New Zealand Banking Group Limited,* http://eresources.hcourt.gov.au/downloadPdf/2012/HCA/30, para. 78 (HCA 6 September 2012). This position was criticised in the *Cavendish Square* case. The Court indeed held that it is 'a radical departure from the previous understanding of the law' (*see supra* n. 90, at 41).
168. *Andrews* case, *id.*, at para. 78.

It is clear that this principle could have relevant consequences also with regard to take or pay clauses in gas sale agreements (and, more in general, in any kind of contract). Indeed, the decision of the High Court in *Andrews* case is in contrast with the argument that such provisions cannot be considered as penalties since no breach of contract occurred if the buyer does not actually take the Minimum Bill Quantity. However, if take or pay clauses are considered as providing for two alternative ways for the buyer to perform the contract, it could be objected that such provisions do not in any case amount to penalties since they remain primary obligations (as said, the buyer has an option with regard to how to perform the contract: it can choose whether to order, take and pay the gas or just pay for it). The "pay" alternative is not a secondary obligation with the function to secure the first option, i.e., take (and pay) the gas.

The issue of penalties was addressed again by the Australian High Court in a very recent decision in which it had to establish whether the late payment fees charged by the bank upon the failure of the credit card accounts' holder to pay the minimum monthly payment provided by the contract amounted to unenforceable penalties.[169] In reaching its decision, the Court referred to the same test as in the *Cavendish Square* case,[170] i.e., whether there is a legitimate interest of the party in which favour the clause was provided and, in the affirmative case, if it is exatravagant with regard to such interest. The Court held that the fees were not penalties since they were provided in order to protect the interest of the bank to receive the timely payment of the minimum monthly sum provided by the contract and they were not out of all proportion with regard to such interest.

[B] The Civil Law Approach

To our knowledge, in civil law systems, few decisions addressed the issue of the qualification of take or pay clauses included in gas sale agreements.

One of them is the decision of the Supreme Commercial Court of the Russian Federation of 28 May 2009 that considered such provisions as penalties.[171] In particular, in this case the buyer took the 11% less than the Minimum Bill Quantity agreed in the contract and, consequently, the seller asked for the payment of the amount corresponding to such missing quantity of gas (almost RUB 4 million). The Court considered such request not proportioned to the damages suffered by the claimant and, in application of Article 333 of the Russian Civil Code (that provides judges with the power to reduce penalties which result to be excessive), lessened the amount claimed of around RUB 3 million.

In this regard, it has to be noted that provisions similar to Article 333 of the Russian Civil Code can be found in general in other civil law countries. Indeed, the approach towards penalties is different in civil law from that adopted in common law since such clauses are usually considered valid and enforceable save for the power of

---

169. *Paciocco v. Australia and New Zealand Banking Group Limited*, http://eresources.hcourt.gov.au/downloadPdf/2016/HCA/28 (HCA 27 July 2016).
170. See *supra* n. 90.
171. See *supra* n. 77.

courts and arbitrators[172] to reduce the amount therein provided in case it results to be excessive and not reasonable. For instance, Article 343 of the German Civil Code provides that:

> If a payable penalty is disproportionately high, it may on the application of the obligor be reduced to a reasonable amount by judicial decision. In judging the appropriateness, every legitimate interest of the obligee, not merely his financial interest, must be taken into account. Once the penalty is paid, reduction is excluded.[173]

According to such provision, the court cannot reduce ex officio the penalty, but an express request of the obligor is necessary. Moreover, the court in deciding whether the amount is excessive has to take into account the interest of the obligee.

A similar provision can be found in both French and Italian law. As to the first, the Civil Code disciplines penalties clauses from Article 1226 to Article 1233. In particular, Article 1231 provides that, in case of partial performance of the contract, 'the agreed penalty may, even of his own motion, be lessened by the judge in proportion to the interest which the part performance has procured for the creditor, without prejudice to the application of Article 1152. Any stipulation to the contrary shall be deemed not written'.[174] In its turn, Article 1152 states that:

> Where an agreement provides that he who fails to perform it will pay a certain sum as damages, the other party may not be awarded a greater or lesser sum. Nevertheless, the judge may even of his own motion moderate or increase the agreed penalty, where it is obviously excessive or ridiculously low. Any stipulation to the contrary shall be deemed unwritten.[175]

As it appears from the above-mentioned provisions, according to the French law, the court has the power not only to reduce the penalty in case it is excessive or the contract was partially executed, but also to increase such amount when it is ridiculously low. Moreover, such power can be exercised ex officio.

With regard to Italian law, Article 1384 of the Civil Code provides that:

> The penalty can be reduced on equity ground by the judge, in case the main obligation has been performed in part or in case the relevant amount is manifestly

---

172. In light of the principle of synchronised competence, the power conferred upon courts by the law has to be deemed as also granted to arbitrators (see Ch. 3, §3.01).
173. Available in English on www.gesetze-iminternet.de. See also Art. 6:94.1 of the Dutch Civil Code and Art. 163.3 of the Swiss code of obligations that contain similar provisions. As to the Swedish legal system, the courts' and arbitrators' power to reduce the penalty is considered to derive from s. 36 of the Swedish Contracts Act that, as seen more in detail in Ch. 3, §3.03[C][3], provides for the power to adjust the contract in case of supervening events altering its balance (see, in this regard, L.A. DiMatteo, *A Theory of Efficient Penalty: Eliminating the Law of Liquidated Damages*, in 38 Am. Bus. L.J. 633, 654–655 (2001)).
174. Available in English on www.legifrance.gouv.fr.
175. *Ibid.* The Belgian Civil Code is different from the French one since Art. 1231 just provides for the power of the judge, *ex officio* or upon the request of the debtor, to reduce the penalty that is excessive.

excessive, having taken into account the interest of the creditor to the performance.[176]

Such provision, on the one hand, is similar to Article 343 of the German Civil Code since both of them do not provide for the court's power to increase the penalty in case it is too low, contrary to French law, and establish that the interest of the creditor has to be taken into account by the judge. On the other hand, Article 1384 is similar to the French Civil Code since it provides that the reduction of the penalty can be done not only when it is excessive but also in case the main obligation of the debtor was partially performed.

As to the power of the court to reduce the penalty ex officio the aforementioned article is silent, however, according to the case law, it is possible for the court to intervene on his own motion.[177] In light of such scope, it was held that the judge can reduce the penalty clause even in case the contract provides that it cannot be reduced.[178] It was, however, specified that in order for the court to exercise the above-mentioned power, even without a specific request by the party, it is necessary that the latter has provided the evidence showing that the penalty is excessive (on the basis of such proof the court will form its decision on whether or not to reduce the penalty).[179] Provided that the general approach towards penalty clauses is different between common and civil law, we have seen above that in the *Jobson* case the decision of the court was, instead, similar to the position of civil law legal systems. Indeed, in such case, the penalty clause included in the contract was not struck down, but it was enforced only for the part corresponding to the actual loss suffered by the claimant. Thus, in such case, the Court de facto reduced the amount of the penalty.[180] The qualification of take or pay clauses not as main obligations but as penalties/liquidation of damages can also be found in a decision of the Court of Appeal of Venice not regarding a gas sale agreement but a supply contract of silicon wafers for the manufacturing of solar cells entered into by Helios Technology ("Helios") and Jiangxi LDK Solar Hi-Tech ("LDK").[181] The Italian Court had to decide on the Helios' challenge of the exequatur order by which an ICC arbitral award was declared enforceable in Italy. In particular, Helios argued that such award was contrary to public policy since, among others, it condemned Helios to pay LDK the amount provided by the take or pay clause included in the contract notwithstanding it was an excessive and punitive penalty. The Court in rejecting the challenge held that such amount was a

---

176. As freely translated.
177. *Sidoti v. Condominio via Di Castro 25 Roma*, I Foro It, 2985 (*Corte di Cassazione* n. 18128 13 September 2005).
178. *Tre Monti Residence v. F. M.*, 3 Obbligazioni e Contratti, 260 (*Corte di Cassazione* n. 21066 28 September 2006).
179. *Caccamo v. Teglia*, 3 Obbligazioni e Contratti, 476 (*Corte di Cassazione* n. 8071 28 March 2008).
180. *Jobson* case, *supra* n. 93.
181. *Helios Technology s.p.a. v. Jiangxi LDK Solar Hi-Tech Co. Ltd*, unpublished (Court of Appeal of Venice 16 January 2013). For a comment on this decision, *see* M. Lorefice, *Il mercato del gas: il quadro attuale e le prospettive - Le clausole di take or pay nei contratti di compravendita di idrocarburi*, in *Il mercato del gas tra scenari normativi e interventi di regolazione*, 220–223 (M.S. De Focatis & A. Maestroni, Giuffrè 2013).

legitimate liquidation of damages for the breach of contract by Helios (confirming the qualification made by the arbitral tribunal).

The qualification of the take or pay clause included in a natural gas sale agreement as a clause providing for two main alternative obligations (i.e., take and pay for the Minimum Bill Quantity or just pay for it and take it later) was, instead, affirmed by the Court of Appeal of Angers by in the *Styrpac* case.[182] In particular, it was held that 'Styrpac's obligation to take, as described above, is reciprocal to GDF's supply obligation. The payment of the remainder of gas not taken during the annual period constitutes a mode of performance of the obligation to take'.[183]

§2.04 CONCLUSIONS

In light of the analysis carried out above, take or pay clauses can be qualified as penalty clauses or as clauses providing for two alternative main obligations, i.e., take (and pay for) the minimum quantity agreed (i.e., the Minimum Bill Quantity in gas sale agreements) or just pay for it (and take it later). Each of such qualifications has different impacts on the arbitrators' adaptation power of long-term gas sale contracts.

With regard to the first interpretation, we have seen that it has relevant consequences especially in the common law area where penalties are usually not enforceable. On the contrary, in civil law systems such provisions are generally considered valid and enforceable save for the courts' and arbitrators' power to reduce the relevant amount when it is excessive.[184] Therefore, in an arbitration proceeding, in which the law applicable to the merits of the dispute is that of a country where penalties are not enforceable, a gas purchaser not complying with its take or pay obligation could oppose the non-enforceability of the above-mentioned provisions against the seller claiming for the payment of the Minimum Bill Quantity not taken by the buyer. The same problem could also arise in relation to the enforcement of an arbitration award in case the relevant judgment is held before a court belonging to a country where penalties are considered as not recoverable. However, it was underlined that, in general, courts are usually cautious when they have to decide the issue of the enforceability of a penalty clause. In particular, before striking down a clause as a penalty, courts carry out a careful analysis of the circumstances of the case and of the relevant contractual terms (indeed, the qualification of a provision as a penalty is a matter of construction of the contract independent of the definition adopted by the parties). The scope of such analysis is to see whether the sum of money to be paid by a party in case of breach of contract can be considered as a genuine pre-estimate liquidation of damages that is commercially justifiable, proportionate to the loss suffered by the complying party and without the function to just "terrorise" the other. In the affirmative case, such, amount is qualified as liquidated damages and, therefore, it is considered enforceable. Moreover, even if a clause is qualified as a penalty, the

---

182. *Supra* n. 80.
183. *Ibid.*, at 7, note 34.
184. *See* ss §2.03[A] and §2.03[B].

normal rules for the assessment of damages will apply and, consequently, the seller will still be able to recover the damages that it can prove to have suffered.[185]

Such approach is the one also adopted with regard to take or pay clauses. Indeed, we have seen that in both the *E-Nik* and *M&J* decisions the court, first, held that such provisions in theory could amount to penalties, but then it considered them enforceable since, after the relevant analysis of the contract and of the facts of the case, the criteria above mentioned were met and, therefore, the take or pay clause was qualified as a genuine pre-estimate of damages, commercially justifiable.[186] With regard to the aforementioned decisions, it is interesting to note that, although the conclusion was for the interpretation of take or pay clauses as penalties, the qualification of the relevant claim provided by the Court was in debt and not in damages. In particular, we have noted that such qualification was in contradiction with the application of the law of penalties since a claim in debt does not find its justification in a breach of contract, as instead a penalty does, but in the main performance carried out by the counterparty.[187] It follows that the qualification of the minimum payment request pursuant to a take or pay clause as a claim in debt (as provide in the above-mentioned cases) implies that such provision is considered not as a penalty but as a provision establishing two main alternative obligations upon the buyer, i.e., take and pay for the minimum quantity agreed or just pay for it. Both of them are due in return for the execution of the main performance of the seller (in the *M&J* case, to supply the minimum quantity of products agreed, while, in the *E-Nik* case, to keep its services available for the counterparty in any moment of the year for the minimum number of days agreed in the contract). In light of the above, in our opinion, the Court should have excluded *in toto* the application of the law of penalties and considered the take or pay clause included in the contract as main alternative obligations.

A contradiction between the qualification of the claim and that of the take or pay clause can also be found in the US law. Indeed, we have seen that, although US courts usually qualified such clauses as providing for main alternative obligations, in some cases the minimum payment obligation therein established was considered as (and applied for) the determination of the damages for the buyer's failure to take and pay for the Minimum Bill Quantity.[188] In some other cases, instead, the qualification of take or pay clauses provided by the court was conforming with the remedy adopted.[189]

As said above, the qualification of take or pay clauses as penalties has also relevant consequences on the adaptation of long-term gas sale contracts by arbitrators. Indeed, we have said that in common law countries penalties are either not enforceable at all or enforceable, if they are a genuine liquidation of damages, but the relevant amount cannot be adjusted. Therefore, although in some circumstances a penalty

---

185. See *Lake River* case, *supra* n. 77.
186. See §2.03[A][1][c]. The same principle can be found in *Lake River* case with regard to take or pay clauses included in gas sale agreements.
187. According to the main view, the law of penalties, indeed, does not apply to claim in debts (*see* §2.03[A][1][b].
188. See §2.03[A][2][a].
189. See §2.03[A][2][b].

clause was adapted,[190] in common law the general principle is that there is no power of arbitrators and courts to adjust the Minimum Bill Quantity or the relevant price upon the occurrence of unforeseen events altering the contract's balance and not making such conditions sustainable for the parties (and, usually, for the buyer anymore).

In civil law country, instead, usually penalties are considered valid, and courts and arbitrators have the power to modify ex officio the relevant amount.[191] Therefore, if the procedural applicable law to the arbitration is one of a civil law system, arbitrators should be entitled to adjust the take or pay clause.[192] However, the extent of such power is limited for two reasons. First, it is generally provided for just the authority to reduce the sum due under the penalty clause when it is considered excessive compared to the loss suffered by the innocent party. Only few legal systems (like the French one) also grant the power to increase such amount.[193] Second, the arbitration tribunal could only intervene on the sum of money due under the take or pay clause and not, for instance, also on the Minimum Bill Quantity.

Moreover, another limit to the adjustment power of arbitrators in case the qualification of take or pay provisions as penalties is represented by the necessary occurrence of a breach of contract that, in case of take or pay clauses, is the buyer's failure to take the Minimum Bill Quantity. Indeed, by interpreting the take or pay provision as a penalty it would not be possible for arbitrators to modify the relevant amount unless the buyer breaches the contract by failing to take (or order) the Minimum Bill Quantity (all or in part) and the seller claims for the relevant payment. In other words, the arbitration tribunal, upon the request of the parties, could not intervene on such clause just to rebalance the contractual *equilibrium* – that in a long-term agreement could be affected by the change of the market conditions – independent of a breach of contract. In light of the above, it can be said that, with regard to the adaptation issue, the aforementioned view presents several limits.

Furthermore, it would be difficult to justify such interpretation in light of the structure of long-term gas sale agreements. In particular, first of all, it would be in contrast with the so called "make-up clauses",[194] that are generally included in such contracts.[195] According to these provisions, the buyer is still obliged to pay for the Minimum Bill Quantity at the agreed deadline, but it is entitled to postpone the actual withdrawal of such quantity to a later moment (such mechanism is often established in the same take or pay provision). Usually, the gas is taken in a subsequent contractual year. This mechanism, therefore, grants the buyer a certain degree of flexibility and mitigates its obligation pursuant to the take or pay clause without interrupting the flow of payments in favour of the seller. Thus, it is clear that it would be difficult to justify

---

190. See *Jobson v. Johnson* case, *supra* n. 93.
191. See §2.03[B].
192. As seen in Ch. 3, the adaptation power of arbitrators is a procedural power and, as such, the relevant law to be considered is the procedural one (whose provisions can be included in the Civil Code).
193. See §2.03[B].
194. *See* Holland & Ashley, *supra* n. 80, at 616; Oladotun, *supra* n. 80, at 16. For a definition of make-up clauses *see* §2.02.
195. *See*, for instance, the contracts dealt with in the US decisions analysed at §2.03[A][2].

the presence in the contract of make-up clauses if take or pay provisions are interpreted as penalties for the buyer's failure to take the Minimum Bill Quantity and not as establishing main alternative obligations. In other words, if the obligation to take the Minimum Bill Quantity can be postponed to a later moment, by means of a make-up clause, it is not possible to consider the duty to pay the relevant price in case such quantity is not taken as a secondary obligation deriving from a breach of contract represented by the failure to take the minimum quantity agreed.

Second, the interpretation of take or pay clauses as penalties has the effect to confuse them with a different kind of provisions always characterising gas sale contracts: take *and* pay clauses.[196] The latter provides for only one obligation of the buyer, i.e., take the gas delivered and pay for it, and, consequently, in this case the failure to take the Minimum Bill Quantity is a breach and the relevant payment represents the relevant damages. Thus, it is clear that, if we interpret a take *or* pay clause as providing for a penalty in case the buyer fails to take the Minimum Bill Quantity, we would actually treat it as a take *and* pay provision. As a consequence, the effects of these two kinds of clauses would be the same in spite of the different names and the parties' autonomy would be limited since they would have just one option to include in the contract: take and pay the Minimum Bill Quantity.

Finally, it has to be noted that the interpretation of take or pay clauses as penalties could also have the consequence to put the seller in a position even better than that in which it would have been in case the buyer had performed the contract. Indeed, the seller not only would receive the price for the Minimum Bill Quantity not taken by the buyer but also it would keep such gas.[197]

The second interpretation of take or pay clauses considers, instead, the latter not as penalties, providing for a liquidation of damages in case of breach of contract (i.e., the buyer's failure to take the Minimum Bill Quantity), but as clauses establishing two main alternative obligations upon the buyer, i.e., take (and pay for) the Minimum Bill Quantity or just pay for it and take it in a later moment. It follows that each of such obligations is carried out in return for the main performance of the seller, i.e., to supply/make available the gas.[198] Thus, the fact that the buyer does not take the Minimum Bill Quantity is not a breach of contract but it is the consequence of its choice of how to perform the contract. In this case, it elected to just pay for such quantity without taking it at the same time. The first consequence of this interpretation is that the minimum sum to be paid by the buyer is not damages, since it does not derive from a breach of contract (i.e., the failure to take the Minimum Bill Quantity), but it is a debt due in return for the seller's main performance (with no consequent application of the discipline concerning damages: duty to mitigate, burden of proof, remoteness, etc.).[199] Such amount has not to be confused with any damages that the seller is entitled to claim as a consequence of the buyer's failure to comply with its minimum payment obligation.

---

196. *See* case cited at §2.03[A][2].
197. *See* Leonardo, *supra* n. 73.
198. *See* §2.03.
199. *See* §2.03[A][1][b].

It could be objected that, in case the buyer fails to order/nominate the minimum quantity of goods agreed, there is no delivery/supply by the seller and, therefore, the minimum sum (to be paid by the buyer) could not be considered as a debt, due in return for the seller's performance, but as damages deriving from the buyer's breach to order/nominate the aforementioned minimum quantity. However, even in this case, the qualification of the buyer's payment obligation pursuant to a take or pay provision as a main obligation could still be justified on the basis of the scope pursued by such clause and, more in general, by the contract including it. In this regard, it was underlined (and it will be seen more in detail in the third chapter) that take or pay clauses – and, more in general, take or pay contracts (such as, long-term gas sale agreements) – accomplish a double functions.[200] First, they provide the seller with a stable and constant flux of money independent on the fluctuations and variations of the actual demand of gas in the market where the buyer operates. In this way, the seller can at least recover the investments made in view of the performance of the contract (for instance, for the infrastructures) that, especially in the gas field, are particularly relevant. Moreover, the seller can fulfil its payment obligations deriving from any loan agreements entered into with banks to finance such investments. Second, take or pay clauses grant the buyer a regular and steady supply of gas in order to meet the relevant demand in the market without the need to negotiate the relevant conditions with the seller any time. Thus, even without the delivery by the seller of the minimum quantity agreed as a consequence of the buyer's failure to order it, the minimum payment obligation could be justified in light of what is probably the main scope pursued by a take or pay clause: the possibility for the seller to recover, at least, the costs borne in order to perform the contract and to be able and ready to supply the minimum quantity agreed to the buyer. In particular, the seller, in order to do that, has to plan its activity and to employ the necessary resources to be ready to deliver the gas when it is requested. In other words, the seller has to keep its services available in order to provide the buyer with the minimum quantity agreed. It is clear that such activity is costly and time consuming. What above mentioned is even more relevant with regard to long-term gas sale agreements. Indeed, such contracts imply huge investments for the seller and the necessity to organise its activity on the basis of the Minimum Bill Quantity provided in the different agreements concluded with different buyers.

As it will be seen more in detail in the next chapter, the interpretation of take or pay clauses based on the scope pursued by such provisions has also consequences on the powers of arbitrators to modify the relevant contracts (especially those not including a specific adaptation/renegotiation clause). In this regard, it has to be underlined that the adaptation of take or pay long-term gas sale agreements aims to maintain them in force and to rebalance the contractual *equilibrium* that, due to its duration, can be affected by the occurrence of unforeseen events. In this way, it is possible for the parties to reach the above-mentioned scope pursued when entered into such contracts (i.e., to guarantee a constant flux of money to the seller and a stable supply of goods to the buyer). Without the possibility for arbitrators to adapt these

---

200. *See* §2.02.

agreement in light of the new market conditions in order to rebalance them, the most probable consequence would be the termination of the contract. However, such solution would frustrate the parties' expectations and would have relevant negative economic effects for them. For this reason, it can be said that the adaptation of long-term contracts (like gas sale agreements), aiming to keep a balanced relationship between the parties for the entire duration agreed, is a better and preferable solution than the termination or conservation for the contract without adjusting it to the new market circumstances. Indeed, it would allow to reach the scope pursued when entered into the contract and to meet the parties' will. The adaptation of gas sale agreements by arbitrators can be deemed to find its justification on the principle of good faith.[201] In light of the above, the interpretation of take or pay clauses as providing for main alternative obligations, in our opinion, has to be preferred as to the one qualifying them as penalties.

It could be said that the situation is different if the take or pay contract expressly provides for the buyer's obligation to order/nominate the Minimum Bill Quantity. In this case, the failure of the buyer to comply with such duty could be seen as a breach of contract and the consequent payment of the minimum sum agreed could be considered a penalty or liquidated damages becoming due upon such breach. However, it could be objected that the failure to order/nominate the gas just means that the buyer has chosen the second alternative way to perform the contract provided by the take or pay clause, i.e., the "pay" alternative. Furthermore, the above-mentioned considerations made with regard to the scope of take or pay contract and on the activity of the seller apply even in this case.

Finally, in addition to meet the parties' expectations and to comply with the principle of good faith, other three aspects make the interpretation of take or pay clauses as providing for two main alternative obligations a better solution compared to that qualifying such provisions as penalties. First, the fact that it is not in contrast with the presence in the contract of make-up clauses. Second, such view allows to distinguish a take *or* pay clause from a take *and* pay clause which provides for only one obligation for the buyer, i.e., take the gas delivered and pay for it, and, consequently, in this case the failure to take the Minimum Bill Quantity is a breach. Third, the adaptation by the arbitration tribunal of take or pay provision could be carried out even in absence of a buyer's breach or failure to perform its contractual duties (e.g., as a consequence of the failure of the parties renegotiations of agreement aiming to rebalance it upon the occurrence of unforeseen events altering its *equilibrium*).

---

201. As seen in Chs 3 and 4.

CHAPTER 3
The Adaptation of Long-Term Gas Sale Agreements by Arbitrators Contracts Without an Adaptation Clause

§3.01 INTRODUCTION

The issue of the arbitrators' power to adapt or modify contracts is still a controversial and an un-resolved matter. The question whether arbitrators can intervene on contractual terms in order to fill in the gaps or to adapt them in case of supervening unforeseen circumstances has given rise to a huge debate without finding a definitive answer yet. This problem assumes even more relevance in case of long-term contracts. Indeed, such agreements can be affected by the occurrence of unforeseen events that change the market conditions existing at the moment of the conclusion of the agreement and representing the framework within which the parties had negotiated it and the basis on which they found the relevant balance.[202] Such events (usually defined as "hardship") do not make the parties' performance impossible (like in case of force majeure) but alter the contract's *equilibrium*.

As it was noted:

> The long-term nature of the contracts at issue makes them vulnerable to disruption from unforeseen events or events which the parties - for whatever reason - did not and perhaps could not deal with in the contract with sufficient time and in sufficient detail. The longer-term an agreement and the more exposed to geological, commercial and political risk, the more it becomes vulnerable to external events. Such events can make the operation of the contract partially impracticable or, from a commercial and financial perspective, no longer viable for one party. One consequence is for the parties to terminate the agreement or for one party to

---
202. The term "market conditions" is meant to include not only the economic conditions characterising the market but also other conditions (political, technological, etc.) that have consequences on the market and the relevant contracts.

withdraw. However, such complete destruction of the contract would then also destroy the contractual relationship which often would have continuing benefits for both parties. Parties can also suspend operations under the contract, which if the issues are not solved will, in many cases, equally result in the destruction of the contract. Finally, both parties will often welcome being seen as reasonable partners with whom one can do business, and salvaging a contractual relationship from the destructive impact of unforeseen and unregulated external events tends to contribute to the parties' reputation as "good to do business with" in the international business community-here the natural resources industry. As a rule, such reputation becomes known quite rapidly in the rather narrow community of the international petroleum industry.[203]

Although long-term contracts (especially the international ones) tend to be exhaustive and complete in term of disciplining future events that may occur during the contract's life and affect the relevant *equilibrium*, it is impossible for the parties to foresee all such circumstances. Besides, it would not be rationale to assume that the original conditions on which basis this kind of agreement was concluded remain the same for its entire duration. Thus, it is necessary to characterise such contracts with a certain degree of flexibility in order to adapt their terms to changes and evolutions of the relevant market conditions. This is usually done by providing for the so called "adaptation or adjustment clauses" which aim to maintain the contract alive by restoring its balance upon the occurrence of unforeseen events altering it. In other words, the scope of such clauses is to provide the parties with a remedy different from termination or specific performance of the original contract.[204]

It can be generally said that such provisions find their justification in the scope pursued by the parties when they entered into long-term contracts (like those for the sale of gas) and in the principle of good faith. Indeed, by means of such agreements, the parties aim to build up and maintain for several years (usually around 20–25) a relationship that satisfies the reciprocal interests and expectations. In particular, with regard to gas sale agreements, the scope is to provide, on the one hand, the supplier

---

203. A. Kolo & T.W. Walde, *Renegotiation and Contract Adaptation in International Investment Projects*, 1 JWIT 5, 5–6 (2000). *See also* E. McKendrick, *The Regulation of Long-Term Contracts in English Law*, in *Good Faith and Fault in Contract Law*, 306 et seq. (J. Beatson & D. Friedmann, Clarendon 1995); W.L. Craig, W.W. Park, & J. Paulsson, *International Chamber of Commerce Arbitration* vol. 3, 142 (Oceana Publications 1990), who affirm that '[m]odifying the contract may be particularly vital to the success of long-term projects, with respect to which the evolution of the product market, rates of currency exchange, technological developments, politics, relative competitive advantages, and the like, may make, it highly desirable to provide for an arbitral adjustment of the contract. Otherwise, the sole alternative to a negotiated solution would be the termination of the contract with a possible award of interest, and both parties may agree at the time of negotiating the contract that such an end to their association would be in the interest of neither'.
204. As seen in §3.06, long-term contracts (and, in particular, gas sale agreements), due to their characteristics can be considered as 'relational contracts', i.e., contracts that aim to create and maintain over the time a stable and profitable relationship between the parties. For this reason, they need to be flexible in order to be adapted in light of the change of the market conditions that occur during their life. Therefore, parties are supposed to cooperate and adjust the contract when such events occur. Indeed, only in this way, it is possible to preserve a balanced relationship between the parties. On the contrary, termination is not the solution that better suit their expectations.

with a stable flux of money in order to recover from the huge investments made and, on the other, the buyer with a stable flux of gas in order to cope, in a profitable way, with the relevant market demand without the need to negotiate every time the quantity of gas to be supplied. In consideration of such scope – upon the occurrence of supervening unforeseen events that affect the original market conditions and, consequently, the contractual *equilibrium* – the best solution for the parties is not the termination or the specific performance of the contract as it is, but its adaptation to the new circumstances. Indeed, without the possibility to adapt the long-term contract, the will of the parties would be frustrated since they could not achieve the purpose pursued by entering into such agreements. Moreover, to deny such possibility would be contrary to the principle of good faith. As seen more in detail below, the rebalancing of the contract in order to meet the parties' expectations is based on the generally recognised principle that contracts have to be performed in good faith.[205] Besides, it would be contrary to such principle to constrain the disadvantaged parties, that is negatively affected by the change of circumstances, to keep on performing the original agreement or to terminate the latter. Indeed, both such remedies would have negative economic effects and consequences for the parties. Moreover, in case of termination by one of the parties, the other would be deprived of the possibility to count on a commercial relationship on which it thought it could rely for several years and, consequently, on which it based and planned its business activity by, among the other, spending a considerable amount of time and money.

The need to adapt contracts is even more relevant in the gas field due to the huge investments that the relevant sale contracts imply. In particular, the necessity to modify and revise such agreements concerns the price and the minimum bill quantities provided by take or pay clauses. With regard to the price, usually the parties set an automatic adaptation mechanism represented by a specific formula that indexes the gas price to that of other competing sources of energy and, most frequently, oil products (some of the most used indexes are: Brent crude, gas oil, high or low sulphur oil). In some other cases, the price formula links the gas price to that of coal or electricity.[206] An example of a common price formula is the following:

$P = P_0 \times [0.5 \times P_G/P_{G0} + 0.25 \times P_{LSF}/P_{LSF0} + 0.25 \times P_{HSF}/P_{HSF0}]^2$. Where P = the price of gas at the delivery point; P_0 = the price of gas as at the date the GSA [gas sale agreement] was signed; P_{G0} = the average price of gas oil in a [specified] market during the six-month period preceding the date the GSA was signed; P_G = the average price of gas oil in a [specified] market during the six-month period preceding the Delivery Date (as defined in the GSA); P_{LSF0} = the average price of low sulphur fuel oil in a [specified] market during the six-month period preceding the date the GSA was signed; P_{LSF} = the average price of low sulphur fuel oil in a [specified] market during the six-month period preceding the Delivery Date; P_{HSF0} = the average price of high sulphur fuel oil in a [specified] market during the

---

205. *See*, in particular, §3.06.
206. *See* G. von Mehren, *The Arbitrator's Role*, in *Gas Price Arbitration*, 91 et seq. (M. Levy, Global Law and Business 2014). As seen in the Ch. 1, the oil indexation is still the most common in long-term gas sale agreements in continental Europe. However, in some cases, also in such contracts it is possible to find some references to spot markets price, as it happens in UK and US.

six-month period preceding the date the GSA was signed; P_{HSF} = the average price of high sulphur fuel oil in a [specified] market during the six-month period preceding the Delivery Date.[207]

However, such indexation mechanism does not reflect all the possible variations and future changes affecting the price and, consequently, during the contract's life, it can result in not being adequate anymore in keeping the price competitive and in maintaining the balance originally found by the parties. In particular, 'the relevant market or economic conditions may eventually cause the value of gas in the end-user market to change in a way that is significantly different from the value of the other product(s) used in the formula'.[208] For this reason, it is frequent to find in gas sale agreements an adaptation mechanism represented by the so called "price review clauses" or "price re-opener clauses". As seen in paragraph §3.02 below, by means of such provisions, the parties can keep the contract balanced by reviewing the price formula in order to adapt it in light of the new market conditions and, consequently, they can maintain a profitable relationship and achieve the purpose pursued by entering into the contract.

Another kind of adaptation provision that can be found in long-term gas sale agreements (and, more in general, in long-term contracts) is the so called "hardship clause" whose application is not limited to price terms (even this clause will be analysed in paragraph §3.02 below). However, it can happen that a gas sale agreement does not provide for an adaptation clause.

In the above-mentioned scenarios, it becomes crucial to determine, in case the parties are not able to agree on the adaptation of the contract, which are the arbitrators' powers and, in particular, whether and to what extent they can modify and adjust the price formula or other contractual terms in order to restore the *equilibrium* between the parties affected by the occurrence of unforeseen events that changed the original market conditions.[209] In other words, it has to be understood if, in some exceptional circumstances, the arbitration tribunal can overcome the principles of parties' autonomy and *pacta sunt servanda* in order to keep the contract in force and to avoid its termination. Indeed, as said above, the latter is not the best solution for long-term gas agreements in consideration of the specific scope pursued by the parties. In this regard, it has to be underlined that the answer to such questions aims to determine whether arbitrators are entitled to adapt gas sale contracts in carrying out their "judicial" task (and, therefore, not as mediators or experts) and, consequently, whether they can adjust such agreements by means of a "judicial" award enforceable pursuant to the 1958 New York Convention on the Recognition and Enforcement of Foreign Arbitral Awards ("New York Convention"). In other words, it is not considered the adaptation carried out by an arbitrator as an independent and impartial expert or mediator issuing a contractual decision.

---

207. A. Stanic & G. Weale, *Changes in the European Gas Market and Price Review Arbitration*, 25 J.E.R.L. 324, 325 (2007).
208. von Mehren, *supra* n. 206, at 92.
209. Usually long-term gas sale agreements refer to arbitration either directly in the adaptation clause or in the general arbitration clause.

Chapter 3: Arbitrators Contracts Without an Adaptation Clause   §3.01

In general, it can be said that the issue of the arbitrators' power to adapt the contract has implications on two different levels: the procedural one since the determination of arbitrators' powers is a procedural matter and the arbitrability level since it has to be established whether the adaptation of contract is a dispute that can be submitted to arbitration.[210] Therefore, the applicable laws considered in the analysis carried out in this book will be both the procedural law and that governing the issue of arbitrability. With regard to the first, it has to be underlined that, for the purpose of this work, it will be considered as procedural applicable law not only the *lex arbitri* but also the procedural norms disciplining the courts' powers on the basis of the generally recognised principle of synchronised competence of judges and arbitrators.[211] According to such principle, in the lack of a specific provision in the *lex arbitri* disciplining a

---

210. In the sense that the problem of adaptation of contract by arbitrators is a procedural and arbitrability matter, *see* J.G. Frick, *Arbitration and Complex International Contracts*, 193–194 (Kluwer Law International 2001), who affirms, in relation to the procedural perspective, that 'contract adaptation by arbitrators in form of an enforceable arbitral award requires that the Lex arbitri does not restrict the arbitrators power in this respect, and additionally, that the applicable substantive law allows such adaptation under certain conditions ... While the lex arbitri determines the power of the tribunal, the substantive law determines the conditions of contract adaptations. Contrary to Berger, the question of the power of the arbitrators, in our opinion is solely answered by the lex arbitri. According to Berger, if arbitration law does not provide relevant procedural rules, one must refer to the competence of the domestic courts, whose rules are then applied to the arbitral tribunal; if the domestic procedural law does not provide a rule for national courts, one had to go back to the substantive law, which serve as "an indicator for contract adaptation and gap-filling by national courts, and accordingly, for arbitral tribunal"'. The Author refers to K.P. Berger, *International Economic Arbitration*, 86 (Kluwer Law and Taxation 1993), who affirms the same concept also in *Power of Arbitrators to Fill Gaps and Revise Contracts to Make Sense*, 17 Arb Intl 1, 10 (2001). As seen below, in our opinion, the fact that the issue of the arbitrators' power is a procedural matter (as correctly sustained by Frick) also requires to analyse the power of courts provided by the applicable procedural law on the basis of the principle of synchronised competence of courts and arbitrators. As to the substantive applicable law, instead, we consider that it has a role with regard to the determination of the procedural powers of courts and arbitrators only to the extent that it physically contains procedural law provisions. In the sense that the adaptation of contracts issue depends on the applicable procedural law *see also* C. Brunner, *Force Majeure and Hardship under General Contract Principles*, 492 et seq. (Kluwer Law International 2009).

With regard to the arbitrability perspective, Frick affirms that, in case no applicable procedural law rule expressly denying the arbitrators' power to adapt the contract exists, 'arbitration is a legally authorized dispute resolution mechanism in which all question can be decided as long as their arbitrability is not excluded by the underlying legal system. In our opinion, the basic question of whether arbitrators are authorized to adapt contracts is a question of arbitrability of the dispute, and of the scope of the arbitration agreement' (*id.*, at 197). The Author, therefore, concludes that in the silence of the *lex arbitri* on the issue of the arbitrators' power to adapt contracts, such authority can be deemed to exist on the basis of the general arbitration clause with no need of an express adaptation clause: '[i]n our opinion, if there is no rule of the lex arbitri prohibiting adaptation of contracts, one can assume that arbitrators in fact have such authority as part of their general decision making power derived from the arbitration clause' (*id.*, at 197). As to the issue of whether the procedural law can be considered as actually silent on the problem of the arbitrators' adaptation power, *see* §3.06.
211. The principle of synchronised competence of courts and arbitrators is generally recognised. See, for instance, P. Sanders, *Arbitration*, in *International Encyclopedia of Comparative Law* vol. XVI, Ch. 12, 70 (Mauro Cappelletti, Mohr Siebeck 1987); Berger, *Power of Arbitrators to Fill Gaps and Revise Contracts to Make Sense*, *id.*; Berger, *International Economic Arbitration*, *id.*; F. Nicklish, *Agreement to Arbitrate to Fill Contractual Gaps*, 3 Arb Intl 35, 38 (1988); C.M. Schmitthoff, *Hardship and Intervener Clauses*, J.B.L. 82, 88 (1980).

particular issue (like the adaptation of contract), if courts are entitled to exercise a specific power also arbitrators should be deemed to have the same authority. Similarly, in case the firsts are not provided with a power also the seconds are considered as not having it. Besides the synchronised competence principle, it seems correct to also take into account the procedural law provisions regarding courts' powers since, on the one hand, they belong to the same procedural law system including the *lex arbitri* that was chosen by the parties as applicable to the specific case and, on the other, the arbitration law is often silent on the issue of the adaption power. Moreover, such analysis does not affect the nature of the matter in question since both the *lex arbitri* and the provisions dealing with courts' powers have a procedural character.

In addition, the substantive applicable law will also be analysed since in some cases the procedural powers of courts and arbitrators are provided by the *lex causae*.[212] However, the fact that the procedural norms are physically placed in civil codes does not affect or change their nature. Therefore, for the purpose of this work, we consider that if a party chooses a particular law to govern the arbitration proceeding, this choice will also include the provisions that have a procedural nature and content but that are included within the body of substantive law norms belonging to the same legal system of the *lex arbitri*. The law applicable to the contract is also relevant with regard to the issue of whether, independent of the arbitrators' or courts' adaptation power, the concept of hardship is in general recognised by a specific legal system and, in the affirmative case, which are the conditions required for its applications and the remedies granted to the parties.[213] Moreover, it will be necessary to determine if the concept of legal dispute, mentioned in the arbitration clause, can also include the conflict between the parties that arise out of the contract's adaptation and, as a consequence, whether the scope of the arbitration clause can be also deemed to encompass the latter.

Provided the above, the issue of the arbitrators' power to adapt contracts will be analysed by considering two different situations: (1) contracts without an adaptation clause, (2) contracts with an adaptation clause.

The first category is not so uncommon due to the parties' reluctance to include an adaptation clause in the contract and to difficulties in the negotiating process that may arise. Indeed, it was noted that:

> The legal provisions will normally come up at a later stage of the negotiations and will often be considered by the non-lawyers as an unwelcome but unavoidable part of the negotiations. This is partly due to the fact that the economic relevance of many of the legal provisions in a contract are not obvious to a non-lawyer at first glance. In addition, in legal discussions between lawyers, other members of the negotiating teams will normally feel excluded by the professional and, from their point of view, often extremely complicated language involved. The pressure on the

---

212. *See*, for instance, the French, the Italian and the German Civil Codes with regard to the power of courts to increase or reduce the amount of penalties established by the parties in case of breach of contract.
213. The analysis of the different concept of hardship and the relevant standards for its application would go beyond the scope of this work that is focused on the issue of the arbitrators' power to adapt the contract.

lawyer will become even greater if the agreement has been reached on all the technical and economic aspects of the contract ... A lawyer attempting to include hardship, *force majeure* and/or special risks clauses is especially susceptible to this experience, since they deal with circumstances which, at the time of contract negotiations, the parties neither wish to occur nor can even foresee in any detail ... These aspects of the negotiating atmosphere will more often than not result in a compromise over these contractual clauses: but, in this case, it often may not be a compromise between the opposing interests of the parties but a compromise of the legal precision with which the clause is drafted owing to the pressure on the lawyer.[214]

Moreover, with the emergence of agreements with a shorter duration (due, for instance, to the development of spot markets) parties tend not to provide for an adaptation clause considering more rare the occurrence of events requiring a revision of their contract.[215]

With regard to this kind of contract, the issue is whether the general arbitration clause can be considered sufficient to confer the power to adjust the contract upon arbitrators. In order to answer such question it is necessary, first of all, to determine whether the procedural applicable law allows arbitrators or courts to adapt the contract. The answer to such question implies a brief overview of some of the most relevant European legal systems and of the US one. As shown below,[216] provided that the general principle remains *pacta sunt servanda*, the analysis reveals that the approach to this problem is different not only between civil law and common law countries but also within legal systems of the same area. Indeed, it will be seen that in the civil law family the French, Belgian and Swiss legal systems adopt a stricter and more conservative approach than the German, Dutch and Swedish ones and do not provide courts and arbitrators with such power. Furthermore, in some cases, they do not even recognise the concept of hardship and, consequently, not even parties can adjust the contract but only terminate it (if the supervening events make the performance impossible) or perform it without modifications (unless the contract provides for a specific clause allowing the parties to adapt or to terminate the contract in case of hardship). However, even in the most conservative legal systems, the case law, in some circumstances, has expressed a favourable opinion towards the possibility that contracts, whose balance is altered by unforeseen events, are adapted by parties and, upon the failure of the renegotiation, by courts and arbitrators. Such conservative

---

214. K.H. Bockstiegel, *Hardship, Force Majeure and Special Risks Clauses*, in *Adaptation and Renegotiation of Contracts in International Trade and Finance* vol. III, 161 (N. Horn, Kluwer, 1985). *See also* S. Macaulay, *An Empirical View of Contract*, Wis.L.Rev. 465, 467 (1985), who affirms that '[c]ontract planning and contract law, at best, stand at the margin of important long-term continuing business relations. Business people often do not plan, exhibit great care in drafting contracts, pay much attention to those that lawyers carefully draft, or honor a legal approach to business relationships'; W.C. Whitford, *Ian Macneil's Contribution to Contracts Scholarship*, Wis.L.Rev., 545 (1985); A. Frignani, *La hardship clause nei contratti internazionali e le tecniche di allocazione dei rischi negli ordinamenti di civil law e di common law*, Riv Dir Civ, 680 (1979).
215. *See* Ch. 1. *See also* T.K. Harper, *The client's perspective*, in *Gas Price Arbitration*, *supra* n. 206, at 105.
216. *See* §3.03.

approach is similar to that adopted in the common law area. However, even in this case, it is necessary to draw some distinctions and, in particular, between the US and the English system. Indeed, in the former, prevailing position is less strict than that adopted in the second, since, first of all, it is recognised the concept of commercial impracticability (i.e., the excessive onerousness) and, second, courts in some cases found in favour of the judicial adjustment of the contract.

Moreover, the approach adopted by arbitration tribunals to the issue of the adaptation of long-term gas sale contracts without an adaptation clauses will be analysed. However, it has to be noted that, due to the difficulty in sourcing and collecting such awards,[217] the analysis will also consider courts decisions issued in proceedings for the setting aside or the enforcement of commercial arbitration awards rendered in energy disputes as well as courts and arbitration decisions concerning different kinds of long-term contracts whose principles can also be applied to gas sale agreements.

As said above, the other aspect to be analysed is if the adaptation of contracts can be considered an arbitrable dispute. The answer to such question implies again the analysis of the legal systems above mentioned in order to see how they discipline the issue of arbitrability. Moreover, it is necessary to consider the concept of legal dispute.

The second category of contract analysed is that including an adaptation clause. Such analysis will deal with both the case in which this provision or the arbitration clause expressly provides for the powers of the arbitrators to adjust the contract terms and the case in which such authority is not expressly conferred. The main issues that arise in relation to this kind of agreement are, on the one hand, the possible conflict between the arbitrators' authority provided by the contract and the relevant applicable procedural law (when it does not entitle arbitrators to intervene on contract's terms) and, on the other, the extent of this power.[218] In other words, it has to be determined whether the will of the parties expressed in the contract prevail on the applicable law. Moreover, with regard to contracts including an adaptation clause but not expressly providing the arbitrators with the power to adjust the contract, it has to be determined whether such authority can be implicitly inferred from the combination of the adaptation clause and the general arbitration clause. In both cases, it will be necessary, like for contracts without an adaptation clause, to consider the arbitrability issue and the concept of legal dispute. Even in relation to this second category of contracts, the procedural and arbitrability law considered will be that of the legal systems analysed in relation to contracts with no adaptation clause. In this regard, it has to be noted that, due to the availability of some arbitration awards dealing with the adaptation power, the analysis will mainly be focused on such decisions.

Before proceeding with the above-mentioned analysis, it is necessary to clarify the meaning of adaptation. For the purpose of this book, the concept of adaptation is used to identify the activity of adjusting and amending the contract upon the occurrence of unforeseen events changing the market conditions and affecting the contract's

---

217. Usually they are not published for confidentiality reasons.
218. This book just briefly addresses the issue of the extent of the arbitrators' adaptation powers by analysing some international arbitration awards issued in the energy field.

balance (so called "supervening gaps"). Therefore, it does not include the function of filling the gaps voluntarily left by the parties at the moment of the conclusion of the contract (so called "initial or original gaps").[219]

Furthermore, it is important to underline that the unforeseen events taken into account in this book are those, beyond the parties' control, that determine changes in the original conditions without rendering the performance of the parties impossible (like in case of a force majeure event) under the relevant long-term contract but extremely burdensome and onerous. It follows that a force majeure provision or any other provision with the effect of terminating the contract in case one of the parties' performance becomes impossible is not considered an adaptation clause.

§3.02 PRICE REVIEW AND HARDSHIP CLAUSES

As said above, price review or price re-opener clauses aim to adapt the price to the current market conditions when they change compared to those existing at the moment of the conclusion of the long-term gas sale contract altering its balance. In this way, it is possible to restore the *equilibrium* of the agreement and to maintain a profitable relationship between the parties instead of terminating it.[220] In particular, '[f]or the buyer, price review provisions are a mechanism to align its supply costs to achieve

---

219. In such cases, the parties decided to let the determination of some contractual terms to a future moment or to determine such elements only for an initial period leaving at the future renegotiation their specification for the following years (for instance, the price could be determined only for the first year with the provision that for the other years it will be negotiated by the parties at a specific date). In favour of a distinction between supervening and original gaps, see also P. Sanders, Quo Vadis Arbitration?, 166 et seq. (Kluwer Law International 1999). In other contexts, instead, the concept of adaptation is used in a wider meaning and it also includes the case of open contracts. *See* in this sense, for instance, N. Horn, *The Concepts of Adaptation and Renegotiation in the Law of Transnational Commercial Contracts*, in *Adaptation and Renegotiation of Contracts in International Trade and Finance*, supra n. 214, at 7, who affirms that '[f]or practical reasons, however, it appears advisable to use the term adaptation in a somewhat wider sense and also to include contractual gap-filling. Where this is necessary to keep the contract in line with new developments. Such gaps may be expressly anticipated, as is typical for "open" contracts as discussed above, or they may be inadvertent'. In any case, it has to be noted that the filling the gaps activity and the adaptation of contracts upon the occurrence of supervening events altering its balance are based on different conditions. Indeed, the first implies the failure of the parties to discipline a specific aspects of their relationship that occurs at the moment of the conclusion of the agreement (so called "original gap"). While in case of adaptation the contract is complete but one (or more) of its elements does not reflect anymore the actual market conditions due to their modifications upon the occurrence of unforeseen events (so called "supervening gaps"). However, these two situations in practice are not so different as to their consequences since, in both situations, arbitrators (or judges) have to intervene on the contract instead of the parties. In this sense, *see also* A. Redfern & M. Hunter, *International Arbitration*, 536 et seq. (Oxford University Press 2015).
220. In this regard, it is interesting to note that two approaches have been identified as underlying such provisions: the evolutionary and the revolutionary approach. The first has its point of reference in the original economic balance of the contract and, therefore, by means of the adaptation of the price tends to re-establish such balance when the market conditions change and alter it. The second, although always aiming at maintaining the contract balanced, does not tend to restore the original *equilibrium* but to determine a new one on the basis of the new market conditions (see P. Griffin & F. van Eupen, *The Future for Price Reviews*, in *Gas Price Arbitration*, supra n. 206, 146–147).

economically viable operations, given that the buyer has a substantial, monetary take-or-pay commitment every year, irrespective of whether it can sell the required volumes at a profit. For the seller, price review provisions are a mechanism to ensure that the buyer does not benefit exclusively from increased values in the end-user market that are not appropriately allocated by an existing price formula'.[221]

Price review clauses can provide for periodic reviews of the price formula in order to adapt it to the current market conditions and/or for reviews to be carried out upon the occurrence of unforeseen changes of the market conditions (usually that of the buyer) that are not reflected in the original formula. As to the first category, the condition triggering the renegotiation and adaptation of the contract (so called "trigger event") is the passing by of time. An example of this kind of clause can be found in the LNG contract concluded in 1976 between Sonatrach and Distrigas, providing that:

> parties agree to meet regularly to proceed with the revision of the Contractual Sales Price defined in Article 9 above. They shall so meet for the first time during the first quarter of the year 1980 and thereafter every four (4) years. The revision of the price shall consist in adapting it in a reasonable and fair manner to the economic circumstances then prevailing on the imported Natural Gas market and on the market for the other imported energy supplies competing with its production in the East Coast and Gulf Coast areas of the United States of America within the framework of long-term contracts.[222]

With regard to the second category of price review clause, the trigger events are the changes of the market conditions that have to be: (1) substantial; (2) unforeseen; and (3) beyond the control of the parties. Moreover, such changes have not to be reflected in the original price formula and their effect on the value of natural gas has to be lasting.[223] An example of such clause is that provided in the contract concluded in 1995 between Atlantic LNG Company of Trinidad and Tobago ("Atlantic") and Gas Natural Aprovisionamentos ("GNA"), according to which:

> [i]f at any time either Party considers that economic circumstances in Spain beyond the control of the Parties, while exercising due diligence, have substantially changed as compared to what it reasonably expected when entering into this Contract or, after the first Contract Price revision under this Article 8.5, at the time of the latest Contract Price revision under this Article 8.5, and the Contract Price resulting from application of the formula set forth in Article 8.1 does not reflect the value of Natural Gas in the Buyer's end-user market, then such Party may, by notifying the other Party in writing and giving with such notice information supporting its belief, request that the Parties should forthwith enter into negotiations to determine whether or not such changed circumstances exist and justify a revision of the Contract Price provisions and, if so, to seek agreement on a fair and

---

221. von Mehren, *supra* n. 206, at 92–93.
222. See *Gas Price Arbitration*, *supra* n. 206, at 173.
223. See *Gas Price Arbitration id.*; Roberts, *supra* n. 73; T. Greeno & C. Kehoe, Contract Pricing Disputes, in *Dispute Resolutions in the Energy Sector*, 109 (R. King, Global Law and Business 2012); S. Sarzana, *The Rise of Price Revision Arbitrations*, https://www.cdr-news.com/categories/expert-views/european-energy-disputes:-the-rise-of-price-revision-arbitrations (31 October 2012); A. Brautaset, *Norwegian Gas Sales* part II, para. 6.2.3 (Sjørettsfondet 1998).

equitable revision of the above-mentioned Contract Price provisions in accordance with the remaining provisions of this Article 8.5.[224]

Another example of the second kind of price review clause can be found in the ICC cases n. 9812/1999 and n. 13504/2007 that dealt with the same contract. In particular, such agreement provided for a revision of the price '[i]f the economic circumstances in the country of the Buyer which are beyond the control of the Parties should change significantly compared to what is reflected in the prevailing price provisions under Articles 6.1-6.4 hereof, then each Party shall be entitled to an adjustment of the price provisions under Articles 6.1-6.4 hereof, reflecting such changes, in particular the value of Natural Gas in the end user market of the buyer as such value can be obtained by a prudent and efficient gas company'.[225]

In general, it is important to note that usually the parties in the price review clauses recall the good faith principle by referring to the concepts of fairness and reasonableness. Moreover, the review can only be asked a limited number of times during the contract life (for instance, every three or four years as of the starting date of the contract or the last price review), by providing the other party with a written request to be sent within a fixed date, and has to be referred to a specific period of time (the so called "price revision period").[226] In addition, price review clauses contain some guidance for the parties (and arbitrators) on how to carry out the review of the price. For example, the Sonatrach and Distrigas contract provided that the parties 'shall take into account the individual characteristics of each of the above products [i.e., the other competing energy products] including the quality, the continuity of deliveries,

---

224. Clause extracted from *Atlantic LNG Company of Trinidad and Tobago v. Gas Natural Aprovisionamentos* unpublished (final arbitration award 17 January 2008). *See also.* von Mehren, *id.,* affirming that '[i]f circumstances beyond the control of either of the Parties have induced significant changes in the energy market of the Buyer as compared to such market at the time [the existing price formula was established], then either Party may request, in the manner hereinafter described, a Regular Price Review or a Special Price Review'. For other examples *see Gas Price Arbitration, id.,* at 173 et seq.
225. ICC case n. 9812/1999, 2009 20 ICC Int'l Ct.Arb.Bull. 69, 69–70 (1999); ICC case n. 13504/2007, 2009 20 ICC Int'l Ct.Arb.Bull., 93, 94–95 (2007).
226. von Mehren, *supra* n. 206, at 94 et seq.; M. Leijten & M. de Vries Lentsch, *The Trigger Phase,* in *Gas Price Arbitration, supra* n. 206, at 36 et seq. *See also* the price review clause included in the Sonatrach and Distrigas contract, *supra* n. 223, as well as those referred to in the *Atlantic* case, *supra* n. 224, at 3 ('Neither Party shall request a Contract Price revision to be effective as of the date which is earlier than twelve (12) Months following the Date of First Commercial Supply and no Party shall request any further to be effective as of a date which is earlier than three (3) Calendar Years after the date as of which such Party has last requested a revision to be effective') and in the ICC cases n. 9812/1999 and 13504/2007, *id.* ('Either Party shall be entitled to request a review of the price provisions under Articles 6.1–6.4 hereof for the first time with effect as of 1 April 1992 or earlier if necessary in order to perform a price review six (6) months prior to start of deliveries, for the second time with effect as of 1 October 1995 and thereafter with effect as of 1 October every three (3) years after 1 October 1995. In addition each Party shall be entitled to request a review of the price provisions under Articles 6.1–6.4 hereof once within each such three-year interval with effect from the first day of the month next following the request for price review, provided that the total number of such additional requests shall be limited to three (3) for each Party during the term of this Agreement').

the production and transportation costs, etc.'.[227] Similarly, the Atlantic and GNA contract provided that:

> [the parties] shall take into account levels and trends in price of supplies of LNG and Natural Gas ... such supplies being sold under commercial contracts currently in force on arm's length terms, and having due regard to all characteristics of such supplies (including, but not limited to quality, quantity, interruptability, flexibility of deliveries and term of supply ... The Contract Price as revised in accordance with this Article, shall in any event, allow the Buyer to market the LNG supplied hereunder in competition with all competing sources or forms of energy ... in the market of the Buyer at the point of consumption, taking into account, *inter alia*, all appropriate operations, services and risks which are usual within the Natural Gas industry from the points of import for handling and marketing the Natural Gas in all market segments when due regard is given to all characteristics of the LNG supplied under this Agreement ... and on the basis that sound marketing practices and efficient operations on the part of the Buyer are assumed and such Contract Price shall allow the Buyer to achieve a reasonable rate of return on the LNG delivered hereunder.[228]

Price review clauses usually, provide, upon the parties failure to find an agreement, for arbitration in order to adapt the price. As it was noted, '[i]t is common for price review clauses to refer to a separate arbitration provision that applies generally to all disputes arising under the agreement. These arbitration clauses are of the kind normally found in commercial agreements'.[229] However, it may happen that the parties do not expressly referred to arbitration in case of failure of the negotiations and, consequently, they do not expressly confer the powers to modify the contract on arbitrators. Therefore, as said, in such situation it has to be determined whether arbitrators are entitled to adjust the price formula on the basis of the combination of the adaptation and the general arbitration clauses.

Another kind of adaptation provision that can be found in long-term gas sale agreements is the hardship clause. An example of such provision is the following:

> If a substantial change that was not predicted at the time of execution takes place in the circumstances on which the Agreement was based so that a party suffers or is foreseen to suffer substantial hardship, which is likely to continue, arising from that change, then the parties shall immediately consult and make mutually acceptable revision of the terms and conditions appropriate to alleviate or eliminate the hardship, in a spirit of mutual understanding and cooperation.[230]

---

227. Sonatrach and Distrigas contract, *id.*
228. *Atlantic* case, *supra* n. 224, at 2–3. *See also* ICC cases n. 9812/1999 and 13504/2007, *supra* n. 225, at 69–70 and 94–95 ('in any case the price provisions hereunder shall allow the Buyer to economically market the Processed gas delivered hereunder in the market of the Buyer in competition with all competing sources of energy in the end user market always assuming sound marketing practices and efficient operations on the part of the Buyer').
229. von Mehren, *supra* n. 206, at note 4. *See also* the *Atlantic* case, *id.*, at 3 ('If agreement is not reached within six (6) months from the date of notifying the request for Contract Price revision, either Party may submit the matter to arbitration for decision in accordance with the criteria set out in sub-Articles (b) and (c) above').
230. M. Polkinghorne, *Predicting the Unpredictable: Gas Price Re-openers* http://documents.jdsupra.com/673d6d07-c6ad-4c11-b85a-2204fd15cfe4.pdf (2011).

Even in this case the triggering events are changes in the market conditions that alter the contract's balance, by making the performance of one of the parties excessively onerous, and that have to be: (1) substantial; (2) unforeseen; and (3) beyond the control of the parties.

An accurate definition of the principle of hardship and description of the relevant triggering conditions are provided by both the International Institute for the Unification of Private Law Principles of International Commercial Contracts ("UNIDROIT Principles") and the Principles of European Contract Law ("PECL").[231] In particular, Articles 6.2.1 and 6.2.2 of the UNIDROIT Principles provide that:

> Where the performance of a contract becomes more onerous for one of the parties, that party is nevertheless bound to perform its obligations subject to the following provisions on hardship and that
>
> There is hardship where the occurrence of events fundamentally alters the equilibrium of the contract either because the cost of a party's performance has increased or because the value of the performance a party receives has diminished, and (a) the events occur or become known to the disadvantaged party after the conclusion of the contract; (b) the events could not reasonably have been taken into account by the disadvantaged party at the time of the conclusion of the contract; (c) the events are beyond the control of the disadvantaged party; and (d) the risk of the events was not assumed by the disadvantaged party.

In its turn, Article 6:111 of the PECL provides that:

> (1) A party is bound to fulfil its obligations even if performance has become more onerous, whether because the cost of performance has increased or because the value of the performance it receives has diminished. (2) If, however, performance of the contract becomes excessively onerous because of a change of circumstances, the parties are bound to enter into negotiations with a view to adapting the contract or terminating it, provided that: (a) the change of circumstances occurred after the time of conclusion of the contract, (b) the possibility of a change of circumstances was not one which could reasonably have been taken into account at the time of conclusion of the contract, and (c) the risk of the change of circumstances is not one which, according to the contract, the party affected should be required to bear.

Like for price review clauses, the aim of the hardship clause is to rebalance the contract in order for the parties to maintain their relationship instead of terminating it and, even in this case, parties usually referred to the principle of good faith. Therefore, also hardship clauses provide for the renegotiation between the parties upon the occurrence of the hardship event. However, unlike price review clauses, they do not often expressly provide for the possibility to recourse to arbitration or courts in case no agreement is found by the parties. Thus, in such situation, the issue is whether arbitrators can still be entitled to intervene on contract's terms in light of the combination of the general arbitration clause and the hardship provision. As seen in

---

231. UNIDROIT Principles (2010), available in English on http://www.unidroit.org/english/principles/contracts/principles2010/integralversionprinciples2010-e.pdf; PECL (2002), available in English on http://www.transnational.deusto.es/emttl/documentos/Principles%20of%20European%20Contract%20Law.pdf.

paragraph 6 below, Article 6.2.3 of the UNIDROIT Principles and Article 6:111, paragraph 3, of the PECL, instead, provide that, upon the failure of the renegotiation, it is possible for the parties to resort to courts that can terminate the contract or adapt it in order to rebalance it.

Finally, it has to be underlined that the extent of hardship provisions is not limited to the revision of the price but is broader and can regard any contract condition. Due to this general application, usually such clauses do not provide for specific parameters on how to adjust the contract, as, instead, it often happens in price review clauses.

§3.03   THE PROCEDURAL APPLICABLE LAW PERSPECTIVE

The issue of the arbitrators' power to adapt long-term gas sale agreements (and contracts in general), when their balance is altered upon the occurrence of unforeseen events, has to be analysed under a procedural law perspective due to the procedural nature of such power. Therefore, in the next paragraphs, an overview of some of the most significant European legal systems and of the US one will be provided in order to see whether, and how, they approach this matter.[232] In particular, such systems will be divided into the following categories:

(1) conservative legal systems, i.e., those that, in general, do not recognise the concept of hardship or *imprèvision* and, consequently, the relevant power to adjust the contract (although, as seen below, the case law in some decisions adopted a different approach);
(2) semi-conservative legal systems, i.e., those that recognise the concept of hardship or *imprèvision* and the possibility for parties to adjust the contract but do not expressly provide for the judges and arbitrators' adaptation power (even in this case some decisions expressed a different view);
(3) non-conservative legal systems, i.e., those that expressly provide for the courts and arbitrators power to adapt contracts.

Before proceeding with such analysis, it is important to underline that, although the parties are free to choose a *lex arbitri* of a country different from that of the seat of arbitration, it is rare that they opt for this solution ('an agreement providing that one country will be the site of the arbitration but the proceedings will be held under the arbitration law of another country [is] "exceptional"; "almost unknown"; a "purely academic invention"; "almost never used in practice"; a possibility "more theoretical than real"; and a "once-in-a-blue-moon set of circumstances"').[233]

---

232. As already noted, also the substantive law will be considered to the extent that, in some cases, the procedural powers of courts and arbitrators are thereby provided (*see* §3.01).
233. *Karaha Bodas v. Perusahaan Pertambangan Minyak Dan Gas Bumi Negara*, 364 F.3d. 274, 291 (5th Cir. 23 March 2004). In the same sense, *see*, *ex multis*, *Naviera Amazonica Peruana v. Compania Internacional de Seguros del Peru*, 1988 1 Lloyd's Rep. 116, 120 (EWCA 10 November 1987); ICC case n. 5505/1987, 1988 XIII YBCA 110, 115 (preliminary award 1987),.

The application of the law of the seat as *lex arbitri* is also the general approach followed in the lack of the parties' choice of the law governing the arbitration ('if the parties have specifically chosen the law governing the conduct and procedure of arbitration, the arbitration proceedings will be conducted in accordance with that law so long as it is not contrary to the public policy or the mandatory requirements of the law of the country in which the arbitration is held. If no such choice has been made by the parties, expressly or by necessary implication, the procedural aspect of the conduct of arbitration (as distinguished from the substantive agreement to arbitrate) will be determined by the law of the place or seat of arbitration').[234] Such approach is mainly based on the fact that the majority of arbitration laws embraces the so called "territorial criterion" according to which the choice of the seat implies the application of the relevant *lex arbitri*. Such criterion, for instance, is the one adopted by the UNCITRAL Model Law which provides that '[t]he provisions of this Law, except Articles ... apply only if the place of arbitration is in the territory of this State'.[235]

The reasons justifying the aforementioned principle are represented by 'the sake of certainty'[236] and the fact that in:

> 'most legal systems, the place of arbitration is the exclusive criterion for determining the applicability of national law and, where the national law allows parties to choose the procedural law of a State other than that where the arbitration takes place, experience shows that parties rarely make use of that possibility. Incidentally, enactment of the Model Law reduces any need for the parties to choose a "foreign" law, since the Model Law grants the parties wide freedom in shaping the rules of the arbitral proceedings. In addition to designating the law governing the arbitral procedure, the territorial criterion is of considerable practical importance in respect of Articles 11, 13, 14, 16, 27 and 34, which entrust State courts at the place of arbitration with functions of supervision and assistance to arbitration. It should be noted that the territorial criterion legally triggered by the parties' choice

---

See also A. van den Berg, *The Application of the New York Convention by the Courts*, in *Improving the Efficiency of Arbitration Agreements and Awards: fourty Years of Application of the New York Convention*, 25–26 (A. van den Berg, ICCA Congress Series n. 9 1999); M. Mustill & S. Boyd, *Commercial Arbitration*, 64 et seq. (Butterworths 1989).

234. *National Thermal Power v. The Singer*, 1993 XVIII YBCA 403, 407 (Indian Supreme Court 7 May 1992). In the same sense see, ex multis, *Steel Corporation of Philippines v. International Steel Services*, 354 Federal Appendix 689, 692–93 (3d Cir. 19 November 2009); *Karaha Bodas* case, id.; *American Diagnostica v. Gradipore, Centerchem*, 1999 XXIV YBCA 574, 580 (NSW Supreme Court 26 March 1998); *Naviera Amazonica* case, id.; *Compagnie Tunisienne de Navigation v. Compagnie d'Armement Maritime*, AC 572, 604 (UKHL 1971). The same position is taken by arbitration awards. In this regard, see *Wigan Athletic AFC v. Heart of Midlothian*, 26 ASA Bull., 513 (final award 30 January 2008); ICC case n. 5294/1988, 1989 XIV YBCA, 137 (final award 1988); ICC case n. 5485/1987, 1989 XIV YBCA, 156 (final award 1987).

235. Article 1.2 of the UNCITRAL Model Law, http://www.uncitral.org/pdf/english/texts/arbitration/ml-arb/07-86998_Ebook.pdf. For a comment on such provision, see S. Brekoulakis, J. Riberiro & L. Shore, *UNCITRAL Model Law on International Commercial Arbitration*, in *Concise International Arbitration*, 836–849 (L. Mistelis, Kluwer Law International 2015). In the same sense, see, for instance, Art. 1073.1 of the Dutch Code of Civil Procedure; s. 2 of the English Arbitration Act; Art. 1509 of the French Code of Civil Procedure; Art. 1025 of the German Code of Civil Procedure; Arts 816 and 832 of the Italian Code of Civil Procedure; Art. 47 of the Swedish Arbitration Act; Art. 176.1 of the Swiss Private International Law Act.

236. Explanatory Note to the UNCITRAL Model Law, http://www.uncitral.org/pdf/english/texts/arbitration/ml-arb/07-86998_Ebook.pdf, 27, para. 14.

regarding the place of arbitration does not limit the arbitral tribunal's ability to meet at any place it considers appropriate for the conduct of the proceedings, as provided by article 20'.[237]

As said, although providing for a territorial approach, the Model Law – with regard to some issues (and, in particular, in relation to the conduct of the proceeding) – recognises a broad procedural autonomy to parties and, in the lack of the parties' agreements, to arbitrators.[238] The same approach is adopted by the most part of arbitration laws[239] and rules,[240] as well as by international

---

237. *Ibid.*
238. Article 19.1 provides that: '[s]ubject to the provisions of this Law, the parties are free to agree on the procedure to be followed by the arbitral tribunal in conducting the proceedings' and Art. 19.2 provides that: '[f]ailing such agreement, the arbitral tribunal may, subject to the provisions of this Law, conduct the arbitration in such manner as it considers appropriate. The power conferred upon the arbitral tribunal includes the power to determine the admissibility, relevance, materiality and weight of any evidence'.
239. *See*, for instance, Art. 594.1 of the Austrian Code of Civil Procedure ('Subject to the mandatory provisions of this Chapter, the parties are free to agree on the rules of procedure. In doing so they may also refer to arbitration rules ... Failing such agreement, the arbitral tribunal shall proceed in accordance with the provisions of this Title, and in other respects in such manner as it considers appropriate'); Art. 1700, paras 1 ('The parties are free to agree on the procedure to be followed by the arbitral tribunal in conducting the proceedings') and 2 ('Failing such agreement, the arbitral tribunal may, subject to the provisions of Part 6 of this Code, determine the rules of procedure applicable to the arbitration in such manner as it considers appropriate') of the Belgian Judicial Code; Art. 1036 of the Dutch Code of Civil Procedure ('Subject to the provisions of this Title, the arbitral proceedings shall be conducted in such manner as agreed between the parties or, to the extent that the parties have not agreed, as determined by the arbitral tribunal'); ss 1.b ('parties should be free to agree how their disputes are resolved, subject only to such safeguards as are necessary in the public interest') and 34.1 ('It shall be for the tribunal to decide all procedural and evidential matters, subject to the right of the parties to agree any matter') of the English Arbitration Act; Arts 1509.1 ('The arbitration agreement may, directly or by reference to arbitration rules or to procedural rules, govern the procedure to be followed for the arbitral proceedings') and 1509.2 of the French Code of Civil Procedure ('Unless the arbitration agreement provides otherwise, the arbitral tribunal shall define the procedure as required, either directly or by reference to arbitration rules or to procedural rules'); Art. 1042, paras 3 ('Otherwise, subject to the mandatory provisions of this Book, the parties are free to determine the procedure themselves or by reference to a set of arbitration rules') and 4 ('Failing an agreement by the parties, and in the absence of provisions in this Book, the arbitral tribunal shall conduct the arbitration in such manner as it considers appropriate. The arbitral tribunal is empowered to determine the admissibility of taking evidence, take evidence and assess freely such evidence') of the German Code of Civil Procedure; Art. 816-*bis* of the Italian Code of Civil Procedure ('The parties are free to determine in the arbitration agreement ... the rules on the procedure to be followed by arbitrators and the language of the arbitration. Failing such agreement arbitrators may conduct the proceeding in such manner as they consider appropriate'); Art. 182, paras 1 ('The parties may, directly or by reference to rules of arbitration, determine the arbitral procedure; they may also submit the arbitral procedure to a procedural law of their choice') and 2 ('If the parties have not determined the procedure, the arbitral tribunal shall determine it to the extent necessary, either directly or by reference to a statute or to rules of arbitration') of the Swiss Law on Private International Law.
240. *See*, for instance, Arts 1.1 ('Where the parties have agreed that disputes between them in respect of a defined legal relationship, whether contractual or not, shall be referred to arbitration under the UNCITRAL Arbitration Rules, then such disputes shall be settled in accordance with these Rules subject to such modification as the parties may agree') and 17.1 ('Subject to these Rules, the arbitral tribunal may conduct the arbitration in such manner as it considers appropriate, provided that the parties are treated with equality and that at an

conventions.[241] The procedural autonomy of parties and arbitration tribunals is subject to the mandatory rules of the law of the seat of arbitration,[242] that usually are 'restricted to those considered necessary to guarantee that the parties have the opportunity to present their case and answer the case against them. This is generally known as due process and is a fundamental element of international arbitration'.[243]

---

appropriate stage of the proceedings each party is given a reasonable opportunity of presenting its case') of the UNCITRAL Arbitration Rules. With regard to the latter provision, it was noted that it 'fairly clearly suggests the possibility that the arbitral tribunal, in conducting the arbitral proceedings, need not give effect to the parties' procedural agreement if doing so would conflict with its obligations to treat the parties with equality, to afford each party a reasonable opportunity to present its case and conduct the arbitration fairly and efficiently. Rather than a pure affirmation of the parties' procedural autonomy, Arts 1(1) and 17(1) of the UNCITRAL Rules, read together, acknowledge both the parties' autonomy and the arbitrators' procedural authority, with the latter being capable, in some cases, of overriding the former. (In general, the arbitrators' procedural authority is limited to matters of procedure and does not extend to basic substantive aspects of the parties' arbitration agreement (e.g., location of arbitral seat, choice of arbitrators, choice of applicable law)' (G. Born, *International Commercial Arbitration*, 2139 (Wolters Kluwer 2014)); Art. 19 of the ICC Rules ('the proceedings before the arbitrator shall be governed by these Rules, and, where these Rules are silent, by any rules which the parties or, failing them, the arbitral tribunal may settle on, whether or not reference is thereby made to the rules of procedure of a national law to be applied to the arbitration'); Arts 14.2 ('The parties may agree on joint proposals for the conduct of their arbitration for consideration by the Arbitral Tribunal') and 14.5 ('The Arbitral Tribunal shall have the widest discretion to discharge these general duties [impartiality, due process, equitable treatment of the parties, avoidance of undue delays and expenses], subject to such mandatory law(s) or rules of law as the Arbitral Tribunal may decide to be applicable') of the LCIA Rules. Such rules, compared to the others, limit the procedural autonomy of the parties, while grant the arbitration tribunal a broad discretion in the determination of the procedure to be followed.

241. *See* Art. V.1.d of the New York Convention (providing that the enforcement of an award may be refused in case '[t]he composition of the arbitral authority or the arbitral procedure was not in accordance with the agreement of the parties, or, failing such agreement, was not in accordance with the law of the country where the arbitration took place'); Arts IV.1.b.iii (providing that parties are free 'to lay down the procedure to be followed by the arbitrators') and IV.4.d 'the President or the Special Committee shall be entitled as need be ... to establish directly or by reference to the rules and statutes of a permanent arbitral institution the rules of procedure to be followed by the arbitrators, provided that the arbitrators have not established these rules themselves in the absence of any agreement between the parties') of the European Convention; Arts 2 'Arbitrators shall be appointed in the manner agreed upon by the parties') and 3 ('In the absence of an express agreement between the parties, the arbitration shall be conducted in accordance with the rules of procedure of the Inter-American Commercial Arbitration Commission') of the Inter-American Convention.

242. *See, ex multis*, Art. 1.3 of the UNCITRAL Arbitration Rules providing that: 'These Rules shall govern the arbitration except that where any of these Rules is in conflict with a provision of the law applicable to the arbitration from which the parties cannot derogate, that provision shall prevail'. *See also* J.E. Castello, *UNCITRAL Arbitration Rules*, in *Concise International Arbitration*, *supra* n. 235, 179–182.

243. J. Lew, L. Mistelis & S. Kroll, *Comparative International Commercial Arbitration*, para. 21.16 (Kluwer Law International 2003). In general on this point, *see* Born, *supra* n. 240, at para. 15.04. As to arbitration laws, *see, ex multis*, Art. 18 of the UNCITRAL Model Law providing that ['t]he parties shall be treated with equality and each party shall be given a full opportunity of presenting his case'. The same principle can also be found in arbitration rules (*see*, for instance, Art. 17 of the UNCITRAL Arbitration Rules). *See also* Art. V of the New York Convention that includes the violation of the due process principle among the grounds to resist to the enforcement of the award. However, it has to be noted that the mandatory rules of the law of the seat of arbitration are not always limited to the due process and equality of treatment of the parties (*see*, for instance, s. 4 and Sch. 1 of the English Arbitration Act).

In light of the above, it follows that, if the parties choose a *lex arbitri* different from that of the place of arbitration, the former applies only in case the latter allows the parties to opt out of its (non-mandatory) rules and, consequently, provides them with the autonomy to determine specific procedural issues.[244] Therefore, it is clear that the choice of a *lex arbitri* different from that of the seat of arbitration would be limited to some procedural aspects, would require a coordination with the law of the seat and would have the consequence that two different procedural laws will govern the same proceeding. Furthermore, the choice of a different arbitration law from that of the seat has implications in relation to the award. Indeed, Article V.1.e of the New York Convention provides that the recognition and enforcement of an award may be refused if it was set aside by the court of the place of arbitration or by the court of the state under whose law the award was made (i.e., the *lex arbitri*).[245] Thus, if the arbitration law is not that of the arbitral seat, there are two competent authorities to set it aside. It follows, on the one hand, that the probability for the award to be annulled is higher and, on the other, that there is the risk of having two conflicting decisions concerning the same award. However, in this regard, it has to be noted that the majority of national arbitration laws provide that the competent authority to set aside an award is the court of the seat.[246]

In consideration of the above, it can be concluded that the choice of the law of the seat as arbitration law is the most convenient and practical option and, therefore, it would be unwise for the parties to select a different *lex arbitri* also taking into account that generally arbitration laws provide them with a quite broad procedural autonomy.

[A] Conservative Legal Systems

[1] The French Legal System

The French legal system, at least with regard to civil and commercial law, is one of the most conservative in relation to the possibility to amend the contract upon the occurrence of unforeseen events that alter its balance (so called *"imprèvision"*).[247]

---

244. See, for instance, s. 4.5 of the English Arbitration Act providing that '[t]he choice of a law other than the law of England and Wales or Northern Ireland as the applicable law in respect of a matter provided for by a non-mandatory provision of this Part is equivalent to an agreement making provision about that matter'. See also Born, *id.*, at 1567–1570 and 1605 et seq.
245. See Born, *id.*, at 1626.
246. See, *ex multis*, Art. 34 of the UNCITRAL Model Law. For further reference see, Born, *id.*, at 1627; Lew, Mistelis & Kroll, *supra* n. 243, at para. 25.15.
247. In this regard, see D. Philippe, *France and Belgium*, in, *Foreseen and Unforeseen Circumstances*, 157 et seq. (A.G. Castermans, K.J.O. Jansen, M.W. Knigge, P. Memelink & J.H. Nieuwenhuis, Kluwer 2012); H. Beale, B. Fauvarque-Cosson, J. Rutgers, D. Tallon & S. Vogenauer, *Cases, Materials and Text on Contract Law*, 1127 et seq. (Hart Publishing 2010); E. Steiner, *French Law – A Comparative Approach*, 334 et seq. (Oxford University Press 2010); C. Kessedjian, *Competing Approaches to Force Majeure and Hardship*, 25 International Review of Law and Economics, 415–433 (2005); B. Nicholas, *The French Law of Contract*, 200 et seq. (Clarendon Press Oxford 1992); A. Frignani, *Hardship Clause*, VI Digesto Discipline Privatistiche sez. Commerciale, 446(1991); P. Gallo, *Revisione del Contratto*, XVII Digesto Discipline Privatistiche sez. Civile 431 (1998); M. Bessone, *Adempimento e rischio contrattuale*, 8 et seq. (Giuffrè

Indeed, not only French procedural law does not provide courts and arbitrators with the power to adjust the contract in such situation but also the civil code does not contain any provision disciplining the *imprèvision*. Therefore, not only judges and arbitrators but also the parties are not entitled to modify the contract terms upon the occurrence of unforeseen events that alter the original contractual *equilibrium*. The fundamental principle in French civil and commercial law is, therefore, *pacta sunt servanda*, as stated by Article 1134.1 of the French Civil Code according to which '[a]greements lawfully entered into take the place of the law for those who have made them'.[248] As a consequence, unless a specific adaptation clause is included in the agreement or a force majeure event occurs[249] or there is an express statutory exception,[250] parties remain bound by the original agreement even if its balance has been altered.

The principle of *pacta sunt servanda* and the lack of arbitrators' and judges' power to adapt the contract upon the occurrence of unforeseen events has been also affirmed by the case law. In this regard, the leading decision is the *Canal de Craponne* case[251] concerning a dispute arising out of a series of long-term contracts, signed between 1560 and 1567, providing for the supply of water destined to an irrigation canal located in *Pélissanne*, at a fixed price (including the maintenance of the canal). Almost three centuries later, due to the rising of the inflation and labour costs, the price became too low and not adequate anymore to cope with the costs for the maintenance and, therefore, it was claimed for an increase of the fixed charge. In the first judgment, the Tribunal granted the increase requested and the Court of Appeal of Aix upheld such decision. In particular, it, first of all, affirmed the general principle of sanctity of contracts and, then, it held that:

> the position is not the same in relation to contracts of a continuing nature ... it is recognized in law that these contracts, which are based upon periodic charges, can be modified by the courts when a fair relationship no longer exists between the charges on the one hand and the costs incurred on the other ... in the present case, the sum owed by the waterers represents the use of the water of the canal, having for its counterpart the maintenance and expenses in respect of the canal ... from the day that this balance ceases to exist, the original law of the contract is broken and it is for the courts to re-establish the initial position of equality ... this charge of 3 sols per unit of water, which could have been sufficient at that time, was no longer sufficient today as the costs of maintaining the canal had increased

---

1975). It is, instead, different the position taken by courts in administrative law that uphold the doctrine of *imprèvision* and, consequently, admit the possibility to adapt the contract in such case. In this regard, *see* the *Compagnie du Gaz de Bordeaux* case, III Sirey, 17 (Cons. d'État 20 March 1916). Also part of the doctrine supports the theory of *imprèvision*. *See*, for instance, J. Savatier, *La théorie de l'imprèvision dans les contrats*, II Études de droit contemporain 1 (1959); C. Renard, *La théorie de l'imprèvision dans les contrats*, II R.D.I.D.C., 17 (1950). For further references, *see* M. Bessone, *id.*

248. Available in English on www.legifrance.gouv.fr.
249. *See* Art. 1148 of the French Civil Code.
250. In this regard, *see* Arts 1152 and 1231of the French Civil Code dealing with the power of judges to increase or decrease the amount of penalties; Art. 131-5 of the French Code of Intellectual Property Rights. *See* for more references Philippe, *supra* n. 247.
251. *Case De Gallifet v. Commune de Pélissanne*, as cited in H. Beale, Fauvarque-Cosson, Rutgers, Tallon & Vogenauer, *supra* n. 247, at 1131 et seq. (*Cour de Cassation* 6 March 1876).

significantly ... the judges of first instance, in setting this increase at 60 centimes per unit of water, had properly assessed the facts of the case ....[252]

The Court of Appeal, therefore, established an exception to the principle of sanctity of contracts in relation to long-term agreements when the relevant economic balance is altered and the relationship between the parties is not fair anymore. In this situation, courts should be allowed to modify the contract in order to rebalance it. However, as said above, the *Cour de Cassation* reversed this decision by affirming the *pacta sunt servanda* principle with regard to any kind of agreements and, consequently, denying any power of courts to intervene on the contractual terms in place of the parties. In particular, the *Cour de Cassation* held that:

> the rule that this Article [1134 of the French Civil Code that the Court considered applicable even to contracts concluded before the civil code entered into force] consecrates is general, absolute and governs contracts whose performance extends to successive periods, just as it governs of all other types ... under no circumstances is it for the courts, however fair their decision may appear to them to be, to take into account the time and the circumstances in order to substitute new terms for those which have been freely accepted by the contracting parties ... in deciding the contrary and in increasing the watering charges ... under the pretext that this charge no longer bore any relation to the costs of maintaining the canal de Craponne, the judgment under challenge had categorically violated Article 1134.[253]

The principle stated by the *Cour de cassation* in the *Canal de Craponne* case has been followed by the majority of the case law.[254] However, it has to be noted that in

---

252. *Case De Gallifet v. Commune de Pélissanne*, as cited in Beale, Fauvarque-Cosson, Rutgers, Tallon & Vogenauer, *ibid.* (Court of Appeal of Aix 31 December 1873).
253. See *Canal de Craponne* case, *supra* n. 251, at 1131–1132.
254. *See, ex multis, Soffimat et Mayennecogen v. Laitière de Mayenne*, https://www.legifrance.gouv .fr/affichJuriJudi.do?oldAction = rechJuriJudi&idTexte = JURITEXT000007508427&fastReqId = 1786293691&fastPos = 1 (*Cour de Cassation* 3 October 2006). Such case deals with a contract for the supply of heat providing for an indexation clause linking the heat price to that of the fuel and for an adaptation clause by which, upon the occurrence of a supervening event beyond the parties' control changing the contract's *equilibrium*, the parties should have met in order to renegotiate the agreement. During the course of the contract, the price of natural gas excessively increased (by around 87%) and, consequently, the sellers asked for a revision. However, the buyer refused any proposal in this sense. Therefore, the suppliers stopped delivering the gas, and the buyer started a litigation proceeding claiming for the termination of the contract and the relevant damages. The *Cour de Cassation* upheld such claim holding that the contract did not provide for an obligation to adapt it and that, in the lack of a conduct representing an abuse of right by the buyer, the failure of the renegotiation and adjustment process could not be ascribed to the latter. Moreover, the suppliers could not claim for a revision of the price since the *imprèvision* had to be borne by them having chosen to index the heat price to that of fuel and no to the natural gas one. *See also Cour de Cassation* 18 March 2009, RTDCiv 528; *Cour de Cassation* 30 May 1996, https://www.legifrance.gouv.fr/ affichJuriJudi.do?idTexte = JURITEXT000007304993; *Cour de Cassation* 18 December 1979, 339 Bull.C.C., stating that when a long-term contract does not contain any adaptation clause (in this case providing for the adjustment of the rate of payment for deposit) courts are not allowed to modify the terms of the contract on the basis of equity principle; ICC case n. 2708/1976, Collection of ICC Arbitral Awards 1974–1985 297 (1976), regarding a dispute that arose out of an international sale contract governed by French law, upon the seller's refusal to deliver the goods without an increase of the price (that was not accepted by the buyer). In such case, the

Chapter 3: Arbitrators Contracts Without an Adaptation Clause   §3.03[A]

some decisions, although no judge's powers to adapt contracts have been recognised, the concept of hardship or *imprèvision* was given some relevance. In particular, the case law has affirmed that changes in the original economic conditions altering the contract's balance can render the agreement null and void or can give rise to a duty of cooperation and renegotiation on the basis of the principle of good faith provided by Article 1134.3 ('[t]hey [contracts] must be performed in good faith') of the French Civil Code.[255]

The reference to the principle of good faith with regard to the adaptation of contracts, governed by French law, was also made in international commercial arbitration. In particular, in the ICC case n. 9994/2001[256] a dispute arose out of a long-term license and sale agreement (governed by French law and not including an adaptation clause), concluded between a US ("Defendant") and a French ("Claimant") company, upon the determination of a new price asked by the Claimant in consideration of the increase of the costs of the raw material it supplied to the Defendant. Such increase was due to the more severe conditions and control imposed by a government agency in relation to collection of the human placenta of which the raw material supplied under the contract was made. The parties did not reach an agreement on the new price and upon the Defendant's termination of the contract, the Claimant started an arbitration proceeding. The tribunal stated that, upon the occurrence of unforeseen events altering the contract balance, the parties, according to French law, have the duty to renegotiate and adapt the contract on the basis of the principle of good faith and regardless of the existence of an adaptation clause. In addition, the arbitrators stated that such principle is even more relevant in case of international contracts. In particular, it was held that:

---

arbitration tribunal, seating in Paris, due the lack of a specific contract clause denied the application of the *rebus sic stantibus* doctrine, invoked by one of the parties in order to justify the non-execution of its obligations, since it is not recognised in French law; *Bacou v. Saint Pé*, as cited in Beale, Fauvarque-Cosson, Rutgers, Tallon & Vogenauer, *supra* n. 247, at 1132 (*Cour de Cassation* 6 June 1921), in which it was held that 'no equitable consideration permits the courts to vary the contracts'.

255. See *Soffimat v. Sec*, https://www.legifrance.gouv.fr/affichJuriJudi.do?idTexte = JURITEXT000 022430481 (*Cour de Cassation* 29 June 2010). Such case concerned a long-term contract providing for the maintenance of industrial equipment upon the payment of a fixed annual price. Soffimat, that was in charge of the maintenance, claimed for an adaptation of such price since the relevant costs had increased of more than the triple in the period from 1998 (when the contract was signed) to 2008 for reasons independent of its control and will (and, namely, the irresistible and incredible increase of the prices of the spare parts imposed by the producer). Upon the refusal of Sec to review the price, Soffimat, in its turn, refused to perform the contract alleging that the latter had become null and void due to the change in the economic conditions altering the balance of the agreement. Sec then started a litigation proceeding claiming for the specific performance of the contract. The *Cour de Cassation* reversed the decisions issued in the first instance and in the appeal judgment (that were in favour of Sec) holding that 'the upheaval in the economy of the contract due to changes in the economic circumstances render the obligation seriously questionable, since the creditor refuses to renegotiate in good faith the contract became un-balanced' (as freely translated from the original French version); *Cour de Cassation* 16 March 2004, D.S. 1757; *Cour de Cassation* 24 November 1998, IV Bull.C.C., 232; *Société française des pétroles v. Huard*, II 1993 J.C.P., 22614 (*Cour de Cassation* 3 November 1992).
256. ICC case n. 9994/2001, 2005 ICC Int'l Ct.Arb.Bull. – *Special Supplement*, 79 (2001).

French law requires from each party to perform the agreement in good faith (see c. civ. 1134, al. 2). Good faith imposes upon the parties the duty to seek out an adaptation of their agreement to the new circumstances which may have occurred after its execution, in order to ensure that its performance does not cause, especially when the contract at stake is a long term agreement, the ruin of one of the parties ... This principle is also prevailing in international commercial law (see Unidroit Principles, art. 6.2. and 6.2.3).[257]

Although the arbitration tribunal affirmed that the execution of long-term agreements (like gas sale contracts) in good faith implies the duty of the parties to adjust them when their balance is altered, it did not go further by recognising that, upon the parties' failure to adapt the contract, they have the authority to carry out such task. This further step seems, instead, to have been made by the Court of Appeal of Paris in *Electricitè de France* ("EDF") *v. Shell France* ("Shell") case.[258] Indeed, in such decision the Court not only ordered the parties to renegotiate the contract upon the occurrence of unforeseen events, notwithstanding there had already been a previous (failed) attempt to modify it, but it also held that, upon the failure of the renegotiations, it would have adapted the contract by means of the determination of a new price formula, on the basis of the solutions proposed by the parties, provided that the latter would have not implied any alteration of the contract terms other than the price. In particular, the *EDF* case concerns a contract for the supply of oil by Shell to EDF including an adaptation clause providing that the parties' duty to renegotiate the contract in case of an increase of the fuel price of six francs per tonne. Due to the oil crisis, the price increased much more than six francs per tonne and, consequently, Shell claimed for the application of the adaptation clause. However, the renegotiation failed and a litigation proceeding was started. The Tribunal held that the contract was null and void since the price did not exist anymore. The Court of Appeal reversed such decision affirming, first of all, that the contract was still in force since the parties, notwithstanding the failure of the renegotiation, continued to perform it upon the payment of the old price that was considered as an account of the new price to be determined. Thus, it was clear that the parties wanted to maintain the agreement alive and to adapt it to the new market situation. Provided that, the Court held that the parties had to renegotiate the contract (under the supervision of a third party) in order to find a new price formula and, upon the failure of such renegotiation 'and bearing in mind the proposed solution, that the Court will say if the formula which might possibly be suitable from the financial point of view modifies the elements of the current contracts and consequently prohibits the judge from imposing it, or whether, as the parties intended, it restricts itself to adjusting the price to the fluctuations of the market

---

257. *Ibid.*
258. *Electricitè de France v. Shell France*, 1978 J.C.P., 18810 (Paris Court of Appeal 28 September 1976). *See also* Beale, Fauvarque-Cosson, Rutgers, Tallon & Vogenauer, *supra* n. 247, at 1166 et seq.; A.H. Puelinckx, *Frustration, Hardship, Force Majeure, Imprèvision, Wegfall der Geschaftsgrundlage, Unmoglichkeit, Changed Circumstances*, 3 J. Int'l Arb. 47, 57 (1986). *See also Novacarb v. Socoma*, 2008, J.C.P., 10091 (Court of Appeal of Nancy 26 September 2007).

(without altering the economy of the contract) and may therefore be substituted automatically'.[259]

Therefore, the power to adapt the contract, although hypothetical and limited to the price formula in light of the parties' proposals, was recognised by the Court. In particular, the latter took into account, on the one hand, the parties' will to keep the contract alive as manifested by their conduct (as said, the parties, notwithstanding the failure to renegotiate the price kept on performing the agreement) and, on the other, the fact that EDF was performing a public service. The latter consideration recalled the argument adopted by administrative courts that usually recognise the *imprèvision* theory on the basis of the public interest pursued by contracts concluded with public bodies and, consequently, invite the parties to renegotiate them.[260] However, in this case the agreement between Shell and EDF was not an administrative contract but a private one (as also confirmed by the fact that the competent court to decide the dispute was a civil court and not an administrative one) .[261] Therefore, the reference made by the Court to the fact that EDF was performing a public service was not so crucial for the justification of the recognition of the *imprèvision* and the adoption of the consequent decision. Thus, such case can be considered one of the rare decisions in which French courts have recognised the possibility for judges to adapt a commercial contract upon the occurrence of unforeseen events altering its balance (although such authority was subject to the previous renegotiations of the parties and to strict limits). This power was acknowledged in order to fulfil the parties' will and expectations aiming to keep the contract alive. The justification of such adjustment can be found again in the principle of good faith. In particular, as seen more in detail below, the application of such principle to the execution of contracts (and, especially, long-term agreements) can be deemed to imply the duty to adapt them when their balance is altered upon the occurrence of unforeseen events. To deny the adjustment would be contrary to good faith since the parties would be deprived of the possibility to reach the scope pursued by means of the contract. Indeed, without adaptation the parties could only terminate the agreement or perform it in its original terms. However, both of these remedies would frustrate the parties' expectations (i.e., the preservation of the agreement).[262]

In addition to the above-mentioned less conservative position taken by part of the case law, it has to be noted that, on 22 September 2005, a project of reform of the French Civil Code was proposed by Professor Catala[263] providing for a modification of Article 1135 by introducing the concept of hardship or *imprèvision*. Indeed, Article 1135.1 of the reform project, by providing that the parties may include in a long-term contract a renegotiation clause, makes specific reference to supervening events that can alter the original balance of such agreement so that the latter 'loses its

---

259. *Electricitè de France* case, *id.*, as translated by Puelinckx, *id.*, at 58.
260. As noted by Puelinckx, it was 'the Court of Appeal's way of walking in the footsteps of the *Conseil d'Etat*', *id.*, at 57.
261. *See* Beale, Fauvarque-Cosson, Rutgers, Tallon & Vogenauer, *supra* n. 247, at 1168; Puelinckx, *id.*
262. *See* §3.04.
263. P. Catala, *Proposal for Reform of the Law of Obligations and the Law of Prescription*, http://www.justice.gouv.fr/art_pix/rapportcatatla0905-anglais.pdf (2005).

point'[264] for one of the parties. It is interesting to underline that this article is quite general since it does not expressly provide that the supervening events have to be unforeseen and beyond the control of the parties. Furthermore, there is no reference to the fact that the performance had become extremely or excessively burdensome for one of the parties but to the fact that the contract loses it point without clarifying the meaning of such expression.[265] The project also contemplates the case in which no renegotiation clause has been included in the contract by providing in Article 1135.2 that in such situation 'a party for whom a contract loses its point may apply to the President of the *tribunal de grande istance* to order a new negotiation'. Thus, no power of the courts to adapt the contract instead of the parties is recognised in the proposal of reform of the Civil Code but '[t]he solution to the problem of supervening circumstances is therefore found in negotiation, thereby solving a contractual difficulty through contract itself'.[266] Finally, Article 1135.3 states that the remedy in case of failure of the negotiations, as long as they were conducted in good faith, is the termination of the contract with no costs or loss.

Notwithstanding the recognition of the concept of hardship or *imprèvision* (mainly on the basis of the principles of good faith) provided by the case law and the project of reform of the French Civil Code proposed by Professor Catala (that expresses the need to provide the parties with a statutory remedy different from termination and specific performance of the contract), the prevailing position in French civil and commercial law is still represented by the principle of *pacta sunt servanda*. In addition, the steps taken towards the recognition of the concept of hardship does not go so far to directly empower courts and arbitrators to adapt the contract terms. Indeed, as seen above, in case of supervening events altering the balance of the agreement the remedy identified is represented by the parties' renegotiation of the latter.

[2] The Belgian Legal System

Similarly to French law, the Belgian legal system adopts a conservative approach towards the possibility for the parties and courts and arbitrators to adjust the contract in case it becomes unbalanced and applied strictly the principle of *pacta sunt servanda*,[267] enshrined in Article 1134 of the Civil Code, that also affirms the principle of the execution of contracts in good faith.[268] At the same time, also the Belgian

---

264. *Ibid.*, at 104.
265. *See* the comment on the reform project by A. Ghozi *ibid.* at 47, who underlines that 'this test acts both as a measure of the seriousness of the imbalance and as its proof'.
266. *Ibid.*, 47.
267. In this regard, *see*, in general, D. Philippe, *CESL: Change of Circumstances and Prescription – A Belgian Perspective*, in *The Draft Common European Sales Law: Towards an Alternative Sales Law?*, 299 et seq. (Intersentia 2013); *Id.*, *France and Belgium*, *supra* n. 247; A. Frignani, *supra* n. 247.
268. Such article provides that '[a]greements lawfully entered into take the place of the law for those who have made them. They can only be revoked by mutual agreement or if provided by the law. They have to be executed in good faith' (as freely translated). Similarly to the French Civil Code, Art. 1135 of the Belgian Civil Code provides that agreements are binding not only as to

legislator provides for some specific statutory exceptions allowing in some cases to modify the contract.[269]

Provided that, it has to be pointed out that the Belgian case law in a quite recent case has recognised not only the concept of hardship or *imprévision* but also (although not always expressly) the power of judges to adapt contracts in such situation.[270] Indeed, in all the three levels of jurisdiction (first instance, appeal and *cassation*) the relevant court, although in different ways, adapted the contract in contrast to the prevailing position of the Belgian jurisprudence that has constantly affirmed the principle of *pacta sunt servanda* with no possibility to amend the contract upon the occurrence of supervening unforeseen events unless a specific adaptation clause is included in the contract.[271]

In the above-mentioned case, a Dutch company, Scafom International ("Buyer"), and a French company, Exma ("Seller") – later replaced by another French company, Lorrain Tubes –, entered into several contracts for the sale of steel tubes governed by the Vienna Convention on the International Sale of Goods ("CISG"). In the absence of a framework agreement, such contracts were concluded every time by means of the acceptance by the Seller of the single Buyer's purchase order including the indication of the number, quantity, delivery date, price and quality standards of the steel. Moreover, upon the receipt of the Seller's acceptance, the Buyer inserted the order in specific lists that was sent to the Seller. The latter, upon the receipt, provided the Buyer with a second confirmation with attached its general conditions including a price review clause. However, no further document was sent by the Buyer in response to such confirmation and, consequently, the price review provision was not expressly accepted by the Buyer. On 18 March 2004, the Seller informed the Buyer that, with regard to the products already ordered and to be delivered during the month of April, it had to modify the price originally agreed by increasing it by almost 50% due to the unforeseeable rise (nearly 70%) of the steel's price. However, the Buyer did not accept the new price and asked the Seller to proceed with the delivery of the steel already ordered at the original price. The Seller refused to perform the contract without the Buyer's acceptance of the new prices. The latter refused to accept the prices' modification requested by the Seller and, consequently, sued the latter for breach of contract.

The Court of First Instance recognised that the Seller had proved the unforeseeable increase of the steel price but held that no adaptation of the latter could be allowed since the CISG only disciplines cases of force majeure and not of hardship or *imprévision*.[272] As a consequence, in order to protect the contract from supervening

---

what is therein expressed, but also as to all the consequences which equity, usage or statute give to the obligation according to its nature.
269. See, for instance, Art. 1231 of the Civil Code that allows the judge to reduce the amount of the penalty that is manifestly excessive. For more references see Philippe, supra n. 267.
270. See the *Scafom International* case.
271. See, ex multis, Cour de Cassation 20 April 2006, www.juridat.be; Cour de Cassation 4 September 2000, www.juridat.be; *Cour de Cassation* 14 April 1994, 1994–1995 R. W., 434; Cour de Cassation 7 February 1994, 1994–1995 R.W., 121; Court of Appeal of Antwerp 6 May 1987, 1990 Tijds Belg Burger R, 299; Court of First Instance of Brussels, 1994JLMB, 358.
272. See Art. 79 of the CISG providing that '[a] party is not liable for a failure to perform any of his obligations if he proves that the failure was due to an impediment beyond his control and that

events altering its economic balance, the Court pointed out that it is necessary for the parties to provide in the agreement for a specific price review clause. In the case *de quo*, however, such provision was considered to be absent since each contract was concluded upon the acceptance by the Seller of the Buyer's purchase order that did not contain any price review clause. As said, the latter was, indeed, included only in the Seller's general conditions sent for the first time to the Buyer as attachment of the second order's confirmation and was never expressly accepted by the Buyer. Thus, since the general conditions could not apply, in the lack of a price adjustment clause in the purchase order no adaptation upon the occurrence of supervening unforeseen events could be allowed. However, it has to be noted that the Court, although it considered that the Seller breached the contract in stopping the deliveries already accepted, affirmed that:

> original price agreements cannot be maintained, and it should be ordered that deliveries, both those performed after the order[273] and the future ones, can be charged at the price as determined in summary procedure, being the original price plus one-half of the extra price. An exception should be made for the orders that should have been delivered before the decision on summary procedure: these should be charged according to the original price agreements, without increase ... This solution is also compatible with equity.[274]

In light of the above, it can be said that, although the Court stated that no contract adaptation could be allowed in the lack of a specific clause, it de facto modified the contract terms by granting the Seller half of the price increase requested to the Buyer during renegotiations (with regard to both the deliveries already performed by the Seller upon the issuing of the interim injunction and to the future ones). Therefore, it seems that the Court, implicitly, recognised the judge's power to adapt the contract upon the occurrence of hardship events (represented in this case by the extraordinary increase of the steel price).

The Buyer appealed such decision before the Court of Appeal of Antwerp[275] which, first of all, resolved the problem of the determination of the law applicable to the dispute pursuant to Article 7.2. of the CISG. Such provision establishes that, in case of matters governed by the CISG but not thereby disciplined, it is necessary to refer to the general principles on which the CISG is based or, in the lack of them, to the applicable law as determined by private international law rules.

The Court considered that no general principles could be found in relation to hardship cases and, consequently, by resorting to the rules of private international law, identified French law (i.e., the one of the Seller) as that applicable to issue at hand.

---

he could not reasonably be expected to have taken the impediment into account at the time of the conclusion of the contract or to have avoided or overcome it or its consequences'.
273. The Court, before the decision on the merits, issued an interim order by which the Seller was compelled to deliver the products.
274. *Scafom International v. Lorrain Tubes*, http://cisgw3.law.pace.edu/cases/050125b1.html, 12 (Commercial Court of Torengen 25 January 2005).
275. *Lorrain Tubes v. Scafom International*, as cited in the decision of the *Cour de Cassation* 29 June 2009, http://cisgw3.law.pace.edu/cases/090619b1.html (Court of Appeal of Antwerp 15 February 2007).

Although French law, as seen above, does not recognise the concept of hardship, the Court held, in adherence to the position taken by some French decisions of the *Cour de Cassation*,[276] that, upon the occurrence of supervening events altering the economic balance of the contract, the parties had the duty to renegotiate the latter according to the principle of good faith ('[u]nder French law the good faith with which contracts must be performed requires re-negotiation of the contractual conditions in certain situations. This is, *inter alia*, the case if, after the conclusion of the contract unforeseeable circumstances occur, which create a serious unbalance between the obligations, such that the further performance of the contract becomes excessively onerous for one of the parties').[277] On the basis of such principle, the Court stated that the Buyer, by rejecting the price adaptation request of the Seller, had breached the above-mentioned duty and, therefore, it was condemned to pay, in addition to the price already received by the Seller, the sum of EUR 450,000, as damages determined, *inter alia*, on the basis of the market situation and of the offer made by the Seller to the Buyer before the legal proceeding. In particular, it was held that:

> the [Seller] has not committed a breach by refusing to deliver without a reasonable adaptation of the price ... The [Seller] would be forced to continue delivering according to the requirements of the interim injunction. This, the [Seller] had clearly indicated it was no longer willing to do unless the price was adapted. [Seller] has suggested a price at which it had been willing to deliver in the month of April 2004. Taking the concrete market situation into account, that offer of the Seller was not unreasonable and it provided a sound basis for re-negotiation. Thus, the Seller proved that it has suffered damage. Given the fact that the eventual result that would have come out of re-negotiations is uncertain, the exact figure of this damage cannot be correctly calculated ... is determined in equity to the amount of 450,000 Euro above the price the Seller has already received [plus interests].[278]

Moreover, with regard to the Seller's incidental appeal, the Court considered that 'the [Seller]'s claim for payment of an addition to the price is justified up to the amount of 450,000.00 Euro'.[279]

In light of the above, it seems possible to consider the amount of EUR 450,000 as an actual adjustment of the contract since such sum was granted to the Seller not only as damages (deriving from the Buyer's breach of the obligation to renegotiate the contract upon the occurrence of unforeseen events) but also as an increase of the price in partial upholding of the Seller's incidental appeal.[280] Therefore, this amount could be considered as an indication of the price for the future orders and deliveries until a new change of the economic conditions on which the balance of the contracts is based.

The Buyer challenged the Court of Appeal's decision before the *Cour de Cassation* which upheld it but grounded its judgment on different reasons. First of all, the Supreme Court considered Article 79.1 of the CISG as applicable also to hardship cases by stating that changes in the 'circumstances that were not reasonably foreseeable at

---

276. *See supra* n. 255.
277. *Scafom International* case, *supra* n. 275, at para. 14.
278. *Id.*, at paras 17–18.
279. *Ibid.*
280. In this regard, *see also* Philippe, *supra* n. 247, at 162.

the time of the conclusion of the contract and that are unequivocally of a nature to increase the burden of performance of the contract in a disproportionate manner, can, under circumstances, form an impediment in the sense of this provision of the Convention'.[281] As to the problem of the filling of contractual gaps contained in the CISG, the Court affirmed that, in light of the combination of Article 7.1 ('[i]n the interpretation of this Convention, regard is to be had to its international character and to the need to promote uniformity in its application and the observance of good faith in international trade')[282] and of the above-mentioned Article 7.2, the general principles of international trade law on which the CISG is based have to be applied in the first place and, only in case of their absence, it is possible to resort to the conflict of law rules. The Court then considered as included in such general principles also the UNIDROIT Principles that recognise the hardship concept and provide for the consequent right of the parties to request to renegotiate the contract. Moreover, such principles, in case no agreement is found and a litigation proceeding is started, provide that the court can either terminate the agreement or adapt it to the new circumstances.[283] In light of the above, the Court held that 'the party who invokes changed circumstances that fundamentally disturb the contractual balance, as mentioned in paragraph 1, is also entitled to claim the renegotiation of the contract'.[284]

Therefore, the Supreme Court considered correct the principle stated by the Court of Appeal that the Buyer had the duty to renegotiate the agreement upon the request of the Seller.

Such decision, although not expressly recognising the judge's power to adapt the contract in case of hardship, represents an important step towards this direction since it considered the UNIDROIT Principles, which expressly provide courts with the aforementioned power, as part of the international general principles on which the CISG is based. It follows that the disadvantaged party not only has the right to request for the renegotiation upon the occurrence of unforeseen events altering the contract *equilibrium*, as stated by the Supreme Court, but in theory it also has the right to claim for the adaptation of the contract by the judge. Thus, implicitly, the *Cour de Cassation* recognised the possibility for judges to adjust the terms of the parties' agreement. Moreover, the recognition by the Supreme Court of the UNIDROIT Principles as general

---

281. *Scafom International* case, *supra* n. 274, at para. IV.1. For comments on such decision and the previous judgments, *see* Philippe, *id.*, *supra* n. 274; *Id.*, *CESL: Change of Circumstances and Prescription – A Belgian Perspective*, *supra* n. 267; A. Veneziano, *UNIDROIT Principles and CISG: Change of Circumstances and Duty to Renegotiate According to the Belgian Supreme Court*, Revue de Droit Uniforme, 137 (2010).
282. *Scafom International* case, *id.*, at para. IV.2.
283. As *seen* at §3.02.
284. *Scafom International v. Lorrain Tubes, Cour de Cassation*, *supra* n. 275, at para. IV.2. In this regard, *see* Veneziano, who underlines that the right of the disadvantaged party to request for the renegotiation of the contract 'could follow from the application of good faith, were the latter considered as one of the general principles underlying the Convention' as maintained by part of the doctrine and case law according to which 'good faith in the performance of the contract is already at the bottom of specific rules in CISG and may well be construed as a general principle of the entire Convention, were the latter considered as one of the general principles underlying the Convention' (*supra* n. 281, at 146–147).

principles applicable to the international trade has to be given a broader extent than the case at hand by also including international sale contracts not governed by the CISG.

Provided the new position taken by the court in the *Scafom* case compared to the traditional view adopted by the Belgian case law, it has to be underlined that such case regarded an international sale contract and, consequently, the question is whether in a domestic case dealing with hardship such concept would be also recognised by courts[285] and, moreover, whether judges would be considered entitled to adapt the contract. In any case, for the purpose of this work, the above-mentioned decision represents an important (although not binding) precedent for arbitrations dealing with the problem of adaptation of international gas sale agreements (and, in particular, in cases of price review dispute).

[3] The Swiss Legal System

In the same vein as French and Belgian laws, the Swiss legal system does not provide for the possibility for the parties to adapt a contract upon the occurrence of unforeseen events changing the relevant balance (and making its performance for one party extremely burdensome)[286] but only to be discharged of a contractual obligation if 'where its performance is made impossible by circumstances not attributable to the obligor'[287] or in the event 'there is a clear discrepancy between performance and consideration under a contract concluded as a result of one party's exploitation of the other's straitened circumstances, inexperience or thoughtlessness'.[288] Accordingly, the case law in some circumstances recognised the possibility to terminate long-term contracts on the basis of the doctrine of *rebus sic stantibus*.[289] However, the case law is particularly cautious and strict in applying such doctrine and requires several conditions to be met. An example of this restrictive approach is represented by the award of 9 September 1983 rendered in an ad hoc arbitration between a German

---

285. See M. Polkinghorne, who underlines that '[o]ne might therefore ask whether Belgium will move towards a more general principle of hardship over and beyond the CISG' (*Changes of Circumstances as a Price Modifier*, in *Gas Price Arbitration*, supra n. 206, at 76).
286. Even in the Swiss legal system, there are some exceptions expressly provided by the legislator. For instance, Art. 272.c of the Swiss Code of Obligations, providing that '[e]ither party may ask the court to modify the lease in line with changed circumstances when deciding on the lease extension'. *See also* Art. 373 of the Swiss Code of Obligations, concerning construction contracts, that grants judges the discretional power, not only to terminate the contract, but also to increase the price in case 'performance of the work was prevented or seriously hindered by extraordinary circumstances that were unforeseeable or excluded according to the conditions assumed by both parties impede the completion or render it exceedingly difficult' (available in English on www.admin.ch). For a general comment on the Swiss Civil Code, *see* I. Williams, *The Sources of Law in the Swiss Civil Code* (Oxford University Press 1923).
287. *See* Art. 119 of the Swiss Code of Obligations available in English on www.admin.ch.
288. *See* Art. 21 of the Swiss Code of Obligations available in English on www.admin.ch.
289. Such doctrine is an exception to the principle of *pacta sunt servanda* since it allows a party to be discharged of its obligations upon the occurrence of unforeseen and extraordinary changes of the circumstances.

engineering company ("Claimant") and a state Polish trading company ("Defendant").[290] Such case regarded a contract for the construction and deliver by the Claimant of a plant and equipment destined to the production of fuel gas from coal in Poland. The agreement was governed by Swiss law and provided, at Article 19, for the exoneration of parties from their obligations upon the occurrence of force majeure events (i.e., unforeseen circumstances beyond the control of the parties, occurred after the conclusion of the contract and making the performance of the latter impossible), among which the parties indicated the adoption of governmental orders.

In January 1982, the Polish government (which participated to the negotiations of the contract) issued an order prohibiting the import of industrial investment goods, including gas production plants. Consequently, the Defendant informed the Claimant of such circumstance and asked for the application of the aforementioned force majeure clause. However, the Claimant rejected such argument and since the contract was still in force it informed the counterparty that it was ready to deliver the products. Upon the refusal of the Defendant to accept the delivery, the Claimant started an arbitration proceeding.

First of all, the arbitration tribunal underlined, on the one hand, that force majeure was not recognised by Swiss law 'as a general ground for cancellation of contracts ... Statutes merely contain provisions on impossibility of contract performance ... These provisions ... refer to the situation that an obligation cannot be performed as agreed'[291] and, on the other, that 'based on doctrine, a detailed practice has developed regarding the so-called *clausola rebus sic stantibus*. This concept refers to the right of a party to be discharged from an obligation as a whole or in part, when after the making of the contract, extraordinary and unforeseeable events have occurred, which create a situation in which a performance according to the text of the contract can, by virtue of good faith, absolutely not expected'.[292] As to the conditions to be met for the application of such doctrine (as developed by the Swiss case law), the arbitrators, after having observed that they were the same as those provided in Article 19 of the contract, affirmed that:

- the risk of changed circumstances should not have been distributed among the parties in the contract; if so, such a provision would prevail;
- the change should not be due to the fault of the obligated party;
- changes should not have been foreseeable, nor have actually been foreseen by the parties;
- the obligated party should not have recognised either *expressis verbis* or, e.g., by negotiations about the performance of its obligations, that the performance may be imputed to him;
- the changes should objectively be extraordinary; in practice, strict requirements are applied;

---

290. *F.R. German v. Polish Buyer*, 1987 XII YBCA, 63 (9 September 1983).
291. *Ibid.*, at 66.
292. *Ibid.*

- the changes should have caused an extraordinary shift of the balance of obligations, making the performance appear objectively unacceptable;
- the court intervention should not lead to results which are unacceptable for the creditor, i.e., the burden may not simply be shifted entirely from the debtor to the creditor.[293]

It is clear from the above that the application of the *rebus sic stantibus* doctrine by the Swiss case law and by arbitrators (even in case of international arbitration) is very limited and strict when the applicable law is the Swiss one. After having summarised the conditions required to apply the aforementioned doctrine, the arbitration tribunal had to answer the question whether Article 19 of the contract could be deemed to refer to all the orders issued by the government 'regardless of the relationship between a party and the ordering State or authority which issued the order'.[294] In this regard, the arbitrators recognised the possibility for a state enterprise, like the Defendant, to invoke force majeure if the order is 'general in nature and not connected with the economic planning'.[295] However, the arbitration tribunal noted that in this case the order issued by the Polish Government was not general and, consequently, it was affirmed that the Defendant could not claim for the application of Article 19 of the contract in order to be discharged from its obligation to purchase the plant and the equipment. In particular, the arbitrators held that:

> The Order of 21 December 1981 bans import of investment goods for certain projects listed in the annex. It concerns 24 industrial projects of mainly industrial nature. The Order cancels the licence granted for the import of goods in connection with these projects. It follows from the wording of the Order that is a governmental act of economic planning which is not of a general character, but affecting certain projects.[296]

Moreover, it has to be underlined that the Defendant did not comply with the time limit provided by the contract for the notification to the counterparty of the occurrence of the force majeure event.

A different principle was, instead, affirmed by the Swiss Federal Tribunal in the decision of 10 October 1933.[297] Such case regarded a long-term lease contract (fifteen years) of a restaurant providing for a progressive increase of the rent. Upon the defendant's refusal to reduce the rent due to the economic depression, as requested by the plaintiff, the latter started a litigation proceeding claiming for a modification of the contract (by decreasing the fixed rentals or by replacing them with contingent rentals) or, as an alternative, for the recognition of its right to rescind the contract. The claim was dismissed by the Commercial Court of the Zurich Canton whose judgment was confirmed by the Federal Tribunal that affirmed that long-term contracts are speculative agreements and, therefore, the parties are assumed to have accepted the risk of

---

293. *Ibid.*, at 66–67.
294. *Ibid.*, at 67.
295. *Ibid.*, at 79.
296. *Ibid.*
297. Swiss Federal Tribunal 10 October 1933, as cited in R. Schlesinger, U. Mattei, T. Ruskola & A. Gidi, *Comparative Law*, 964 (Foundation Press 2009).

'substantial fluctuations of the general level of prosperity'.[298] Moreover, the Tribunal underlined that the claimant in this case 'was conscious of the possibility of bad years, and that he tried to impress the defendant with his ability to cover losses from the restaurant in the instant premises by the use of his other revenues ... Moreover, plaintiff has not even alleged that the objective rental value of the leased premises has fallen since the time when the contract was made, or that similar space in Zurich would today be available for a substantially lesser rental'.[299]

Provided the above, the Tribunal recognised in general the possibility for courts to adapt the contract upon the occurrence of unforeseen events changing the contract's balance and not just to terminate it. The Tribunal also considered the termination of the contract with no retroactive effects as a sort of adaptation. In particular, it was stated that:

> From the standpoint of Swiss law, however, there is no decisive objection against permitting judicial modification of a contract in lieu of its termination. It should be pointed out in the first place that, if termination only is permitted, and modification is not, such termination can, in certain cases, be declared only for the future. In such event, the termination has no retroactive effect ... Such prospective termination of the contract, having effect only for the future, is in the last analysis equivalent to judicial adjustment of the contract.[300]

By not excluding a priori the possibility of a judicial adjustment of the agreement in case of hardship, such decision affirms an innovative principle compared to the prevailing position adopted in the Swiss legal system. Indeed, the latter uphold the *pacta sunt servanda* principle upon the occurrence of supervening events affecting the contractual balance or of termination of the contract on the basis of the *rebus sic stantibus* doctrine (upon the occurrence of all the conditions above mentioned). As seen below, a further step towards the recognition of the arbitrators' power to adapt contracts was taken by the Federal Tribunal in the *Belgische Sceehpvaartmaatschappij-Compagnie Maritime Belge v. Distrigas* case that rejected the recourse for the annulment of an arbitration award by which the arbitral tribunal amended the contract between the parties.[301] Moreover, with regard to international contracts governed by Swiss law, it was affirmed the possibility for arbitrators to depart from the principle of *pacta sunt servanda* upon the occurrence of a hardship event.[302]

[4] The Common Law

The principle of sanctity of contracts is also a cornerstone of the Common Law which considers contracts as absolute and, consequently, to be performed even in case of

---

298. *Ibid.*, at 968.
299. *Ibid.*
300. *Ibid.*, at 965.
301. *Belgische Sceehpvaartmaatschappij-Compagnie Maritime Belge v. Distrigas*, 20 ASA Bull., 493 (Swiss Federal Tribunal 19 December 2001), that is analysed at §3.04.
302. ICC case n. 2508/1976, in Collection of ICC Arbitral Awards 1984-1985, 292 (1976), that is analysed at §3.04.

supervening events unless a specific clause in the contract expressly excuses one party from carrying out its performance.[303] However, such principle has been mitigated during the years by the introduction of the doctrine of frustration that allows the parties to be discharged of their obligations by means of termination of the contract upon the occurrence of a specific event rendering its performance impossible.[304] The concept of impossibility – and, consequently, the application of the doctrine of frustration – have been progressively extended. Indeed, at the beginning, the performance was considered impossible only in two cases: (1) when the contract was characterised by the so called *"intuitus personae"* and the party, that had to carry out the personal performance, died or became permanently incapacitated; (2) when the specific thing, representing the subject matter of the contract, perished. Such principle was affirmed in the well-known *Taylor v. Caldwell* case regarding a contract for the hire of a music hall.[305] However, before the date provided in the contract for the first concert, a fire destroyed the hall and, although none of the parties was responsible, the hirer claimed for damages in order to cover the cost borne for the advertising of the concerts. The Court rejected such claim and considered the contract frustrated, discharging the parties from their obligations. In particular, it was held that:

> 'in contracts in which the performance depends on the continued existence of a given person or thing, a condition is implied that the impossibility of performance arising from the perishing of the person or thing shall excuse the performance'.[306]

As said above, gradually the case law departed from the strict principle stated in *Taylor v. Caldwell* case and the application of the doctrine of frustration was extended to cases where the performance was not physically impossible but where the purpose and the conditions that the parties implicitly placed at the basis of the contract disappeared upon the occurrence of unforeseen events. For instance, in the famous *"Coronation* Case",[307] the defendant hired a room perfectly located to see the procession of the incoronation of King Edward VII (such purpose was not expressly indicated in the contract but was implicitly recognised by the parties). The procession was postponed due to the illness of the King, but the plaintiff claimed in any case for the payment of the rent. However, the Court considered the contract frustrated, discharging the parties from their obligations, although the performance was not physically impossible since the room could still be occupied by the defendant during the days in which the procession was supposed to be taken. Thus, the doctrine of frustration was extended to 'cases where the event which renders the contract incapable of performance is the cessation or non-existence of an express condition or state of things, going

---

303. *See, ex multis, Paradine v. Jane*, Aleyn's Reports, 26 (EWHC (KB) 26 March 1647), in which it was affirmed that the lessee was obliged to pay the rent although the lands it was supposed to occupy were held by the King's enemies.
304. In this regard, *see*, in general, E. McKendrick, *Contract Law*, 700 et seq. (Oxford University Press 2012); Treitel, *supra* n. 98, at 920 et seq.; Beale, Fauvarque-Cosson, Rutgers, Tallon & Vogenauer, *supra* n. 247, at 1106 et seq.
305. *Taylor v. Caldwell*, 3 B.& S., 826 (EWHC (QB) 6 May 1863). *See also, ex multis, Appleby v. Myers*, 3 B.& S., 826 (EWHC (QB) 21 June 1867).
306. *Taylor* case, *id.*, at 833.
307. *Krell v. Henry*, 2 K.B., 740 (EWCA 11 August 1903).

to the root of the contract, and essential to its performance'.[308] Moreover, the Court specified that it was not necessary for such condition or state of things to be expressly provided in the contract being sufficient that the latter 'clearly appears by extrinsic evidence to have been assumed by the parties to be the foundation or basis of the contract'.[309] In the *Coronation* case, the Court extended the application of the doctrine of frustration on the basis of the concept of the foundation of the contract representing an implied term or condition that is essential for the parties for the conclusion and maintaining of the agreement.[310]

However, the theory of implied terms as a justification of the frustration of the contract was criticised due to the difficulty in finding out the intention of the parties with regard to the effects on the contract of a supervening unforeseen event since 'there is something of a logical difficulty in seeing how the parties could even impliedly have provided for something which *ex hypothesis* they neither expected nor foresaw; and the ascription of frustration to an implied term of the contract has been criticized as obscuring the true action of the court which consists in applying an objective rule of the law of contract to the contractual obligations that the parties have imposed upon themselves'.[311] It was, instead, considered necessary a radical objective change of the obligation to be performed according to the contract due to supervening events. In particular, it was held that:

> frustration occurs whenever the law recognises that without default of either party a contractual obligation has become incapable of being performed because the circumstances in which the performance is called for would render it a thing radically different from that which was undertaken by the contract ... The data for decision are, on the one hand, the terms and construction of the contract, read in the light of the then existing circumstances, and, on the other hand, the events which have occurred.[312]

The same position was taken in the ICC case n. 1512/1971 that confirmed the strict application of the frustration doctrine according to English law.[313] In particular, it was expressly made reference to the occurrence of a modification of the foundation of the contract in order to be considered the latter frustrated and it was specified that it is not just a matter of a substantial change in the circumstances but also in the obligation.[314] Moreover, the same strict approach was adopted in relation to the *rebus sic stantibus* doctrine (that was also referred to by the claimant). In this regard, the

---

308. *Ibid.*, at 748.
309. *Ibid.*
310. The theory of the foundation of the contract was also affirmed, for instance in *W F Tatem v. Gamboa*, 1 K.B., 132 (1939); *Tamplin Steamship v. Anglo-Mexican Petroleum*, 2 AC, 39 (EWCA 1 January 1916).
311. *Davis Contractors v. Fareham Urban DC*, 1 AC 696, 729 (UKHC 19 April 1956).
312. *Ibid.*
313. ICC case n. 1512/1971, Collection of ICC Arbitral Awards 1974–1985, 3 (1971).
314. It was held that 'English law rejects the criteria of hardship, commercial inconvenience or material loss as such but insists that there must be such a radical change of circumstances ... *that the foundation of the contract has gone* ... [that is] not simply a question whether there had been a radical change in the circumstances, but whether there has been a radical change in the *obligation*' (*Ibid.*, at 3–4).

arbitral tribunal held that for the application of the latter (that, as underlined by arbitrators, sometimes is called *"imprèvision"*, "frustration" or "force majeure") it has to be limited 'to cases where *compelling reasons* justify it, having regard not only to the fundamental character of the changes, but also to the particular type of the contract involved, to the requirements of fairness and equity and to all circumstances of the case'.[315]

At the end, the arbitrators found that the conditions for the application of the frustration and the *rebus sic stantibus* doctrines were not met in such case.

As regard to the above-mentioned theories employed to justify the application of the frustration doctrine (i.e., implied terms or radical change of the contractual obligations), it was underlined that they are not so different since at the end they all imply and are based on the construction and interpretation of the contract.[316] Such process is, indeed, necessary in order to either find out which was the foundation of the contract or determine whether the performance upon the occurrence of unforeseen events has radically changed. Moreover, it has to be noted that English courts usually do not apply the frustration doctrine upon the occurrence of unforeseen events that render the contract just commercially impracticable, i.e., excessively burdensome to perform due to hardship events (such as, for instance, a high increase of prices or a severe inflation)[317] unless there is a specific clause in the contract disciplining such situation. The principle behind this position is the allocation of risks between the parties. Indeed, if the latter did not provide anything in the contract in order to face hardship events, it is assumed that they decided to accept the risk that the performance of the contract can become excessively burdensome upon the occurrence of unforeseen circumstances. This principle has been, in particular, affirmed with regard to market and price fluctuations. If the contract does not provide for an index or a price review clause, it is supposed that the parties have accepted the risk of variations of the price on the basis of the change of market conditions.[318]

With regard to gas sale agreements, an example of the courts' refusal to frustrate the contract when the performance become commercially impracticable is represented

---

315. *Ibid.*, at 4.
316. *See* McKendrick, *Contract Law*, *supra* n. 304, at 711; Treitel, *supra* n. 98, at 983.
317. Treitel, *id.*, at 922. *See also Davis Contractors* case, *supra* n. 311, at 729 in which it was stated that 'it is not hardship or inconvenience or material loss itself which calls the principle of frustration into play. There must be as well such a change in the significance of the obligation that the thing undertaken would, if performed, be a different thing from that contracted for'; *Britishmovietonews v. London and District Cinemas*, 1952 AC 166, 185 (UKHL 26 July 1951), in which it was held that '[t]he parties to an executory contract are often faced, in the course of carrying it out, with a turn of events which they did not at all anticipate – a wholly abnormal rise or fall in prices, a sudden depreciation of currency, an unexpected obstacle to the execution, or the like. Yet this does not in itself affect the bargain which they have made'; *Tennants (Lancashire) v. C S Wilson & Co*, AC, 495, 510 (UKHL 21 July 1917), in which it was stated that '[t]he argument that a man can be excused from performance of his contract when it becomes 'commercially' impossible seems to me a dangerous contention which ought not to be admitted unless the parties have plainly contracted to that effect'.
318. *See*, in general, Treitel, *supra* n. 98, at 940; *Superior Overseas Development v. British Gas*, 1982 1 Lloyd's Rep., 262 (EWHC (QB) 27 March 1981). *See also* F.R. Fucci, *Hardship and Changed Circumstances as Grounds for Adjustment or Non-Performance of Contracts*, http://www.cisg. law.pace.edu/cisg/biblio/fucci.html (2006).

by *Thames Valley Power v. Total Power Gas* case[319] regarding a long-term contract for the supply of gas entered into between Thames Valley Power ("Claimant") and Total Power Gas ("Defendant") by which the latter had to provide the Claimant with gas to be used for the production of heat and electricity destined to Heathrow airport. The agreement provided that the party unable to perform the contract upon the occurrence of a force majeure event would be relieved from its obligations. A dispute arose upon the request of the Defendant to be released from its obligations, according to such clause, due to the increase of the gas price. The Court rejected this argument holding that:

> Total is unable to carry out that obligation if some event has occurred as a result of which it cannot do that. The fact that it is much more expensive, even very greatly more expensive for it to do so, does not mean that it cannot do so. To interpret clause 15 [the force majeure clause] as applicable in circumstances where performance is "commercially impractical" or Total is "commercially unable" to supply is to enforce a qualification highly uncertain in ambit and open ended in reach which is neither necessary nor obvious and which is inconsistent with the express terms of the GSA. Total's obligation under the GSA to supply gas in return for the price is not dependent on nor is it related to the market price of gas. Nor is Total's obligation an obligation to supply gas provided that the cost to it of doing so is not commercially unacceptable or impracticable. In those circumstances if Total can supply gas it cannot be said that they are unable to perform their obligations under the agreement.[320]

On the contrary, in the US, the principle of commercial impracticability, to be intended as an extreme and unreasonable hardship, has been recognised by courts[321] and legislator.[322]

Such section, therefore, by referring to the concept of impracticability and not to impossibility, extends the cases in which a party can be excused from the performance (or from the timely performance) of its obligations since such concept also includes situations in which the latter, upon the occurrence of unforeseen events, has become

---

319. *Thames Valley Power v. Total Power Gas*, 2006 1 Lloyd's Rep. 441, (EWHC (QB) 27 September 2005).
320. *Ibid.*, at 449.
321. The concept of commercial impracticability was affirmed for the first time in *Mineral Park Land v. P.A. Howard*, 172 Cal. 289, 294 (Cal. 13 March 1916) in which it was held that '[a] thing is impossible in legal contemplation when it is not practicable; and a thing is impracticable when it can only be done at an excessive and unreasonable cost'.
322. Section 2-615(a) UCC (dealing with 'Excuse by Failure of Presupposed Conditions' in sale contracts) that provides that '[d]elay in delivery or non-delivery in whole or in part by a seller who complies with paras (b) and (c) is not a breach of his duty under a contract for sale if performance as agreed has been made impracticable by the occurrence of a contingency the non-occurrence of which was a basic assumption on which the contract was made or by compliance in good faith with any applicable foreign or domestic governmental regulation or order whether or not it later proves to be invalid'. *See also* s. 454 Restatement (First) of Contracts and s. 261 Restatement (Second) of Contracts. For a comparison between s. 2-615 and Art. 313 of the German Civil Code *see* E.C. Zaccaria, *L'adattamento dei contratti a lungo termine nell'esperienza giuridica statunitense: aspirazioni teoriche e prassi giurisprudenziale*, 2 Contratto Impresa, 478 (2006).

commercially not sustainable.[323] Moreover, this provision can be deemed to find its justification in the principle of good faith (expressly provided by section 1–203 UCC)[324] since it would be against the latter to ask a party to perform the contract when it has become extremely and excessively onerous (i.e., impracticable) due to supervening events changing the conditions on which the agreement was based and, consequently, altering its balance. However, in order to consider the performance commercially impracticable, it was clarified that it is not sufficient for an increase of costs 'unless the rise in cost is due to some unforeseen contingency which alters the essential nature of the performance'.[325] At the same time, it does not make the performance impracticable 'a rise or a collapse in the market ... for that is exactly the type of business risk which business contracts made at fixed prices are intended to cover'.[326] Therefore, the price or market changes have to be severe and relevant.[327]

Furthermore, in some cases the rejection of the application of the impracticability doctrine was justified on the basis of the concept of foreseeability. In particular, in the *Northern Illinois Gas* ("NI-Gas") *v. Energy Co-operative* ("ECI") case,[328] dealing with a long-term contract for the supply of naphtha from ECI to Ni-Gas, the Court affirmed that '[t]he question of whether the non-occurrence of an event was a basic contract assumption is a question of foreseeability ... adverse shifts in oil and gas prices were foreseeable and NI-Gas was charged with knowledge that it might not always be able to raise its rates'.[329]

Moreover, the Court, in denying the occurrence of impracticability, gave relevance to the take or pay clause and the price escalation clause (linking the price of naphtha to that of oil) included in the contract. Indeed, by means of the first provision, 'NI-Gas specifically agreed to take or pay for naphtha thus guaranteeing performance regardless of the demand for SNG [supplemental natural gas]. The record reveals that NI-Gas understood this provision to mean that it was obligated to pay for the product whether it was delivered and used or not ... Such a provision belies any assertion that the contract was based on the assumption that the buyer would have a continuing need for the sellers product, especially when inserted into a long-term supply contract such as this one'.[330] Instead, by providing for price escalation clause, 'the contract would remain profitable for ECI and indicates that the risk of increased naphtha prices due to increased crude oil prices (which were foreseeable) was shifted to NI-Gas'.[331]

---

323. *See* the official comment n. 3 on s. 2-615 UCC providing that '[t]he additional test of commercial impracticability (as contrasted with "impossibility, "frustration" of performance" or "frustration of the venture") has been adopted in order to call attention to the commercial character of the criterion chosen by this Article'.
324. *See* s. 1-304 UCC providing that '[e]very contract or duty within this Act imposes an obligation of good faith in its performance or enforcement'.
325. Official comment n. 4 on the UCC. *See also*, *W.R. Grace v. Local Union 759*, 461 U.S., 757 (U.S. 31 May 1983).
326. *Ibid.*
327. *See Louisiana Power & Light v. Allegheny Ludlum Industries*, 517 F.Supp., 1319 (E.D. La. 7 July 1981).
328. *Northern Illinois Gas v. Energy Co-operative*, 461 N.E.2d, 1049 (Ill. App. Ct. 27 March 1984).
329. *Ibid.*, at 1054.
330. *Ibid.*
331. *Ibid.*

Another example of the strict interpretation and application of the impracticability doctrine adopted by the case law is the *Iowa Electric Light & Power* ("Iowa") *v. Atlas* ("Atlas") case concerning a contract for the supply of uranium from the second to the first.[332] After the conclusion of the agreement, Atlas suffered serious economic difficulties due to the severe increase of its production costs caused by the oil embargo determined by Arab countries, the OPEC cartel, new federal environmental regulations and the shortage of uranium. For such reasons, Atlas asked for an equitable adjustment of the contract's price according to section 2-615 of the UCC. The Court rejected such claim holding that Atlas did not sufficiently prove that the increase of the production costs was completely beyond its control, and that some of the supervening events to which it referred were not unforeseeable. Thus, the Court denied the existence of the impracticability of the performance and, consequently, the possibility to adjust the contract. However, it has to be underlined that the judge did not expressly exclude the possibility to adjust the contract's price as a matter of principle, provided that the (strict) conditions required for the application of the impracticability doctrine are met.[333]

As said above, the effect of frustration is the termination of the contract with the consequent discharge of the parties from future contractual obligations while the already accrued rights remain enforceable.[334] Therefore, the rule is that no adjustment of the contract to the changed circumstances by courts and arbitrators is recognised.[335] However, in some cases, courts adopted a different approach.

The most famous decision in which the court adapted the contract in light of supervening events – altering the original balance and making the performance for one of the parties still possible but extremely burdensome (i.e., impracticable) – is the *Alcoa* case.[336] The latter regarded a long-term supply contract (so called "Molten Metal Agreement") concluded in 1967 by which Essex Group ("Essex"), undertook to provide Aluminium Company of America ("Alcoa") with alumina to be converted by the latter into molten aluminum and then supplied back to Essex. The price was calculated by means of an escalation formula linking it, in part, to the Wholesale Price Index Industrial Commodities (WPI) and, in part, to an index based on the average hourly

---

332. *Iowa Electric Light & Power v. Atlas*, 654 F.2d, 704 (8th Cir. 30 June 1981).
333. See E.C. Zaccaria, *The Effects of Changed Circumstances in International Commercial Trade*, International Trade & Business Law Review, 145 (2005).
334. In order to mitigate the negative consequences that such rule could determine the Law Reform (Frustrated Contracts) Act of 1943 was enacted. In particular, s. 1 provides that '[a]ll sums paid or payable to any party in pursuance of the contract before the time when the parties were so discharged (in this Act referred to as "the time of discharge") shall, in the case of sums so paid, be recoverable from him as money received by him for the use of the party by whom the sums were paid, and, in the case of sums so payable, cease to be so payable. Provided that, if the party to whom the sums were so paid or payable incurred expenses before the time of discharge in, or for the purpose of, the performance of the contract, the court may, if it considers it just to do so having regard to all the circumstances of the case, allow him to retain or, as the case may be, recover the whole or any part of the sums so paid or payable, not being an amount in excess of the expenses so incurred'. *See also* Treitel, *supra* n. 98, at 970 et seq.
335. In this regard, it has to be noted that the Federal Arbitration Act (enacted on 12th February, 1925 and included in Title 9, ss 1 et seq. of the United States Code) is silent on this issue.
336. See *Aluminium Company of America v. Essex Group*, 499 F.Supp., 53 (W.D. Pa. 1980).

labour rates paid by Alcoa to its employees. The agreement did not provide for a price review clause. A dispute arose between the parties with regard to the WPI index since Alcoa alleged that it did not actually reflect the rise of its non-labour costs (and, in particular, the one for electricity) due to the increase of the oil prices decided by OPEC as of 1973 and the costs for antipollution control established by the government, as instead originally meant by the parties. Due to such supervening events, Alcoa suffered a loss equal to USD 60 million. Therefore, the latter started a lawsuit before the Pennsylvania Western District Court asking for the adjustment of the contract price on the basis of mutual mistake, impracticability and frustration of purpose doctrines. The Court upheld such claim on the basis of the last two doctrines since it affirmed that they apply to events occurred after the execution of the contract (like in the *Alcoa* case) while the mutual mistake theory regards facts already existing at the moment of the conclusion of the agreement. Then, the Court recognised that both the impracticability and the frustration of purpose doctrines are based on the concept of hardship and have the effect to relieve the disadvantaged party of its obligations. In particular, it was held that:

> Performance may be impracticable because *extreme and unreasonable difficulty, expense, injury, or loss to one of the parties will be involved* ... A mere change in the degree of difficulty or expense due to such causes as increased wages, prices of raw materials, or costs of construction, unless well beyond the normal range, does not amount to impracticability since it is this sort of risk that a fixed-price contract ... a party is discharged from performing his contract where his principal purpose is *substantially* frustrated by the occurrence of a supervening event. It is not enough that the transaction has become less profitable for the affected party or even that he will sustain a loss. The frustration must be so severe that it is not fairly to be regarded as within the risks that he assumed under the contract.[337]

The Court then affirmed that the standards of both the above-mentioned theories were met in the case since Alcoa had proved to have suffered a very high loss (USD 60 million) due to unforeseen events that determined a severe increase of its production costs and altered the contractual *equilibrium*. As to impracticability, it was held that the 'wide variation'[338] between the WPI index and the Alcoa's production costs was not foreseeable 'in a commercial sense and was not allocated to ALCOA in the contract'.[339] With regard to frustration, the Court affirmed that the main scope of Alcoa when entering into the contract was to make profit and that such purpose was clearly frustrated since it suffered a very high loss. In this context, the Court considered that the traditional remedy of termination of the contract was not appropriate since it would have had the effect 'to grant ALCOA a windfall gain in the current aluminum market. It would at the same time deprive Essex of the assured long term aluminum supply which it obtained under the contract'.[340] On the contrary, the most appropriate remedy would have been the adjustment of the contract to the new circumstances in order to rebalance it and to allow the parties to reach the purpose on the basis of which they

---

337. *Ibid.*, at 73.
338. *Ibid.*, at 77.
339. *Ibid.*
340. *Ibid.*, at 80.

decided to enter into the agreement (i.e., to guarantee Essex a long-term supply of aluminum at a reasonable price and Alcoa a long-term flux of money). Therefore, the Court held that '[a] remedy modifying the price term of the contract in light of the circumstances which upset the price formula will better preserve the purposes and expectations of the parties than any other remedy. Such a remedy is essential to avoid injustice in this case'.[341]

The Court then, taking into account the terms of the contract, adopted a scheme for the calculation of the price in order to re-establish the contractual *equilibrium*. In particular, the Court affirmed that:

> For the duration of the contract the price for each pound of aluminum converted by ALCOA shall be the lesser of the current Price A or Price B indicated below. Price A shall be the contract ceiling price computed periodically as specified in the contract. Price B shall be the greater of the current Price B1 or Price B2. Price B1 shall be the price specified in the contract, computed according to the terms of the contract. Price B2 shall be that price which yields ALCOA a profit of one cent per pound of aluminum converted.[342]

In its conclusion, the Court recognised that the best solution in this case would have probably been the negotiation between the parties of the contract in order to adapt it to the new circumstances. However, it pointed out that:

> [the parties] have not done so, and a rule that the Court may not act would have the perverse effect of discouraging the parties from resolving this dispute or future disputes on their own. Only a rule which permits judicial action of the kind the Court has taken in this case will provide a desirable practical incentive for businessmen to negotiate their own resolution to problems which arise in the life of long term contracts.[343]

Such decision was criticised and not followed by the majority of the case law since it was considered in contrast with the sanctity of contracts doctrine that represents the prevailing position in US law.[344] However, part of the doctrine expressed a positive opinion in relation to the principle affirmed in the *Alcoa* case[345] and some

---

341. *Ibid.*
342. *Ibid.* It has to be noted that, upon the appeal, the parties settled the dispute and, therefore, the decision of the Pennsylvania Western District Court was not enforced.
343. *Ibid.*, at 92.
344. In this regard, *see* J. Dawson, *Judicial Revision of Frustrated Contracts: The United States*, 64 B.U.L.Rev. 1, 35 et seq. (1984); S.J. Sirianni, *The Developing Law of Contractual Impracticability and Impossibility: Part 1*, 14 U.C.C.L.J. 55, 55–56 (1981).
345. In particular, such position was taken by those supporting the theory of relational contracts, i.e., contracts that, in contrast with the so called "discrete transactions", are characterized by a long-term relationship during which parties cooperate and collaborate with each other in order to achieve the purpose pursued by entering into the contract. As a consequence, this implies that parties should adapt the contract in case of change of circumstances. *See*, for instance, R.A. Hillman, *Court Adjustment of Long-Term Contracts: An Analysis Under Modern Contract Law*, 1 Duke L.J., 2 (1987); R.E. Speidel, *Court Imposed Adjustment Under Long-Term, Supply Contracts*, 76 N.Y.U.L.Rev., 369 (1981); I. Macneil, *Contracts: Adjustment of Long-Term Economic Relations Under Classical, Neoclassical, and Relational Contract Law*, 72 N.Y.U.L-.Rev., 854 (1978) (*see* §3.06). For further references and comments, *see also* R.A.M. Uribe, *The Effect of a Change of Circumstances on the Binding Force of Contracts*, 178 (Intersentia 2011);

authorities³⁴⁶ expressly referred to it affirming that, in case of long-term contracts whose balance is altered by the occurrence of supervening events, the most appropriate solution would be the renegotiation of the agreement by the parties and only '[w]hen that does not work, courts should make themselves available to provide just and equitable resolutions with the primary goal being to maintain the integrity of the long-term contractual relationship'.³⁴⁷ In this regard, it has to be noted that the situations dealt with by such decisions were different from the *Alcoa* case and that at the end the disputes were settled by the parties and, consequently, the Court did not have to intervene on the contract terms. However, in spite of such differences, it is possible to find a characteristic common to all these cases: the recognition by courts that long-term contracts should be adapted upon the occurrence of unforeseen events and that such adjustment should be done, at first, by the parties and, in case of failure of the renegotiations, by courts.³⁴⁸ Furthermore, it has to be underlined that in a recent decision, although not dealing with the occurrence of supervening events beyond the parties' control altering the contract's balance, the Court held in favour of the recognition, in particular circumstances, of the arbitrators' power to adjust contracts even without an adaptation clause.³⁴⁹

In particular, the case concerned a dispute that arose out of a video game publishing agreement entered into by Timegate Studios ("Timegate") and Gamecock Media Group ("Gamecock")³⁵⁰ by which the first undertook to develop a video game (called "section 8") and the second, as a publisher, undertook to provide Timegate with the most part of the investments necessary to develop the videogame. Furthermore, the contract granted Gamecock a non-exclusive temporary license to use the intellectual property rights related to the video game (whose owner was Timegate) and did not authorise it to directly produce the sequels. It is also important to underline that the contract did not include an adaptation clause, but it just provided for a general arbitration clause. Few months after the release of the videogame – whose sales were negative and far from the parties' expectations – Timegate started a litigation proceeding before the Southern District Court of Texas in which each party contested to the other a breach of contract. Moreover, Gamecock asked for the staying of the proceeding since it was filed in spite of the arbitration clause included in the agreement. The District Court upheld such claim.

Zaccaria, *supra* n. 321, at 488 et seq.; F. Macario, *Modificazioni del mercato e disciplina dei contratti di fornitura dell'energia*, 96 et seq. (Maggioli 1991).
346. *See Unihealth v. US Healthcare*, 14 F.Supp.2d, 623 (D.N.J. 10 July 1998); *Florida Power & Light v. Westinghouse Electric*, 485 U.S., 1021 (5th Cir. 2 April 1986); *McGinnis v. Cayton*, 312 S.E.2d, 765 (W. Va. 27 January 1984). In this regard, *see also* Uribe, *id.*; J.J. White & D.A. Peters, *Essay: A Footnote for Jack Dawson*, 100 Mich. L. Rev., 1973 (2002); Macario, *id.*; Zaccaria, *id.*, at 504 et seq.
347. *McGinnis* case, *id.*, at 780.
348. *See* the comment of R. Pardolesi on the *Florida Power & Light* case, *supra* n. 346, IV Foro It, 376 (1981).
349. *Timegate Studios v. Gamecock Media Group*, http://www.ca5.uscourts.gov/opinions%5Cpub%5C12/12-20256-CV0.wpd.pdf (5th Cir. 9 April 2013).
350. Gamecock after the conclusion of the agreement was acquired by Southpeak Interactive.

In the following arbitration proceeding, the arbitrator upheld the counterclaim of Gamecock and found Timegate liable for breach of contract and fraud since it neither spent all the money received by Gamecock to develop the video game nor it complied with its contractual obligation to invest some money for such purpose. However, for such breach, the arbitrator not only awarded Gamecock monetary damages but also amended the contract. In particular, on the one hand, Gamecock was provided with 'a perpetual license for TimeGate's intellectual property in the Game, and Gamecock and [Southpeak] have no obligation to report to TimeGate about sales of the Game that use any of TimeGate's intellectual property, nor do Gamecock and [Southpeak] have any legal obligation to pay any royalties to TimeGate under the Publishing Agreement, and with right to create Sequels, Ports, Add-Ons related to the Game'[351] and, on the other, Timegate was granted the right to 'create sequels, Ports, Add-Ons related to the Game, or other competing products, and ... TimeGate has no legal duty to pay any royalties to Gamecock or [Southpeak] related to the Game'.[352]

In the enforcement proceeding, the District Court vacated the award since, 'although a finding of fraud permits an arbitrator to fashion an award which conflicts with contractual provisions, any such award must still be "rationally inferable from the parties' central purpose in drafting the agreement."',[353] by granting a perpetual license to Gamecock (instead of the temporary one provided by the contract) the arbitrator exceeded its authority since such remedy was 'inconsistent with the fundamental purpose of the contract'.[354]

Gamecock appealed such decision and the Court of Appeals reversed the District Court's judgment and confirmed the award. First of all, the Court affirmed the principle that judges 'must sustain an arbitration award even if we disagree with the arbitrator's interpretation of the underlying contract as long as the arbitrator's decision "draws its essence" from the contract'.[355] In order for a decision to "draw its essence form the contract", it is necessary to investigate which is the purpose pursued by the parties by means of the contract. With regard to the agreement between Gamecock and Timegate, the Court held that the scope of the latter was 'the creation of a mutually beneficial business relationship between two parties with distinct expertise: a video game developer and a video game publisher. The parties were to work jointly to create, market, and popularize a video game whose success would yield financial benefits to be distributed between the two parties in accordance with their respective contributions to the joint effort as required by the contract'.[356]

The Court then considered that the granting of a perpetual license was conform to and in line with the scope of the contract as above identified. In particular, such assertion was motivated on the ground that 'the collaborative relationship presupposed

---

351. *Timegate Studios* case, *supra* n. 349, at 6.
352. *Ibid.*
353. *Ibid.*, at 7.
354. *Ibid.*
355. *Ibid.*, at 8. On this point, the Court referred to *Executone Info. Sys. v. Davis*, 26 F.3d 1314, 1320 (5th Cir. 12 July 1994).
356. *Time Gate Studios* case, *supra* n. 349, at 10.

by the Agreement was no longer possible due to the breaches of Timegate'[357] and, consequently, the 'perpetual license granted to Gamecock represents an attempt by the arbitrator to restore to Timegate and Gamecock the fundamental goal of the Agreement: mutual access to financial benefits derived from their joint creation and distribution of section 8'[358] since the monetary damages were not sufficient considering that was not possible to foresee whether and how the sequels and other iterations of the video game could be successful on the market. In light of the above, the Court concluded that the arbitrator did not exceed its authority since the remedy granted (i.e., the perpetual license) could be included in the broad scope of the arbitration clause and reflected the scope of the contract.[359]

The *Timegate* case, even if in a completely different context, represents a recent affirmation of the principle already stated in the *Alcoa* case and, namely, that, in particular circumstances (and, especially, upon the occurrence of unforeseen events altering the contractual *equilibrium*), judges and arbitrators, even in the lack of an adaptation clause, should be entitled to adjust the contract in order to rebalance it if this is the parties' will. In other words, such authority should be recognised if the parties, due the specific characteristics of the contract and scope pursued by means of the latter, aim to preserve a profitable relationship for the entire duration agreed. In particular, this is the case of long-term contracts implying relevant investments, like gas sale agreements. In this situation, it is clear that both the performance of the contract without adaptation to the new circumstances and its termination would frustrate the parties' expectations. As already mentioned and as it will be seen more in detail below,[360] the adaptation of long-term contracts in order to meet the parties' will is based on the principle of good faith. In particular, it can be said that the execution of such agreements in good faith implies, in light of their characteristics and scope, the necessity to adapt them when their balance is altered upon the occurrence of unforeseen events.

In conclusion, although the prevailing position in Common law is contrary to the arbitrators' and judges' power to amend the contract upon the occurrence of unforeseen circumstances altering the relevant balance (in particular, English law is still reluctant to accept such idea), the *Alcoa* and *Timegate* cases represent an important step towards the recognition of such power aiming to meet the parties' will and expectations. Such approach has to be encouraged since, as noted by Professor Schmitthoff, 'the inability of courts and arbitrators to adapt a contract to uncontemplated fundamental changes of economic, political or social nature, if the parties intend

---

357. *Ibid.*, at 11.
358. *Ibid.*
359. It has also to be noted that the fact that under Texas law (the one applicable to the contract) in case of fraud arbitrators can void some contractual provisions and issue an award in contrast with the original agreed terms was surely a further element in favour of the arbitrator power to amend the contract. However, it was not the main reason on which the award and the Court's decision were grounded.
360. *See* §3.01 and §3.06.

to abide by their contract and to implement it' is 'a serious defect in English commercial law'.[361]

[B] Semi-conservative Legal Systems – The Italian Legal System

The Italian legal system can be considered as a semi-conservative one since it recognises the concept of hardship and the relevant possibility for the parties to adapt the contract when it becomes unbalanced but it does not provide courts and arbitrators with the same power.[362] In particular, Article 1467 of the Civil Code states that:

> (1) In contracts for continuous or periodic performance or for deferred performance, if the performance of one of the parties becomes excessively onerous upon the occurrence of extraordinary and unforeseen events, such party can claim for the termination of the contract, with the effects established by Article 1458. (2) The termination cannot be claimed if the supervening onerousness is part of the normal risk of the contract. (3) The party against whom the termination is claimed can avoid it by offering to equitably modify the conditions of the contract.[363]

According to such provision, courts (and arbitrators) do not have the power to adapt contracts in case of hardship being such possibility only granted to the advantaged party.[364] Indeed, only the latter can offer to equitably modify the agreement in light of the new situation in order to maintain it in force, while the party affected by hardship (i.e., the excessive onerousness due to extraordinary and unforeseen events) can only claim for the termination of the contract.[365] However, it was underlined that also the disadvantaged party could be interested in keeping alive the contract and not

---

361. Schmitthoff, *supra* n. 211, at 91. A further element in this direction is represented by comment n. 6 on s. 2-615 of the UCC stating that '[i]n situations in which neither sense nor justice is served by either answer when the issue is posed in flat terms of "excuse" or no "excuse", adjustment under the various provisions of this Article is necessary, especially the sections on good faith, on insecurity and assurance and on the reading of all provisions in the light of their purposes, and the general policy of this Act to use equitable principles in furtherance of commercial standards and good faith'.
362. According to Art. 2908 of the Civil Code (i.e., a mandatory provision), judges (and, consequently, arbitrators) are entitled to create, modify or extinguish legal relationships (i.e., to issue the so called "constitutive decisions", in which the adaptation of contracts is clearly included) only when it is expressly provided by the law (*see*, for instance, Art. 1384 of the Civil Code granting the judge the power to equitably reduce the amount of the penalty provided by the parties in case of breach of contract; Arts 1657 and 1660 of the Civil Code regarding the determination of the price and the variations to the original project of construction contracts and contracts for the supplying of services).
363. As freely translated.
364. However, as seen below, part of the case law in some circumstances has also considered judges and arbitrators as entitled to adapt the contract according to Art. 1467 of the Civil Code.
365. With regard to the right to request the equitable modification of the contract, *see also Pamedil v. Bruno*, Giur It, 2279 (*Corte di Cassazione* n. 46, 5 January 2000). that confirmed that 'the only party entitled to solicit the equitable modification of the contract's conditions is the one sued by means of the termination claim for excessive onerousness, since it has to be excluded that a request of reduction *ad aequitatem* can be opposed to a request of performance of the contract [i.e., the equitable modification of the contract cannot be asked by the party affected by hardship when it is sued in order to justify its breach of contract]'.

just to terminate it and, therefore, should be entitled to request an equitable modification of the contractual conditions.[366]

As to the determination of whether an offer can be considered equitable, it is possible to identify two main positions. The first considers equitable the modification offer that brings back the contract to the normal risk, i.e., in a situation in which the disadvantaged party would not claim for the termination of the contract.[367] The second theory, instead, affirms that an equitable revision of the contract is the one that rebalances the performances of the parties and re-establishes the contractual *equilibrium* by taking into account, in particular, the actual market values and conditions.[368]

In light of the above, the role of courts and arbitrators, pursuant to Article 1467, is limited to the determination of whether the offer made by the advantaged party is equitable or not without modifying it.[369] Provided that, it has to be noted that the *Corte di Cassazione* in some decisions has considered judges as entitled to amend the contract. Such cases mainly deal with preliminary real estate contracts that became excessively onerous for one of the party in the period of time between their conclusion and the date agreed for the stipulation of the definitive contract. Although these cases do not concern long-term agreements, the principles therein expressed and the approach adopted in favour of the adjustment of contracts can be also applied to the latter. Indeed, in both situations disputes arise out of agreements in which the time is relevant either because the performance of the contract does not immediately follow its conclusion or because the contract has a duration of several years. Therefore, it is clear

---

366. *See Cosarma v. Agip*, I 1974 Giur It, 280 (domestic arbitration award 28 February 1972); *Officina Meccanica di Crosta Mario v. Tintorie Milano di Cozzi & C.*, Foro Pad., 80 (Court of Appeal of Milan 4 July 1950). *See also* F. Macario, *Adeguamento e rinegoziazione*, in *Trattato dei contratti – I contratti in generale* vol. II, 1883 (P. Rescigno & E. Gabrielli, Utet 2006).
367. *See Privitera v. Borsato*, I 1993 Giur It, 2018 (*Corte di Cassazione* n. 247 11 January 1992); *Valentini v. Mantovani*, I Giust.civ., 2564 (*Corte di Cassazione* n. 3347 18 July 1989); *Annoni v. Salvia*, I 1985 Giur It, 362 (*Corte di Cassazione* n. 275 13 January 1984). In this regard, it has to be noted that, according to part of the doctrine, beyond the normal risk there is another area (so called 'anomalous risk') in which the performance cannot still be considered as excessive onerous and, consequently, the termination cannot be claimed. According to such position, only the excessive onerousness entitles the disadvantaged party to ask for the termination of the contract and usually it is considered to occur when the normal risk is doubled. Thus, the reduction offer is not necessarily to bring back the contract within the normal risk to be considered equitable (F. Macario, *Adeguamento e rinegoziazione nei contratti a lungo termine*, 275 et seq. (Jovene 1996); *Id.*, *supra* n. 345, at 44 et seq.).
368. *See Società immobiliare Bravetta v. Barrese*, I 1990 Giur It, 944 (*Corte di Cassazione* n. 4023 11 January 1989), that considered equitable the offer that eliminates the economic imbalance and that brings back the parties' performances to a full objective equivalence. This position was also supported by the doctrine. *See*, for instance, A. Di Majo, *Eccessiva onerosità sopravvenuta e reductio ad aequitatem*, Corriere giuridico, 664 (1992); C.G. Terranova, *L'eccessiva onerosità nei contratti*, in *Il Codice Civile – Commentario*, 196 (P. Schlesinger, Giuffrè 1995).
369. *See*, for instance, *Vettese v. Condominio via Pessina 66, Napoli*, I 1987 Foro It, 2177 (*Corte di Cassazione* n. 6584 11 November 1986); *Corte di Cassazione* n. 1067 24 March 1976, I Giust.civ., 1493; *Corte di Cassazione* n. 2748 18 September 1972, I Giust.civ., 1886; *Società azionaria per la condotta di acque potabili v. Comune di Torino*, I 1960 Foro It, 565 (*Corte di Cassazione* n. 224 27 January 1959). *See also* E. Quadri, *La rettifica del contratto*, 127 (Giuffrè 1973); F. Gazzoni, *Equità e autonomia privata*, 108 (Giuffrè 1970); F. Santoro Passarelli, *La transazione*, 60 (Jovene 1963); A. Pino, *La eccessiva onerosità della prestazione*, 84 (Padova 1952); A. De Martini, *L'eccessiva onerosità nell'esecuzione dei contratti*, 136 (Giuffrè 1950).

that the lapse of time can affect both categories of agreements since supervening events may occur and change the original market conditions making such contracts unbalanced. As a consequence, in both situations judges or arbitrators face the problem of the adjustment of these agreements in light of the new circumstances.

The first case analysed in this regard is the Decision n. 3347 of 18 July 1989,[370] that, as said, concerns a preliminary real estate contract. The sellers started a litigation proceeding before the Tribunal of Ferrara claiming for the termination of such agreement, pursuant to Article 1467 of the Civil Code, due to the fact that, during the period of time between the conclusion of the preliminary contract and the definitive one, the value of the lands had increased fourfold compared to the price provided by the preliminary contract. As a consequence, such disproportion between the actual market value of the lands and the sale price made the sellers' performance excessively onerous. The buyer contested the sellers' claim and, subordinately, offered to equitably modify the price agreed. The Tribunal rejected the sellers' claim. Upon the appeal by the latter, the Court of Appeal of Bologna reversed the first instance decision and upheld the sellers' request. In particular, the Court affirmed that the offer made by the buyer was not adequate to rebalance the contract and the consequent demand to adjust the contract could not be upheld since the Court did not have the power to implement it by means of a judicial decision.

Upon the buyer's appeal, the *Corte di Cassazione* reversed such judgment. First of all, the Supreme Court affirmed the principle that only the party advantaged by the occurrence of the unforeseen event, making the contract's performance excessively onerous for the counterparty, is entitled to offer to equitably modify the agreement. The judge can just ascertain whether such offer is actually equitable or not with no power to amend it by means of a constitutive decision. Therefore, the offer has to be complete and detailed. However, the Supreme Court noted that, in this case, the buyer not only made a specific proposal to modify the sale price, but also (as a subordinate claim) requested the judge to determine any different sum (greater or minor) that the latter considered equitable. In light of such specific request, the *Corte di Cassazione* stated that the Court of Appeal was not only entitled to ascertain whether the buyer's offer was equitable or not but, in the latter case, it also had the power to determine the sale price (by implementing the offer made by the buyer that was considered too low compared to the actual market value of the lands). In particular, it was held that:

> only the party is entitled to make an offer [to equitably reduce the conditions of the contract that became excessively onerous], that has to be specific in all its elements, while the judge, has to limit himself to determine whether the modifications proposed are suitable for normalizing the contractual relationship without being entitled to complete any deficiency of such proposal or to broaden it up. Provided that, the Court of Appeal, in rejecting the offer as clearly not equitable, did not, however, consider that [*the buyer*] requested the Court to declare that the remaining sum due by the counterparty as balance of the sale price re-evaluated amounted to … or, in the worst scenario, to … or to the minor or greater sum that the Court considered equitable, sum that the buyer offered to the sellers. In such case it has to be assumed that the party submitted a subordinate claim for the

---

370. *Valentini* case, *supra* n. 367.

judicial determination of the equitable price due to the sellers, in light of which the judge was entitled to implement the offer proposed on the basis of the elements already acquired in the proceeding.[371]

Thus, the *Corte di Cassazione* affirmed the principle that, in case there is (even subordinately) a specific request to the judge to ascertain in equity the right price or the sum suitable for eliminating the excessive onerousness, the judge has the power to determine such amount (by increasing or diminishing the offer made by the advantaged party) and, consequently, to adapt the contract by issuing a constitutive decision.

The same conclusion was reached in the decision n. 5922 of 25 May 1991.[372] Even this case regarded a preliminary real estate contract that the seller wanted to terminate due to the extraordinary increase of the inflation rate that rendered the contract excessively onerous. The buyer rejected such request and invited the seller to conclude the definitive sale contract. Upon the seller's refusal the buyer started a litigation proceeding before the Tribunal of Santa Maria Capua Vetere asking the latter to issue a decision replacing the effects of the definitive sale agreement contract that the seller refused to conclude. The latter, in its turn, claimed for the termination of the preliminary agreement. The Tribunal upheld such request and its judgment was confirmed by the Court of Appeal of Naples upon the appeal brought by the buyer. It is important to underline that in this proceeding the buyer also offered to equitably modify the contract. However, such proposal was not examined by the Court since it was not specific but general and vague and, consequently, it was not possible for the judges to ascertain whether it was suitable to rebalance the contract.

The *Corte di Cassazione* reversed the Court of Appeal's decision. In particular, the Supreme Court affirmed that part of the case law considered the *reductio ad aequitatem* offer as a contractual proposal addressed to the counterparty that, upon the latter's acceptance, determines the conclusion of a new contract amending the previous one. Only in case of the counterparty's refusal, such adjustment request can be addressed to the judge that, due to its contractual nature, has just the power to accept or reject it without being entitled to modify it. However, according to the Court, it is preferable to follow another view by which the offer of the advantaged party is a unilateral offer that produces its effects when the counterparty becomes aware of it. The latter can adhere to such offer or not. In the last case, the relevant claim proposed by the advantaged party before the Court can be considered as a request to issue 'a constitutive judicial decision aiming to obtain, *ope iudicis*, a modification of the contractual condition sufficient to make the contract equitable'.[373] As a consequence, since the offer is not a contractual proposal, it is not necessary that it specifically indicates the clauses to be adjusted since it is possible to ask the judge to determine which parts of the contract has to be modified. Therefore, according to such view, judges have an adaptation power provided of course that a request (even general and vague) is made by the party.

---

371. *Ibid.*
372. *Moscatiello v. Cerbo*, Rep.Foro.It., 'Contratto in genere', n. 359 (*Corte di Cassazione* n. 5922 25 May 1991).
373. *Ibid.*

In light of the above, the *Corte di Cassazione* affirmed that the Court of Appeal 'should have not considered the offer of *reduction ad aequitatem* as generic, but it should have examined it in the merits, if need by resorting to an expert consultancy ...'.[374]

As said, the aforementioned decisions adopted a new approach in favour to the adaptation power of judges (and arbitrators) in case the contract becomes unbalanced due to tan hardship event. However, they do not explain how such power can be justified according to Article 2908 of the Italian Civil Code. Such mandatory provision establishes that judges (and, consequently, arbitrators) are entitled to create, modify or extinguish legal relationships (i.e., to issue the so called "constitutive decisions", in which the adaptation of contracts is clearly included) only when it is expressly provided by the law.[375] Therefore, it is necessary to find a law provision justifying the adjustment power that the decisions analysed above have recognised to courts (and arbitrators). It seems difficult to consider Article 1467 itself as the "legislative justification" pursued since it does not contain any provision in this sense. Indeed, it only refers to the possibility for the disadvantaged party to propose to adjust the contract without mentioning a similar power upon judges.[376] As seen more in detail below,[377] it seems, instead, possible to justify the adaptation power of courts and arbitrators upon the occurrence of an hardship event – making the contract excessively onerous for one of the parties and, as such, unbalanced – in light of the principle of good faith. In particular, the adjustment power can be deemed to derive from the application of such principle to the execution of contracts (whose performance is continuous, periodic or deferred in time), as provided by Article 1375 of the Italian Civil Code.[378] In particular, this solution consents to meet the parties' will and expectations that, due to the characteristics and scope proper of long-term agreements, aim to maintain alive the contract. Thus, the best remedy in such cases is not the termination of the agreement but its adaptation in light of the new market conditions that consents to rebalance it and to keep it in force.[379]

---

374. *Ibid.* The same principle was also affirmed in *Privitera* case, *supra* n. 367 in which the Supreme Court seems to consider admissible a request made by the advantaged party to the judge to determine the modifications to the contract necessary to render it equitable upon the occurrence of unforeseen events. However, the Court underlines that in case, instead, the party's modification offer is specific in its term the judge can only determine whether it is equitable or not without being entitled to modify it by means of a constitutive decision.
375. *See supra* n. 362.
376. We have seen that the majority of the case law and doctrine consider courts as not entitled to issue a constitutive decision by increasing or decreasing the offer made by the advantaged party in order to rebalance the contract but only to determine whether such offer is equitable or not (and, consequently, to issue a so called 'declarative decision').
377. *See* §3.06.
378. According to such provision, all contracts have to be executed in good faith.
379. In favour of the maintenance of the contract instead of its termination in the above-mentioned situations *see Prisco v. Palumbo*, I Giust.civ., 1630 (*Corte di Cassazione* n. 1720 27 February 1985). As to the doctrine, *see* R. Sacco & G. De Nova, *Il contratto*, 1708 et seq. (UTET 2016); Macario, *supra* n. 367, at 321; Terranova, *supra* n. 368, at 231 et seq. In favour of the adaptation of contracts by courts in light of the principle of good faith in case of supervening events altering their balance, *see* A. D'Angelo, *La buona fede ausiliaria del programma contrattuale*, in *Buona fede e giustizia contrattuale* (A. D'Angelo, P.G. Monateri & A. Somma, Giappichelli

The reference to the principle of good faith as a justification of the courts' power to intervene on the contractual terms was also recently made by the *Corte di Cassazione* in the decisions n. 20106 of 18 September 2009,[380] regarding a case of abuse of right allegedly committed by a car manufacturer that, according to a specific provision of such agreement, withdrew from a license contract for the sale of cars. Although such decision does not deal with a case of hardship altering the original balance of the contract, the principle affirmed by the Supreme Court has a general relevance and is also applicable to different cases, such as the adaptation of long-term agreements. In particular, it was, at first, held that the principle of good faith (to be intended as loyal behaviour between the parties) has to govern, in general, the relationship between creditors and debtors (as provided by Article 1175 of the Civil Code) and, more specifically, the execution of the contract (as provided by Article 1375 of the Civil Code). Furthermore, the Court stated that such principle also found a legislative reference in constitutional law being an expression of the mandatory duties of social solidarity provided by Article 2 of the Italian Constitution. In this context, the Court then affirmed that the principle of good faith consents the judge to control the contract, even by adapting it, in order to guarantee the correct *equilibrium* and proportion. It is, therefore, clear how important is such decision since it provides a general justification of the courts' (and arbitrators') power to adjust a contract, when its balance is altered, on the basis of the principle of good faith. The latter indeed represents the criterion and the means to be used by judges and arbitrators to re-establish the contract *equilibrium* even by modifying its conditions.

Also in the arbitration field, it is possible to find another example of the position taken by the case law in favour of the adaptation of contracts by arbitrators.[381] In particular, the case concerned a domestic charter providing for the determination of the freight rate in pounds on the basis of the Tanker Nominal Freight Scale ("Scale"), increased by 30%,[382] to be converted in Italian lire.[383] Upon the devaluation of the

---

2005). The Author seems to consider possible such judicial intervention only in cases in which the supervening events do not determine an economic disproportion between the parties' performances or the frustration of the contract. Thus, the judicial adjustment is possible when the conditions for the termination of the contract are not met and it is necessary to adapt the agreement in order to preserve, and not to modify, its *equilibrium*. Therefore, it is excluded the judicial adaptation in case of a mere economic disproportion between the parties' performances due to the occurrence of unforeseen events. Indeed, in this situation, if such disproportion amounts to excessive onerousness, according to Art. 1467 of the Civil Code, the remedy for the disadvantaged party is the termination of the contract unless the advantaged party offers to adapt it. In case, instead, the disproportion remains within the normal area of risk the adjustment is still not possible since it would modify the allocation of risks provided by the contract and, consequently, it would change its balance and not just preserve it.

380. *A.G. et al. v. Renault Italia et al.*, I Giust.civ., 2671 (*Corte di Cassazione* n. 20106, 18 September 2009). The reference to the principle of good faith as the tool that courts can employ in order to guarantee the contractual *equilibrium* even by modifying or supplementing the agreement was already affirmed in *Ditta Autocori v. Società Demaca*, 2008 XII Giust.civ., 2807 (*Corte di Cassazione* n. 23726 15 November 2007).
381. See *Cosarma* case, *supra* n. 366.
382. The Tanker Nominal Freight Scale the freight rate is calculated both in pounds and US dollar for any single trip.
383. The currency used before the introduction of Euro.

pound, the owner of the boat modified the method of calculation of the freight rate using, as a reference, the standard rate provided by the Scale expressed in dollar. It converted such sum, first, in pounds (at the new exchange rate) and, then, in Italian lire in order to avoid the effects of the pounds devaluation. The charterer did not accept such modification and kept on paying the freight rate calculated according to the old method. Upon the owner's claim of the payment of the greater sum due by the charterer (on the basis of the new calculation), a dispute arose between the parties. In particular, the owner claimed for the payment of Italian lire 140,910,535 (that it alleged to be due by the charterer) or of the amount considered equitable by the arbitration tribunal in order to rebalance the contract. The arbitrators, after having clarified that the Scale just provided for standard freight rates, had to face the issue of whether the owner, i.e., the disadvantaged party, was entitled to ask for the reduction *ad aequitatem* of the contract (as it was asked as secondary claim), according to Article 1467 of the Italian Civil Code since, as said above, the latter only grants this right to the advantaged party (in such case the charterer). The answer of the arbitration tribunal was positive. It considers that, on the basis of the principle of solidarity underlying such provision, the charterer should not be precluded from asking a reduction *ad aequitatem* and that the pounds devaluation was an extraordinary and unforeseen event triggering the application of Article 1467. In conclusion, the arbitrators decided that the equitable solution would be to share between the parties the effects of the devaluation and, consequently, it ordered the charterer to pay the owner a sum equal to half of the amount claimed by the latter. Such award is interesting because, first of all, it admits that also the disadvantaged party should be entitled to offer the equitable reduction of the contract and, second, it confirms that arbitrators, upon the specific demand of the party should be entitled to modify the contract by means of a constitutive decision (similarly to what stated in the courts' decision above mentioned).

In light of the above, it can be said that, although Article 1467 of the Italian Civil Code does not expressly provide courts and arbitrators with the power to adapt contracts in case of hardship altering the relevant balance, the case law has shown a tendency during the last decades in favour of the possibility to grant them such power in specific circumstances. As already mentioned, such approach can be justified on the basis of the application of the principle of good faith to the execution of contracts whose performance is continuous, periodic or deferred in time. In this way, in case of long-term contracts (like gas sale agreements) the parties can benefit of a remedy (the adaptation) that is preferable to their termination since it consents to maintain them alive and, consequently, to fulfil the parties' will and expectations.

A final consideration should be made in relation to the issue whether the revision of contracts by arbitrators should be considered as informal arbitration (so called "*arbitrato irrituale*"), i.e., a specific kind of arbitration provided by Article 808-*ter* of the Code of Civil Procedure, by means of which arbitrators, if the parties established so in the arbitration agreement, decide the dispute by issuing a contractual determination. Therefore, the latter cannot be considered as a judicial award and arbitrators are not deemed to act like judges and, consequently, do not exercise the same powers. Moreover, the arbitration tribunal has not to follow the procedural rules provided by Code of Civil Procedure. In this way, it would be possible to avoid the problems arisen in relation to whether arbitrators should be entitled in some circumstances to adapt the contract by means of constitutive judicial decisions. On the other side, as said above, the decision of the arbitration tribunal in an informal arbitration does not have the same effects as a traditional judicial award[384] and, consequently, the non-compliance by one of the party would be the same as a contractual breach. Thus, the non-breaching party will have to start a litigation proceeding in order to make ascertain the responsibility of the counterparty and to claim for the relevant damages.[385]

[C] Non-conservative Legal Systems

[1] The German Legal System

The German legal system can be considered a non-conservative one being favourable to the adaptation of contracts by courts, and consequently by arbitrators, upon the occurrence of unforeseen events changing the contractual *equilibrium*. Indeed, the German Civil Code (BGB), after the reform of 2002, expressly recognises the hardship concept and provides for the courts' authority to adjust the contract in such case.[386] The German legal system is an example of situations in which a procedural power of courts (and arbitrators) is included in the substantive law and not in the procedural one.

---

384. In this regard, it has to be noted that it was recognised the possibility to enforce the decision issued in the informal arbitration under the New York Convention. *See*, for instance, *Pagnan v. Butera*, 1979 I Giur It, 407 (*Corte di Cassazione* n. 416 18 September 1978); *Rocco v. Federal Commerce and Navigation*, 1983 Dir Marit, 774 (*Corte di Cassazione* n. 6915 15 December 1982); *SEB v. Van Raaij Voertuigen*, 1992 Riv Dir Intern Priv & Proc, 574 (Tribunal of Milan 11 November 1991).
385. In this regard, it was noted that, unlike the so called 'arbitraggio' (i.e., the determination by a third party of the gaps of the contract left by the parties) provided by Art. 1349 of the Civil Code, in the informal arbitration, when a dispute arises between the parties with regard to whether or not the events triggering the application of Art. 1467 of the Civil Code occurred, the arbitrator, before revising the contract, carries out the same judgment as in case of the formal arbitration. In other words, it resolves real disputes and 'as such requires that the principles and rules of procedure indispensable in any judging activity be observed' (M.J. Bonell, *Arbitration as a Means for the Revision of Contracts*, in *Italian National Reports to the X International Congress of Comparative Law – Budapest 1978* 221, 242 (Giuffrè 1978). For these reasons, according to the Author, although the award has not the same effects as a judicial decision, in Italy the solution of the problem of the adaptation of contract by a third party is not so difficult as in other countries due to the existence of the informal arbitration (also considering that the relevant decision is enforceable under the New York Convention).
386. The first application by the case law of Art. 313 is represented by the decision of the *Bundesgerichtshof* dated 8 February 2006, VIII BIZR, 304, as cited in R. Pennazio, *La dottrina del fondamento negoziale nel diritto giudiziale europeo*, 1 Contratto Impresa/Europa, 391 (2009). Such case dealt with the violation of a non-competition obligation by the seller of a company's stocks. Such obligation, although not expressly provided in the contract, was considered by the Court as an implicit condition on which basis the contract was concluded. Therefore, the Court adjusted the latter by reducing the price of the stocks to be paid by the seller since the above-mentioned violation had decreased the relevant value (the seller indeed had become the manager of a competitor of the company whose stocks were sold and concluded some contracts with the main client of the latter).

In particular, Article 313 of the BGB establishes that:

(1) [i]f circumstances which became the basis of a contract have significantly changed since the contract was entered into and if the parties would not have entered into the contract or would have entered into it with different contents if they had foreseen this change, adaptation of the contract may be demanded to the extent that, taking account of all the circumstances of the specific case, in particular the contractual or statutory distribution of risk, one of the parties cannot reasonably be expected to uphold the contract without alteration. (2) It is equivalent to a change of circumstances if material conceptions that have become the basis of the contract are found to be incorrect. (3) If adaptation of the contract is not possible or one party cannot reasonably be expected to accept it, the disadvantaged party may revoke the contract. In the case of continuing obligations, the right to terminate takes the place of the right to revoke.[387]

The first paragraph of Article 313 deals with the occurrence of unforeseen events while the second paragraph regards the case in which the circumstances representing the basis of the contract are absent since the beginning due to the mutual error of the parties. In both these situations, the first remedy is the adaptation of the contract that the disadvantaged party can claim to the court unless it is not possible or unreasonable (in such case, the result is the termination of the agreement, as provided by third paragraph of Article 313). The adaptation process has to be carried out by taking into account all the specific circumstances of each case and the contract or law provisions disciplining the distribution of the risk between the parties. In this regard, it was noted that Article 313 is 'strictly subsidiary. The first means of dealing with unforeseen changes should be - as indicated - contractual provisions, such as flexible price clauses and construction of the contract itself. The legal rules governing rescission ..., impossibility of performance ... and the liability for defects ..., amongst other legal remedies, take precedence over [Article] 313 BGB'.[388] Besides its subsidiary nature, Article 313 can be applied when the circumstances representing the foundation of the contract (on which the parties found the relevant economic balance) are not express terms of the latter but are implied conditions.[389] Notwithstanding the aforementioned limits regarding the application of Article 313, German law represents one of the few codifications that recognise the courts' power to adapt the contract in case of supervening events altering the contract's balance. It follows that if the applicable procedural law to arbitration is German law, arbitrators, provided that all the conditions required for the application of Article 313 are met, will have the authority to adapt the agreement upon the occurrence of unforeseen events that alter the relevant balance between the parties even without an express adaptation clause providing them with such power. The possibility for the parties to ask for an adaptation of the contract upon the change of the circumstances representing the basis of such agreements and in light of which they reached a balance between their interests, finds its justification on the principle of good faith. Indeed, it would be against the latter to constrain the parties to

---

387. Available in English on www.gesetze-im-internet.de.
388. *See* H. Rosler, *Hardship in German Codified Private Law – In Comparative Perspective to English, French and International Contract Law*, 3 E.R.P.L. 483, 490(2007).
389. *Ibid.*, at 491.

keep a contract that has become excessively burdensome for them or to terminate it when this is not the scope pursued by the parties. Therefore, Article 313 can be considered as an application of the principle of good faith provided by Article 242 of the German Civil Code,[390] as also confirmed by the case law that, before the introduction of such article, had already recognised the court's power to adapt the contract in case of alteration of its *equilibrium*. Indeed, it can be said that such provision codified the approach adopted during the years by the jurisprudence. In particular, the first recognitions of the courts' adaptation power was the consequence of a specific political and economic situation occurred in Germany after the First World War characterised by a severe inflation that caused a loss of the purchase power of the German currency (the Mark) by almost 80% and depression of the entire German economy. In the first decisions dealing with such issue, the German Supreme Court (that until the Second World War was the *Reichsgericht*) referred to the concept of economic impossibility with the consequent release of the debtor from its contractual duties[391] or to the *clausola rebus sic stantibus* doctrine to adapt the price in a vapour sale agreement due to the excessive increase of the price of natural resources.[392]

In 1922 the German Supreme Court, always facing with the problem of the inflation of the German currency, affirmed, instead, the principle of the collapse of the contract's foundation (*Wegfall der Geschäftsgrundlage*) – inspired to the already developed doctrine of the basis of the transaction[393] – and considered courts entitled to adjust the agreement since it would be contrary to the principle of good faith to maintain it when, due to the occurrence of unforeseen events, the conditions on which it was based are altered and, consequently, the contract was not balanced anymore. In particular, it was noted that:

> [such principle] was founded on the idea that certain crucial matters of wide application to the contract are usually not embodied within the four corners of the contract. The parties negotiating a contract usually do not question that certain legal norms or economic conditions prevailing at the time of the contract will continue to prevail. However, when the economic or legal order undergoes a completely unforeseen change that erodes the "objective" economic bases of the contract, performance may become extremely burdensome. Under these changed circumstances, German law may be unwilling to exact performance from the obligor because to do so would offend against good faith *Treu und Glauben*.[394]

In a case, regarding a contract concluded on 31 May 1919 for the sale of certain assets of a dissolving partnership, a dispute arose between the parties in relation to the fixed price provided in the agreement.[395] The Court recognised the negative serious

---

390. Such article provides that '[a]n obligor has a duty to perform according to the requirements of good faith, taking customary practice into consideration' (available in English on www.gesetze-im-internet.de).
391. *Reichsgericht* 15 October 1918, RGZ, 45.
392. *Reichsgericht* 21 September 1920, RGZ, 100.
393. See P. Oertmann, *Geschaftsgrundlage – Ein neuer Rechtsbegriff* (Deichert 1921).
394. D.W. Rivkin, *Lex Mercatoria and Force Majeure*, in *Transnational Rules in International Commercial Arbitration*, 182 et seq. (E. Gaillard, International Chamber of Commerce 1993).
395. *Reichsgericht* 3 February 1922, RGZ, 103, as cited in Beale, Fauvarque-Cosson, Rutgers, Tallon & Vogenauer, *supra* n. 247, at 1139–1140.

effects deriving from the monetary devaluation and held that this implied to verify if the basis of the contract disappeared. Then, the Court, in setting aside the previous judgment, affirmed the principle that the 'parties will have to enter fresh negotiations before the courts which will have to take account of the disappearance of the contractual basis. However, the courts must be careful to ensure that the defendant M does not avail himself of that opportunity to withdraw completely from its contractual obligations'.[396] Furthermore, the Court held that, in application of the principle of good faith, judges have to try to maintain contracts by means of adaptation.

A similar approach was adopted in another decision dealing with a dispute arising out of the valuation of stocks agreed by the parties due to the monetary depreciation.[397] The Court decided that the price of the stock fixed in the contract had to be adjusted on the basis of equity reasons in light of the severe devaluation of the German currency after the First World War and taking into account the interests of the parties.

These two cases opened the way to the recognition of the courts' power to adapt a contract upon the occurrence of unforeseen events that cause the disappearance of the foundation of the contract on which basis the parties entered into it. As seen, such view is based on the principle of good faith that should govern the execution of any contract and on the idea that the best remedy in case of hardship due to the change of the circumstances is to maintain the latter by means of adaptation to the new economic situation instead of just terminating it or keeping it without modification.

Other two important decisions issued by the *Bundesgerichtshof* (i.e., the German Federal Supreme Court that replaced the *Reichsgericht*), that reaffirmed the principle of adaptation of contracts in light of doctrine of the collapse of the contract's foundation and of the principle of good faith, are those dated 16 January 1953[398] and 14 October 1992.[399]

The first dealt with a contract for the sale of 600 drill hammers ordered by a company located in the West Germany and to be used for mining in Eastern Germany (such circumstance was not expressed in the contract but known to the seller). After the order was issued on 31 May 1948 and before the delivery of the drill hammers, the Berlin blockade occurred (it lasted from 24 June 1948 to 22 May 1949). The seller, which at that time had already manufactured 200 hammers, kept on producing the last 400. However, the buyer did not take the delivery nor pay the price agreed since basically it could not reach the purpose by which it concluded the contract, i.e., the sale of the hammers in Eastern Germany. The seller sued the buyer claiming for the payment of the price and the *Landgericht* (the German lower court) and the Court of Appeal upheld such claim. However, the *Bundesgerichtshof* revised the decision of the Court of Appeal and, on the basis of the good faith principle (provided by Article 242

---

396. *Id.*, at 1140.
397. *Reichsgericht* 27 June 1922, RGZ, 103, as cited in Beale, Fauvarque-Cosson, Rutgers, Tallon & Vogenauer, *supra* n. 247, at 1140–1141.
398. *Bundesgerichtshof* 16 January 1953, as cited in Beale, Fauvarque-Cosson, Rutgers, Tallon & Vogenauer, *id.*, at 1142–1143.
399. *Bundesgerichtshof* 14 October 1992, as cited in Beale, Fauvarque-Cosson, Rutgers, Tallon & Vogenauer, *id.*, at 1144–1146.

of the German Civil Code), held that, upon the disappearance of the contractual basis due to supervening events, the contract should be adjusted to the new circumstances by taking into account the parties' interests. Without such adaptation, the parties' expectations would be frustrated.

The second decision regarded a contract for the sale of pressurised milling machines entered into between two Eastern German companies on 10 January 1990. The parties knew that the 50% of the payment of the sale price would have been financed by the state since such sale was part of an economic plan. Upon the re-unification process of the Germany, the subsidy was not granted anymore and, therefore, the payment of the entire sale price by the buyer became extremely burdensome and unfair. The Supreme Court considered that the German re-unification was an unforeseen event that caused the collapse of the contract's foundation represented by the parties' intentions to enter into a sale agreement in light of the concession of the state financial aid. Therefore, without the latter no contract would have been concluded. In such situation, the Court on the basis of the principle of good faith decided to adjust the contract since it 'is a question as a matter of principle of upholding the contract as far as possible and of adapting it in the interests of the parties to the new circumstances'.[400]

Provided the above, it has to be underlined that the collapse of the contract's foundation doctrine – as first developed by the case law before and as now established by Article 313 of the German Civil Code – is applied restrictively and only in exceptional circumstances.

An example of such restrictive application, before the codification of the doctrine, is represented by the decision of the *Bundesgerichtshof* dated 8 February 1978 dealing with a dispute arising out of an oil sale agreement. In this case, the supplier refused to perform the contract without an adjustment of the original price that had become unreasonable due to the oil crisis. However, the Supreme Court rejected the claim since the crisis was foreseeable and consequently the supplier could have taken proper measures to prevent the relevant effects (such as the creation of adequate reserves). Therefore, the losses suffered by the supplier were considered as caused by its behaviour. Moreover, the Court in reaching its decision took into account other two elements: (i) the fact that the contract was almost expired when the suppliers asked for the adjustment of the price, and (ii) the fact that the contract did not provide for a price review clause in order to adapt it upon changes of the conditions in the relevant market. The failure of including such a clause represented for the Court the allocation of the price risk decided by the parties when entered into the contract and, as such, it was considered as an expression of the parties' will.

[2]   The Dutch Legal System

Another legal system that expressly provides for the arbitrators' power to adapt the contract in case of hardship is the Dutch one. In this case, however, not only courts

---

400. *Ibid.,* at 1145.

(Article 6:258 of the Civil Code, dealing with unforeseen circumstances), but also arbitrators (Article 1020 of the Code of Civil Procedure) are expressly provided with such authority.

In particular, the first provision states that:

> 1. Upon a right of action (legal claim) of one of the parties to an agreement, the court may change the legal effects of that agreement or it may dissolve this agreement in full or in part if there are unforeseen circumstances of such a nature that the opposite party, according to standards of reasonableness and fairness, may not expect an unchanged continuation of the agreement. The court may change or dissolve the agreement with retroactive effect. 2. The court shall not change or dissolve the agreement as far as the unforeseen circumstances, in view of the nature of the agreement or of common opinion, should remain for account of the party who appeals to these circumstances. 3. For the purpose of this Article, a person to whom a right or obligation from the agreement has passed, is equated with an original party to that agreement.[401]

In light of such article, courts, upon the occurrence of unforeseen events altering the contract balance and the party's request, can adapt the contract to the new situation, provided that such events do not depend on the party claiming for the modification of the agreement.

Even in the case of the Dutch legal system, the principle behind the above-mentioned provision is represented by good faith to which Article 6:258 refers by means of the terms "reasonableness and fairness". Therefore, it would be against such principle, in case of supervening circumstances altering the original balance of the contract, to require the disadvantaged party to perform the agreement without adapting it to the new situation. The principle that the relationships between parties have to be governed by good faith can be also found in Articles 6:2 and 6:248 of the Civil Code.[402]

The first provision, regarding in general obligations, establishes that:

> 1. The creditor and debtor must behave themselves towards each other in accordance with the standards of reasonableness and fairness. 2. A rule in force between a creditor and his debtor by virtue of law, common practice or a juridical act does not apply as far as this would be unacceptable, in the circumstances, by standards of reasonableness and fairness'.[403]

Article 6:248, regarding more specifically contracts, provides that:

> 1. An agreement not only has the legal effects which parties have agreed upon, but also those which, to the nature of the agreement, arise from law, usage (common practice) or the standards of reasonableness and fairness. 2. A rule, to be observed by parties as a result of their agreement, is not applicable insofar this, given the

---

401. Available in English on www.dutchcivillaw.com. This provision is another example of a procedural norm included in the Civil Code.
402. As it was noted 'the term of 'reasonableness and fairness' is used instead of 'good faith' in order to prevent confusion with the notion of good faith in the subjective sense (Art. 3:11 BW)'. See D. Busch, E. Hondius, H. van Kooten, H. Schelhaas & W. Schrama, *The Principles of European Contract Law and Dutch Law*, 49 (Kluwer Law International 2002).
403. Available in English on www.dutchcivillaw.com.

circumstances, would be unacceptable to standards of reasonableness and fairness.[404]

The latter provision differs from Article 6:258, first of all, because it is not a procedural norm included in the Civil Code, but it is a truly substantive law provision. Indeed, it does not confer any power upon courts when the contract contains provisions contrary to the principle of good faith. Moreover, the effect and the extent of Article 6:248 are different since, on the one hand, it does not provide for the adjustment of the agreement (by parties) but directly for the non-application of such provisions and, on the other, its application is not limited to the case of unforeseen events. The reason of this choice by the legislator can be found in the peculiarity and delicateness of the issue of contract's adaptation in case of hardship that require the intervention of a court.[405]

As to the events triggering the adjustment of the agreement, according to Article 6:258, it is important to note that it is not necessary that the "unforeseen circumstances" regard the foundation of the contract being possible to claim the adaptation also in relation to other ancillary contact provisions (such as, for instance, place and time of delivery).[406] Moreover, such expression 'must not be taken literally. The decisive factor is whether the parties have made allowance for the occurrence of these circumstances in their contract; if the contract has made sufficient provisions for *those* circumstances. This must be determined by interpretation of the contract'.[407]

As already said, the other necessary condition provided by Article 6:258 is the request of one of the parties. Such demand also fulfils the function to circumscribe the discretionary power of the court since the latter 'is obliged to turn to the solutions mentioned by the parties'.[408] In particular, it was affirmed that the best solution would be for the court to choose the adaptation option proposed by the parties that 'in its opinion, come *closest* to what the parties are entitled to expect from one another according to reasonableness and fairness'[409] instead of rejecting 'any demand which does not (sufficiently) indicate the outcome it considers best'[410] with the consequent refusal to adapt the contract. Furthermore, the Court, in adapting the contract, can fix additional conditions and can provide one or more parties with the right to rescind the

---

404. Available in English on www.dutchcivillaw.com.
405. In this sense, *see* J. Hijma, *The Role of the Court and of the Parties in Adapting a Contract to Unforeseen Circumstances*, in Castermans, Jansen, Knigge, Memelink & Nieuwenhuis, *supra* n. 247, at 19 who affirms that '[t]he difference is considered appropriate because changed circumstances lead to a definitive new arrangement of the contractual relations. This implies a deep intervention; moreover, many cases will be rather complex so that various solutions are possible. So it is for reasons of legal certainty that the legislator here prefers a constitutive court verdict to a declarative one'.
406. *See* A.S. Hartkamp & M.M.M. Tillema, *Contract Law in the Netherlands*, 125 (Kluwer Law International 1995).
407. *Ibid.*
408. Hijma, *supra* n. 405, at 16. *See also* M. Mekki & M. Kloepfer-Pelèse, *Hardship and Modification (or 'Revision') of the Contract*, in *Towards a European Civil Code*, 679 (A.S. Hartkamp, Kluwer Law International 2011).
409. *Ibid.*
410. *Ibid.*

agreement within a specific period of time. In this case, the adaptation will not be effective until such period is expired. Indeed, Article 6:260 provides that:

> 1.When the court has changed or dissolved an agreement on the basis of Article 6:258 or 6:259, it may set additional conditions in its judgment. 2. If the court changes or partially dissolves the agreement on the basis of Article 6:258 or 6:259, it may order that one or more parties may rescind the agreement entirely by means of a written notification within a period to be set in its judgment. In that event the change or partial dissolvement (dissolution) of the agreement shall not take effect before this period has expired.[411]

As said above, in addition to Article 6:258, another law provision that makes the Dutch legal system one of the less conservative with regard to the possibility for arbitrators to adjust the contract upon the occurrence of unforeseen events, is represented by Article 1020 of the Code of Civil Procedure (included in the fourth Book dealing with arbitration). Such provision, besides granting the parties the possibility to settle any dispute arising out of a specified legal relationship (first paragraph), establishes, at paragraph 4, letter c), that the parties may also submit to arbitration 'the filling of gaps in, or modification of, the legal relationship between the parties referred to in paragraph (1)'.[412] Unlike Article 6:258, the application of this norm is not limited either to contracts, since it refers in general to legal relationships, or to hardship since the latter is not mentioned.

Moreover, it has to be noted that the arbitrators' authority to adapt the contract is recognised only in case the parties have expressly provided so in the arbitration agreement or in the contract, not being sufficient the general arbitration clause by which all the disputes related to an agreement will be settled by an arbitration tribunal. However, it was held that in case the substantive applicable law is the Dutch one, it is possible for arbitrators, in light of the above-mentioned Article 6:258, to adapt the contract upon the occurrence of unforeseen events altering the relevant balance even if such specific power has not been expressly conferred upon them by the parties in the arbitration or in the adaptation clause.[413] This is also in consideration of the mandatory nature of such norm as provided by Article 6:250 of the Civil Code.[414] Therefore, according to such view, the above-mentioned authority should also be recognised in case the contract does not include any adjustment clause (provided that the substantive applicable law is the Dutch one). The solution would be different in case the substantive applicable law is not the Dutch Civil Code since in this case it would be necessary for an express provision in the contract granting the arbitrator with the power to adapt the contract. In such situation, an issue could arise in relation to the arbitrators' power to adapt the contract if the applicable substantive law does not

---

411. Available in English on http://www.dutchcivillaw.com/civilcodebook066.htm.
412. Available in English on http://www.dutchcivillaw.com/civilprocedureleg.htm.
413. In this sense, *see* B. Van der Bend, M. Leijten,& M. Ynzonides, *A Guide to the NAI Arbitration Rules: Including a Commentary on Dutch Arbitration Law*, 49 (Kluwer Law International 2009).
414. Such Article provides that '[i]t is possible to derogate by agreement from Articles of this Section that will follow as of now with the exception of Articles ... 6:258'.

Chapter 3: Arbitrators Contracts Without an Adaptation Clause §3.03[C]

recognise such authority or even the concept of hardship.[415] In our opinion, this view can be criticised since, as said, Article 6:258 is a procedural provision in spite of its collocation in the Civil Code. Therefore, in case the parties did not expressly provide arbitrators with the power to adjust the contract, as established by Article 1024(4) of the Code of Civil Procedure, the authority of the arbitration tribunal to modify the agreement cannot derive from the fact that the substantive applicable law is the Dutch one and, consequently, from the application of Article 6:258. It seems, instead, possible to consider the arbitration tribunal as entitled to adapt the contract despite the lack of an express agreement by the parties in light of the recognised principle of synchronised competence[416] and on the mandatory nature of Article 6:258, that for this reason should prevail on Article 1024(4). Thus, like courts, arbitrators should have the power to modify the contract when the conditions provided in such article are met independent of any specific agreement by the parties.

As to the application of Article 6:258, it has to be noted that it is strictly applied by arbitrators in cases where the market conditions change and cause economic difficulties to one of the parties in complying with its original contractual obligations. An example of such strict and cautious approach is the ICC case n. 8486/1996.[417] In such decision, that did not deal with the issue of adaptation of a contract but of its termination upon the occurrence of unforeseen events, the tribunal held that Article 6:258 was not applicable since the relevant conditions were not met. In particular, this case concerned an international contract for the sale of a manufacturing plant entered into between a Dutch company (the seller) and a Turkish (the buyer) and governed by Dutch law. A dispute arose between the parties in relation to the payment of the price. In particular, the buyer paid only 3% of the agreed price, as advance payment, instead of 5%, as provided by the contract, and did not open the letter of credit within the term set forth in the agreement since it was experiencing financial problems due to an excessive fall of the products price in the relevant market. As a consequence, the seller offered to deliver only half of the plant and, upon the acceptance by the buyer, issued an invoice for half of the price originally agreed. However, the buyer then proposed to the seller to pay only 60% of the reduced price. The seller did not accept such proposal and, upon the failure of negotiations, it started an arbitration proceeding. The buyer claimed that 'it was discharged of its obligations under the contract because of the dramatic drop of the price of the relevant product [to be manufactured by means of plant to be sold under the contract] on the Turkish market, which amounted to hardship'.[418] The sole arbitrator rejected such claim holding that:

---

415. In the sense of the impossibility for arbitrators to adapt the contract, see A. Van den Berg, R. Van Delden & H.J. Snijders, *Netherlands Arbitration Law*, 34 (Kluwer Law and Taxation Publishers 1993).
416. See §3.01.
417. ICC case n. 8486/1996, 1999 XXIV YBCA, 162 (1996). The same strict approach in the application of Art. 6:258 was adopted in the award of 10 September 1975 issued by the arbitration tribunal of the Netherlands Oils, Fats and Oilseeds Trade Association, 1977 II YBCA, 156, which did not recognise as a force majeure event the drop of market price of the coconut oil to be sold under the contract with the result that the defendant was not discharged from its obligations and the claimant was granted damages for breach of contract.
418. ICC case n. 8486/1996, *id.*, at 164.

the conditions of [Art. 6:258] are not met in the present case. We start from the premise that [Art. 6:258] must be applied with the utmost restraint because, among others, it is a special rule with respect to the general possibility, under Art. 6:248(2) together with Art. 3:12 of the Dutch Civil Code, to consider certain contractual provisions inapplicable on grounds of reasonableness and fairness in certain circumstances ... This restraint is also in line with international contractual and arbitral practice. It is also to be taken into consideration in the context of Dutch national law.[419]

Moreover, the arbitrator reaffirmed the principle that in international commercial contracts it has to be assumed that 'the parties take the risks of performing under and carrying out the contract upon themselves unless a different allocation of risk is expressly provided for in the contract [for instance, by inserting in the agreement an adaptation clause]'[420] and, consequently, it concluded that '[t]he rising of a private manufacturing sector and the connected fall in the price [of the product] described therein, as well as the general trade situation in Turkey, only concern the economic frame of the Turkish market and thus fall within the risk sphere of the defendant ... it does not seem maintainable that the defendant wants to shift the commercial risks related thereto onto claimant'.[421]

[3] The Swedish Legal System

In the same vein as Dutch law, the Swedish legal system provides for the power of courts and arbitrators to intervene on contracts terms in both the Contract and Arbitration Acts. In particular, Article 36 of the Contract Act (that has a procedural and mandatory nature)[422] consents the adaptation of the contract in case of supervening events changing the contractual *equilibrium* by providing that:

> A contract term may be adjusted or held unenforceable if the term is unreasonable with respect to the contract's contents, circumstances at the formation of the contract, subsequent events or other circumstances. If the term is of such significance that it shall otherwise be enforceable in accordance with its original terms, the contract may also be adjusted in other respects or held unenforceable in its entirety. With respect to the application of the first paragraph, special consideration shall be given to the need for protection of consumers and others who assume an inferior position in the contract relationship. The first and second paragraphs shall be given similar application to terms in other legal relationships than that of contract.[423]

---

419. *Ibid.*, 166.
420. *Ibid.*, at 168. With regard to the principle of assumption of risk in international contracts, *see also* ICC case n. 1512/1971, *supra* n. 312. Such approach is the prevailing view in international arbitration (*see* §3.04).
421. ICC case n. 8486/1996, *supra* n. 417. Moreover, the arbitrator in reaching its decision took into account that the defendant was aware of the Turkish market situation and, consequently, it held that the unforeseeability condition provided for by Art. 6:258 was not met.
422. *See* M. Bogdan, *Private International Law as Component of the Law of the Forum*, 241 (Hague Academy of International Law 2012).
423. As translated by U. Bernitz, *Swedish Standard Contracts Law and the EC Directive on Contract Terms*, http://www.scandinavianlaw.se/pdf/39-1.pdf (moreover, Art. 36 provides that, with

The reference made by such provision to the concept of unreasonableness of contract terms (not only included in standard agreements but also in the those negotiated between the parties) recalls the principle of good faith. Indeed, it would be against the latter to maintain a term of the agreement that upon the occurrence of an unforeseen event has become unreasonable[424] and, as such, not compatible anymore with the new context and conditions within which the contract has to be performed.[425] Moreover, Article 36 provides for the possibility not only to adjust a single term of the agreement but also, in case such condition is so relevant that the rest of the contract could not reasonably be enforced without changing it, to modify other terms of the agreement.

With regard to long-term contracts, Article 36 has been more frequently applied in relation to consumer agreements than to those concluded between companies.[426] Indeed, it seems that only in one case a commercial contract was adapted on the basis of such provision.[427] In this decision, the Supreme Court dealt with a forty-nine years

---

regard to the adjustment of consumer contracts, Art. 11 of the Swedish Act on consumer contracts (1994:215) applies). A similar provision can also be found in the Danish, Finnish and Norwegian Contract Acts.

424. As to the issue of what is considered unreasonable in order to trigger the application of Art. 36 see B. Lehrberg, *Scandinavian Jurisdiction*, in *Unexpected Circumstances in European Contract Law*, 107 (E. Hondius & Christoph Grigoleit, Cambridge University Press 2011), who underlines that '[i]t follows from the above that the application of the pre-requisite "unreasonable" is based on the contractual situation as a whole. However, it is necessary that the application of section 36 is directed at (at least) one specific contract clause. It is not possible to adjust the contract only because it is unreasonable in general, if no specific unreasonable contract clause could be identified. The travaux préparatoires to the section and case law provide clear and simple solutions only in a few cases. In other cases the application of the pre-requisite "unreasonable" is often a rather complicated task. However, some important guidelines are suggested in the preparatory works. A contract clause can be judged as unreasonable solely on basis of the content of the contract. A contract clause can also be considered as unreasonable per se, even if it is not accompanied by any aggravating circumstances. Some contractual clauses are even considered unreasonable regardless of the circumstances. Clauses that are in conflict with the law or morals are usually mentioned, although all of those are not considered as unreasonable. However, the judgment in respect to a specific contract clause often depends on the contents of the contract as a whole. A party who seems to have been treated unfairly in one clause is often compensated in another. A clause which hands over the right to decide upon important issues to one of the parties is often to be considered as unreasonable'. *See also Id., Unexpected Circumstances – National Report from Sweden*, www.unexpected-circumstances. org (2005); *Id., Renegotiation Clauses, the Doctrine of Assumptions and Unfair Contract Terms*, 3 E.R.P.L., 265 (1998).
425. *See* C. Ramberg, *Obligations, Contracts and Sales*, in *Swedish Legal System/Contract Law and Obligations*, 284 (M. Bogdan, Norstedts Juridik 2010), who, however, underlines that '[t]he application of this provision is very restricted. It has to be an unforeseen supervening event which ought not have been foreseen at the time of conclusion of the contract. Furthermore, the change must be so fundamental that the new situation in effect entails a wholly new contractual relationship'. The implication of a different contractual relationship upon the occurrence of unforeseen events seems to recall the doctrine of frustration applied in Common law.
426. *Ibid.*; *Id., Sweden*, 12 ERCL, 506–513 (2006); Lehrberg, *Unexpected Circumstances – National Report from Sweden, supra* n. 424, at 6, who notes that '[t]he conditions for an adjustment under section 36 are enhanced if the contract is between two consumers rather than between two businesses. Section 36 has been rarely and cautiously applied in commercial relations'.
427. *See* NJA case 1983, 385 et seq., as cited in Ramberg, *Sweden, id.*, at 511 and in Lehrberg, *id*, at 9.

agreement for the lease of land whose rent was indexed to the price of wheat. During the life of the contract, the leaseholder claimed for an increase of the rent and for the application of the consumer price index since the one provided in the contract had resulted not to be suitable for the determination of land's rents. The Court upheld such claims and adjusted the contract (although the rent was increased by an amount lower than that asked by the leaseholder). The limited application of Article 36 to business to business long-term contracts is also due to the fact that in such cases parties are supposed 'to foresee the possibility of changing circumstances and consequently to address such possibilities in their contract (by including hardship-clauses, index-clauses, termination-clauses or *force majeure*-clauses). Parties failing to insert such clauses in their long-term agreement may be considered to have undertaken the risk of supervening events'.[428] Therefore, it is likely that, in gas sale disputes, the arbitration tribunal, even if the applicable procedural law is the Swedish one, would not easily adapt the contract upon the occurrence of unforeseen events affecting the balance of gas sale agreements on the basis of Article 36.

As said above, the Swedish legal system expressly provides grants arbitrators the power to intervene on contracts terms by providing, at Article 1(2) of the 1999 Swedish Arbitration Act, establishes that:

> Disputes concerning matters in respect of which the parties may reach a settlement may, by agreement, be referred to one or several arbitrators for resolution. Such an agreement may relate to future disputes pertaining to a legal relationship specified in the agreement. The dispute may concern the existence of a particular fact. In addition to interpreting agreements, the filling of gaps in contracts can also be referred to arbitrators.[429]

However, unlike the Dutch Arbitration Act, such article only refers to the possibility for the arbitration tribunal to fill the gaps originally left open by the parties at the moment of the conclusion of the contract (provided that the parties have expressly conferred such power on arbitrators)[430] and not to adapt the latter upon the occurrence of unforeseen events. In this regard, it was underlined that in practice it is

---

428. Ramberg, *Obligations, Contracts and Sales*, supra n. 425, at 285.
429. Available in English on www.sccinstitute.com.
430. It was held that such authorisation could also be implied by the interpretation of the contract, for instance, in case 'the substantive clauses of a contract with an arbitration clause are written in such a way as to presuppose a subsequent supplementation, then the arbitrators are empowered to fill gaps'. *See* L. Heuman, *Arbitration Law of Sweden*, 152–153 (Jurisnet 2003). *See also* K.I. Hobér, *Arbitration Reform in Sweden*, 17 Arb Intl 351, 357 (2001), who notes that 'it is doubtful that the provision adds very much to the already existing powers of the arbitrators. It would seem that interpretation of and gap-filling with respect to contracts form part of the customary methods of interpretation of contracts and as such would normally be covered anyway by the arbitration agreement in question. It should be pointed out in this connection that while arbitrators have the right to fill gaps in contracts, they can exercise such a right only within the limits set by the parties. Consequently, the arbitrators may not, e.g. ruler *ultra petita*'. As to the issue of whether the arbitrators' decision amending or supplementing the contract constitutes an award enforceable under the New York Convention or it is a mere contractual decision, *see* J. Sekolec & N. Eliasson, *The UNCITRAL Model Law on Arbitration and the Swedish Arbitration Act: A Comparison*, in *The Swedish Arbitration Act of 1999, Five Years On*, at 178 (L. Heuman & S. Jarvin, Jurisnet 2006), who affirms that, although in principle such award should be recognized as a judicial decision, due to its declaratory nature '(i.e.,

Chapter 3: Arbitrators Contracts Without an Adaptation Clause §3.03[D]

not so simple to distinguish the filling of gaps left open by the parties when concluding the contract and the adaptation of the latter's terms upon the occurrence of unforeseen events changing the contract's balance.[431] Moreover, in light of the principle of synchronised competence, it has to be considered possible for arbitrators to adjust the contract upon the occurrence of unforeseen events in light of Article 36 of the Swedish Contract Act, bearing, of course, in mind all the above-mentioned limits regarding its application to commercial contracts.

[D] Conclusions on the Procedural Law Perspective

The legal systems analysed above have shown a different approach towards the issue of the adaptation of contracts by courts and arbitrators upon the occurrence of unforeseen events that alter their balance. Such differences do not only depend on the belonging to the civil or common law area since we have seen that within the same legal family the position towards the problem of the adjustment of contracts considerably varies from a conservative approach – that in general does not recognise the power of judges and arbitrators to intervene on contract's terms – to a less conservative view that, instead, considers possible such intervention upon the occurrence of specific conditions. In particular, the first position, in the civil law area, is adopted by the French, Belgian and Swiss legal systems and, in the common law area, by the English and US systems (although with some differences). Therefore, these laws provide two solutions in case of supervening events making the contract unbalanced by rendering the performance of one of the parties excessively burdensome: termination of the contract or performance without adaptation to the new circumstances. However, from the analysis carried out it has also emerged that, even in the most conservative legal systems, there are some openings by the case law towards the adaptation of contracts mainly based on the principle of good faith.

The second approach is, instead, taken by the German, Dutch and Swedish laws that expressly provide courts and arbitrators with an adaptation power (even in this case the solution of the legislator is mainly based on the principle of good faith). Moreover, we have seen that the position of the Italian system can be considered in-between the two mentioned views since there is a statutory recognition of the concept of hardship (Article 1467 of the Civil Code) and of the consequent possibility for the advantaged party to offer to adjust the contract in order to rebalance it, while, the legislator does not confer the authority to adjust the contract upon judges and arbitrators. However, even in this system, the case law, in some circumstances, has recognised such power.[432]

---

declaring the existence of a contract term binding on the parties as compared to condemning a party to perform an obligation)' it should not be considered enforceable.
431. See N. Horn, *The Procedures of Contract Adaptation and Renegotiation in International Commerce*, in *Adaptation and Renegotiation of Contracts in International Trade and Finance*, supra n. 214, at 173 et seq.
432. As seen at §3.03[B], the general rule in the Italian legal system is that provided by Art. 2908 of the Civil Code, whereby judges (and, consequently, arbitrators) are entitled to create, modify or extinguish legal relationships (i.e., to issue the so called "constitutive decisions"), in which

In light of the above, we can conclude that, from a procedural perspective, if the applicable law is the German, Dutch or Swedish one (or a different law containing similar provisions in term of adaptation of contracts) arbitrators should be entitled to adjust long-term gas sale agreements without an adaptation clause, provided that all the relevant triggering conditions established by the applicable law and the relevant case law are met. The same conclusions can be made in case the place of arbitration is one of the above-mentioned countries on the basis of the relevance given to the arbitral seat with regard to the determination of the *lex arbitri*.[433] Therefore, the problem arises when the procedural arbitration law or the place of arbitration is not one of those aforementioned or one with the same characteristics. As a consequence, in such situations, it has to be determined whether it is still possible for arbitrators to adjust the contract even if the applicable arbitration law does not provide them with such power.

Before proceeding with the analysis, two controversial scenarios that can occur have to be mentioned. The first is the case in which the parties select as place of arbitration a country whose legal system does not recognise the arbitrators' power to adapt the contract and as *lex arbitri* a law that, instead, provides for such authority. Although this situation is rare since usually parties do not choose as *lex arbitri* a law different from that of the seat of arbitration,[434] it can nevertheless occur. In this regard, the question is whether the choice of an arbitration law providing for the aforementioned power can be considered equal to the inclusion in the contract of an adaptation clause granting such authority to arbitrators. Indeed, in both cases there is an element in the agreement that is the expression of the parties' will to adapt the contract when it becomes unbalanced. As seen below,[435] the general approach in international arbitration is in favour of contract's adjustment if the parties provided so on the basis of the *pacta sunt servanda* principle. In other words, arbitrators tend to fulfil the parties' will as expressed in the agreement and, consequently, if there is a contract's provision representing an indication of the parties' intention to adapt the agreement it should be upheld. Since it seems possible to consider the choice of a *lex arbitri* that provides arbitrators with the power to intervene on contract's terms as an indication of such will, consequently the arbitration tribunal should be entitled to adapt the contract.

However, it has to be noted that a conflict could arise with the arbitration law of the seat if the denial of the arbitrators' adjustment power is provided by mandatory rule of such law. Indeed, the parties' procedural autonomy is limited by the compliance with the mandatory rules of the law of the place of arbitration. Although the latter usually just concerns the principles of due process and equality of treatment of the parties, there are some exceptions.[436] Therefore, it will be necessary to carry out a

---

the adaptation of contracts is clearly included, only when expressly provided by the law (*see*, for instance, Art. 1384 of the Civil Code granting the judge the power to equitably reduce the amount of the penalty provided by the parties in case of breach of contract; Arts 1657 and 1660 of the Civil Code regarding the determination of the price and the variations to the original project of construction contracts and contracts for the supplying of services).

433. *See* §3.03.
434. *Ibid.*
435. *See* §3.04.
436. *See* §3.03.

case-by-case analysis in order to see which are the mandatory norms of the arbitration law of the seat. An example of a mandatory provision not granting arbitrators the authority to adjust the contract is represented by Article 2908 of the Italian Civil Code. Such norm – that has a procedural nature although placed in the substantive law's body of rules – establishes that courts (and, consequently, arbitrators in light of the principle of synchronised competence) can issue the so called "constitutive decisions" (i.e., decisions creating, modifying or extinguishing legal rights), in which the judicial adjustment of the contract is included, only when it is expressly provided by statutes. Among these cases, however, it is not comprised, as a general rule, the adaptation of agreements in case of hardship. As seen, Article 1467 of the Civil Code only consents the advantaged party to offer the counterparty to reduce the contract in order to rebalance it, although some decisions recognised in particular circumstances the power of judges and arbitrators to adjust the contract in such situation.[437] A similar problem can also be found in case the procedural applicable law, although not expressly denying the power of arbitrators to adjust the contract, belongs to a legal system that in general does not recognise the concept of hardship or *imprévision* and only in some exceptional cases expressly provides courts and arbitration tribunals with the power to modify agreements.[438] In this situation, it seems possible to identify, in light of the general characteristics of the legal system, a sort of implicit mandatory provision denying the adaptation power of courts and arbitrators.

In this regard, it has to be underlined that the problem of the possible conflict between the contract and parties' will, on one side, and the procedural law, on the other, seems not to be addressed (or not deemed to be relevant and critical to the purpose of the decision of the case) by arbitration tribunals when facing disputes regarding long-term gas sale agreements providing for an adaptation clause. In this situation, the parties' will expressly affirmed in the contract seems to be considered as prevailing on any other element. In light of such view, although no specific decisions were found on this point, it seems possible to adopt the same approach even in case the agreement provides as *lex arbitri* a law entitling arbitration tribunals to adapt it while the law of the seat does not grant such authority. However, in both cases, it would remain the problem in the event that such denial is established by a mandatory norm. As seen below[439] in the Author's opinion, the answer to the question of whether arbitrators are entitled to adjust long-term gas sales agreements, despite that the procedural applicable law does not grant them such authority and the presence of an adaptation clause in the contract, has to be found in the principle of good faith. This also in consideration of the fact that the choice of the arbitration law and of the seat could not be determined by the intention of the parties to adjust or not the contract but by other factors like, for example:

- the need to find a compromise between the parties' requests when negotiating the contract;

---

437. *See* §3.03[B].
438. An example of such case is the French law (*see* §3.03[A][1]).
439. *See* §3.06.

- the importance of particular place with regard to international arbitrations;
- the neutrality and impartiality reasons.

Such elements, indeed, could be the real justifications of the parties' choice and not the possible consequences that the latter might have in terms of the possibility to adapt or not their agreement. Provided that, the above-mentioned conclusion, generally adopted by arbitration tribunals, at the end is correct since it meets the parties' expectations and will when entering into a long-term contract with the characteristics of a gas sale agreement, that is to maintain it alive for all the duration agreed and, consequently, to consent its adaptation if it becomes unbalanced. In such case, therefore, one could say that the nature, structure, scope and characteristics of a long-term sale agreement are better indications of the parties' will than the choice of a procedural law or a seat that, as said, are often made for reasons independent of the relevant provisions in terms of adjustment of contracts by arbitrators.

Moreover, if we apply the above-mentioned reasoning – that allows the adaptation of the contract by arbitrators only if there is a specific clause providing for such power directly or by referring to a procedural law recognising such power – to the opposite situation (i.e., the case in which the parties choose an arbitration law that does not entitle arbitrators to modify the contract and an arbitral seat whose procedural law, instead, recognises such authority), the solution would be different. Indeed, the choice of a *lex arbitri* denying the aforementioned power could be considered as an indication that the parties do not want their agreement to be adapted upon the occurrence of unforeseen events altering its balance in spite of the nature and characteristics of long-term gas sale agreements. Therefore, since arbitration tribunals tend to enforce and fulfil the parties' will, they should not adapt the contract unless such power is provided by a mandatory rule of the procedural law of the seat. Therefore, it would be necessary to carry out a case-by-case analysis of the *lex fori*. As said above, usually the mandatory rules of the law of the seat just concern the principles of due process and equal treatment of the parties. Even when such rules are not limited to these aspects, it is difficult that they regard the courts' and arbitrators' power to adjust the contract. However, there are some exceptions. For instance, Article 6:258 of the Dutch Civil Code analysed above is one of them. Indeed, this provision, that expressly grants courts (and, consequently, arbitrators) with the adaptation power is a mandatory norm that cannot be opt out by the agreement of the parties as stated by Article 6:248.[440]

Even in such case, the considerations made above – in relation to the choice of the *lex arbitri* and the seat as well as to the characteristics and scope of long-term gas sale agreements and the different solution that would turn out in light of the principle of good faith – can apply.

The second scenario in which a conflict could arise due to the parties' choice of the applicable law is the case in which they select a procedural law not providing arbitrators and courts with the power to adapt the contract (as, for instance, French law) and a substantive law, instead, granting such authority (as, for instance, Article

---

440. *See* §3.03[C][2]. Another example is Art. 36 of the Swedish Contract Act, as seen at §3.03[C][3].

313 of the German Civil Code). We have seen above that the fact that a procedural norm is physically contained within the body of substantive law provisions does not change its nature.[441] Therefore, in our example, Article 313 of the German Civil Code has to be considered as part of the German procedural law that is not applicable to the arbitration proceeding since the party chose French law as the relevant procedural law. For the same reason, such article cannot find application as part of the substantive applicable law chosen by the parties (German law) since, as said, it has a procedural nature even if it is located in the German Civil Code. Even in this case, according to the Author, the solution to the issue of the adaptation of contracts by arbitrators has not to be found in the substantive law but in the good faith principle.

[E] Arbitration Rules

A final consideration has to be made with regard to arbitration rules. Institutional arbitration rules, usually, are silent on the issue of the arbitrators powers to adapt the contract. The same approach is adopted by the UNCITRAL Arbitration Rules. However, in some cases, arbitration institutions provide for specific rules for the adaptation of contracts separate and distinct from those regarding arbitration proceedings. Such solution clearly denotes the idea that the adjustment of contracts is not considered as traditional arbitration and, consequently, is not part of the judicial task of arbitrators.

This approach, for instance, is adopted by the Belgian Centre for Arbitration and Mediation (CEPANI), that provides for Adaptation of Contracts Rules.[442] In particular, Article 1 establishes that such rules applies only if the parties 'have so agreed with a specific clause' and if they 'wish to have recourse to a third person whose mission shall be to complete the contract on items unforeseen by them, or to adapt their common intent to new situations'. The third appointed party issues a written recommendation or a decision that is binding for the parties but that does not constitute a judicial decision or an arbitral award.

Similarly, the International Chamber of Commerce (ICC) issued specific rules for adaptation of contract by publishing in 1978 The Rules for the Regulation of Contractual Relations,[443] providing for the possibility for the parties to ask the Standing Committee for the Regulation of Contractual Relations to appoint a third party who, upon parties' request, could issue either a recommendation or a binding decision becoming part of the contract. However, it was specified that parties could also opt for traditional arbitration in order to obtain the adjustment of the contract. The same approach was adopted in the 1985 version of the document providing guidelines for the drafting of an hardship clause.[444] Such document proposed three options in case no agreement could be found by the parties: (1) the maintenance of the original contract; (2) the recourse to courts or arbitrators; (3) the recourse to the Standing Committee for

---

441. *See* §3.01.
442. Available in English on www.cepani.be (currently under revision by a study group).
443. *Adaptation of Contracts* (ICC Publication n. 326 1978).
444. *Force Majeure and Hardship* (ICC Publication n. 421 1985), http://www.trans-lex.org/700650 /_/icc-(ed)-force-majeure-and-hardship-paris-1985-(icc-publ-no-421)/.

the Regulation of Contractual Relations. Therefore, notwithstanding the provision of specific rules and proceeding for contracts' adaptation, the ICC seemed to consider arbitration as a suitable alternative means to obtain the adjustment of the agreement. However, the last version of the hardship clause suggested by the ICC does not provide either for arbitration or the Standing Committee upon the parties' failure to find an agreement. Indeed, the only option proposed in such situation is the termination of the contract. The change in respect to the previous document was justified by the ICC on the basis of the fact that termination 'would in most cases provide an incentive towards' negotiation.[445]

In other cases, although not specific contracts' adaptation rules are provided, mediation or conciliation rules are adopted in order to help the parties to settle their dispute without the issuing of an award.[446]

§3.04 THE INTERNATIONAL ARBITRATION PERSPECTIVE

The problem of the adjustment of long-term contracts not including an adaptation clause was also addressed by international arbitration awards. In general, it can be said that the prevailing position in international commercial arbitration is to strictly apply the principle of *pacta sunt servanda* and, consequently, arbitrators (even when they are acting as *amiable compositeurs*) tend not to intervene on the contract in case of hardship, unless the latter provides for an adaptation clause (or, at least, the applicable law allows them to do so). The main reason behind such strict approach is that parties in international commercial contracts are presumed to be skilled and competent professionals and, therefore, to have the capacity to include in the agreement all the necessary clauses to protect their interests against the occurrence of unforeseen events altering the contract balance (as, for instance, price review and hardship clauses). It follows that, in the lack of such provisions, parties are considered as having accepted the risk that during the contract life, its *equilibrium* might change and that such risk will be borne by the disadvantaged party. The only exception is the suspension or termination of the contract when the supervening circumstance is a force majeure event making the performance impossible. However, even towards such events the approach in international commercial arbitration is strict and, consequently, the relevant remedy is only granted in exceptional circumstances.[447] The same severe approach is adopted with regard to the application of the *rebus sic stantibus* doctrine.

---

445. *ICC Force Majeure Clause 2003, ICC Hardship Clause 2003* (ICC Publication n. 650), http://www.trans-lex.org/700700/_/icc-force-majeure-clause-2003-icc-hardship-clause-2003-icc-publication-no-650/.
446. *See*, for instance, the UNCITRAL Conciliation Rules; the International Mediation Rules of the International Centre for Dispute Resolution (the international division of the American Arbitration Association) or the equivalent Mediation Rules of the American Arbitration Association; the Mediation and Conciliation Rules of the Arbitration Chamber of Milan.
447. *See, ex multis*, ICC case n. 3267/1975, Collection of ICC Arbitral Awards 1974–1985 76, 85 (partial award 1975), in which it was affirmed that 'it is a generally accepted principle in international arbitration that the paramount duty of the arbitrator, even as 'amiable compositeur', is to apply the contract of the parties, unless it is shown that the provisions relied on are clearly against the true intent of the parties, or violate a basic commonly accepted principle of

However, it has to be underlined that in some cases arbitrators found in favour of the adaptation of contracts even without a specific clause. In particular, such principle was affirmed in the ICC case n. 2508/1976 regarding an international contract for the supply of fuel governed by Swiss law.[448] The claimant started an arbitration proceeding (with seat in Geneva) upon the defendant's failure to deliver a certain quantity of fuel due to the increase of the oil price that, according to the latter, should imply an adaptation of the contract by modifying the agreed price.

The arbitration tribunal rejected the defendant's allegations on the basis of the *pacta sunt servanda* principle as recognised by Swiss law (unless the maintenance of the contract as it is represents an abuse of right). Provided that, the tribunal specified that such principle can be applied less strictly in relation to international commercial contracts (like the one in dispute). However, in such case, the defendant failed to provide adequate proofs to support its position, in particular, with regard to the serious negative consequences deriving from the increase of the oil price and, in addition, it admitted that the contract represented just a small part of its business. Thus, due to these circumstances, it was not possible for the arbitration tribunal to consider whether or not the contract had to be adjusted. In any case, the principle stated in such decision represents an important recognition in the international arbitration field of the possibility for arbitrators, independent of the existence of an adaptation clause, to depart from the sanctity of contract doctrine when the contractual balance is altered by the occurrence of unforeseen events.[449] It has also to be underlined that such principle was affirmed in a case in which the substantive and procedural[450] applicable law was Swiss

---

public policy'. Such principle was also confirmed by the final award, 1987 YBCA, 87 (1984); ICC case n. 2404/1975, Collection of ICC Arbitral Awards 1974-1985 280, 281 (1975), in which it was held that 'such notion [the rebus sic stantibus principle] has to be strictly applied in particular in case the intention of the parties has been clearly expressed in the contract. And this even more in international contracts where in general parties are aware of the risks that can occur ...' (as freely translated); ICC case n. 1512/1971, *supra* n. 312, at 4 in which it was affirmed that '[t]he principle *'Rebus sic stantibus'* is universally considered as being of strict and narrow interpretation, as a dangerous exception to the principle of sanctity of contracts ... As a general rule, one should be particularly reluctant to accept it [the rebus sic stantibus doctrine] when there is no gap or lacuna in the contract and when the intent of the parties has been clearly expressed ... Caution is especially called for, moreover, in international transactions where it is generally much less likely that the parties have been unaware of the risk of a remote contingency or unable to formulate it precisely'. *See also* Redfern & Hunter, *supra* n. 219, at 536 et seq.; Zaccaria, *supra* n. 333, at 159 et seq.; Berger, *Power of Arbitrators to Fill Gaps and Revise Contracts to Make Sense*, *supra* n. 210, at 1 et seq.; P. Fouchard, E. Gaillard & B. Goldman, *Fouchard, Gaillard, Goldman on International Commercial Arbitration*, 24 et seq. (G. Gaillard & J. Savage, Kluwer Law International 1999); N. Nassar, *Sanctity of Contracts Revisited*, 204 et seq. (Martinus Nijhoff Publishers 1995); Craig, Park & Paulsson, *supra* n. 203, at 142-144; B.G. Poznanski, *The Nature and Extent of an Arbitrator's Powers in International Commercial Arbitration*, 4 J. Int'l Arb., 71 (1987).

448. *See, supra* n. 302.
449. In this case, we do not know which would have been the arbitration tribunal's decision if the defendant had submitted adequate proofs: if the direct adjustment of the contract or just the order to the parties to renegotiate it and, only in case of failure, a direct adaptation by the tribunal.
450. Although in the published extract of the award there is no indication as to the procedural applicable law, we can assume that it is the Swiss one since usually the parties choose the law of the seat (*see* §3.03).

law that we have seen is one of the most conservative with regard to the adaptation of contracts.[451] However, the tribunal did not specify which was the principle of law justifying the possibility to adapt (international) contracts in case of supervening events.

Although in relation to a different situation, the same approach in favour to the adaptation of contracts was taken by the Court of Appeal of Paris in *Intrafor Cofor v. Gagnant*.[452]

In particular, Intrafor Cofor and Gagnant were members of a group of companies and on 24–25 March 1980 concluded an agreement, governed by French law, providing that in case of termination of such contract, Intrafor Cofor could exercise a purchase option of 49% of the holding's stocks (it already owned the remaining 51%). Moreover, it was established that the relevant price should have been reduced by 50% in case Gagnant would terminate the contract within the first five years. Furthermore, the agreement included a general arbitration clause by which all the disputes concerning its validity, interpretation and execution should have been settled by a three-member arbitration tribunal, entitled to act as *amiable compositeur*, with seat in Geneva.

Upon the contract's termination by Gagnant on 12 December 1981, Intrafor, on 22 December 1981, informed the first of its intention to exercise the above-mentioned purchase option, also specifying that the price should have been reduced by 50% (since Gagnant terminated the agreement within the first five years). Furthermore, the parties agreed that Gagnant should have continued its activity until the end of 1982 in order to conclude the works not yet completed. A dispute arose between the parties in relation to the determination of the stocks' price. The arbitration tribunal, considered valid the purchase option exercised by Intrafor Cofor and established that such price should have been determined by a third party on the basis of the group's consolidated net assets on 31 December 1982 and reduced by 25%.

Intrafor Cofor appealed the *exequatur* order of the arbitration award, issued by the President of The Tribunal of Paris, alleging, among the other, that the arbitration tribunal exceeded its jurisdictional function and the relevant powers by modifying the contract and deciding on aspects not provided by the latter nor asked by the parties. In particular, Intrafor Cofor claimed that the arbitration tribunal, instead of considering 22 December 1981 (i.e., the date of the exercise of the purchase option by Intrafor Cofor), as the date for the calculation of the stocks' price, as provided by the agreement, wrongly referred to 31 December 1982 (i.e., the date of the termination by Gagnant of its activity) and reduced the price by only 25% instead of 50%, as set in the contract. However, the Court of Appeal of Paris rejected the Intrafor Cofor's claims holding that the arbitration tribunal did not violate its jurisdictional function since it was entitled to temper the effects deriving from the strict application of the contract's conditions in light of the circumstances of the case and of the equity powers granted to them by the parties. In particular, they correctly considered 31 December 1982 as the date for the evaluation of the stocks' price to be purchased by Intrafor Cofor since until such day

---

451. *See* §3.03[A][3].
452. *Intrafor Cofor v. Gagnant*, Revue de l'Arbitrage, 299 (Court of Appeal of Paris 12 March 1985).

Chapter 3: Arbitrators Contracts Without an Adaptation Clause §3.04

Gagnant worked for the group of companies and, consequently, the sale price had also to reflect the value of such activity. As to the price's reduction by only 25%, according to the Court, the arbitrators correctly held that it was justified in light of the fact that Intrafor Cofor was in part responsible for the termination of the contractual relationship with Gagnant. In this regard, the arbitration tribunal referred to the courts' power to reduce the amount of penalties (notwithstanding, in this case, the reduction of the price was not provided upon the occurrence of a breach of contract) as recognised by French law.[453]

In this case, the position taken, first, by arbitrators and, then, by the Court of Appeal of Paris, in favour of the adaptation of contracts was mainly justified on the fact that the arbitration tribunal was granted *ex aequo et bono* powers that are recognised as allowing arbitrators to temper the effects of the contract in light of the particular facts of the case.[454]

Another relevant decision to be mentioned is the one issued by the Swiss Federal Tribunal in the *Compagnie Maritime* case.[455] Although it concerned a problem of filling the gaps and not of adaptation of contracts due to change of circumstances, it is, however, worth to be analysed for the reference made to the principle of good faith. Such case regarded a long-term charter-party (twenty years) of a ship, to be used for the transportation of LNG from Algeria to Belgium, concluded on 31 October 1973 between *N.V. Belgische Sceehpvaartmaatschappij-Compagnie Maritime Belge* ("CMB"), the owner of a ship, and *N.V. Distrigas* ("Distrigas"), the charterer. The contract was governed by Belgian law and included a general arbitration clause providing for ICC arbitration with seat in Geneva.

On 29 March 1981, the parties entered into an *addendum* to such contract providing that, upon the charterer's request made within the end of the eighteenth year, the parties would have negotiated an extension of the charter-party. In case of no agreement, the charterer would be entitled to exercise a purchase option of the ship at a price equal to its scrap value.

In 1996, the parties started the negotiations for the extension of the charter-party (until 2014) and found an agreement on all the conditions except for a different purchase option clause that Distrigas wanted to include. As a consequence, on 30 August 1998 Distrigas, according to the above-mentioned *addendum*, exercised the purchase option therein provided and, therefore, stopped paying the rent and asked CMB to cooperate in order to transfer the property of the ship. However, CMB contested the exercise of the option by Distrigas and did not deliver the ship. The latter, after having obtained by the Tribunal of Aversa a provisional measure ordering CMB to

---

453. *See* §3.03[A][1]. This is an example of the application of the principle of synchronised competence (*see* para §3.01).
454. The same approach was taken, for instance, in the ICC case n. 4972/1989, Collection of ICC Arbitral Awards 1986–1990, 380 (1989), in which it was underlined that arbitrators, acting as *amiable compositeurs*, are entitled to temper the effects of a contractual clause or to rule out it even in cases where no abuse of right is committed by a party. Indeed, the tribunal specified that in some situations also the legitimate exercise of a right can have inequitable consequences.
455. *See supra* n. 301.

provide it with the ship as of 2 December 1998, started an arbitration proceeding. Among the other, Distrigas requested the tribunal to declare that it validly exercised the purchase option and, as a consequence, that since 1 November 1998 it had become the owner of the ship whose price was equal to its scrap value at such date. However, the arbitrators rejected the Distrigas' claim since, in its opinion, the latter did not validly exercise the purchase option provided by the *addendum*. In particular, such conclusion was based on the fact that the parties had found an agreement on each clause of the prolongation of the charter-party apart from just the new purchase option proposed by Distrigas. From such circumstances, the tribunal inferred that the parties' will was to keep the contract by extending it and not to terminate it (and, consequently, to allow Distrigas to buy the ship). In the opposite case, indeed, the disagreement between the parties would have concerned more than just a clause. Therefore, the arbitrators, in light of the principle of good faith, completed the contract that was under negotiation by the parties (i.e., the extension of the charter-party) in order to fulfil their expectations and added the only missing provisions, i.e., the purchase option clause. In particular, it included in the new contract the old clause that was provided by the *addendum*. In this regard, it was affirmed that:

> Belgian law consents to complete a contract on the basis of the good faith principle, in particular in case of long-term contracts, like the one in dispute. As a consequence, the agreement on the extension of the charter-party has to be completed by including the purchase option already provided in the charter-party that had to be extended.[456]

Distrigas challenged such award before the Swiss Federal Tribunal alleging, among the other, that the arbitration tribunal, by completing the contract, exercised a power that had not been conferred to it by the parties by means of the arbitration clause and had decided on an issue that was not submitted to arbitration by the parties. The Federal Tribunal rejected such claim holding that the arbitrators did not exceed their jurisdictional powers since the arbitration clause was enough broad to embrace any dispute related to the charter-party and to provide the arbitrators with the authority to adopt the remedy they granted. In particular, the arbitrators had to decide whether the contract had to be considered as terminated or, according to the will of the parties, as still in force. The arbitral tribunal opted for the second solution since the parties' intention to keep the contract alive was demonstrated by the fact that they had found an agreement on all the conditions of the extended charter-party except for just the purchase option clause proposed by Distrigas. As a consequence, the arbitrators had to answer the question of what the parties would have done if they had known that the purchase option clause proposed by Distrigas could have not been included in the new contract. The answer, according to the arbitration tribunal, was that Distrigas would have proposed to include the old purchase option clause provided in the original charter-party (and, namely, in the *addendum*) and that CMB in good faith would not have refused such proposal. Thus, the arbitrators completed the contract by means of interpretation of the parties' intentions and the Federal Tribunal considered that also

---

456. *Ibid.*, at 500.

such activity was included in the arbitration clause. Moreover, the Federal Tribunal affirmed that neither the *lex arbitri* (i.e., the Swiss international private law) nor the *lex fori* (i.e., Swiss law) nor the *lex causae* (i.e., Belgian law) prevented arbitrators to complete a contract, even without an express authorisation of the parties. In particular, it was specified that Belgian law only prevents to modify a contract on the basis of the principle of good faith but not to complete it (as it happened in such case).

The Federal Tribunal also rejected the Distrigas' claim by which it alleged that the arbitrators exceeded their authority by deciding beyond the parties' submissions. In particular, it was underlined that Distrigas in its conclusions, subordinately, requested the arbitrators to grant it any remedy considered equitable and appropriate. Therefore, upon the rejection of the main claim of Distrigas (i.e., that it correctly exercised the purchase option) by the arbitration tribunal, the latter adopted the remedy it considered more equitable and, consequently, the Federal Tribunal affirmed it did not decide beyond what the parties claimed.[457]

As said, this decision is particularly relevant since it recognised the possibility of arbitrators to intervene on long-term contracts on the basis of the good faith principle, independent of an adaptation clause, provided that the applicable law does not prevent it. Although, the reference to good faith was made in relation to the filling the gaps activity, it also seems possible to employ the same principle with regard to the adaptation of contracts upon the occurrence of unforeseen events. Indeed, the filling the gaps, adaptation and integrative interpretation often overlap and are not so clearly distinct and different.[458] However, it has to be underlined that, in our opinion, the Tribunal, in determining whether the arbitrators were entitled to intervene on the contract, should have not also considered the substantive applicable law (Belgian law) but only the procedural applicable law (Swiss law). Indeed, as seen, the latter is only relevant in order to determine the arbitrators' powers.[459] Moreover, with regard to the procedural applicable law, the Tribunal affirmed an important principle: if the procedural applicable law is silent on the issue of the arbitrators' power to intervene on a contract, it does not mean that they are prevented from doing it.[460] In this case, the Tribunal considered silent the Swiss law although we have seen that the latter adopts a conservative approach towards the issue of the courts' and arbitrators' adaptation power and, in general, with regard to the possibility to adjust the contract.[461]

The reference to the principle of good faith was also made in the ICC case n. 9994/2001,[462] above analysed, concerning a long-term license and sale agreement between a US company ("Defendant") and a French company ("Claimant"), governed by French law and not including an adaptation clause. In such case, a dispute arose

---

457. It is interesting to note that the reference to the fact that the subordinate claim of the claimant entitled the arbitrators to intervene on the contract (by requesting to grant any remedy considered equitable and appropriate) was the same used by the Italian case law (*see* §3.03[B]).
458. *See* Horn, *supra* n. 219.
459. *See* §3.01.
460. On the issue of when the procedural applicable law is actually silent with regard to the arbitrators' power to adapt the contracts *see* §3.06.
461. *See* §3.03[A][3].
462. *See supra* n. 256.

between the parties upon the determination of a new price of the raw material supplied by the Claimant to the Defendant in consideration of the increase of the costs due to the more severe conditions and control imposed by a government agency in relation to the collection of the human placenta of which such material was made. The parties did not reach an agreement on the new price and, upon the Defendant's termination of the contract, the Claimant started an arbitration proceeding. In this case, the tribunal affirmed that, even under French law (i.e., one of the most conservative systems), parties, upon the occurrence of unforeseen events altering the contract balance, have the duty to renegotiate and adjust it on the basis of the principle of good faith and regardless of the existence of an adaptation clause. Moreover, it held that such principle 'is also prevailing in international commercial law'.[463] Although the tribunal adopted a cautious approach since it did not directly adapt the contract by fixing the new price on the basis of good faith, such decision represents a further recognition of the fact that such principle is deemed to govern the execution of long-term commercial contracts. As a consequence, the latter can be considered as implying a duty of the parties to adjust the agreement in order to rebalance it. Indeed, it would be against good faith to force a party to perform a contract without adapting it upon the occurrence of unforeseen events altering its balance and making such performance excessively burdensome. Moreover, the tribunal recognised that the termination of the contract is not the best solution in these cases since the intention of the parties is to maintain their relationship.

§3.05 THE SCOPE OF THE ARBITRATION AGREEMENT AND ARBITRABILITY

The analysis of the issue of the arbitrators' power to adjust contracts upon the occurrence of unforeseen events involves, in addition to the procedural aspect, other two elements: the scope of the arbitration agreement and the notion of arbitrability.

With regard to the first, it has to be noted that usually arbitration agreements are quite broad and general. They normally provide that all, or any, disputes related to, or arising out of, a contract shall be settled, or decided, by arbitration according to a specific set of rules or a national procedural law (as an alternative, parties can choose an ad hoc arbitration providing for a specific discipline applicable to that specific dispute). The same arbitration standard clause provided by the most important arbitration institution are broad and extended. For instance, the one suggested by the ICC provides that:

> All disputes arising out of or in connection with the present contract shall be finally settled under the Rules of Arbitration of the International Chamber of Commerce by one or more arbitrators appointed in accordance with the said Rules.[464]

In the same vein, the London Court of International Arbitration (LCIA) recommended clause provides that:

---

463. *Ibid.*, at 1 (the arbitrators referred to the UNIDROIT Principles).
464. Available in English on www.iccwbo.org.

Chapter 3: Arbitrators Contracts Without an Adaptation Clause §3.05

Any dispute arising out of or in connection with this contract, including any question regarding its existence, validity or termination, shall be referred to and finally resolved by arbitration under the LCIA Rules, which Rules are deemed to be incorporated by reference into this clause.[465]

Leaving aside for a moment the question whether arbitrators have the procedural power to adapt the contract, it has to be determined if the reference to the notion of dispute contained in the general arbitration clause also encompasses the adaptation of the contract when no agreement can be reached by the parties by means of renegotiation. In other words, it has to be determined whether the traditional notion of legal dispute can also include the adjustment of the contract.

The negative answer to such question is based on the idea that a legal dispute is traditionally considered as a conflict with regard to existing rights and obligations with the consequence that its resolution is 'the adjudication of pre-existing rights in a yes-or-no decision'.[466] According to such view, the adaptation of a contract (as well the gaps-filling task) is not considered as arbitration since it does not deal with existing rights and obligations but with future ones. By means of adaptation, arbitrators would create the content of the future relationship between the parties and '[s]uch creative exercise is traditionally deemed incompatible with the nature and essence of arbitration'[467] being, instead, considered more as an expert's task. It follows that the relevant award would not be a traditional judicial award and, consequently, it could not be enforced under the New York Convention.

---

465. Available in English on www.lcia.org. Similar clauses are those suggested, among the others, by the UNCITRAL Arbitration Rules; the American Arbitration Association and the International Centre for Dispute Resolution (the international division of the American Arbitration Association); the Belgian Centre for Arbitration and Mediation (CEPANI); the Arbitration Chamber of Milan.
466. Berger, *Power of Arbitrators to Fill Gaps and Revise Contracts to Make Sense*, supra n. 210, at 1-2, who does not agree on such view and affirms that 'it is the changing paradigm of international contract law which speaks in favour of a broad competence of international arbitrators to adapt contracts and fill gaps' (16). In the same sense, *see* Brunner, *supra* n. 210, at 496, who affirms that the adaptation by arbitrators would depend on parties' request that has to be exhaustive and sufficiently proved. As a consequence, 'the outcome of the adaptation process by the tribunal is not open that it would not be suited to classical arbitral adjudication in the sense of a "yes or no" decision'. With particular regard to long-term contracts, contrary to a distinction between two types of arbitrations and in favour of the so called "oneness of arbitration, *see* R. David, *Arbitration in International Trade*, 411 (Kluwer Law and Taxation Publishers 1985), who affirms that '[i]t is artificial and it is in many respects deplorable that a distinction should be drawn and contrast made between two varieties of arbitration: the one aiming at the settlement of a legal dispute, the other at the regulation of a contractual relationship. In both cases the same technique is resorted to, the same result is aimed at, the application of the same rules is desirable. The development of a new type of complex and long-term contracts, made necessary by today's technology, adds a special weight to this consideration'. *See also* the discussion at the Conference on Force Majeure and Hardship, organised by the ICC in Paris on 8 March 2001, 6 Unif.L.Rev., 104 (2001), in which it was affirmed that 'the problem of informational asymmetry seems exaggerated: in the exercise of their adaptation powers, arbitrators act within a contractual framework and cannot rewrite or re-invent the contract for the parties. They are bound to restore an original contractual equilibrium and rely in doing so on verifiable data'.
467. *See* L. Beisteiner, *The (Perceived) Power of the Arbitrator to Revise a Contract – The Austrian Perspective*, in *Austrian Yearbook on International Arbitration*, 84 (C. Kalusegger & P. Klein, Manz'sche Verlags- und Universitätsbuchhandlung 2014).

However, this position can be criticised for two reasons. First, the concept of dispute clearly refers to and includes any conflict or difference between the parties on a particular matter that could not be solved by mutual agreement.[468] With regard to adaptation, it can, therefore, be said that such element is present since there is a difference or conflict between the parties concerning how to adjust a specific term of the contract in light of supervening events. Upon the failure of parties' renegotiations, such difference can be submitted to arbitration as any other dispute in order to be settled. This principle has to be applied, in particular, in case of long-term contracts that, due to their nature, require to be adjusted over the time. In such situation, the standard arbitration clause does not have:

> to receive a standard, or restrictive interpretation. The clause must always be interpreted as part of, and in the light of, the particular contract in which it appears. Here it is used in a long-term contract, with a number of provisions which may require adjustment over the period of that contract. If the conclusion is that the parties contemplated arbitration with a view to their adjustment, and if the language itself of clause 20 is general or wide enough to enable clause 20 to apply to such adjustment, as it certainly is ('all disputes arising in connection with this contract'), then this clause should be interpreted even though in other contexts it might be given a narrow scope.[469]

Second, in our opinion, the statement that, by means of adaptation, arbitrators would not deal with existing rights and obligations, but with future ones, is not correct. Indeed, if an arbitration tribunal revises the price or the Minimum Bill Quantity provided by a take or pay clause (i.e., the most common adjustments regarding a gas sale contract), it does not create new rights or obligations since the obligations to pay the price (and the consequent right to receive the money) and to take a certain amount of gas at a certain date (and the corresponding obligation to make such gas available for the delivery) were already provided in the original agreement and remained unaltered. What changes is the price formula or the amount to be paid for the gas or the minimum quantity of gas to be taken compared to the original contractual provisions. Therefore, the arbitrator does not cancel or establish a right or obligation that before was, or was not, provided by the parties but he just reshapes and modifies existing rights and

---

468. *See*, for instance, s. 82(1) of the English Arbitration Act that provides that '"dispute" includes any difference'. *See also*, D.J. Sutton, J. Gill & M. Gearing, *Russell On Arbitration*, 10–11 (Sweet & Maxwell 2007), who affirm that '[s]ince an arbitrator can be given such powers as the parties wish, he can be authorized to make a new contract between the parties. The parties to a commercial contract often provide that in certain events their contract shall be added to or modified to fit the circumstances then existing, intending thereby to create a binding obligation although they are unwilling or unable to determine just what the terms of the new or modified agreement shall be. To a court such a provision is ineffective as being at most a mere "agreement to agree"; but a provision that the new or modified terms shall be settled by an arbitrator can without difficulty be made enforceable'; R. Merkin & L. Flannery, *Arbitration Act 1996* (Informa 2008).
469. ICC case n. 5754/1988 (unpublished), as cited by Craig, Park & Paulsson, *supra* n. 203, at 112. *See also* the *Timegate* case, *supra* n. 349 and analysed at §3.03[A][4]; the *Compagnie Maritime* case, *supra* n. 301 and analysed at para §3.04.

obligations. Moreover, 'this narrow interpretation of the arbitrator's role does not reflect the practice or indeed the current needs of international trade'.[470]

The second aspect to be considered is the arbitrability issue. It has, indeed, to be determined whether the adaptation of contracts is a matter that can be submitted to arbitration (so called "objective arbitrability"). Without analysing in detail the different criteria for the determination of the law governing the arbitrability,[471] that would go beyond the scope of this work, it is enough to underline that, if the arbitrability issue arises at a pre-award stage (and, and namely, when it has to be decided on the validity of the arbitration agreement), in some cases it was held that the applicable law is that ruling the validity of the arbitration agreement.[472] However, the prevailing view seems to be that supporting the application of the law of the place of the court or of the arbitration tribunal deciding on the question of arbitrability.[473] Such position is based on the fact that the same criterion is employed to resolve the arbitrability issue when it arises at a post-award stage (and, namely, at the moment of the enforcement of the award) according to the New York Convention.

Usually national laws directly identify the disputes that are arbitrable. With regard to the legal systems above analysed in relation to the procedural law, it has to be underlined that they provide for a broad notion of arbitrability by considering arbitrable the dispute concerning a right of which the parties can freely dispose or the dispute characterised by an economic interest. Such broad notion can, therefore, be deemed to encompass the request of adaptation of a gas sale agreement.

The first approach is adopted by French, Italian, Dutch and Swedish law. In particular, Articles 2059 and 2060 of the French Civil Code provide that:

> All persons may make arbitration agreements relating to rights of which they have the free disposal ... One may not enter into arbitration agreements in matters of status and capacity of the persons, in those relating to divorce and judicial separation or on controversies concerning public bodies and institutions and more generally in all matters in which public policy is concerned. However, categories of public institutions of an industrial or commercial character may be authorized by decree to enter into arbitration agreements.[474]

---

470. *See* Fouchard, Gaillard, Goldman, *supra* n. 447, at 25. *See also* the Resolutions of the Fifth International Arbitration Congress on Arbitration, organised by the International Council for Commercial Arbitration (ICCA) in New Delhi on 10 January 1975, available on www.arbitration-icca.org.
471. For an in-depth explanation of the different criteria *see* Born, *supra* n. 240, Ch. 4; Lew, Mistelis & Kroll, *supra* n. 243, Ch. 9.
472. *See Company M v. M SA*, 1989 XIV YBCA, 618 (Court of Appeal of Brussels 4 October 1985).
473. *See, ex multis, Matermaco v. PPM Cranes*, 2000 XXV YBCA, 673 (Tribunal of Commerce of Brussels 20 September 1999); *Fincantieri v. Ministry of Defence of Iraq*, 1996 XXI YBCA, 494 (Court of Appeal of Genoa 7 May 1994); *V. v. G.*, 1993 XVIII YBCA, 143 (Swiss Federal Tribunal 28 April 1992). As to international arbitration awards, *see*, for instance, ICC case n. 8420/1996, 2000 XXV YBCA, 330 (partial award 1996); ICC case n. 6149/1990, 1995 XX YBCA, 41 (1990); ICC case n. 6162/1990, 1992 XVII YBCA, 153 (1990); ICC case n. 4604/1984, 1985 X YBCA, 975 (1984).
474. Available in English on www.legifrance.gouv.fr. The concept of public policy, that potentially can be applied broadly due to its vagueness, has been narrowly interpreted by French Courts in the field of international arbitration in order to favour the arbitrability of disputes regarding international commercial matters (*see* Born, *supra* n. 240, at 962–963).

As said, the same approach is taken by the following provisions: Article 806 of the Italian Code of Civil Procedure ('Parties can submit to arbitration the disputes that arose between them that do not deal with rights of which they cannot freely dispose');[475] Article 1020 of the Dutch Code of Civil Procedure ('All persons may make arbitration agreements relating to rights of which they have the free disposal'.[476] Moreover, as seen above, such provision also consents the parties to ask arbitrators to fill the gaps or to modify their legal relationship);[477] Article 1 of the Swedish Arbitration Act ('Disputes concerning matters in respect of which the parties may reach a settlement may, by agreement, be referred to one or several arbitrators for resolution'.[478] Such provision, as seen above, allows the parties to submit to arbitration the filling of gaps in contracts).[479]

The second approach (i.e., the one referring to the economic interest of the dispute) is, instead, adopted by the Swiss Private International Law (PIL) that, at Article 177(1), provides that '[a]ny dispute of financial interest may be the subject of an arbitration'.[480]

A combination of the above-mentioned approaches characterised the Belgian and German legal systems.[481] In particular, Article 1676 of the Belgian Code of Civil Procedure provides that '[a]ll financial disputes can be submitted to arbitration. The non-financial disputes can be submitted to arbitration if they can be settled'.[482]

In the same vein, Article 1030(1) of the German Code of Civil Procedure establishes that 'Any claim under property law may become the subject matter of an arbitration agreement. An arbitration agreement regarding non-pecuniary claims has legal effect insofar as the parties to the dispute are entitled to conclude a settlement regarding the subject matter of the dispute'.[483]

---

475. As freely translated.
476. Available in English on http://www.dutchcivillaw.com/civilprocedureleg.htm.
477. See §3.03[C][2].
478. Available in English on http://swedisharbitration.se/wp-content/uploads/2011/09/The-Swedish-Arbitration-Act.pdf. In a recent decision, the Swedish Supreme Court gave a broad interpretation of such provision in favour of arbitrability holding that '[a] dispute amenable to out-of-court settlements could include non-arbitrable elements, and include the application of peremptory rules of law ... That a field of law includes peremptory provisions does not, however, automatically imply that issues within that field of law are exempt from settlement by arbitration. The issue to be resolved also in these situations is whether the dispute is amenable to out-of-court settlement. If the peremptory provisions do not prevent the parties from reaching a settlement, then the dispute may be resolved by arbitration ... As noted in the preparatory works to the Swedish Arbitration Act, this view is in line with the international development entailing that an international dispute may be resolved by arbitration, even if a corresponding domestic dispute could not have been resolved in the same matter' (*Moscow City Golf Club v. Nordea Bank*, https://www.arbitration.sccinstitute.com/Views/Pages/GetFile.ashx?portalId=89&cat=79572&docId=1450921&propId=1578, 5-6 (Supreme Court n. T 49 82-11 23 November 2012),).
479. See §3.03[C][3].
480. Available in English on https://www.swissarbitration.org/files/34/Swiss%20International%20Arbitration%20Law/IPRG_english.pdf.
481. The same approach is adopted by Art. 582(1) of the Austrian Code of Civil Procedure.
482. As freely translated.
483. Available in English on http://www.gesetze-im-internet.de/englisch_zpo/englisch_zpo.html#p3542.

The concepts of free disposition and of economic interest are interpreted broadly in order to encompass all commercial disputes and, in particular, those involving international commercial contracts.[484] The same favourable approach towards arbitration is adopted by the US and English legal systems although the relevant arbitration laws are silent on such issue. In particular, the courts have adopted a narrow interpretation and application of the concept of non-arbitrability and, consequently, consider subject to arbitration the most part of disputes.[485]

In light of the above, it can be concluded that, with regard to the arbitrability perspective and the scope of the arbitration agreement, if the arbitration clause is broad it can be deemed to also include the adjustment of the relevant contract that is characterised by the conflict between the parties and by freely disposable economic interests.

§3.06 CONCLUSIONS

The analysis carried out above has shown that the approach to the issue of the adaptation of long-term contracts by courts and arbitrators upon the occurrence of unforeseen events that alter their balance, is different not only between common law and civil law but also within legal systems of the same area. Indeed, we have seen that in the civil law the French, Belgian, Swiss and Italian legal systems adopt a stricter and more conservative approach than the German, Dutch and Swedish laws and do not provide courts and arbitrators with such power. Furthermore, some of them do not even recognise the concept of hardship and, consequently, not even the parties can adjust the contract but only terminate it (if the supervening events make the performance impossible) or perform it without modifications (unless the contract provides for a specific clause allowing the parties to adapt or to terminate the contract in case of hardship). Such approach is similar to that taken by the common law. However, even there, we have seen that the US case law position is less strict than the English one, since, first of all, it recognises the concept of commercial impracticability (i.e., the excessive onerousness) and, second, in some cases courts were granted the authority to adjust the contract.[486]

As mentioned above, in other civil law countries (Germany, Netherlands, Sweden), instead, the position adopted by the legislator and case law is less conservative since the adaptation of the contract by courts and arbitrators is recognised. Provided that, it was also underlined that, even in the most conservative legal systems, the case law, in some circumstances, has expressed a favourable opinion towards the adaptation of contracts, whose balance is altered by unforeseen events, by courts and arbitrators (in some cases, upon the failure of the parties' negotiations).

---

484. For a detailed account on the extensive interpretation of these concepts as adopted by case law and doctrine in order to favour international commercial arbitration *see* Born, *supra* n. 240, at 959 et seq.
485. *Ibid.*
486. *See* §3.03[A][4].

In light of such analysis, it can be concluded that, if the procedural law applicable to the arbitration is the German, Dutch or Swedish one (or other laws containing similar provisions granting arbitrators or judges the power to adjust the contract), the arbitral tribunal should be entitled to adjust gas sale agreements not including an adaptation clause upon the occurrence of unforeseen events altering their balance (as long as the relevant triggering conditions are satisfied). Indeed, although we have seen that the main position in international commercial arbitration is a conservative one since arbitrators tend not to intervene on contracts unless the parties expressly provided so, the arbitrators' adaptation power has a procedural nature and, consequently, the applicable procedural law has to be taken into account.[487] Therefore, in case the latter expressly conferred such authority upon arbitrators, even if the arbitration agreement (or more in general the contract) is silent on this point, they can be considered allowed to adjust the contract as long as all the conditions required for such adaptation are met.

The problem then arises in case the procedural applicable law is silent or expressly prevents courts and arbitrators from adjusting the contract.

As to the first scenario, it is assumed that, if the procedural law is silent, arbitrators are entitled to adapt the contract on the basis of the arbitration agreement.[488] Although, as seen below, the reason justifying the arbitrators' adaptation power, in our opinion, is different, such conclusion can be considered correct since it meets the parties' expectations. Furthermore, it is supported by the observations made above in relation to the arbitrability and scope of arbitration agreement according to which the parties' conflict regarding the adjustment of the contract should be deemed arbitrable and included in the scope of the general arbitration clause.[489]

Provided that, according to the Author, in order to consider the procedural applicable law to arbitration really silent on the issue of adaptation of contracts by arbitrators it is also necessary that the legal system, to which it belongs, in general recognises the concept of hardship (or *imprèvision* or impracticability). Moreover, the procedural law provisions dealing with courts' powers have to be taken into account on the basis of the principle of synchronised competences and of the fact that they belong to the same procedural law system as the arbitration law chosen by the parties.[490] Therefore, it seems difficult, for instance, to consider arbitrators as entitled to adjust the contract in case the procedural applicable law is the French one. Indeed, we have seen that the French legal system, although not containing a provision expressly denying the courts' and arbitrators' contract adaptation power, can be considered as one of the most conservatives in relation to such issue for two main reasons. First of all, the French civil and commercial law in general does not recognise the principle of

---

487. In this regard, it was noted that the procedural law to be taken into account not only includes the *lex arbitri* but also the provisions regarding courts' power. Moreover, the procedural norms can be physically included in the *lex causae*. However, such circumstance does not affect their nature and, therefore, they apply as procedural law provisions and not as substantive law provisions (*see* §3.01).
488. See Frick, *supra* n. 210, at 197.
489. See §3.05.
490. See §3.01.

imprèvision (except for specific statutory provisions) but only the concept of force majeure that makes the performance impossible. Moreover, when the French legislator intended to grant courts (and, consequently, arbitrators) the power to adjust the agreement, it expressly provided so. Therefore, French law expressly recognises such authority only in exceptional cases.[491] It follows that, notwithstanding there is not a norm expressly forbidding, as a general rule, the adaption of contracts by courts and arbitrators, such rule can be implicitly inferred from the aforementioned characteristics of the French legal system.

In light of the above, a procedural law could be deemed silent on the issue of the courts' and arbitrators' power to adjust the contract in case: (1) the legal system to which it belongs in general recognises the concept of hardship (or *imprèvision* or impracticability); (2) neither the arbitration law nor the norms disciplining the courts' procedural powers expressly or implicitly provide, as a general rule, that judges or arbitrators have not the authority to adapt the agreement. If such conditions are not met, the procedural applicable law cannot be considered silent but as not granting arbitrators with the adjustment power.

An example of law that, instead, can be deemed to expressly deny such authority is the one affirming the general rule that courts and arbitrators can issue the so called "constitutive decisions" (i.e., decisions that create, modify or extinguish legal relationships), in which the one adapting the contract can be included, only if it is consented by statutory provisions and the latter do not refer to the adjustment of contracts upon the occurrence of unforeseen events altering their balance (i.e., in case of hardship).[492]

Therefore, in all the aforementioned situations it remains the question whether it is still possible for arbitrators to intervene on the contract in order to rebalance it on the basis of the general arbitration clause despite the procedural applicable law.

In order to answer such question it is, first of all, necessary to remind the peculiarity of gas sale agreements. As seen, the scope pursued by the parties when entering into such contracts is, on the one hand, to guarantee the seller a stable flux of money in order to recover the investments made and, on the other, to provide the buyer with a stable flux of gas in order to meet the market demand without the need to negotiate any time the conditions of the supply. The achievement of such purpose necessarily implies a continuative commercial relationship between the parties. As a consequence, gas sale contracts are characterised by a long duration (around 20–25 years) and by take or pay clauses.[493]

It is, therefore, evident that such agreements are different from the so called "discrete transactions", i.e., contracts that are concluded and executed in a limited

---

491. *See*, §3.03[A][1].
492. *See*, for instance, the Italian legal system that includes such rule in Art. 2908 of the Civil Code and that does not allow, in general, courts and arbitrators to issue a constitutive decision in order to adapt the contract in case of hardship. Indeed, as seen above, Art.1467 of the Civil Code only consents the advantaged party to offer the counterparty to reduce the contract in order to rebalance it, although part of the case law in some circumstances has also considered judges and arbitrators as entitled to adapt the contract according to such provision (*see* §3.02).
493. *See* Ch. 2 and §3.01.

lapse of time and do not require a stable relationship between the parties.[494] For this reason, it is easier for the contractors to foresee and provide for any possible event that might affect the contract which, consequently, tends to be complete and specific. The emphasis is on the provisions of the agreement that remain binding for the parties no matter what changes occur in the market over the time. In this way, the contract tends to be isolated from supervening events that will not determine any modification or adjustment of its terms (the negative or positive effects will be borne by the parties). As Professor Macneil underlined, a pure discrete transaction is characterised, among the other, by a limited parties' personal involvement and communication between them, as well as by 'short agreement process; short time between agreement and performance; short time of performance'. Moreover, this kind of contract 'can be very complete and specific; only remote contingencies (if those) are beyond reasonable planning capacity' (planning that 'is entirely binding') and does not require future cooperation. In particular, unless specifically planned and, consequently, disciplined, there are no parties' 'expectations about trouble in performance or among the participants'. Therefore, 'a truly discrete exchange transaction would be entirely separate not only from all other present relations but from all past and future relations as well' and not flexible.[495] Such contracts give emphasis on the concept of promise and on the idea that the relationship between the parties finds its sole discipline in the agreement. They tend to maximise the predictability of future risks and events at the moment of the conclusion of the contract.[496] As a consequence, in case the contract does not discipline a specific contingency or does not provide for an adaptation clause, it is assumed that the parties decided to allocate the risk on the party negatively affected by such event. This is the approach usually adopted in international arbitration where arbitrators tend to strictly apply the principle *pacta sunt servanda*.[497]

On the contrary, in a gas sale agreement, it is difficult for the parties to do the same since the long duration makes it impossible to foresee all the supervening events that can change the original market conditions on which basis the parties found a specific balance satisfying the reciprocal interests.[498] In particular, the will of the

---

494. Discrete transactions characterised the classical and neoclassical contract law theories.
495. Macneil, *supra* n. 345, at 902–905 However, the Author observes that a pure discrete transaction is rare to be found in practice since a relational component is always present. As a consequence, 'we do find in real life many quite discrete transactions: little personal involvement of the parties, communications largely or entirely linguistic and limited to the subject matter of transaction, the subjects of exchange consisting of an easily monetized commodity and money, little or no social or secondary exchange, and no significant past relations nor likely future relations' (856–857). *See also*, *Id.*, *The Many Futures of Contracts*, 47 S.Cal.L.Rev. 691, 738–740 (1974).
496. The so called "presentation of a transaction", i.e., the 'restricting its expected future effects to those defined in the present' (*Id.*, *Contracts: Adjustment of Long-Term Economic Relations Under Classical, Neoclassical and Relational Contract Law*, 72 N.Y.U.L.Rev. 854, 863 (1978)).
497. See §3.04.
498. Such contracts clearly do not fit the model of discrete transactions typical of classical contract law since they presuppose a relationship between the parties that lasts in time and that are characterised by investments and complexity. They can be included in the kind of contract that Professor Macneil defines as "relational contracts". Due to their characteristics, they require flexibility and cooperation between the parties in order to adapt them upon the occurrence of supervening events altering their balance. An attempt to respond to such needs is made by the

Chapter 3: Arbitrators Contracts Without an Adaptation Clause §3.06

parties, as said, is to build up and maintain a stable profitable relationship guaranteed by the above-mentioned *equilibrium*. Both the latter and the parties' will and expectations are crystallised in the contract that, consequently, can be deemed to represent their objective expression.[499] More in general, due to the fact that gas sale agreements are usually characterised by some standard clauses, it can be said that they crystallise the expectations and will of those operating in such market. It follows that the parties' expectation is to adapt the gas sale contract upon the occurrence of an unforeseen change of the market conditions that altered its *equilibrium* during its life.[500] Such expectation, and the consequent duty to adjust the agreement, find its justification on the principle of good faith that is generally considered applicable to the execution of contracts. Indeed, the analysis carried out above shows that such principle is recognised either by statutory provisions or case law and scholars.[501]

---

neoclassical contract law by recurring to some techniques (in particular, frustration and impossibility doctrines) that allow the parties to be discharged of their obligations without being in breach of contract when the latter is affected by supervening events that make it something different from what originally provided or impossible. However such response is not sufficient, and it is still based on a discrete transaction model. Indeed, relational contracts require to be adjusted during time instead of being terminated since the scope of the parties is to preserve their relationship (*see*, Macneil, *supra* n. 345, at 854 et seq.). For an analysis of discrete and relational transactions and of their application with reference to long-term international commercial contracts, *see* Nassar, *supra* n. 447, 170–171, who affirms that in such transactions 'the operations regulated by the parties' agreement are simply too complex to be all-encompassing and fixed at one point in time as envisaged by the classical theory. Discreteness is difficult to satisfy. There are too many considerations that cannot be finalized at the time of contracting because they depend on the occurrence of a future contingency, or because the parties – due to a lack of, or insufficient information – may be unable to make a final decision regarding some aspects of their relationship. Moreover, the passage of time might simply render the agreement incomplete. In other instance a specific aspect of the contractual content is expected to develop over the course of time ... In such cases, future review of the agreement is inevitable'. *See also* McKendrick, *supra* n. 203; U. Draetta, R.B. Lake & V.P. Nanda, *Breach and Adaptation of International Contracts*, 169 et seq. (Butterworth Legal Publishers 1992).

499. It can be said that the overall contract is the objectification of the parties' will and expectations.
500. *See* ICC case n. 2291/1975, Collection of ICC Arbitral Awards 1974–1985, 274 (1975), in which it was held that 'all commercial transactions are based on the balance of the reciprocal performances and to deny such principle would transform a commercial contract in an aleatory contract based on speculation and hazard. There is a rule of *lex mercatoria* by which the performances shall remain economically balanced and, as a consequence, in almost all the international contracts, the price is, therefore, fixed in consideration of the conditions existing at the moment of the conclusion of the contract and it shall vary in light of the parameters that reflect the variations of the values of the different elements that form the product or the performance' (as freely translated from the original French version). *See also* ICC case n. 2443/1975, *id.*, 276 affirming the principle that the parties have a general duty to cooperate on the basis of the principle of good faith.
501. *See*, for instance, Art. 1134 of the French and Belgian Civil Codes; Art. 2 of the Swiss Civil Code; Art. 1375 of the Italian Civil Code; Art. 242 of the German Civil Code; Art. 6:248 of the Dutch Civil Code (moreover, as seen above, both Art. 313 of the German Civil Code and Art. 6:258 of the Dutch Civil Code, that entitle courts and arbitrators to adapt the contract, contain references to the principle of good faith). With regard to the Denmark, Finland, Norway and Swedish legal systems, *see* O. Lando & H. Beale, *Principles of European Contract Law*, 117–118 (Kluwer Law International 2000). Moreover, like for German and Dutch laws, Art. 36 of the Contract Act, providing for the courts and arbitrators power to adapt the contract, contains, as seen above, a reference to the principle of good faith. As to the US, *see* s. 1-304 UCC ('[e]very contract or duty within this Act imposes an obligation of good faith in its performance and enforcement')

It would be against the principle of good faith to constrain a party to keep on performing a contract that became excessively onerous and unbalanced for it. Indeed, in such case, '[o]nly one party bears the consequences of the unexpected change, while the other is permitted to act opportunistically, unjustly enriching himself by taking advantage of his partner's hardship. This is not to say that contractual parties are required to alleviate each other's hardships. They are expected, however, not to use the

---

and s. 205 of Restatement (Second) of Contracts ('[t]he phrase "good faith" is used in a variety of contexts, and its meaning varies somewhat with the context. Good faith performance or enforcement of a contract emphasises faithfulness to an agreed common purpose and consistency with the justified expectations of the other party; it excludes a variety of types of conduct characterized as involving "bad faith" because they violate community standards of decency, fairness or reasonableness. The appropriate remedy for a breach of the duty of good faith also varies with the circumstances'). More, in general, it has to be noted that references to the concepts of good faith and reasonableness are included in many other sections of the UCC (*see* Zaccaria, *supra* n. 322, at 484). With regard to English law, it has to be noted that, although it does not expressly recognise a general doctrine of good faith, it employs other theories in order to guarantee fairness in contract or fair dealing. In particular, courts obtain such result by means of construction and interpretation of contracts and by the implied terms doctrine. In some cases, courts implicitly recalls the principle of good faith by referring to the term "justice". For instance, in *J. Lauritzen v. Wijsmuller, The Super Servant Two*, 1 Lloyd's Rep. 1, 5 (EWCA 12 October 1989) in which the Court, in describing the doctrine of frustration, held that '[t]he object of the doctrine was to give effect to the demands of justice, to achieve just and reasonable result, to do what is reasonable and fair, as an expedient to escape from injustice where such would result from enforcement of a contract in its literal terms after a significant change in circumstances'. Moreover, it has to be noted that in a recent decision the High Court expressly recognised that in English law there is an implied duty to perform the contract in good faith (*see Yam Seng v. International Trade*, 1 Lloyd's Rep., 526 (EWHC (QB) 1 February 2013). The principles therein affirmed were recalled in *Bristol Groundschool v. Intelligent Data Capture*, http://www.bailii.org/ew/cases/EWHC/Ch/2014/2145.html (EWHC (Ch) 2 July 20 14); *Mid-Essex Hospital Services NHS Trust v. Compass Group UK and Ireland*, http://www.bailii.org/ew/cases/EWCA/Civ/2013/200.html (EWCA 15 March 2013). Moreover, also the Supreme Court of Canada has recently recognised the existence of a duty to perform the contract in good faith in *Bashin v. Hrynew*, https://scc-csc.lexum.com/scc-csc/scc-csc/en/item/14438/index.do (13 November 2013). Furthermore, eminent scholars hold in favour of the recognition of a general principle of good faith in English law. See, in particular, R. Brownsword, *Positive, Negative, Neutral: the Reception of Good Faith in English Contract Law*, in *Good Faith in Contract*, 13 et seq. (R. Brownsword, N.J. Hird & G. Howells, Ashgate/Dartmouth 1999), who refers to "a good faith requirements model" based on 'the standards of fair dealing already recognised in particular contracting context' (35); J. Wightman, *Good Faith and Pluralism in the Law of Contract*, in *id.*, at 41 et seq., who, expresses a similar idea by referring to "contextual good faith" that 'derives the content of good faith from the reasonable expectations of the parties. These expectations are based on norms which are widely observed in their contracting community' (42); H. Collins, *The Law of Contract*, 251 et seq. (Butterworths 2003); Nassar, *supra* n. 447; R. Brownsword, *Contract Law, Co-operation, and Good Faith: The Movement from Static to Dynamic Market-Individualism*, in *Contracts, Co-operation and Competition*, 255 et seq. (S. Deakin & J. Michie, Oxford University Press, 1997); *Id., Good Faith in Contracts Revisited*, 49 C.L.P., 111 (1996); *Id., Two Concepts of Good Faith*, 7 JCL, 197 (1994); R. Powell, *Good Faith in Contracts*, 9 C.L.P., 16 (1956). For additional indications and a comparative analysis of the topic *see also* R. Zimmermann & S. Whittaker, *Good Faith in European Contract Law* (Cambridge University Press 2000); Beatson & Friedmann, *supra* n. 203. As to international arbitration, *see* ICC case n. 2291/1975, *supra* n. 500, at 274 et seq.; ICC case n. 4761/1987, Collection of ICC Arbitral Awards 1986–1990, 519 (1987). Moreover, the recognition of good faith as a general principle of contract law finds an additional confirmation in the UNIDROIT Principles and in the PECL.

hardship of others to further their own interests unjustifiably, thus undermining the joint interest of the contractual project'.[502]

The same consideration can be made in relation to the termination of the contract. Indeed, even in this case, the principle of good faith would be violated since the non-terminating party would be deprived of the possibility to count on a commercial relationship on which it thought it could rely for several years and, consequently, on which it based and planned its business activity by, among the other, spending time and money. With regard to the costs, it has to be noted that, usually, it is possible to recover the relevant investments made by the parties (and, above all, by the supplier) only after a certain number of years and that such money cannot be easily transferred and destined to other operations. Moreover, it would not be easy for the parties to find in a short time a new suitable commercial partner.[503]

Thus, in light of the specific characteristics and scope of gas sale agreements, the fairness in the execution of contracts deriving from the principle of good faith means that the parties have to maintain a balanced and profitable relationship during the years as originally planned and expected by them when concluding the contract. It follows that the principle of good faith can be deemed to imply, with reference to the execution of such particular contracts, a duty of the parties to adjust the agreement upon the occurrence of unforeseen events altering its balance, independent of a specific adaptation clause. As said, without adaptation, it would not be possible to rebalance the agreement and the will of the parties would be frustrated since they could not achieve the scope pursued by means of the contract. Therefore, for these particular kinds of transactions, the execution of contracts in good faith is the means consenting the parties to fulfil their expectations. In other words, to execute this kind of contract in good faith means to execute it according to the parties' will. Thus, the same idea of fairness applicable to such contracts can be deemed to overlap the parties' expectations since both of them are represented by the maintenance of a balanced relationship over the years. As Professor Collins noted:

> The idea of reasonable expectations differs from a simple fairness criterion, for its reference is not to an independent standard of a fair price, but rather to the unexpressed intentions of the parties. But the circle becomes almost closed once it is accepted that those intentions are likely to be construed as a desire to enter a contract with reasonable balance of obligations on both sides ... The best interpretation of this standard is one which takes fairness in the sense of the preservation of the balance of advantage of the contract as the unacknowledged but vital guide to interpretation.[504]

---

502. Nassar, *supra* n. 447, at 219.
503. *Ibid.*, at 206 et seq. Moreover, the Author underlines that it is difficult to know to 'what extent potential contracting parties prepared to invest in feasibility studies and other information-generating activities to ensure that they have provided for every possible eventuality' and that 'revealing the potential disruptive effect of some future eventuality is beyond the state of art and available technology' (207).
504. Collins, *supra* n. 501, at 258, 279. *See also* ICC case n. 9994/2001, *supra* n. 256, in which it was affirmed that the application of the principle of good faith implies the duty of the parties to adjust the contract to the supervening events.

The adoption of a general doctrine of good faith could, therefore, allow courts to meet and better protect the parties' expectations. Indeed:

> with such a principle, the courts are better equipped to respond to the varying expectations encountered in the many different contracting contexts - and, in particular, it might be argued that the courts are better able to detect co-operative dealing where it is taking place ... if English contract law adopted a doctrine of good faith, it would pose questions of contractual interpretation and implication in a context, not only of background standards of fair dealing, but more immediately of the concrete expectations of the parties. Such expectations would be based as much on the way that the parties related to one another (whether they dealt with one another in an adversarial or non-adversarial manner) as on the express provisions of the agreement. As a result, English law would recover the ability to give effect to the spirit of the deal in a way that prioritized the parties' own expectations.[505]

Such position was recently upheld by the case law.[506] In particular, in a case dealing with a dispute arising out of an alleged breach of a distribution agreement, the Court, contrary to the traditional position adopted by English law, recognised the existence of a general implied duty to perform contracts in good faith whose content has to be determined case by case since it 'is heavily dependent on context and is established through a process of construction of the contract'.[507] However, the Court specified that, even if 'its requirements are sensitive to context, the test of good faith is objective in the sense that it depends not on either party's perception of whether particular conduct is improper but on whether in the particular context the conduct

---

505. Brownsword *Positive, Negative, Neutral: The Reception of Good Faith in English Contract Law*, supra n. 501, at 27). *See also* Wightman, supra n. 501, at 41 et seq.
506. *See Yam Seng* case, supra n. 501. The same principles were also affirmed in the *Bristol Groundschool* and *Mid-Essex Hospital Services NHS Trust* cases, supra n. 501, in which the Court, although not recognising the existence of a general principle of good faith, considered possible to imply it with regard to particular categories of contracts. Also the Supreme Court of Canada has recently recognised the existence in common law of a general principle to perform the contract in good faith, affirming that '[t]wo incremental steps are in order to make the common law more coherent and more just. The first step is to acknowledge that good faith contractual performance is a general organizing principle of the common law of contract which underpins and informs the various rules in which the common law, in various situations and types of relationships, recognizes obligations of good faith contractual performance. The second step is to recognize, as a further manifestation of this organizing principle of good faith, that there is a common law duty which applies to all contracts to act honestly in the performance of contractual obligations ... Taking these two steps will put in place a duty that is just, that accords with the reasonable expectations of commercial parties and that is sufficiently precise that it will enhance rather than detract from commercial certainty ... The organizing principle of good faith exemplifies the notion that, in carrying out his or her own performance of the contract, a contracting party should have appropriate regard to the legitimate contractual interests of the contracting partner' (*Bashin* case, supra n. 501, at paras 33, 65).
507. *Yam Seng* case, *id.*, at para. 147. Furthermore, the Court specifies that, for this reason, the recognition of the good faith duty 'is entirely consistent with the case by case approach favoured by the common law. There is therefore no need for common lawyers to abandon their characteristic methods and adopt those of civil law systems in order to accommodate the principle' (*ibid.*).

would be regarded as commercially unacceptable by reasonable and honest people'.[508] Moreover, it was confirmed that the strict connection between good faith and parties' expectations since 'the basis of the duty of good faith is the presumed intention of the parties and meaning of their contract'.[509] It follows that the recognition of such duty 'is not an illegitimate restriction on the freedom of the parties to pursue their own interests. The essence of contracting is that the parties bind themselves in order to co-operate to their mutual benefit. The obligations which they undertake include those which are implicit in their agreement as well as those which they have made explicit'.[510] In particular, the Court underlined the relevance of such principles with regard to contracts involving 'a longer term relationship between the parties which they make a substantial commitment' by stating that:

> Such "relational" contracts, as they are sometimes called, may require a high degree of communication, cooperation and predictable performance based on mutual trust and confidence and involve expectations of loyalty which are not legislated for in the express terms of the contract but are implicit in the parties' understanding and necessary to give business efficacy to the arrangements. Examples of such relational contracts might include some joint venture agreements, franchise agreements and long term distributorship agreements.[511]

In light of the above, in case the parties fail to find an agreement, the same principle of good faith entitles judges or arbitrators (usually gas sale agreements include an arbitration clause) to carry out the adjustment. In case the parties fail to adjust the contract by means of renegotiation, they have the right to recur to judicial adaptation in order to rebalance the agreement. Indeed, why they should be deprived of a remedy that could give them the possibility to achieve the purpose pursued? Judicial adaptation is, therefore, another tool, besides renegotiation, that the parties can employ in order to obtain compliance with the duty to adjust the contract (implied in the principle of good faith) and to realise their main interest, i.e., to re-establish the *equilibrium* necessary for the maintaining of a profitable commercial relationship. As a consequence, since the adaptation of gas sale agreements (by parties or arbitrators) depends on the application of the principle of good faith to the execution of contracts, the lack of an adaptation clause or of a discipline for any supervening event that can affect the contract, does not mean that the party decided to allocate the risk to the disadvantaged party and that did not want to adjust the contract on the basis of the market's changes.

In addition to the request of adjustment, a party, in case the failure of the renegotiation depended on the unfair behaviour of the other (that, for instance, refused to start the renegotiation process or refused any proposal made by the counterparty or did not propose itself any reasonable offer of modification), could claim for damages resulting from the counterparty's breach of the duty of good faith as including the duty to adjust the contract upon the occurrence of events altering its balance.

---

508. *Ibid.*, at para. 144.
509. *Ibid.*, at para. 148.
510. *Ibid.*
511. *See ibid.*, at para. 142.

It could be objected that the above-mentioned solution could not be applicable with regard to those legal systems analysed that allow judges and arbitrators to intervene on contracts or, more in general, to issue the so called "constitutive decisions" (i.e., the decisions that create, modify or extinguish legal rights), like the one adapting the contract, only when expressly provided by the law. Such objection can be overcome by the recourse to the principle of good faith. Indeed, all the above-mentioned legal systems, provide, as seen, that the contract has to be executed in good faith. Moreover, they establish that the agreement is binding for the parties not only in relation to its provisions but also to all the consequences deriving from it according to the law, usages and equity.[512] It follows that the parties are bound by the above-mentioned duty to execute the contract in good faith. As a consequence, judges or arbitrators, by adapting the contract in light of good faith, are just giving execution to a statutory provision affirming that contracts are binding to the parties also as to the legal consequences deriving from it. In such case the legal consequence is the duty to perform the contract in good faith that, as seen, with regard to some particular agreements (like gas sale contracts) and in a specific context, can be deemed to imply a duty to adjust the contract. Therefore, there is no violation of the principle established in some legal systems by which judges and arbitrators can issue constitutive decision only if expressly provided by the law.

Other objections that can be made are that the revision of contracts by courts or arbitrators violates the principle of party autonomy, and that they do not have the expertise necessary to adjust the contract since they do not have the technical skills required in a field complex like the energy sector.

As to the first, it can be rebutted that the adaptation according to the principle of good faith is, instead, the way to comply with the principle of party autonomy. Indeed, as seen, by means of such principle it is possible to fulfil the parties' expectations and to respect their will since they want to adjust the contract in order to keep their relationship over the years.[513]

---

512. In this regard, *see, ex multis*, Art. 1135 of the French and Belgian Civil Code ('[a]greements are binding not only as to what is therein expressed, but also as to all the consequences which equity,usage or statute give to the obligation according to its nature'); Art. 1374 of the Italian Civil Code ('The contract is binding to the parties not only as to what is therein expressed, but also as to all the consequences deriving from it according to the law or, in the lack of the latter, to usages and equity'); Art. 2, para. 1 of the Swiss Civil Code ('Every person must act in good faith in the exercise of his or her rights and in the performance of his or her obligations'). The duty provided by such article is considered as an ancillary one implied to the contract and complementary to the main contractual duties (*see Guiding Principles of European Contract Law*, in *European Contract Law*, 421 et seq., 464–465 (B. Fauvarque-Cosson & D. Mazeaud, Sellier 2008)).
513. *See* Brownsword, *Positive, Negative, Neutral: the Reception of Good Faith in English Contract Law, supra* n. 501, at 37 et seq.; Collins, *supra* n. 501, at 251 et seq.; Hillman, *supra* n. 345, at 27 et seq. *See also* J.M. Perillo, *Hardship and its Impact on Contractual Obligations: A Comparative Analysis*, http://www.cisg.law.pace.edu/cisg/biblio/perillo4.html (1996), who affirms that there is no violation of the principle of autonomy of contract since when a supervening event is unforeseen and beyond the parties' control and it radically changes the nature of the performance, it can be deemed that the parties have never provided their consent to the execution of the contract in such situation. Therefore, without consent there is no conflict with the principle of freedom of contract and party's autonomy.

Chapter 3: Arbitrators Contracts Without an Adaptation Clause §3.06

With regard to the second objection, it is true that the best solution would be the adaptation of the agreement by the parties since they know better the economic and technical reality in which they operate, as well as the issues connected to this kind of contract. However, first of all, it has to be noted that, if the parties fail to find an agreement for the adaptation of the contract, they should not be deprived of the possibility to obtain the adjustment only because a successful renegotiation is a better solution than judicial adjustment. Indeed, as said, the latter is another tool for the parties to comply with their expectation and with the duty to adjust the contract provided by the principle of good faith. Therefore, it would be against such principle to deprive the parties of one of the remedies that could allow them to comply with the duty to adjust the contract and, consequently, with the possibility to maintain their relationship and to reach the scope that led them to conclude the contract.

An additional consideration to be made is that, at the end, the adaptation of a contract implies the same activity as that required to arbitrators or judges when they have to decide about termination or ordering the specific performance, i.e., the interpretation of the contract in light of the parties' will and the evaluation of facts and proofs. In carrying out this activity, arbitrators can recur to the general power to conduct the proceeding as they consider appropriate that is usually provided by arbitration laws[514] and rules.[515] Indeed, in general, the arbitration tribunal has a wide discretion in determining the procedure to be followed in case the parties did not specifically agree on this matter. However, it is difficult that the arbitration agreement contains a detailed and specific discipline on how to conduct the proceeding. It is more common for the parties to generally refer to an arbitration law or to a set of arbitration rules. Such discretion 'enables the arbitral tribunal to meet the needs of the particular

---

514. In this regard, *see, ex multis,* Art. 19 of the UNCITRAL Model Law that provides that '(1) Subject to the provisions of this Law, the parties are free to agree on the procedure to be followed by the arbitral tribunal in conducting the proceedings. (2) Failing such agreement, the arbitral tribunal may, subject to the provisions of this Law, conduct the arbitration in such manner as it considers appropriate. The power conferred upon the arbitral tribunal includes the power to determine the admissibility, relevance, materiality and weight of any evidence'. The same provision can be found in the majority of the arbitration laws. *See,* for instance, Art. 1036 of the Dutch Code of Civil Procedure; Art. 1700 of the Belgian Code of Civil Procedure; s. 34 of the English Arbitration Act; Arts 1464 (applicable to domestic arbitration) and 1509 and 1511 (applicable to international arbitration) of French Code of Civil Procedure; Art. 1042 of the German Code of Civil Procedure; Art. 816-*bis* of the Italian Code of Civil Procedure; Art. 182 of the Swiss PIL.
515. In this regard, *see, ex multis,* Arts 19 and 22 of the ICC Arbitration Rules; Art. 20 of the ICDR arbitration Rules; Art. 14 of the LCIA Arbitration Rules; Art. 17 of the UNCITRAL Arbitration Rules. *See also* the Code of Ethics for Arbitrators in Commercial Disputes of the American Arbitration Association that provides that '[d]uring an arbitration, the arbitrator may engage in discourse with the parties or their counsel, draw out arguments or contentions, comment on the law or evidence, make interim rulings, and otherwise control or direct the arbitration. These activities are integral parts of an arbitration. Paragraph D of Canon I is not intended to preclude or limit either full discussion of the issues during the course of the arbitration or the arbitrator's management of the proceeding' (para. I of Canon I). Para. D of Canon I above mentioned provides that '[a]rbitrators should conduct themselves in a way that is fair to all parties and should not be swayed by outside pressure, public clamor, and fear of criticism or self-interest. They should avoid conduct and statements that give the appearance of partiality toward or against any party'.

case and to select the most suitable procedure when organizing the arbitration, conducting individual hearings or other meetings and determining the important specifics of taking and evaluating evidence. In practical terms, the arbitrators would be able to adopt the procedural features familiar, or at least acceptable, to the parties (and to them) ... Above all, where the parties are from different legal systems, the arbitral tribunal may use a liberal 'mixed' procedure, adopting suitable features from different legal systems and relying on techniques proven in international practice, and, for instance, let parties present their case as they themselves judge best. Such procedural discretion in all these cases seems conducive to facilitating international commercial arbitration, while being forced to apply the 'law of the land' where the arbitration happens to take place would present a major disadvantage to any party not used to that particular and possibly peculiar system of procedure and evidence'.[516]

Due to the general discretion granted to the arbitration tribunal, it can be said that they have the power to hear the parties in order to ask them questions and clarifications. Moreover, it has to be noted that in some cases arbitration laws and rules expressly confer such authority on the arbitration tribunal. For example, Article 1043 of the Dutch Code of Civil Procedure provides that '[a]t any stage of the proceedings the arbitral tribunal may order the parties to appear in person for the purpose of providing information or attempting to arrive at a settlement'.[517] In the same vein, section 34 of the English Arbitration Act states that the arbitration tribunal, save for any agreement of the parties, shall decide all the procedural and evidential matters among which, paragraph 2, letter (e) of such provision, includes 'whether any and if so what questions should be put to and answered by the respective parties and when and in what form this should be done'. In this regard, it was noted that:

> 'Although questions may, and indeed often will, be put to the parties by the tribunal during the oral phase of the proceedings, the primary purpose of this example of an arbitrator's procedural powers is directed at the use of 'interrogatories', a term used in the rules of court. In court, the rules contemplate the exchange of written questions and answers between the parties. This procedure may also be adopted in arbitration. However, it is sometimes more useful for the tribunal itself to pose questions to the parties during the written phase of the proceedings. Again, the guiding principle for a tribunal in determining whether or not to adopt such a procedure is cost-effectiveness and, in particular, the reduction of hearing time'.[518]

A similar approach is taken by the CEPANI Arbitration Rules that, at Article 23(4), provides for the power of the arbitration tribunal, upon the request of the parties or ex officio, to 'summon the parties to appear before it on the day and at the place that it specifies'.[519]

---

516. United Nations, *document A/CN.9/264* (*Analytical Commentary on Draft Text of a Model Law on International Commercial Arbitration*), remarks 5 and 6 on Art. 19, as cited in 1985 XVI UNCITRAL Yearbook Part II, para. I.B., 125.
517. Available in English on www.dutchcivillaw.com.
518. J.M. Hunter, *The Procedural Powers of Arbitrators Under the English 1996 Act*, 13 Arb Intl 345, 350 (1997).
519. Available in English on www.cepani.be.

Chapter 3: Arbitrators Contracts Without an Adaptation Clause §3.06

Furthermore, even in the lack of a specific provision included in the arbitration law, arbitrators, in addition to the general discretion in conducting the proceeding, can rely on the powers granted to judges by the procedural applicable law on the basis of the principle of synchronised competence.[520] For example, Articles 8 and 13 of the French Code of Civil Procedure give judges the power to invite the parties to provide explanations on facts and legal arguments when it is considered necessary for the resolution of the dispute. Therefore, arbitrators could rely on such provisions and ask the parties the necessary questions and clarifications in order to adapt long-term gas sale agreements.[521] Similarly, Article 183 of the Italian Code of Civil Procedure provides judges not only with the power to ask the parties, usually by means of their counsels, the clarifications considered necessary (paragraph 4) but also to summon them in person in order to freely interrogate them.[522]

In light of the above, it is clear that arbitrators could use their discretion in conducting the proceeding in order to obtain directly from the parties any clarification they may need in the contract's adaptation process. Of course the arbitration tribunal has to limit its discretion and authority to what it is really necessary for the adjustment of the contract in order to meet the parties' will and expectations avoiding to make the arbitral proceeding excessively time consuming and expensive.[523]

In addition, in order to overcome the difficulties that can arise in the adaptation process due to technicalities, the parties could appoint an arbitrator that has an expertise in the field. In case he is not, it is still possible to appoint an expert that can help the arbitration tribunal in relation to the technical aspects. Besides, the documents submitted by the parties and their proposal of adaptation formulated during the renegotiation are elements that can help arbitrators in reaching its decision on technicalities. Even in this case, the arbitration tribunal can recur to its procedural powers to appoint ex officio an expert and to ask the parties to produce documents it considers necessary for its decision. Indeed, usually, arbitration laws[524] and rules[525]

---

520. See §3.01. For a general recognition of arbitrators to ask parties clarifications, see Lew, Mistelis & Kroll, *supra* n. 240, at para. 21.44. See also Brunner, *supra* n. 210, at 496 and the discussion at the ICC Conference on Force Majeure and Hardship, *supra* n. 466.
521. In this regard, it has to be underlined that Art. 1464 of the French Code of Civil Procedure, dealing with arbitration, expressly refers to Art. 13 above mentioned.
522. See also Art.139 of the German Code of Civil Procedure.
523. See, *ex multis*, s. 33(1), letter b), of the English Arbitration Act providing that 'the tribunal shall adopt procedures suitable to the circumstances of the particular case, avoiding unnecessary delay or expense, so as to provide a fair means for the resolution of the matters falling to be determined'. See also, Arts 22 of the ICC Arbitration Rules, 14 of the LCIA Arbitration Rules and 17 of the UNCITRAL Arbitration Rules.
524. See, *ex multis*, Art. 26 of the Model Law; Arts 1700 and 1707 (that allows the arbitration tribunal to appoint expert unless the parties have agreed otherwise) of the Belgian Code of Civil Procedure; Arts 1039 and 1042 of the Dutch Code of Civil Procedure; ss 34 and 37 and of the English Arbitration Act; Arts 232 and 1467 of the French Code of Civil Procedure; Art. 1049 of the German Code of Civil Procedure (that allows the arbitration tribunal to appoint expert unless the parties have agreed otherwise); Arts 61, 191 and 210 of the Italian Code of Civil Procedure (that allows courts to order the production of documents only upon the party's request); s. 25 of the Swedish Arbitration Act. However, with regard to experts, it has to be noted that the arbitrators' power to appoint an expert is subject to the approval of the parties.
525. See, for instance, Art. 23 of the CEPANI Arbitration Rules; Art. 25 of the ICC Arbitration Rules; Arts 20 and 25 of the ICDR Arbitration Rules; Arts 21 and 22 of the LCIA Arbitration Rules;

provide arbitrators with such authority. Even in this case, the same considerations made with regard to clarifications and interrogatories in term of time and money apply. Therefore, 'the argument that arbitrators lack sufficient information and expertise to determine when a contract should be adjusted ... is not convincing either'.[526]

Finally, it has to be noted that the possibility for courts and arbitrators to adapt the contract can encourage parties to reach an agreement by means of renegotiation before an arbitral or litigation proceeding or can help them to find an agreement on the basis of the judicial decision.[527]

The above-mentioned conclusions on the recognition of the arbitrators' power to adapt contracts, in addition to be shared by some of the decisions *supra* analysed,[528] seem to find a further support in the so called "relational contract theory". As said, such doctrine, developed by some US scholars,[529] has elaborated a model of contract that differs from that developed by classical and neoclassical theories, represented by the so called "discrete transaction", i.e., contracts that are concluded and executed in a limited lapse of time and that do not require a stable relationship between the parties. Such contracts maximised the predictability of future risks and events at the moment of their conclusion (so called "presentation"). Therefore, there is no room for adaptation of the agreement upon the occurrence of unforeseen events. Indeed, it is assumed that if the parties did not set a discipline for a specific supervening circumstance, they decided that the risk has to be borne by the disadvantaged party. However,

---

Arts 27 and 29 of the UNCITRAL Arbitration Rules. *See also* Arts 3 and 6 of the IBA Rules on the Taking of Evidence in International Arbitration.

526. *See* Brunner, *supra* n. 210, at note 2447.
527. As it happened, for instance, in the *Alcoa* case (*see* §3.03[A][4]). Moreover, courts and arbitrators, in some cases, first ordered the parties to renegotiate and, upon their failure, they directly adjusted the contract (*see*, for instance, the *Electricitè de France* case, *supra* n. 258 and ICC case n. 10351/2001, 2009 20 ICC Int'l Ct.Arb.Bull., 76 (partial award 2001), analysed in Ch. 4).
528. *See* §3.03 and §3.04.
529. *See*, in particular, Macneil, *The Many Futures of Contracts*, *supra* n. 495, at 691 et seq.; *Id. supra* n. 345, at 854 et seq.; *Id. Restatement (Second) of Contracts and Presentation*, 60 Va.L.Rev., 589 (1974); S. Macaulay, *Relational Contracts Floating on a Sea of Custom? Thoughts About the Ideas of Ian Macneil and Lisa Bernstein*, 94 N.Y.U.L.Rev., 775 (2000). Other contributions to this doctrine came also from English scholars, such as, I. Macneil & D. Campbell, *The Relational Theory of Contract: Selected Works of Ian Macneil* (Sweet & Maxwell 2001); H. Collins, D. Campbell & J. Wightman, *The Implicit Dimensions of Contract* (Hart 2003); R. Austen-Baker, *A Relational Law of Contract*, 20 JCL, 125 (2004); *Id.*, *Comprehensive Contract Theory: A Four-Norm Model of Contract Relations*, 25 JCL, 216 (2009), who proposes a variant of the relational contract doctrine compared to the original idea developed by Professor Macneil. In favour of considering long-term gas sale contracts as relational contracts and, as such, characterised by 'consistent cooperation rather than the optimisation of the separate positions of each party', *see* Griffin & van Eupen &,*supra* n. 220, at 147, who, however, underline that 'recent events in the gas market have shown that if their financial and economic interests diverge, the parties are likely to put their own interests first and seek to strengthen their own position ... Market forces have strained the relational and cooperative nature of long-term LNG contract arrangements'. The Authors support the idea that due to the relational nature of long-term gas contracts as well as the substantial investments made by the parties in term of money and time 'the price review clause should provide for a mechanism which encourages the reapportionment of the value of the shared enterprise, in a way which reflects the risk-sharing nature of the long-term LNG contract' (*ibid.*). For a recent definition of relational contracts, *see* also the *Yam Seng* case, *supra* n. 501.

Chapter 3: Arbitrators Contracts Without an Adaptation Clause §3.06

as it was noted, this model does not fit all the different kinds of transactions that can occur in the reality and, in particular, long-term contracts that, due to their characteristics and particular scope, presuppose the creation and preservation of a stable relationship between the parties for several years[530] (for this reason, they are considered relational contracts). It follows that relational contracts are characterised by flexibility and require to be adapted during their life since termination is not the solution appropriate for long-term relations and does not fit the purpose pursued by the parties. In this regard, Professor Macneil underlined that when changes occur 'it is well to remember that we are dealing with situations where the desire is to continue the relation, not to terminate it'.[531] However, that does not mean to keep the contractual relationship as it is in spite of changes. Indeed, it was also observed that the 'status quo in a dynamic society does not mean a static status quo; ... the status quo itself may very well be one in which changes in a certain direction are expected. If they do not come or come less than expected, then the interest-dispute-resolver is faced with a situation where the status quo calls for change, not for simply sticking to patterns now viewed as obsolete'.[532] Moreover, 'changes typically can be harmonized with the remainder of the relation only by making them consistent with the status quo ... But it must be noted that if the status quo is a dynamic one moving over time in certain directions ... change in accord with those patterns is essential to preserve the status quo itself'.[533]

Therefore, it could be said that it emerges the idea that adjustment is one of the characteristics of long-term contracts. They can be deemed to encompass and include their adaptation over time in order to avoid both termination and performance without modification in light of the changes occurred and affecting their balance since such remedies are in contrast with the nature of such agreements and with the purpose pursued by the parties. Starting from such principle it was affirmed that these kinds of contracts, and in particular energy contracts, presuppose a duty of the parties to adjust them on the basis of good faith.[534] The compliance by the parties with the latter would meet their expectations when entered into the contract, i.e., the preservation of a long-term profitable relationship that could not be achieved without adaptation. Indeed, the principle of good faith 'requires cooperation on the part of one party to the contract so that another party will not be deprived of his reasonable expectations'.[535]

---

530. The preservation of the relationship is one of the so called "relational norms" identified by Professor Macneil as specifically applicable to relational contracts (*see supra* n. 345, at 862, 895 et seq.).
531. *Ibid.*, at 896.
532. *Ibid.*
533. *Ibid.*, at 897. The harmonisation of conflicts within the relation is another relational norm identified by Professor Macneil.
534. *See* Hillman, *supra* n. 345, at 1 et seq. A position in favour of courts and arbitrators' adjustment can also be found in Brownsword, *Positive, Negative, Neutral: the Reception of Good Faith in English Contract Law*, *supra* n. 501, at 13 et seq.; Nassar, *supra* n. 447, at 216–220, 234–242. See also D'Angelo, *supra* n. 379. As to the case law, *see*, in particular, the *Timegate Studios* and *Belgische Sceehpvaartmaatschappij-Compagnie Maritime Belge* cases, *supra* n. 301; the *Electricité de France* case, *supra* n. 250; ICC case n. 2508/1976, *supra* n. 302.
535. E.A. Farnsworth, *Good Faith Performance and Commercial Reasonableness Under the Uniform Commercial Code*, 30 U.Chi.L.Rev. 666, 669 (1962). *See also* Nassar, *id.*, at 141 et seq.; ICC case n. 2443/1975, *supra* n. 500.

In light of the duty to adjust long-term contracts, courts, in case the parties fail to agree on adaptation, should be entitled to do it.[536] Indeed, it was affirmed that:

> The goal of court adjustment is to preserve the parties' purposes and to avoid unbargained-for gains by one party or losses by the other. In situations ripe for adjustment, the supplier sought an assured market and cost coverage and the buyer sought an assured supply at a reasonable price. The parties did not intend to permit the supplier to raise prices without a corresponding increase in its costs. Similarly, the parties did not intend to permit the buyer to take advantage of an exigent market situation by raising its own prices to third parties (such as a utility increasing its rates or spot selling on the market), while at the same time insisting on the supplier's performance at pre-inflation prices.[537]

The idea that arbitrators should adjust long-term international contracts in order to maintain their balance is also affirmed by the so called "contractual *equilibrium* theory" that also recognises that the relational model is the most appropriate for long-term agreements and aims at the preservation of a balanced relationship between the parties on the basis of the principle of good faith.[538] In particular, according to such theory, arbitrators determine the content of the duties of good faith and fair dealing (that rule the adjustment process) in light of the specific context in which the parties operate ("surrounding circumstances"). Moreover, in carrying out such task, arbitrators have to consider the purpose of the contract. It is affirmed the idea that, contrary to the classical contract law doctrine, in addition to contract provisions other elements have to be considered in order to determine the parties' obligations; Elements that complement the rights and duties provided by the agreement. In other words, arbitrators have a discretionary power to determine the content of the contract on the basis of the "surrounding circumstances" that they reasonably consider relevant. However, this:

> does not deprive individuals of the power to regulate their own relationships. It merely allows tribunals to examine the contractual context and apply general legal standards to define the content of contractual relationships … merely tries to remedy the shortcomings of the promise principle. Thus, there are few general standards, such as good faith and fair dealing, which apply to supplement the promise principle regardless of an agreement to that effect … under the contractual

---

536. *See* Hillman, *supra* n. 345, at 19. Although the Author recognises that the best solution would be parties' adaptation of the contract and that 'a court is far from ideally suited to adjust long-term contracts' (*ibid.*). In favour of the adaptation of international long-term contracts by courts and arbitrators on the basis of the principle of good faith, *see also* Berger, *Power of Arbitrators to Fill Gaps and Revise Contracts to Make Sense*, *supra* n. 210, at 16 et seq.
537. Hillman, *id.*, at 19–20. As to the criticism that courts do not have the expertise and knowledge necessary to adapt long-term contracts, the Author underlines that judges have different sources to employ in order to carry out the adjustment, such as, other similar contracts, parties' documents and experts. Moreover, it was noted that 'a judge has the benefit of hindsight. Hindsight provides judges with accurate, current information that not only helps them to adjust the contract to reflect present conditions, but also provides clues as to the likelihood of future events' (26).
538. Nassar, *supra* n. 447, at 237–242. In this regard, the Author underlines that, although long-term agreements presuppose the existence of common interests and of a common scope, the individualistic different interests of the parties, that are proper of any commercial transaction, remain and are not merged in one unique common interest (149).

equilibrium theory, tribunals must interfere to ensure the business efficiency of LTICT's [long-term international commercial contracts] by maintaining an equitable contractual balance.[539]

In consideration of the above, it seems possible to conclude that, in some circumstances, arbitrators (and courts), upon a party's request, should be entitled to adapt long-term gas sale contracts (and, in particular, the price and take or pay clauses), even in the absence of an adaptation clause, on the basis of the principle of good faith and independent of whether or not the procedural applicable law provide them with such power. As seen, in consideration of the particular characteristics of gas contracts (long duration, complexity, huge investments) and of the relevant scope pursued by the parties (to build up and preserve a stable relationships in order to guarantee the seller a constant flux of money to recover the investments made and the buyer a constant flux of gas to meet the market demand without the need to negotiate for every supply), the generally recognised principle of good faith can be deemed to provide for a duty to adjust such agreements upon the occurrence of unforeseen events altering the relevant balance. Without such adjustment, it would, indeed, be impossible to rebalance the contract and, consequently, to preserve a profitable relationship and to allow the parties to achieve the scope pursued when entering into the contract. Both termination and performance without adaptation would be against the will of the parties and the principle of good faith in the execution of the contract. For this reason, if the parties fail to adapt the contract by means of renegotiation, arbitrators should be allowed to do it. In order to reach its decision, the arbitration tribunal will have to determine whether the triggering conditions provided by the applicable law (and the relevant case law) are met[540] and, in general, whether the alteration of the contract's balance actually occurred and was proved (it is obvious that not any economic difficulty in the performance of the contract or any non-convenient transaction could legitimate a modification of the agreement). Moreover, arbitrators can employ different sources (such as, parties' documents and submissions, expert, other similar contracts) that can help them to carry out this task. In addition, it was underlined, that adaptation requires the arbitration tribunal to interpret the contract in light of parties' will and to evaluate the facts and proofs submitted by the parties, similarly to when the arbitration tribunal has to decide on termination or specific performance of the agreement.

Finally, it has to be noted that the above-mentioned approach is also the one adopted by international law and, namely, by the UNIDROIT Principles and the PECL. In particular, Article 6.2.3 of the UNIDROIT Principles provides that:

> (1) In case of hardship the disadvantaged party is entitled to request renegotiations. The request shall be made without undue delay and shall indicate the grounds on which it is based. (2) The request for renegotiation does not in itself entitle the disadvantaged party to withhold performance. (3) Upon failure to reach agreement within a reasonable time either party may resort to the court. (4) If the court finds hardship it may, if reasonable, (a) terminate the contract at a date and

---

539. *Ibid.*, at 242.
540. Usually the events altering the contract balance have to be: (1) substantial; (2) unforeseen; and (3) beyond the control of the parties.

on terms to be fixed; or (b) adapt the contract with a view to restoring its equilibrium.[541]

In its turn, Article 6:111 of the PECL provides that:

(1) A party is bound to fulfil its obligations even if performance has become more onerous, whether because the cost of performance has increased or because the value of the performance it receives has diminished. (2) If, however, performance of the contract becomes excessively onerous because of a change of circumstances, the parties are bound to enter into negotiations with a view to adapting the contract or terminating it, provided that: (a) the change of circumstances occurred after the time of conclusion of the contract, (b) the possibility of a change of circumstances was not one which could reasonably have been taken into account at the time of conclusion of the contract, and (c) the risk of the change of circumstances is not one which, according to the contract, the party affected should be required to bear. (3) If the parties fail to reach agreement within a reasonable period, the court may: (a) terminate the contract at a date and on terms to be determined by the court; or (b) adapt the contract in order to distribute between the parties in a just and equitable manner the losses and gains resulting from the change of circumstances. In either case, the court may award damages for the loss suffered through a party refusing to negotiate or breaking off negotiations contrary to good faith and fair dealing.[542]

The above-mentioned principles are soft law and, as such, they apply only if the contract refers to them or if arbitrators consider them as general principles of international law, and, therefore, they are applicable without the necessity of a specific reference in the contract. However, they express the need of the international business community to have, independent of what provided in the agreement, a general recognition of the courts' and arbitrators' power to adjust long-term contracts, when the relevant *equilibrium* is altered upon the occurrence of unforeseen events.[543] Indeed, it was noted that:

the emphasis on good faith and fair deal signals the transition to a new form of contractual morality in international business. The "all or nothing rule" of the sanctity of contract principles is being replaced by a more flexible, pragmatic approach. This approach seeks to produce results that are perceived to be just and fair and in consonance with commercial common sense. Modern commercial contract doctrine is developing away from the discrete model of the one-time exchange of goods and money to the co-operative and complex long-term transactions where the parties are depending to a substantial extent on the compliance of their counterparts with good faith and fair dealing as conduct-related legal standards over a long period of time.[544]

---

541. *See supra* n. 231.
542. *Ibid.*
543. In this regard, *see* the ICC Conference on Force Majeure and Hardship and in the Resolutions of the ICCA Fifth International Arbitration Congress on Arbitration, *supra* n. 466 and n. 470.
544. Berger, *Power of Arbitrators to Fill Gaps and Revise Contracts to Make Sense*, *supra* n. 210, at 17–18.

CHAPTER 4

The Adaptation of Long-Term Gas Sale Agreements by Arbitrators Contracts with an Adaptation Clause

§4.01 INTRODUCTION

The second category of long-term contracts analysed, in relation to the issue of the arbitrators' power to adapt the contract upon the occurrence of unforeseen events altering their balance, is represented by long-term gas sale agreements providing for an adaptation clause. The most common kinds are price review and hardship clauses. The first provide for the adjustment of the price formula in case the latter does not reflect the actual market conditions anymore and, consequently, makes the contract unbalanced. The second, instead, consent to adapt the contract whose balance is altered by supervening circumstances without limitation to the price conditions. Therefore, both these provisions aim to rebalance the contract in order to allow the parties to keep their relationship for the entire duration agreed and, as a consequence, to meet their expectations. Usually these clauses set out, as triggering event, the change of market conditions, which alters the contract's balance and has to be: (1) substantial; (2) unforeseen; and (3) beyond the control of the parties. Moreover, in case of price review clauses, the triggering condition can be just the passing of time. Indeed, they can provide for periodic reviews of the price formula in order to adjust it in light of the actual market conditions.

The analysis of this second category of contracts, will deal with both agreements that, in the adaptation or arbitration clause, expressly provide for the powers of arbitrators to adjust the contract terms and agreements that, instead, do not expressly confer such authority. Like for contracts without an adaptation clause, the problem has to be considered under both the procedural and arbitrability perspective. In particular, the main issues to be taken into account are, on the one hand, the conflict that may arise between the arbitrators' authority provided by the contract and the relevant applicable procedural law in case it does not entitle arbitrators to intervene on contract's terms and, on the other, the extent of this power.[545] In other words, it has to be determined whether the will of the parties expressed in the contract prevails on the applicable law. Moreover, in case of agreements not expressly providing the arbitrators with the power to adjust them, it has to be determined whether such authority can be implicitly inferred from the combination of the adjustment clause and the general arbitration clause. In addition, even for the category of agreements with an adaptation clause, it will be necessary to consider the concept of legal dispute. In this regard, it has to be noted that the considerations made on the application of the principle of good faith to the execution of contracts without an adaptation clause – and, the consequent, possibility for arbitrators to adjust such agreements – can also be applied to contracts including this provision. Indeed, such agreements have the same characteristics (long duration, take or pay clauses, huge investments) and purpose (to build up and maintain a profitable relationship between the parties in order to provide the supplier with a stable flux of money and the buyer with a stable flux of gas) as the former category. In addition, the presence of an adaptation clause makes even more evident the intentions and will of the parties to rebalance the contract when its *equilibrium* is altered upon the occurrence of unforeseen and to avoid its termination. Such provisions, therefore, can be deemed to represent the expression of the generally recognised duty to execute contracts in good faith.[546] Indeed, we have seen that the application of such duty to long-term gas sale agreements, due to their characteristics and purpose, can be considered as implying an obligation of the parties to adapt them (when their balance is altered upon the occurrence of unforeseen events) from which it derives, in case they fail to find an agreement, the possibility to ask courts and arbitrators to carry out such task in order to fulfil the parties' expectations. In light of the above, even in case the applicable procedural law does not provide arbitrators with adaptation powers, a gas sale agreement can be modified. Therefore, the possible conflict between the procedural applicable law and the contract including an adaptation clause has to be resolved in favour of the latter. Such provision just makes more evident the will of the parties to maintain their relationship over the entire duration of the contract; Will that, however, emerges already from the peculiar nature and structure of long-term gas sale agreements even without the adjustment clause. As a consequence, the difference between these two categories of contracts is not that in a case the agreement can be adjusted and in the other not, but that, by means of the adaptation provision, the parties can better define the adjustment process by determining the conditions and criteria that they want to be met. For instance, they can set out: which terms of the agreement they want to be adapted, the triggering events, the limits of the arbitrators' power, the parameters to be followed in conducting the adjustment of the agreement, etc. In other words, the adaptation clause consents to better identify and determine the concrete application of the principle of good faith, and the consequent adjustment process deriving from it, to the specific contract concluded between the parties. The

---

545. This book just briefly addresses the issue of the extent of the arbitrators' adaptation powers.
546. Adaptation clauses often contain an express reference to the good faith principle (*see* Ch. 3, §3.02).

more such clause detailed is, especially with regard to the triggering conditions and the criteria to be followed for the review, the easier the task to be carried out by arbitrators is since there are more elements to which they can refer. Similarly, the parties could be advantaged with regard to both the renegotiation process and the proofs to be submitted before the tribunal upon the failure to reach an agreement. In conclusion, the presence of the adaptation clause is not a condition to recognise their power to adjust the contract. As said, the existence of such authority derives from the application of the principle of good faith to this particular kind of contract.

In the same vein, the considerations concerning the arbitrability issue, the scope of arbitration agreement and the notion of legal dispute, made with regard to contracts without an adaptation clause, can also be applied to agreements including such provision.

Provided the above, this part, due to the availability of arbitration awards specifically dealing with gas contracts including an adaptation clause, will focus on the analysis of such decisions in order to see whether and how they dealt with the aforementioned issues and, in particular, if they refer to the principle of good faith.

§4.02   ICC CASE N. 10351/2001

The first award to be considered in our analysis with regard to the issue of the adjustment of a long-term gas sale contract is the one rendered in the ICC case n. 10351/2001.[547] Before examining such decision, it has to be noted that its relevance is mainly due to the fact that the arbitration tribunal expressly referred to the principle of good faith as a principle that is generally applicable to international contracts and that implies the duty of the parties to adapt the agreement in order to rebalance it, upon the occurrence of unforeseen events altering its *equilibrium,* independent of the applicable law and the provision of an adaptation clause.

In the case at issue the parties concluded a long-term contract for the sale of liquid natural gas (LNG) and, at Article VIII, agreed to use as reference prices the FOB Breakeven prices published by Platts[548] linking the LNG price to that of crude oil.[549] Furthermore, the contract included a renegotiation clause providing for the obligation of the parties to meet in order to agree on a new index for the calculation of the price (granting a result as much as possible equivalent to that resulting out of the application of the previous index) in three cases:

---

547. *See* ICC case n. 10351/2001, *supra* n. 527.
548. Platts is 'a leading global provider of energy, petrochemicals, metals and agriculture information, and a premier source of benchmark price assessments for those commodity markets' (*see* www.platts.com).
549. In particular, Art. VIII provided that '[l]a formule de calcul de prix comprenait un paramètre B, étant la moyenne arithmétique pendant le semestre précédant le trimestre d'application des prix moyens par baril des pétroles bruts le semestre précédant le trimestre d'application des prix moyens par baril des pétroles bruts originaires de huit pays différents, tells que publiés par [Platts Oilgram Price Report]' (*see* ICC case n. 10351/2001, *supra* n. 527, at 76).

(1) if one of the parties contests the publication of the above-mentioned Platts' Breakeven prices; or
(2) if Platts ceases to publish reliable information with regard to such prices; or
(3) if Platts ceases to publish such prices at all.

Furthermore, it has to be underlined that, during the course of the contract, the parties amended Article VIII several times. In particular, by means of the last modification, it was introduced a new element aiming to correct any possible distortion caused to the contract price by the application of the reference formula used by Platts. In addition, the agreement provided for a price review (Article IX) and an arbitration clause. The parties also expressly granted the arbitration tribunal the power to adjust the agreement (although it was not specified which provision provided for such authority).[550] According to Article IX, the parties, every four years, could request a revision of the agreed price in case the latter did not reflect the actual economic conditions of the LNG market as well as of the Western European markets of natural gas and other competing energy sources. Furthermore, it was established that, during the renegotiation phase, the old conditions remained in force.

The arbitration clause referred to the ICC Rules and fixed as a seat of arbitration Geneva. In consideration of the fact that the extract of the award published does not provide information of whether the parties referred to a specific *lex arbitri* different from the one of the seat and of the fact that usually this choice is very rare,[551] we can assume that the procedural law applicable to the arbitration was Swiss law that is silent on the issue of the adaptation power of arbitrators. However, we have seen that, in order to consider a law really silent and neutral, it is also necessary to take into account both the procedural provisions regarding the powers of courts and, more in general, the approach adopted by the legal system to which the arbitration law belongs in relation to the concept of hardship and to the possibility to adjust the contract.[552] In this regard, the Swiss legal system can be considered as a conservative one since, in general, it does not recognise the power of courts and arbitrators to adapt the contract (apart from some statutory exceptions) and, consequently, Swiss procedural law cannot be considered as actually silent and neutral.[553] However, in case the parties provide for an adaptation clause, the prevailing view in international arbitration is in favour of the adjustment of the agreement by arbitrators independent of the applicable procedural law. Moreover, in some cases, in which the *lex arbitri* was the Swiss law, arbitrators considered themselves entitled to intervene on contract's terms even in the lack of an adaptation clause.[554]

In light of the above, it can be concluded that the possible conflict between the agreement providing arbitrators with the adaptation power and the Swiss procedural law could be overcome and, therefore, the arbitration tribunal correctly assumed to

---

550. *Ibid.*, at para. 201.
551. *See* Ch. 3, §3.03.
552. *See* Ch. 3, §3.06.
553. *See* Ch. 3, §3.03[A][3].
554. *See* Ch. 3, §3.04. This tendency is also confirmed by the awards analysed in this chapter.

have the power to adjust the contract. However, it has to be underlined that the arbitrators did not address (at least as it results from the extract of the award published) such issue.[555]

Having said that, the dispute between the parties arose out of the modification by Platts of the method of calculation of its reference prices starting from January 1996 (in particular, the change regarded the oil products used as a reference to fix the price). Such amendment determined the increase of the LNG contract price. Moreover, Platts did not publish the new method. As a consequence, the claimant asked the counter-party to use the old formula and, upon the latter's refusal, it started an arbitration proceeding.

First of all, the tribunal affirmed that, in contrast to what alleged by the claimant, none of the three aforementioned hypothesis provided by Article VIII – in which the parties had the obligation to meet and agree on a new index replacing the old one – applied to the case at issue. Therefore, the claimant could not ask for the revision of the price according to such clause. However, the tribunal pointed out that in such case Article IX could apply since it disciplined the situation in which the contract price did not reflect anymore the market conditions. Moreover, the arbitrators noted that, by introducing the price-correcting factor, the parties recognised that, due to the link of such element with the Platts' price calculation formula, the modification of the latter also determined the modification of the former. Therefore, according to the tribunal, in this case since a change of the Platts' formula occurred the correcting factor had to be adjusted as a consequence. In affirming that the arbitrators referred to the principle of good faith. In particular, it was held that the obligation to execute contracts in good faith, in addition to be provided by the applicable law, is a general principle of international contract law (being provided by Article 1.7 of the UNIDROIT Principles) and that, according to such obligation, the parties have to adjust the contract in order to rebalance it when the original conditions change. Moreover, the tribunal noted that, in this case, the parties explicitly provided for two renegotiation clauses (Articles VIII and IX) that clearly could be considered as the expression of the above-mentioned principle. According to the arbitrators, the same could be said in relation to the correcting factor that, as seen, was supposed to be reviewed in case of modifications of the Platts' formula to which it was linked. In this regard, the arbitrators affirmed a second relevant principle. They underlined that the amendment of the correcting factor upon the change of the Platts' formula could occur independent of Article IX, i.e., independent of an adaptation clause, since it was based on the above-mentioned general duty to execute the contract in good faith. In conclusion, the tribunal ordered the parties to renegotiate and determine a modification of the correcting factor. Moreover, it was specified that, upon the renegotiation failure, the tribunal itself would have determined such amendment taking into account the parties' observations and any useful information provided by them.

As mentioned above, two important aspects emerge from the analysis of this case. First, the recognition of the parties' obligation to execute contracts in good faith

---

555. The same approach is also adopted in the other cases analysed in this chapter.

as generally applicable to international contracts independent of the relevant law. Second, the recognition of such obligation implies the duty to adjust the contract, when it becomes unbalanced due to the occurrence of unforeseen events, independent of the existence of an adaptation clause. As to the latter point, it has to be noted that the tribunal did not go so far as to also recognise the power of arbitrators to adapt the contract in the lack of an express provision in this sense. Therefore, it seems possible to say that, if the parties had not granted the arbitrators with such authority, the solution might have been different. In particular, the tribunal probably would have not affirmed that, upon the failure of the parties' renegotiations, it would have determined the modification of the correcting factor. However, as seen above, in the Author's opinion, also arbitrators and judges should be entitled to adapt long-term contracts on the basis of the principle of good faith since in this way it is possible to fulfil the parties' will and expectations that aim to maintain a balanced contract for all the duration agreed.

A further aspect has to be underlined with regard to this case. The latter is an example of how the arbitration tribunal can overcome the technical difficulties that may arise when adjusting complex contract, like long-term gas sale agreements, i.e., by referring to the parties' documents and allegations as well as to any useful information that they could, and should, provide in order to help arbitrators in reaching the decision.[556] This approach is in compliance with the will of the parties to find a suitable solution in order to maintain their relationship instead of terminating it and, consequently, it is always expression of the principle of good faith.

§4.03 THE *ATLANTIC* CASE

The problem of the adaptation of contracts was also addressed by the UNCITRAL arbitration award issued in the *Atlantic* case.[557] The dispute arose out of a long-term LNG sale agreement concluded in 1995 between Atlantic LNG Company of Trinidad and Tobago ("Atlantic"), the claimant, and Gas Natural Aprovisionamientos ("GNA"), the defendant. Such agreement provided for the supply of LNG produced by Atlantic, at its Caribbean facility ("Train1 LNG"), to GNA that was entitled to transport it to Spain or New England. Moreover, the agreement included a price review clause providing that:

> If at any time either Party considers that economic circumstances in Spain beyond the control of the Parties, while exercising due diligence, have substantially changed as compared to what it reasonably expected when entering into this Contract or, after the first Contract Price revision under this Article 8.5, at the time of the latest Contract Price revision under this Article 8.5, and the Contract Price resulting from application of the formula set forth in Article 8.1 does not reflect the value of Natural Gas in the Buyer's end-user market, then such Party may, by notifying the other Party in writing and giving with such notice information

---

556. *See* Ch. 3, §3.06.
557. *See supra* n. 224.

supporting its belief, request that the Parties should forthwith enter into negotiations to determine whether or not such changed circumstances exist and justify a revision of the Contract Price provisions and, if so, to seek agreement on a fair and equitable revision of the above-mentioned Contract Price provisions in accordance with the remaining provisions of this Article 8.5 … In reviewing the Contract Price … the Parties shall take into account levels and trends in price of supplies of LNG and Natural Gas … such supplies being sold under commercial contracts currently in force on arm's length terms, and having due regard to all characteristics of such supplies (including, but not limited to quality, quantity, interruptability, flexibility of deliveries and term of supply … The Contract Price as revised in accordance with this Article, shall in any event, allow the Buyer to market the LNG supplied hereunder in competition with all competing sources or forms of energy … in the market of the Buyer at the point of consumption, taking into account, inter alia, all appropriate operations, services and risks which are usual within the Natural Gas industry from the points of import for handling and marketing the Natural Gas in all market segments when due regard is given to all characteristics of the LNG supplied under this Agreement … and on the basis that sound marketing practices and efficient operations on the part of the Buyer are assumed and such Contract Price shall allow the Buyer to achieve a reasonable rate of return on the LNG delivered hereunder.[558]

It is important to note that the events triggering the possibility for the parties to request the price review were represented by changes of the economic conditions occurred only in the Spanish market, although the contract also gave GNA the possibility to sell the LNG in New England. Moreover, such changes, as usually provided by adjustment clauses, had to be: (1) substantial, (2) beyond the parties' control, (3) unforeseeable at the moment of the conclusion of the contract. Besides, the price formula agreed had not to reflect the aforementioned changes and, consequently, the contract price had not to reflect anymore the value of the natural gas in the Buyer's end-user market. The price review clause also provided the parties with some guidance to carry out the revision. In particular, they had to take into account the levels and trends of the price of supplies of LNG and natural gas, as well as the characteristics of such supplies. In addition, parties had to consider the other energy sources present in the GNA market in order for the reviewed price to be competitive and to allow GNA to obtain a reasonable return. The contract also referred to good faith by stating that such review had to be equitable and fair. Finally, the adaptation clause expressly granted arbitrators the power to adapt the contract, according to the criteria set therein, in case the parties would have not found an agreement within six months from the date of the price revision request. In its turn, the arbitration clause provided for an arbitration governed by the UNCITRAL Arbitration Rules with seat in New York.

Due to the liberalisation of the Spanish natural gas market, occurred after the conclusion of the contract, the relevant price decreased and, consequently, from October 2002 GNA have stopped selling the LNG supplied by Atlantic in Spain and focused its business on the New England market. For this reason, on 21 April 2005, Atlantic sent GNA a request to review the price alleging that the contract 'was negotiated on the assumption that the LNG would be delivered to and sold in Spain.

---

558. *Ibid.*, at 2–3.

This is reflected in many provisions of the Contract, which contain specific reference to Spain.[559] In addition, the pricing provision was negotiated in the context of the Spanish market, focusing on the Spanish tariff structure and the price of competing fuels'.[560] However, since the parties were not able to find an agreement, on 21 October 2005, Atlantic, according to the contract, started an arbitration proceeding claiming for the revision of the price (and, more specifically, for an increase of the latter) by considering the New England market as the GNA's actual end-user market, instead, of the Spanish one since, as said, the buyer was not operating there anymore. On 17 January 2007, the three-member arbitration tribunal issued the relevant award.[561]

Before analysing the solution adopted by the tribunal, it is important to note that the latter, first of all, addressed the issue of its authority to modify the price provision. As seen above, the contract in question is an example of long-term gas sale agreement that includes an adaptation clause expressly providing for the arbitrators power to adjust it (in this case the price) upon the failure of the parties' renegotiation. In light of such provision, the tribunal affirmed that it had the authority, not just to determine whether the events triggering the review of the price occurred, but also to actually revise it, according to the criteria fixed in the contract. In particular, it was held that:

> A price re-opener proceeding imposes on the Tribunal obligations that are broader than a traditional arbitration proceeding because the Tribunal is instructed to make commercial decisions based on very general standards and criteria. The Tribunal is required not just to determine whether there is a basis to reopen the price, but to actually decide what the new price should be - in effect revising a key provision of the Contract [...] The Tribunal interprets Article 8.5(f) as authorizing it to revise the price provisions of Article 8, but does not believe that it is empowered to revise any of the other provisions of the Contract.[562]

Thus, the tribunal considered sufficient the contract's provisions (i.e., the parties' will) to establish its authority to adjust the agreement and did not expressly address the issue of whether the applicable procedural law also provided it with such power and, consequently, whether a possible conflict with the parties' will could arise. Provided that such conclusion can be considered correct in light of the principle of good faith and its application to long-term gas sale agreements, it is in any case interesting to examine whether a conflict with the procedural law could actually arise in the *Atlantic* case. As said, the parties did not choose the law governing the arbitration. Therefore, the *lex arbitri* has to be considered that of the place of arbitration, i.e., the Federal Arbitration Act and the New York Arbitration Law since the seat chosen was New York. Furthermore, the arbitration proceeding, within the limits provided by the applicable *lex arbitri*, is governed by the UNCITRAL Arbitration Rules. The Federal Arbitration Act and the New York Arbitration Law (as well as the UNCITRAL Rules) are silent on the issue of the arbitrators' power to adapt the contract. However, as mentioned above,

---

559. *See*, in particular, the above-mentioned price review clause that expressly referred to the change of the economic conditions in the Spanish market.
560. *See* the *Atlantic* case, *supra* n. 224, at 5.
561. The arbitration tribunal clarified and corrected the award on 27 March 2008 upon the request of Atlantic.
562. *Atlantic* case, *supra* n. 224, at 8.

even in the lack of a specific provision on such issue in the *lex arbitri*, the latter can actually be considered silent and neutral if also the procedural norms regarding the powers of courts do not contain any provision in this regard. In addition, the approach adopted by the legal system to which the arbitration law belongs in relation to the concept of hardship and to the possibility to adjust the contract has to be taken into account. In this regard, we have seen that the common law system adopts a conservative approach by not providing courts and arbitrators with the power to adjust and modify contracts (apart from few exceptions made by the US case law) and by not recognising in general the concept of hardship (except, again, for the US legal system that recognises the notion of impracticability even if it is applied strictly and that its effect is usually the termination of the contract).[563] As a consequence, in the *Atlantic* case a conflict could be deemed to exist between the legal system including the procedural applicable law and the will of the parties. However, as said, the arbitration tribunal did not consider such issue and just relied on the contract provisions (and, namely, the three adaptation clauses and the arbitration clause) that was deemed sufficient to provide it with the authority to review the price.[564]

After having established their power to review the price, the arbitrators proceeded to determine whether the triggering conditions provided by the contract were met and, namely, whether a 'meaningful departure from the relationship between the Contract Price and the price of natural gas in the Buyer's end-user market'[565] occurred. The answer was positive since the tribunal affirmed that the original price formula, that was determined taking into account the Spanish market, did not reflect anymore the value of the natural gas due to the liberalisation of such market that had the effect to make GNA sell the gas supplied by Atlantic in New England. For this reason, the tribunal held that, in order to review the price formula, it was fair and equitable to consider which was the actual GNA's end-user market in which it was selling the gas. In light of the above, the arbitrators established a dual pricing scheme in order to construe the price 'in a manner that will be adaptable depending on the Buyer's end-user market at the time'.[566] Therefore, the tribunal, on the one hand, maintained the Spanish price formula since 'the Contract was clearly intended to be Spanish based, and [...] it should always have a Spanish based price'[567] (although it modified the relevant base price component) and, on the other, introduced a New England market price adjustment clause to be applied in relation to quarters in which more than a specific quantity of the LNG gas supplied by Atlantic was sold by GNA in New England market.[568]

Atlantic resisted to the enforcement proceeding of such award before the competent US District Court[569] by challenging it on the grounds that the arbitration

---

563. *See* Ch. 3, §3.03[A][4].
564. This seems to be the common approach adopted by arbitrators when the contract provides for an adaptation clause.
565. *See* the *Atlantic* case, *supra* n. 224, at 10.
566. *Ibid.*, at 16.
567. *Ibid.*
568. The exact percentage determined by the tribunal remained confidential.
569. *See GNA v. Atlantic*, www.westlaw.com (S.D.N.Y. 16 September 2008).

tribunal exceeded its authority and violated its due process rights, on which basis, according to Article V of the New York Convention and the Federal Arbitration Act (9 U.S.C. §10(a)(3) and (4)), the recognition and enforcement of the award may be refused or it may be vacated. The Court rejected both the Atlantic's claims and confirmed the award.

In particular, as to the first ground, Atlantic argued that the tribunal exceeded its powers since:

(1) it reviewed the price notwithstanding the triggering conditions were not met since, as also the tribunal affirmed, the liberalisation of the Spanish market was not an unforeseen event as required by the adaptation clause. Therefore, the arbitrators only relied on the second triggering event, i.e., the departure of the contract price from the actual value of the gas in the GNA's end-user market; and

(2) it rewrote the contract by imposing a dual-price scheme.

The Court rejected the first argument since the tribunal, in affirming that the liberalisation of the Spanish market was not unexpected, it also specified that the real test was whether the consequent developments significantly disrupted the expected relationship between the contract price and the value of natural gas. Therefore, according to the tribunal, the elements to be considered were the consequences (i.e., the developments) deriving from such liberalisation on the contract price that, instead, were unexpected. This was also confirmed by Atlantic which recognised that 'the impact of U.S. prices on the Spanish market price of LNG'[570] was not expected.

The Court also rejected the second argument made by Atlantic stating that:

> [it is] undisputed that the Tribunal was specifically charged with the duty to revise the pricing scheme once it determined that the contractual preconditions were met. The Tribunal having made that determination, Article 8.5(a) required it to reach "a fair and equitable revision" of the contract price. Neither this standard nor any other contractual provision set a structural limitation on permissible price revisions. Indeed, Atlantic's submissions to the Tribunal acknowledged the Tribunal's broad authority in this regard. In them Atlantic opined that the relevant contractual terms "do not appear to expressly limit this Tribunal's award to the imposition of a single pricing formula".[571]

Thus, the Court recognised that the parties did not set any limit to the arbitrators' power to review the structure of the price formula as long as the latter resulted in being fair and equitable, i.e., in compliance with the principle of good faith. Since we have said that the application of such principle to long-term gas sale agreements implies the adjustment of the contract in order to rebalance it, the tribunal was entitled to adopt any solution necessary to reach such purpose in order to allow the parties to keep their relationship (even the determination of a dual-price scheme). Furthermore, the Court rejected the due process violation argument proposed by Atlantic.

---

570. *Ibid.*, at 5.
571. *Ibid.*

In light of the above, it can be said that this case represents a correct application of the principle of good faith to long-term gas sale agreements by both the arbitration tribunal and the Court that confirmed the award. Moreover, such decision is an example of the extensive interpretation given to the scope of arbitrators' adaptation power. Indeed, unless the parties set out express limits, the adjustment clause is deemed to provide arbitrators with a broad authority to intervene on the contract in order to rebalance it and, consequently, the excess of power allegation made by a party when challenging the award or resisting to its enforcement is usually rejected.

§4.04   ICC CASES N. 9812/1999 AND N. 13504/2007

Other two relevant decisions to be analysed with regard to the adaptation of gas sale agreements are the ICC cases n. 9812/1999 and n. 13504/2007,[572] that both dealt with the same contract. The latter was a long-term agreement (with a duration from 1986 to 2026) for the sale of gas whose price was determined according to a formula that indexed it to the price of oil products in order to reflect the increases and decreases of competing energy sources in the buyer's market. In particular, such clause provided for 'two elements: a base price (P0) and a specific price element to be added or deducted from the base price. This specific price element is calculated for each quarter on the basis of the development of the prices for two competing sources of energy-light and heavy fuels oils'.[573] Moreover, the contract specified that 'the level of the base price can be seen as reflecting an average of all differently priced market opportunities available to the Buyers in the various segments of the gas market in [Buyers' State] at the time of conclusion of the [Contract]. Consequently, there is no direct relation between the base price and the prices obtained by the Buyers when reselling the case [sic] in the various customer segments'.[574]

The contract also included a price review clause (Article 6.10) providing that:

> (a) If the economic circumstances in the country of the Buyer which are beyond the control of the Parties should change significantly compared to what is reflected in the prevailing price provisions under Articles 6.1–6.4 hereof, then each Party shall be entitled to an adjustment of the price provisions under Articles 6.1–6.4 hereof, reflecting such changes, in particular the value of Natural Gas in the end-user market of the buyer as such value can be obtained by a prudent and efficient gas company. In any case, the price provisions hereunder shall allow the Buyer to economically market the Processed gas delivered hereunder in the market of the Buyer in competition with all competing sources of energy in the end-user market always assuming sound marketing practices and efficient operations on the part of the Buyer.[575]

The triggering condition of the price review was the occurrence of a substantial change of the economic circumstances in the buyer's market that was beyond the

---

572. *See supra* n. 225.
573. *See* ICC case n. 13504/2007, *id.*, at 93.
574. *Ibid.*
575. ICC case n. 9812/1999, *supra* n. 225, at 69; ICC case n. 13504/2007, *supra* n. 225, at 69.

parties' control and not reflected in the actual price formula. However, it was not mentioned the unforeseeability of such changes, that usually is a condition required by the adaptation provisions. Moreover, such clause provided the parties with some guidance for the revision by establishing that the parties had to take into account the value of natural gas in the buyer's end-user market and the other energy sources present in such market in order for the price reviewed to be competitive and for the gas to be marketable (so called "marketability requirement"). Then, the clause set out the frequency of the price review and the period of time to be taken as a reference by providing that either party was 'entitled to request a review of the price provisions under Articles 6.1–6.4 hereof for the first time with effect as of 1 April 1992 or earlier if necessary in order to perform a price review six (6) months prior to start of deliveries, for the second time with effect as of 1 October 1995 and thereafter with effect as of 1 October every three (3) years after 1 October 1995. In addition each Party shall be entitled to request a review of the price provisions under Articles 6.1–6.4 hereof once within each such three-year interval with effect from the first day of the month next following the request for price review, provided that the total number of such additional requests shall be limited to three (3) for each Party during the term of this Agreement'.[576] Upon the failure of the parties to find an agreement within 120 days from the request of the review, they could start an arbitration proceeding in order to have the price formula adapted according to criteria set out above. The extract of the two awards in question do not provide any indication neither of the substantive applicable law nor of the procedural one, apart from the indication of the ICC rules. However, we can assume that the arbitration was governed by the Swedish Arbitration Act since Stockholm was the seat of the arbitration and by the ICC rules when compatible with such act.

A first review of the price was negotiated by the parties upon the request of the sellers in 1992 that determined an increase of the price. Some years later, both parties asked for a second price amendment. However, this time, they did not reach an agreement and, therefore, they started the first arbitration proceeding (i.e., the ICC case n. 9812/1999).

[A] ICC Case n. 9812/1999

Before analysing the decision adopted by the arbitration tribunal in case n. 9812/1999, it is important to underline two aspects. First, like in the other decisions above mentioned, the arbitrators did not address (at least expressly) the issue of whether, according to the applicable procedural law, they were entitled to adapt the contract but they considered sufficient the will of the parties enshrined in the adaptation clause that, as seen, expressly provided them with such power. However, in this case, under a procedural law perspective the arbitration authority to adapt the contract could not find any objection and, consequently, no conflict with the parties' will could arise since we

---

576. *Ibid.*

have seen that the Swedish legal system recognises such authority upon courts and arbitrators.[577]

Second, the arbitration tribunal correctly affirmed that its decision was based on 'the grounds and circumstances invoked by the parties, the statements made, the expert opinions and other evidence submitted'.[578] This aspect is important since it shows that the resolution of disputes that arose out of adaptation of contracts implies the same activity as that required for the resolution of any other dispute, i.e., the analysis and interpretation of the contract, facts and evidence submitted by the parties, as well as expert opinions. In this way, arbitrators can address and resolve technical questions and difficulties that characterise complex contracts as gas sale agreements. As seen below, in such case the arbitrators affirmed that neither parties properly substantiated their price review requests by submitting adequate and appropriate evidence.

Said the above, the arbitration tribunal had to establish whether the aforementioned trigger events occurred in order to justify the price review claimed by the parties. The first step was the determination of the period of time within which the changes of the economic circumstances in the buyers' market occurred. In this regard, the arbitrators pointed out that the relevant years to be considered were those referred to by the parties in the amendment n. 4 to the contract entered into on 7 July 1994, i.e., from 1 October 1985 to 1 April 1994. Once established the period of time to be taken as a reference, the arbitration tribunal had to determine whether any changes in the economic circumstances in the buyers' market occurred during the above-mentioned years and whether such changes were significant and beyond the control of the parties. First of all, it was clarified that changes in the economic circumstances 'cover any fluctuation, variation or modification. Examples of such changes are a devaluation or revaluation of the [currency], a changed competitive situation, a tax on one or several sources of energy, an imposed price control and a changed legal environment with an economic effect, e.g., new environmental requirements'.[579] Then the tribunal had to interpret the meaning of significant change since, as said, only in this case the price review mechanism could be applied. The arbitrators in deciding this issue considered the definitions given by the parties in their claims and their conduct and concluded that 'a change, which implies an adjustment of P0 [i.e., the base price for gas] with approximately 15%, is without any doubt a significant change in the terms of the [Contract]'.[580]

As to the second condition (the fact that changes had to be "beyond the control of the parties"), the tribunal excluded 'changes within a sphere where it is possible for one or both parties to influence or command a certain level, including, but not limited to, contractual relationships'.[581] With regard to the last condition to be met (the fact that the change in the economic circumstances in the buyers' market had not to be

---

577. *See* Ch. 3, §3.03[C][3].
578. ICC case n. 9812/1999, *supra* n. 225, at 70.
579. *Ibid.*
580. *Ibid.*, at 71.
581. *Ibid.*

reflected in the price formula provided by Articles 6.1-6.4 of the contract), the tribunal stated that:

> In the adjustment formula, the changes of the prices for gasoil and heavy fuel oil in comparison with the base price for gas (P0) are the relevant factors ... Therefore, a relevant economic change as referred to in Article 6.10(a)(1) only occurs if there has been fluctuation, variation or modification in the economic circumstances in [Buyers' State] not reflected in the price calculated according to the price adjustment formula in Articles 6.1-6.4 [by which the gas price was indexed to the that of gasoil and heavy fuel oil].[582]

Before examining whether the trigger events indicated in the contract had occurred in the specific case, the arbitrators analysed the meaning of the provision included in Article 6.10, letter (a), first and second paragraph, according to which in adjusting the price the parties had to take into account the value of natural gas and the other energy sources in the buyer's end-user market in order for the price reviewed to be competitive. In this regard, with regard to first paragraph, the tribunal held that:

> The words "in particular" in Article 6.10(a)(1) imply that not only changes in the market value of natural gas may be relevant for an adjustment of the contract price ... One example of a change in the economic circumstances unrelated to the value of natural gas might be the entry of a powerful and independent competitor on the [Buyers' State] market, ... which would not necessarily change the market value of gas, but may nevertheless influence the price of gas. Another example could be the introduction of a governmental price control forcing sellers of gas to end-users in [Buyers' State] not to exceed a certain price, so that the sellers were unable to obtain the market value of gas. In this situation, the market value of gas as such is not affected for the time being, but a significant change, not reflected in the price provisions, in the meaning of Article 6.10(a)(1) would nevertheless have occurred.[583]

With regard to the second paragraph, the arbitrators affirmed that it had to be interpreted all together with the first since:

(1) the second paragraph did not indicate the mechanism for the price adjustment in case the buyer could not economically market the gas;
(2) the second paragraph did not provide in which situations the buyer could claim for the "non-marketability" of the gas;
(3) the second paragraph, if considered independent, would provide the buyer with an additional mechanism to adjust the price not linked to the trigger events included in the first period of Article 6.10, letter (a), i.e., the significant and beyond the parties' control change of the economic conditions in the buyer's market. On the contrary, the only possibility for the seller to request a price review would depend on the occurrence of such triggering events.

---

582. *Ibid.*
583. *Ibid.*

In particular, the tribunal held that:

> a consolidation of both paragraphs has to take place. Such consolidation entitles the buyer to invoke Article 6.10(a)(2) if an application of Article 6.10(a)(1) leads to a result where he cannot economically market the natural gas. Accordingly, the second paragraph therefore works as a protection of the buyer against upward adjustments of the price considering his market situation.[584]

In light of this interpretation, the arbitrators rejected the buyers' claim to adjust the price based on the "non-marketability" ground, provided by the second paragraph of Article 6.10, letter (a), since such 'allegation ... cannot be used by the Claimants as an independent basis for its request for price review, but can only be invoked as a defense against the Respondents' request for price increase according to Article 6.10(a)(1)'.[585]

Then, the tribunal examined the other claim of the buyers by which they asked for a reduction of the price due to the occurrence (from 1 April 1994) of the following changes in the economic circumstances of their market: '(i) the reaction in the end-user market based on the awareness of the intention by the Government to impose a tax on natural gas; (ii) the change in the border value of processed gas; (iii) the change in the movements in [Buyers' State] oil prices relative to [neighbouring] oil prices which indicate a decline in the [Buyers' State] oil prices and (iv) the decline in the premium of natural gas'.[586] The buyers alleged that such changes were significant, beyond the control of the parties and not reflected in the price formula. Furthermore, it was sustained that they caused a decrease of the value of the gas in the end-user market. However, it has to be noted that the tribunal considered only the first change alleged by the buyers (i.e., the future introduction of a tax on gas that 'will increase the consumers price of natural gas and will therefore worsen the competitive position of natural gas')[587] since the allegations and evidence they submitted in the price review request regarded just such circumstance. The tribunal did not consider possible the later introduction of new arguments to support the claimants' position since Article 6.10, letter (b), of the contract expressly provided that the price review had to substantiate the reasons why a party was asking it with no possibility to reserve the right to submit further issues and evidence, as asked by the buyers.

As to the merits, the tribunal rejected the buyers' claim since the latter failed to prove that 'the announced intention [to introduce a new tax on gas] constituted a change - and even less a significant change - in the economic circumstances'.[588]

Then, the arbitrators examined the defendants' request to review the price based on the introduction of an oil tax affecting the prices of energy sources in competition with gas. In particular, it was alleged that such tax 'had an effect on the prices for the relevant oil products and the significant relative changes in the prices of such products

---

584. *Ibid.*, at 72.
585. *Ibid.*, at 73.
586. *Ibid.*, at 74.
587. *Ibid.*
588. *Ibid.*, at 75.

in the [Buyers' State] market'.[589] The defendants based such allegation on the indices provided by institutions of the buyers' country and 'then used the three-month average process, calculated in the basis of these indices, for the three-month period immediately preceding the price review period (i.e., January to March 1994) and compared them with the prices for the three-month period in the end of the period (i.e., July to September 1995)'.[590] Even in this case, the tribunal rejected the claim for lack of proof and held that:

> In order to succeed with their claim, the Respondents furthermore have to prove that the oil tax caused a significant change of the economic circumstances not reflected in the price provisions of the [Contract]. As the oil tax was introduced [date], it would, in the view of the Arbitral Tribunal, have been more appropriate to measure its effect subsequent to that date as only a change caused by the introduction of the oil tax and not any other factors should be taken into account. An assessment of the changes in the prices during the whole price review period does not reflect the relative impact of the oil tax. The evidence submitted by the Respondents regarding the effects of the introduced oil tax only purports to show that a change in the prices has occurred during the price review period, but not to what extent the change was due to the oil tax. But even if a tax on oil presumably had at least some effect on the oil prices it has not been proven that any change of the market value of natural gas resulting from such price increases on gasoil and heavy fuel oil has been significant.[591]

[B] ICC Case n. 13504/2007

As previously said, the award issued in case n. 13504/2007 was the second decision regarding the long-term gas sale agreement described above. In this case, the dispute between the parties referred to changes of the economic circumstances in the buyers' market that occurred in the period from 1 October 1998 to 1 October 2001. In particular, the claimants (the buyers) requested a reduction of the price, while the defendants (the sellers) asked for an increase of the latter. Even in this decision, the arbitration tribunal did not expressly address the question of whether the procedural applicable law empowered it to adjust the contract and, consequently, to resolve the possible conflict between such law and the will of the parties. Due to the fact that the contract is the same as in case n. 9812/1999, it is possible to draw the same conclusions as those made in the latter in relation to such issue.

Said that, before analysing the decision adopted by the arbitrators, it is interesting to underline what they affirmed in relation to the purpose of adaptation clauses. In this regard, the arbitrators, after having specified that natural gas meant 'natural gas in general, including but not limited to the "Processed Gas" delivered under the [Contract]',[592] held that:

---

589. *Ibid.*, at 76.
590. *Ibid.*
591. *Ibid.*
592. ICC case n. 13504/2007, *supra* n. 225, at 96.

This means that the adjustment to be made should "in particular" have the effect to re-establish a reasonable difference between [Contract] prices and market values. This does not mean, however, that "the value of Natural Gas" is the only relevant consideration when an adjustment of the price provisions is to be made. The Arbitral Tribunal considers that the general purpose of price review provisions such as Article 6.10 [Contract] and the like provisions in long-term contracts, is to facilitate appropriate adjustments to counter unexpected economic developments not reflected in the price provision or which could distort the long-term viability of the [Contract].[593]

In such statement, therefore, the arbitrators made it clear that the scope of adaptation clause (like price review provisions) is to re-establish the balance and the *equilibrium* of a long-term contract altered by the occurrence of unforeseen events. Moreover, with the expression "re-establish a reasonable difference", they underlined that the adjustment of long-term contracts derives from and is based on the application of the principle of good faith (of which the adaptation clause is an expression) to the execution of such agreements.

As to the meaning of the expression "value of natural gas" (on which the parties had different opinions), the tribunal affirmed that, since the contract did not provide for any useful indication in this regard, it would have literally interpreted such expression by taking into account in any case the 'context in which the relevant terms were used by the Parties'.[594] Accordingly, the arbitrators considered that the value of natural gas meant 'the ordinary market value of gas, and that the market value of gas is to be determined on the basis of prices obtained or obtainable in actual transactions in the various market segments constituting the end-user market of the Buyer ... the ordinary market value of the gas is a key element when considering whether or not the gas can be marketed "economically"'[595] and it 'shall be reflected by an adjustment of the price provisions, provided that such change is not already reflected in the prevailing price provisions'.[596] In order to determine the value of the gas in the end-user market of the buyers, according to the tribunal, it was necessary to take into account all the different parts (and different prices) forming such market.

Then, the arbitrators clarified that the changes in the buyers' market occurred during the price review period met the triggering conditions provided by the price review clause since they were significant (on the basis of the parties' allegations, it was considered significant a change of the market value of natural gas that gave the Buyers the right to claim for a reduction of the contract price at least by 6.9%) and beyond the control of the parties (as seen below, the changes were due to the introduction of a new legislation, both in the electricity and gas sectors, that was considered an event independent of the parties).

As to the merits of the dispute, the tribunal upheld the request of the buyers to reduce the gas price due to the changes occurred in the relevant end-user market during the price review period that 'have had the effect of reducing the ordinary market value

---

593. *Ibid.*
594. *Ibid.*, at 99.
595. *Ibid.*, at 100.
596. *Ibid.*

of gas ... compared to what was reflected in the prevailing [Contract] price provisions'.[597] Such changes were mainly represented by the introduction, at the same time, of new laws regarding the gas and electricity[598] fields during the price review period that affected the market structure and, consequently, the value of the gas. In particular, it was noted that, due to the enactment of the new legislations, the buyers' market passed from a sort of monopoly protecting the suppliers there operating (this was the situation at the time of the conclusion of the contract) to a market open to competition favouring the entrance of new energy suppliers. This situation affected the gas price since the buyers had to reduce the sale prices in order not to lose their market shares. Moreover, it was considered relevant the increase of the contract gas price due to the growth of oil products' price to which it was indexed (due to the new market situation above described it was not possible for the claimants to transfer such increase to their customers).

Finally, it is interesting to analyse the approach adopted by the arbitrators in addressing one of the technical issues that may arise when carrying out the adaptation of long-term gas agreement and, namely, the quantification of the price reduction asked by the claimants. In order to assess such reduction, it was necessary to determine the market value of gas in the buyers' end-user market, i.e., 'the volume-weighted average of all obtained or obtainable prices in the various market segments'.[599] Even in this case, the arbitration tribunal, in resolving technical questions, relied on the proofs submitted by the parties. Indeed, the arbitrators held that the parties 'must substantiate a claim for price review by reliable and timely relevant price information from all the various market segments and calculate a volume-weighted average of the total segmental changes, taking into account also segments that are unaffected or have moved in different directions'.[600] In particular, the tribunal pointed out that the determination of the gas market value should be based on 'the relative volume shares (percentages of the total volume) per segment to build a representative average end user realization level'.[601] Then, in light of such data, it would be possible 'to assess ... the relative contribution of each market segment to the average total realization of the Buyer in the end user market'.[602] This process should be 'carried out for the situation at the start and at the end of the review period'[603] in order to obtain 'the change of the gas value during the price review period [i.e., the difference between the two situations]'[604] that 'may be compared with the relative change of the contract prices for [Contract] gas between the same points in time'.[605] However, since neither parties provided adequate evidence for this purpose, the tribunal issued an order requesting the parties to submit further proofs in order to 'ensure that complete volume as well as

---

597. *Ibid.*, at 105.
598. Electricity, on the basis of the evidence submitted, was considered as an energy resource in competition with gas with consequences on the latter's price and value.
599. *Ibid.*, at 102.
600. *Ibid.*
601. *Ibid.*, at 106.
602. *Ibid.*
603. *Ibid.*
604. *Ibid.*
605. *Ibid.*

realization changes over the review period were properly reflected, and that the information was presented in a form allowing adequate comparison'.[606] This is an example of one of the procedural powers that arbitrators can exercise (i.e., the request to the parties to submit further evidence) in order to resolve technical issues that may arise when adapting a long-term gas sale agreement. Moreover, it is interesting to underline the method applied by the tribunal for the evaluation and utilisation of the data provided by the parties. Since the latter were different, the arbitrators adopted the so called "cross-check methodology", that consisted in combining such data and, then, calculating the arithmetic average of such results. Such method was considered by the arbitrators as 'the most reliable basis available for an estimate regarding the extent to which [Contract] prices exceeded the ordinary market value of gas in the end user market during the price review period. Such a change no doubt meets the criteria of significance in Article 6.10(a) [Contract] ... Also, the relative loss of gas market value evidenced thereby is considered to have resulted from changes in the [Buyers' State] market caused by events outside the control of the Parties'.[607]

In light of the above, the tribunal adjusted the price formula provided in the contract by reducing the base price element.

§4.05 THE *QUINTETTE* CASE

Another decision that, although not dealing with a gas sale contract but with a coal sale agreement, is relevant for our analysis is the *Quintette* case.[608] In July 1981, Quintette Coal ("QCL") and Japanese Steel Companies ("JSI") concluded a long-term contract (almost fifteen years) whereby the former supplied the coal to latter at a price of USD 75 per tonne ("Base Price"). Such price was formed by a fixed part (equal to USD 35) and a varying part (equal to USD 40), that was subject to quarterly automatic adjustments by means of an escalating formula that linked it to the costs of labour, material and supplies, diesel fuel. Such indexes were indeed adjusted every three months on the basis of specific parameters.

The contract was governed by the law of British Columbia (Canada) and included two different price review clauses (Articles 7 and 9). Article 7 set out, as triggering condition, only the passing of time by providing, during the entire life of the contract, for three reviews of the Base Price in order to adjust it 'taking into consideration the then prevailing market price of metallurgical coal being supplied and sold to Buyer from major Canadian suppliers under long term contracts and also the quality

---

606. *Ibid.*, at 107.
607. *Ibid.*, at 108–109.
608. *Quintette Coal v. Japanese Steel Companies*, 28 May 1990, unpublished. The information available is that extracted from the decisions of the British Columbia Supreme Court (22 June 1990) and of the British Columbia Court Appeal (24 October 1990), that concern the judgment for the setting aside of the arbitration award and are both available on www.lexisnexis.com. Moreover, a detailed report on and comment to the case is provided by A.W. Neilson, *Price Adjustments in Long-Term Supply Contracts: the Saga of the Quintette Coal Arbitration*, 18 C.B.L.J., 76 9 (1991).

differential, if any, in comparison with those coals'.[609] The reference period of time during which carrying out the price review with effect for the following four years was set out to be the four months before the revision dates (31 March 1987, 31 March 1991, 31 March 1995). Article 9, instead, provided for a so called "iniquity review" by establishing that '[i]f any significant change in the metallurgical coal market takes place at any time during the term of the contract either party shall have the right to request a price review. The parties shall discuss the matter in good faith to reach a fair and reasonable adjustment'.[610] Such clause, therefore, established, as triggering condition, the occurrence of a significant change in the market. However, unlike the standard price re-opener provisions, it did not specify that the change had to be unforeseen, beyond the parties' control and affecting the value of the coal.

It has also to be noted that the agreement, in addition to the aforementioned price review clauses, included a hardship clause (Article 8) providing that '[b]oth Buyer and Seller recognize that circumstances may arise that could not have been foreseen at the time this contract was entered into. Both parties agree to use their best effort to solve any hardships or difficulties arising from such unforeseeable circumstances in the spirit of mutual good will and cooperation'.[611] This provision is very general since it refers to "any hardships or difficulties", and it is not limited to a specific element of the agreement (therefore, it could be applied to all contract terms). The above-mentioned Articles 8 and 9 are examples of the flexibility that characterise long-term contracts and of how the principle of good faith is enshrined in such agreements and is the basis of their adaptation.

As seen, neither the price review clauses nor the hardship provision referred to arbitration upon the parties' failure to find an agreement. It is, therefore, interesting to analyse the arbitration clause (Article 15) to see whether it provided, expressly or implicitly, the arbitrators with the power to adapt the contract. Such clause referred to '[a]ll unresolved disputes, controversies or differences between the parties arising out of or in connection with or resulting from this Agreement, or the breach hereof, any failure of the parties to reach agreement with respect to matters provided for herein and all matters of dispute relating to the sale of Coal by Seller to Buyer'. It is clear from the wording of the arbitration agreement that it also encompassed the power to adjust the contract. Indeed, first of all, the clause generally referred to "all unresolved disputes, controversies or differences". Such element can be considered sufficient to also include the conflict between the parties on the adjustment of the price or of any other contract term.[612] Moreover, the aforementioned provision expressly referred to "any failure of the parties to reach agreement with respect to matters provided for herein and all matters of dispute relating to the sale of Coal by Seller to Buyer". Thus, it is clear that, in light of such specification, no doubt could be deemed to exist with regard to the

---

609. *See* the British Columbia Supreme Court decision, *id.*, at 4.
610. *Ibid.*, at 5.
611. *Ibid.*, at 4-5.
612. *See* Ch. 3, §3.05.

power of the arbitration tribunal to adjust the contract upon the parties' failure to find an agreement (provided that the relevant triggering conditions were met).[613]

As to the procedural law, the arbitration clause provided for the application of the Rules of Procedure of the British Columbia Arbitrators' Institute.[614] Such rules referred to the Domestic Arbitration Act, that in 1986 was replaced, for international commercial arbitrations (like this case), by the International Commercial Arbitration Act that is based upon the UNCITRAL Model Law.

The first request of price review was submitted by JSI, at the beginning of 1985, due to the decrease of the coal price on the Japanese market determined by the oil crisis of the Middle East, the recession affecting such market and the discovery of new supplies of coal obtained by Japanese mines. After fifteen months of negotiations, the parties, in July 1986, reached an agreement and reduced the fixed component of the Base Price by USD 8.50 per tonne. Later, in December 1986, the buyers requested another revision of the price but this time QCL rejected such demand and, after several attempts to find an agreement, JSI, in November 1987, started an arbitral proceeding, basing the notice of request for arbitration mainly on Article 7 of the contract. In particular, JSI claimed that they were paying a price excessively higher than the actual market price and asked the tribunal to determine the price for coal to be supplied from 31 March 1987 to 31 March 1991. The claimants also indicated different price adjustment proposals and, as an alternative, asked the arbitration tribunal to decide the formula or method it considered appropriate.

The arbitration tribunal, on the basis of the above-mentioned clauses, considered itself as entitled to adapt the contract and, consequently, to review the price. Thus, even in this case it did not analyse whether such authority was also provided by the procedural applicable law (i.e., the International Arbitration Commercial Act) and, therefore, whether a possible conflict could arise with the parties' will. In this regard, it has to be noted that such Act is silent on the issue in question. However, as mentioned above, even if the *lex arbitri* does not rule on the arbitrators' adaptation of contracts authority, it is also necessary (in order to consider such law really silent and neutral on this matter) to take into account the procedural provisions regarding the powers of courts and, more in general, the approach adopted by the legal system to which such law belongs in relation to the concept of hardship and to the possibility to adjust the contract. In this regard, we have seen that the common law system adopts a conservative approach by not providing courts and arbitrators with the power to adjust and modify contracts (apart from few exceptions made by the US case law) and by not recognising in general the concept of hardship (except, again, for the US legal

---

613. In this sense, *see* also. Neilson, *supra* n. 608, at 87 (and the decisions therein mentioned), who, in particular, underlines the fact that the combination of the review clauses and the arbitration clause could be considered as providing for the duty to adjust the price upon the parties and, in case they fail to reach an agreement, for the power of the arbitrators to do it.
614. Originally the arbitration clause provided for the application of the Japan-Vancouver Trade Arbitration Agreement of 14 June 1961. In 1984 the parties amended the clause by establishing for the Rules of Procedure of the British Columbia Arbitrators' Institute.

system that recognises the notion of impracticability even if it is applied strictly and that its effect is usually the termination of the contract).[615]

Therefore, in the *Quintette* case (like in the *Atlantic* decision), a conflict could be deemed to exist between the legal system including the procedural applicable law and the will of the parties. However, from the information available, it seems that the arbitration tribunal did not address such issue and just relied on the contract provisions (and, namely, the three adaptation provisions and the arbitration clause) that it considered sufficient to provide it with the authority to review the price formula. As we saw in the analysis carried out above, this seems to be the common approach adopted by arbitrators when the contract provides for an adaptation clause. Two further considerations, supporting the authority of the arbitration tribunal in this case, can be made. First, the general approach in common law countries is in favour of arbitration and, consequently, when the parties choose the latter as the mechanism to settle their disputes arbitrators and courts tend to enforce the relevant arbitration agreement (even in case it is defective).[616] Second, the principle of *pacta sunt servanda*, that is prevailing in common law, is not only applied to deny the adaptation of contract when the parties did not include an adjustment clause, but it is also applied in the opposite case, i.e., when the contract, instead, provides for such clause. Therefore, if the parties also empowered the arbitrators to review the agreement, such provision is usually fulfilled since it meets the parties' will and expectations as enshrined in the contract.

As to the merits of the dispute, the arbitration tribunal upheld the claimants' request of reducing the Base Price. In particular, it amended the fixed part since it did not have the appropriate tools and evidence to revise the escalation formula determining the varying part. However, the arbitrators did not just establish one new Base Price to be applied for the four years following the review request but they fixed fifteen different Base Prices for each of the following fifteen quarters until the next revision date (until 31 March 1991). As a consequence, JSI was entitled to get back the difference between the price it paid to QLC since 1987 and the price calculated by the arbitrators.

For this reason, QLC challenged the award before the Supreme Court in order to set it aside on the ground that the arbitration tribunal exceeded its jurisdiction since it did not have the power to determine fifteen different prices, but only to fix one Base Price for the following four-year period that, consequently, had to remain the same until the next revision date. Therefore, even in this case it was not the general authority of the arbitration tribunal to adjust the contract to be challenged, but the fact that it went beyond the scope of the arbitration agreement. However, the Supreme Court rejected the claim holding that, even if the tribunal 'was wrong in its conclusion on that point, that would constitute a mere error in interpreting the contract and would not, under the International Act [the British Columbia International Commercial Arbitration Act], provide a ground for setting it aside'.[617] The Court also added that it did not

---

615. *See* Ch. 3, §3.03[A][4].
616. *See*, in general, on the approach in favour of the enforceability of arbitration agreements, Born, *supra* n. 240, Ch. 5; Lew, Mistelis & Kroll, *supra* n. 243, Ch. 7.
617. British Columbia Supreme Court decision, *supra* n. 608, *id.*, at 6.

consider that the tribunal's interpretation of the contract was wrong and, consequently, it concluded that the arbitrators were entitled to fix different Base Prices since their jurisdiction was not 'limited to fixing a base price as of the beginning of the period',[618] as contended by QLC.

The latter appealed such decision before the British Columbia Court of Appeal that confirmed the judgment of the Supreme Court referring, in particular, to the fact that the arbitrators were asked by the JSI to determine the formula they considered appropriate. Such issue, according to the judges, was included in the scope of the arbitration agreement. Moreover, the Court affirmed that the approach to be adopted when the parties provide for arbitration is 'to preserve the autonomy of the forum selected by the parties and to minimize judicial intervention when reviewing international commercial arbitral awards in British Columbia. That is the standard to be followed in this case'.[619] Even in this case, therefore, the excess of power argument was not upheld. This seems to be the main approach adopted by arbitration tribunals and courts when the contract includes an adaptation and an arbitration clause that, alone or combined together, provide arbitrators with broad power and do not set particular limits to their authority to review the contract's terms. In case, instead, the language of such provisions is not so general and extensive there is the risk that the authority of arbitrators can be considered as being limited only to certain matters and, consequently, their jurisdiction can be challenged. This is what happened in *Esso* case.[620]

§4.06 THE *ESSO* CASE

This case dealt with a dispute arose out of a fifteen-year natural gas sale agreement concluded on 27 November 1997 between *Esso Exploration & Production UK* ("Esso") and *Electricity Supply Board* ("ESB") and providing for two kinds of review of the price and, namely, of its Energy Charge element (the other component of the price was a Delivery Point Capacity Charge, that was not subject to adjustment). The first was a periodic review (every six months) to be conducted in light of four factors: the price of gasoil, the price of low sulphur fuel oil, the price of natural gas and the rate of inflation in Ireland. Such factors had to be determined by considering the relevant average calculated with regard to a period of twelve months ending three months before the review date. Moreover, the agreement provided that, as reference prices of the above-mentioned energy sources, the spot prices for the delivery in North West Europe had to be taken. The second type of review was, instead, based on the change of the market conditions and, in particular, in case 'it is reasonably satisfied in good faith that the Energy Charge ... is at the time of giving such Price Review Notice eighty five per

---

618. *Ibid.*
619. British Columbia Court of Appeal, *supra* n. 608, at 5. QLC requested the Supreme Court of Canada the leave to appeal from the decision of the British Columbia Court of Appeal. However, on 13 December 1990 the Supreme Court denied such request.
620. See *Esso Exploration & Production UK v. Electricity Supply Board*, as cited in *Gas Price Arbitration*, *supra* n. 206, at 157 et seq. (EWHC (QB) 31 March 2004).

cent (85%) or less than the Comparator'.[621] The latter was defined as '[t]he market price ... at the date of the relevant Price Review Notice for natural gas being supplied on the basis described above, that is, on the basis of the sale of reasonably similar quantities over a reasonably similar period on reasonably similar terms and conditions between parties of reasonably similar commercial and financial standing for use in a reasonably similar type of power station in the UK or Ireland'.[622] In addition, the agreement established that the party requesting a price review had to submit a notice specifying 'the value of the Energy Charge which it is requesting ... a reasonable and detailed explanation of how it has reached that figure and to provide it with all reasonably available published and other non-confidential information to support its position'.[623] Upon the submission of the price review notice, the parties had to negotiate and, in case no agreement could be reached within ninety days, the requesting party had to either withdraw the notice or start an arbitration in order 'to determine the Comparator and the consequent adjustment to the price'.[624]

On 1 November 2002, Esso sent its review notice to ESB claiming that the Energy Charge was 85% or less than the Comparator. As to the determination of the latter, it affirmed to have calculated it by taking as reference other short-term contracts since it was impossible for confidentiality reasons to obtain information on other long-term gas sale contracts similar to that in force between the parties. ESB rejected such request alleging that it did not comply with the contract since the latter provided that the Comparator had to be determined by referring to long-term gas sale agreements ("on the basis of the sale of reasonably similar quantities over a reasonably similar period on reasonably similar terms and conditions between parties of reasonably similar commercial and financial standing for use in a reasonably similar type of power station in the UK or Ireland"). Thus, according to ESB, due to the wrong calculation of the Comparator made by Esso the condition triggering the review (i.e., that the price had to be equal to 85% or less than the Comparator) did not occur and, consequently, the price review request was invalid. Upon the parties' failure to reach an agreement, Esso referred the matter to arbitration. However, ESB challenged the jurisdiction of the arbitration tribunal on the ground that, since the price review request was invalid, the condition necessary to establish its authority was lacking. Esso, then, brought the matter before the High Court. The latter agreed with ESB arguments regarding the calculation of the Comparator and the consequent invalidity of the price review request, on the one hand, and the lack of jurisdiction of arbitrators, on the other. As to the latter issue, the Court made a further consideration. In particular, it affirmed that the part of the review clause providing that, in the lack of an agreement between the parties, the matter could be referred 'to arbitration to determine the Comparator and the consequent adjustment to the price', had to be interpreted as granting arbitrators only the power to determine the amount of the Comparator and not the issue of its nature, i.e., how it had to be calculated. According to the Court, since the real dispute

---

621. *Ibid.*, at 175.
622. *Ibid.*
623. *Ibid.*
624. *Ibid.*

between the parties regarded the latter point (i.e., whether the Comparator had to be determined by taking as a reference long-term or short-term gas sale agreements), the arbitration tribunal did not have the jurisdiction.

In our opinion, the interpretation of the Court was not correct since the words "to determine the Comparator and the consequent adjustment of the price", provided in the review clause, have a broader scope than that given by the Court and, consequently, could be deemed to encompass not just the determination of the amount of the Comparator but also of the issue regarding its method of calculation. Said that, this case is an example of the importance of the choice of the words when drafting an adaptation clause. The decision of the Court would have probably been different if the price review clause in question had just provided, for instance, that, in the lack of the parties' agreement, the dispute or matter could be referred to arbitrators.

§4.07 CONCLUSIONS

The analysis of the decisions carried out in this chapter has shown that, in case the contract provides for the arbitrators' power to adjust it either in the adaptation or in the arbitration clause, arbitrators (and courts when the awards is challenged) usually tend to enforce it independent of the procedural applicable law. In these cases, the will of the parties is considered sufficient to establish their authority to adjust the agreement and arbitrators do not address (at least expressly) the issue of whether also the procedural applicable law provides them with such power and, in the negative case, of how to resolve the consequent conflict. This approach seems to be mainly based on the following elements:

(1) the fact that the arbitrators' jurisdiction derives from the arbitration agreement;
(2) the principle of *pacta sunt servanda* and the consequent fulfilment of the parties' will. The application of such principle is prevailing in international commercial arbitration and, consequently, if the parties do not include an adaption clause in the contract arbitrators do not adjust it and vice-versa;
(3) strictly connected to the previous point, the general favourable approach towards arbitration when the parties select such mechanism to settle the disputes arising out of their contract.

Although the above-mentioned solution eventually results to be correct since it fulfils the parties' will (that want to adapt the contract in order to keep it alive), in our opinion, the procedural perspective should also be considered. Indeed, arbitration has an hybrid nature since, even if the jurisdiction of arbitrators derives from the contract, they carry out a judicial task and, consequently, they deliver an award with the same effects as those of a decision issued by courts. Therefore, the powers that they exercised are procedural like those of judges. For this reason, the procedural applicable law perspective could not be completely ignored in the analysis of the case, although at the end the decision adopted could depart from what therein provided. In this regard, we have seen that, even if such law does not allow arbitrators and courts to adjust the contract, the application of the principle of good faith to the execution of long-term agreements provides them with this power, even not including an adaptation clause. Indeed, its application to long-term gas agreements, due to their characteristics and scope, implies their adaptation (by parties and arbitrators) upon the occurrence of events unbalancing them. In this way, it is possible to meet the parties' will and expectations that aim to maintain their commercial relationship.[625] Such considerations can also be made with regard to contracts with an adaptation clause since they have the same characteristics and scope as those of agreements without such provision and, therefore, in both cases the parties' will is identical. Thus, the presence of the adaptation clause is not a condition necessary for the recognition of their power to adjust the contract. It just consents the parties to better identify and define the adaptation process of their agreement by specifying, for instance, the terms to be modified, the triggering conditions, the limits and extent of the arbitrators' power, the criteria to be followed in carrying out the adjustment of the contract, etc. The more detailed the clause is, especially with regard to the triggering conditions and the criteria to be followed for the review, the easier the task to be carried out by arbitrators is since there are more elements to which they can refer. Similarly, the parties could be advantaged with regard to both the renegotiation process and the proofs to be submitted before the tribunal upon the failure to reach an agreement.[626]

In conclusion, it can be said that the approach adopted in the decisions above analysed seems to be in line with the solution prospected in this book, based on the application of the principle of good faith, since both of them meet the parties' expectations and will to maintain alive their contract. However, even if this is the final result, arbitrators, in reaching their decisions, should not completely omit to consider also the procedural applicable law perspective since, as said, their power to adapt the contract has a procedural nature.

The same solution can be also applied to gas sale agreements including an adaptation clause but not expressly conferring, neither in such provision nor in the arbitration clause, the power to adjust the contract upon arbitrators. Indeed, this element does not change the considerations made above. Moreover, although we did not find awards on this particular kind of agreement, the lawyers and arbitrators involved in gas sale disputes, that were contacted and interviewed by the Author, confirmed that usually arbitration tribunals considered themselves as entitled to adapt the contract on the basis of the combination of the adjustment and the general arbitration clauses, provided, of course, that the latter does not expressly exclude such power.

Another aspect that emerged from the decisions analysed is that the most common adaptation process, and relevant dispute, concerns the review of the price. Indeed, we have seen that all the cases above mentioned dealt with the request of the parties to adjust the price, by modifying the relevant formula, when the market conditions change and make the contract unbalanced. This seems to be also confirmed

---

625. See Ch. 3, §3.06.
626. See §4.01.

Chapter 4: Arbitrators Contracts with an Adaptation Clause §4.07

by the most recent arbitration proceedings regarding long-term gas agreements. Unfortunately, the relevant decisions are not published and, consequently, the information available regarding the contract's clauses and the content of the award is few and, mainly, extracted by press releases or reports and comments published in this regard.[627] However, it is possible to mention the following price review disputes:

(1) *Edison v. Promgaz.* In April 2013, Edison filed an arbitration before a three-member tribunal, governed by the Stockholm Chamber of Commerce. Edison claimed a reduction of the price of the gas supplied by Promgaz in line with the actual market gas price. The award was issued in August 2014 whereby the tribunal partially upheld the claim of Edison by recognising the 35% of its request. The claimant criticised such decision alleging, in particular, that it did not comply with the contract's provisions and with the principles applicable to price reviews. However, Edison declared its intention not to challenge the award.

(2) *Gazprom v. RWE.* This case was an ICC arbitration, with seat in Vienna, filed by RWE that claimed for an adjustment of the price formula since it did not reflect the actual market conditions. In June 2013, the arbitration tribunal handed down the award that partially upheld the claimant's request. In particular, the price formula was modified by replacing the oil price element, to which originally the gas price was linked, with the reference to gas spot prices. Moreover, RWE was awarded a compensation for the price paid in excess for the gas supplied by Gazprom. Such amount seems to be equal to a third of what it claimed.

(3) The same parties faced another arbitration proceeding regarding the same contract filed by RWE this time not in relation to the price but to the take or pay clause included in such agreement and according to which RWE had to buy 9 billion cubic metres of gas per year until 2035. The buyer asked for a reduction of such obligation and the ICC arbitration tribunal, seating in Vienna, with the award issued in October 2012 granted such request. In particular, the tribunal affirmed that the minimum bill quantity provided in the contract had to be reduced of an amount equal to the gas directly supplied by Gazprom in the RWE market (the Czech Republic). Gazprom has challenged the award before the Austrian Courts.

---

627. *See*, in particular, the following articles: C. Spallon, *Edison-Gazprom Pricing Dispute at an End*, http://globalarbitrationreview.com/article/1033884/edison-gazprom-pricing-dispute-at-an-end (19 November 2014); GAR News, *Gas Price Reviews: Is Arbitration the Problem*, http://globalarbitrationreview.com/article/1033224/gas-price-reviews-is-arbitration-the-problem (6 March 2014); K. Karadelis, *ICC Panel Revises Gazprom Export Price Formula*, http://globalarbitrationreview.com/article/1032473/icc-panel-revises-gazprom-export-price-formula (3 July 2013); *Id.*, *Polish-Russian Gas Price Review Case Settles*, http://globalarbitrationreview.com/article/1031744/polish-russian-gas-price-review-case-settles (9 November 2012). *See* also McNair Chambers, *LNG Price Review Disputes*, http://www.mcnairchambers.com/client/publications/2013/LNG_PRICE_REVIEW_DISPUTES_.pdf (10 December 2013) and the report of Russian Today of 17 May 2016, https://www.rt.com/business/343286-gazprom-europe-supplies-price/.

(4) *Edison v. Sonatrach* (the award was issued in April 2013) and *Edison v. Rasgas* (the award was delivered in September 2012). In both cases, Edison claimed for, and obtained, a reduction of the price of the gas supplied by the counterparties. In particular, the arbitration tribunals seems to have modified the price formula by eliminating the link to the oil price and awarded a compensation to Edison for the overpayments made.

(5) *Edison v. Eni*. Edison filed an arbitration claiming, even in this case, for a reduction of the price of the Libyan gas supplied by Eni. The award was handed down in October 2012 and granted Edison a reduction of such price (we do not know if the latter met the exact request of the claimant).

(6) *Polskie Gornictwo Naftowe i Gazownictwo (PGNiG) v. Gazprom*. PGNiG in February 2016 filed an arbitration in Stockholm's Arbitration Court against Gazprom in order to amend the price of the long-term contract signed by the parties in 1996 and in force until 2022. The decision is expected by July 2017.

Moreover, other three recent proceedings against Gazprom were filed: Gas Terra (a Dutch company) started a court proceedings against Gazprom Export on 4 May 2016; Botas (a Turkish company), upon the failure of the negotiations with Gazprom, filed an arbitration claiming for a gas price discount; Shell Energy Europe filed an arbitration against Gazprom whose first hearing should be in February 2018.

Instead E.On Ruhrgas settled its price review dispute with Gazprom.

As said, we do not have information on the contracts and awards concerning the aforementioned cases. In particular, we do not know what the adaptation and arbitration clauses provided and consequently, which was the procedural applicable law (apart from the arbitration rules above mentioned), if the arbitration tribunal addressed the issue of their power to adapt the contract, which was the extent of such powers. As to the latter point, we do not know, for instance, whether the contract already provided for the possibility to replace the oil price index included in the original price formula or whether the parties with their conduct have already modified the agreement *per facta concludentia*. However, it seems possible to affirm, on the one hand, that the approach of arbitration tribunals, in case of contracts including an adaptation clause, is to consider themselves as entitled to review such agreements on the basis of the adjustment provision and, on the other, that the extent of their power is quite broad.

Bibliography

Aissaoui A., *The Political Economy of Oil and Gas* (Oxford University Press 2001).

Austen-Baker R., *Comprehensive Contract Theory: A Four-Norm Model of Contract Relations*, 25 JCL, 216 (2009).

Austen-Baker R., *A Relational Law of Contract*, 20 JCL, 125 (2004).

Beale H., Fauvarque-Cosson B., Rutgers J., Tallon D. & Vogenauer S., *Cases, Materials and Text on Contract Law* (Hart Publishing 2010).

Beatson J., Burrows A. & Cartwrigth J., *Anson's Law of Contract* (Oxford University Press 2010).

Beggs D. & Sapte D. W., *Gas Sales and Supply Contracts*, in *Natural Gas Agreements* (M. R. David, Sweet & Maxwell 2002).

Beisteiner L., *The (Perceived) Power of the Arbitrator to Revise a Contract - The Austrian Perspective*, in *Austrian Yearbook on International Arbitration* (C. Kalusegger & P. Klein, Manz'sche Verlags- und Universitätsbuchhandlung 2014).

Berger K. P., *International Economic Arbitration* (Kluwer Law Taxation 1993).

Berger K. P., *Power of Arbitrators to Fill Gaps and Revise Contracts to Make Sense*, 17 Arb Intl, 1 (2001).

Bernitz U., *Swedish Standard Contracts Law and the EC Directive on Contract Terms*, http://www.scandinavianlaw.se/pdf/39-1.pdf.

Bessone M., *Adempimento e rischio contrattuale* (Giuffrè 1975).

Bockstiegel K. H., *Hardship, Force Majeure and Special Risks Clauses*, in *Adaptation and Renegotiation of Contracts in International Trade and Finance* vol. III (N. Horn, Kluwer, 1985).

Bogdan M., *Private International Law as Component of the Law of the Forum* (Hague Academy of International Law 2012).

Bonell M. J., *Arbitration as a Means for the Revision of Contracts*, in *Italian National Reports to the X International Congress of Comparative Law - Budapest 1978* (Giuffrè 1978).

Born G., *International Commercial Arbitration* (Wolters Kluwer 2014).

Brautaset A., *Norwegian Gas Sales* (Sjørettsfondet 1998).

Brekoulakis S., Riberiro J. & Shore L., *UNCITRAL Model Law on International Commercial Arbitration*, in *Concise International Arbitration* (L. Mistelis, Kluwer Law International 2015).

Brownsword R., *Positive, Negative, Neutral: the Reception of Good Faith in English Contract Law*, in *Good Faith in Contract* (R. Brownsword, N. J. Hird, & G. Howells, Ashgate/Dartmouth 1999).

Brownsword R., *Contract Law, Co-operation, and Good Faith: The Movement from Static to Dynamic Market-Individualism*, in *Contracts, Co-operation and Competition* (S. Deakin & J. Michie, Oxford University Press 1997).

Brownsword R., *Good Faith in Contracts Revisited*, 49 C.L.P., 111 (1996).

Brownsword R., *Two Concepts of Good Faith*, 7 JCL, 197 (1994).

Brunner C., *Force Majeure and Hardship under General Contract Principles* (Kluwer Law International 2009).

Burrows A., *Remedies of Torts and Breach of Contract* (Oxford University Press 2009).

Busch D., Hondius E., van Kooten H., Schelhaas H. & Schrama W., *The Principles of European Contract Law and Dutch Law* (Kluwer Law International 2002).

Castello J. E., *UNCITRAL Arbitration Rules*, in *Concise International Arbitration*, 182 (L. Mistelis, Kluwer Law International 2015).

Chitty J., *Chitty on Contracts* vol. I and II (Sweet & Maxwell 2012).

Cheshire G. C., Fifoot C. H.S. & Furmston M. P., *Cheshire, Fifoot & Furmston's Law of Contract* (Oxford University Press 2007).

Collins H., Campbell D. & Wightman J., *The Implicit Dimensions of Contract* (Hart 2003).

Collins H., *The Law of Contract* (Butterworths 2003).

Corbin A. L., *Corbin on Contracts* (West Publishing Co. 1964).

Correljé A. F. & Odell P. R., *Four decades of Groningen production and pricing policies and a view to the future*, 28 Energy Policy, 19 (2000).

Craig W. L., Park W.W. & Paulsson J., *International Chamber of Commerce Arbitration* vol. 3 (Oceana Publications 1990).

D'Angelo A., *La buona fede ausiliaria del programma contrattuale*, in *Buona fede e giustizia contrattuale* (A. D'Angelo, P.G. Monateri & A. Somma, Giappichelli 2005).

Davenport P., *Construction Claims* (The Federation Press 1995).

Davey H., *"Take or Pay" and "Send or Pay": a Legal Review and Long-Term Prognosis*, 11 O.G.L.T.R., 419 (1997).

David R., *Arbitration in International Trade* (Kluwer Law and Taxation Publishers 1985).

Dawson J., *Judicial Revision of Frustrated Contracts: The United States*, 64 B.U.L.Rev., 1 (1984).

De Martini A., *L'eccessiva onerosità nell'esecuzione dei contratti* (Giuffrè 1950).

Di Majo A., *Eccessiva onerosità sopravvenuta e reductio ad aequitatem*, in Corriere giuridico, 664 (1992).

Draetta U., Lake R. B. & Nanda V. P., *Breach and Adaptation of International Contracts* (Butterworth Legal Publishers 1992).

Estrada J., Bergesen H. O., Moe A. & Sydnes A. K., *Natural Gas in Europe* (Pinter Publishers Limited 1988).

Fauvarque-Cosson B. & Mazeaud D., *European Contract Law* (Sellier 2008).

Farnsworth E. A., *Good Faith Performance and Commercial Reasonableness Under the Uniform Commercial Code*, 30 U.Chi.L.Rev., 666(1962).

Frick J. G., *Arbitration and Complex International Contracts* (Kluwer Law International 2001).

Frignani A., *Hardship Clause*, VI Digesto Discipline Privatistiche sez. Commerciale, 446 (1991).

Frignani A., *La hardship clause nei contratti internazionali e le tecniche di allocazione dei rischi negli ordinamenti di civil law e di common law*, Riv Dir Civ, 680 (1979).

Fucci F. R., *Hardship and Changed Circumstances as Grounds for Adjustment or Non-Performance of Contracts*, http://www.cisg.law.pace.edu/cisg/biblio/fucci.html (2006).

Fouchard P., E. Gaillard &, B. Goldman, *Fouchard, Gaillard, Goldman on International Commercial Arbitration*, (G. Gaillard & J. Savage, Kluwer Law International 1999).

Gallo P., *Revisione del Contratto*, XVII Digesto Discipline Privatistiche sez. Civile, 431(1998).

Gazzoni F., *Equità e autonomia privata* (Giuffrè 1970).

Greeno T. & Kehoe C., *Contract Pricing Disputes*, in *Dispute Resolutions in the Energy Sector* (R. King, Global Law and Business 2012).

Grigoryev Y., *The Russian Gas Industry, Its Legal Structure, and Its Influence on World Markets*, 28 Energy L.J., 125 (2007).

Griffin P. & van Eupen F., *The Future for Price Reviews*, in *Gas Price Arbitration* (M. Levy, Global Law and Business 2014).

Hartkamp A. S. & Tillema M. M. M., *Contract Law in the Netherlands* (Kluwer Law International 1995).

Hayes M. H., *Algerian Gas to Europe: The Transmed Pipeline and Early Spanish Gas Import Projects*, http://www.africanews.it (May 2004).

Heather P., *Continental European Gas Hubs: Are they fit for purpose?*, https://www.oxfordenergy.org/wpcms/wp-content/uploads/2012/06/NG-63.pdf, 1 (2012).

Henderson J., *Evolution of the Russian Gas Market - The Competition for Customers*, www.oxfordenergy.org, 1 (2013).

Heuman L., *Arbitration Law of Sweden* (Jurisnet 2003).

Hobér K. I., *Arbitration Reform in Sweden*, 17 Arb Intl, 351 (2001).

Hijma J., *The Role of the Court and of the Parties in Adapting a Contract to Unforeseen Circumstances*, in *Foreseen and Unforeseen Circumstances* (A.G. Castermans, K.J.O. Jansen, M. W. Knigge, P. Memelink & J. H. Nieuwenhuis, Kluwer 2012).

Hillman R. A., *Court Adjustment of Long-Term Contracts: An Analysis Under Modern Contract Law*, 1 Duke L.J., 2 (1987).

Hognestad G., *The Role of the Norwegian Government when Selling Natural Gas*, in *Natural Gas Markets and Contracts* (R. Golombek, M. Hoel & J. Vislie, Elsevier Science Publishers B.V., North Holland, 1987).

Holland B. & Ashley P., *Enforceability of Take-or-Pay Provisions in English Law Contracts*, 26 J.E.R.L., 615 (2008).

Horn N., *The Concepts of Adaptation and Renegotiation in the Law of Transnational Commercial Contracts*, in *Adaptation and Renegotiation of Contracts in International Trade and Finance* vol. III (N. Horn, Kluwer 1985).

Id., *The Procedures of Contract Adaptation and Renegotiation in International Commerce*, in *Adaptation and Renegotiation of Contracts in International Trade and Finance* vol. III (N. Horn, Kluwer 1985).

Hunter J. M., *The Procedural Powers of Arbitrators Under the English 1996 Act*, 13 Arb Intl, 345.

Hylleberg T. & Pedersen M. A., *Overview of the Norwegian Oil and Gas Industry*, www.offshorecenter.dk, 14 (2009).

Iynedjian M., *Gas Sale and Purchase Agreements under Swiss Law*, in 4 ASA Bulletin, 746 (2012).

Juris A., *Market Development in the United Kingdom's Natural Gas Industry* (The World Bank, Private Sector Development Department, Private Participation in Infrastructure Division 1998) 1998).

Juris A., *Development of Natural Gas and Pipeline Capacity Markets in the United States* Development of Natural Gas and Pipeline Capacity Markets in the United States 1998).

Karadelis K., *ICC panel revises Gazprom Export price formula*, http://globalarbitrationreview.com/article/1032473/icc-panel-revises-gazprom-export-price-formula (3 July 2013).

Karadelis K., *Polish-Russian gas price review case settles*, http://globalarbitrationreview.com/article/1031744/polish-russian-gas-price-review-case-settles (9 November 2012).

Kessedjian C., *Competing Approaches to Force Majeure and Hardship*, 25 International Review of Law and Economics, 415 (2005).

Kolo A. & Walde T. W., *Renegotiation and Contract Adaptation in International Investment Projects*, 1 JWIT, 5 (2000).

Lando O. & Beale H., *Principles of European Contract Law* (Kluwer Law International 2000).

Lehrberg B., *Scandinavian Jurisdiction*, in *Unexpected Circumstances in European Contract Law* (E. Hondius & Christoph Grigoleit, Cambridge University Press 2011).

Lehrberg B., *Unexpected Circumstances - National Report from Sweden*, www.unexpected-circumstances.org (2005).

Lehrberg B., *Renegotiation Clauses, the Doctrine of Assumptions and Unfair Contract Terms*, 3 E.R.P.L., 265 (1998).

Leonardo G., *L'obbligo di take or pay: Qualificazione e gestione delle sopravvenienze*, I Contratti, 605 (2013).

Leijten M. & de Vries Lentsch M., *The Trigger Phase*, in *Gas Price Arbitration* (M. Levy, Global Law and Business 2014).

Levy M., *Gas Price Arbitration* (Global Law and Business 2014).

Lew J., Mistelis L. & Kroll S., *Comparative International Commercial Arbitration* (Kluwer Law International 2003).

Lorefice M., *Il mercato del gas: il quadro attuale e le prospettive - Le clausole di take or pay nei contratti di compravendita di idrocarburi*, in Il mercato del gas tra scenari normativi e interventi di regolazione (M.S. De Focatis & A. Maestroni, Giuffrè 2013).

Macario F., *Adeguamento e rinegoziazione*, in Trattato dei contratti - I contratti in generale vol. II (P. Rescigno & E. Gabrielli, Utet 2006).

Macario F., *Adeguamento e rinegoziazione nei contratti a lungo termine* (Jovene 1996).

Macario F., *Modificazioni del mercato e disciplina dei contratti di fornitura dell'energia* (Maggioli 1991).

Macaulay S., *An Empirical View of Contract*, Wis.L.Rev., 465 (1985).

Macneil I. & Campbell D., *The Relational Theory of Contract: Selected Works of Ian Macneil* Sweet & Maxwell 2001).

Macneil I., *Contracts: Adjustment of Long-Term Economic Relations Under Classical, Neoclassical, and Relational Contract Law*, 72 N.Y.U.L.Rev., 854 (1978).

Macneil I., *The Many Futures of Contracts*, 47 S.Cal.L.Rev., 691 (1974).Mckendrick E., *Contract Law* (Oxford University Press 2012).

Macneil I., *The Regulation of Long-term Contracts in English Law*, in Good Faith and Fault in Contract Law, (J. Beatson & D. Friedmann, Clarendon 1995).

Mekki M. & Kloepfer-Pelèse M., *Hardship and Modification (or 'Revision') of the Contract*, in Towards a European Civil Code (A. S. Hartkamp, Kluwer Law International 2011).

Melling A. J., *Natural Gas Pricing and Its Future*, http://carnegieendowment.org, (2010).

Merkin R. & Flannery L., *Arbitration Act 1996* (Informa 2008).

Mustill M. & Boyd S., *Commercial Arbitration* (Butterworths 1989).

Nassar N., *Sanctity of Contracts Revisited* (Martinus Nijhoff Publishers 1995).

Neilson A. W., *Price Adjustments in Long-Term Supply Contracts: the Saga of the Quintette Coal Arbitration*, 18 C.B.L.J., 76 (1991).

Nicholas B., *The French Law of Contract* (Clarendon Press Oxford 1992).

Nicklish F., *Agreement to Arbitrate to Fill Contractual Gaps*, 3 Arb Intl, 35 (1988).

Oertmann P., *Geschaftsgrundlage - Ein neuer Rechtsbegriff* (Deichert 1921).

Oladotun A., *M&J Polymers Ltd. v. Imerys Mineral Ltd: Can Take or Pay Clause in Gas Contract Be Considered a Contractual Penalty?*, 14 CEPMLP Annual Review 1 (2005).

Osikilo Y., *How Are the Problems of Buyer in Long-Term Take or Pay Contracts in the Gas Industry Mitigated?*, 9 CEPMLP Annual Review, 1 (2005).

Pardolesi R., *Florida Power & Light v. Westinghouse Electric*, IV Foro It, 376 (1981).

Parola L., *Contratti di somministrazione di gas naturale "take or pay" e project financing*, I Contratti, 192 (2002).

Peebles M. V. H., *Evolution of the Gas Industry* (The Macmillan Press Ltd. 1980).

Pennazio R., *La dottrina del fondamento negoziale nel diritto giudiziale europeo*, 1 Contratto Impresa/Europa, 391 (2009).

Perillo J. M., *Hardship and its Impact on Contractual Obligations: A Comparative Analysis*, http://www.cisg.law.pace.edu/cisg/biblio/perillo4.html (1996).

CESL: *Change of Circumstances and Prescription - A Belgian Perspective*, in *The Draft Common European Sales Law: Towards an Alternative Sales Law?* (Intersentia 2013).

Philippe D., *France and Belgium*, in *Foreseen and Unforeseen Circumstances* (A.G. Castermans, K.J.O. Jansen, M. W. Knigge, P. Memelink & J. H. Nieuwenhuis, Kluwer, 2012).

Phillips B., *Examining the Future of Long-Term Take or Pay contracts*, 3 O.G.L.T.R, 73 (1997).

Pino A., *La eccessiva onerosità della prestazione* (Giuffrè 1952).

Polkinghorne M., *Changes of Circumstances as a Price Modifier*, in *Gas Price Arbitration* (M. Levy, Global Law and Business 2014).

Polkinghorne M., *Take-or-pay Conditions in Gas Supply Agreements*, http://www.whitecase.com/sites/whitecase/files/files/download/publications/paris-energy-series-no7_2016.pdf (2013).

Polkinghorne M., *Predicting the Unpredictable: Gas Price re-openers*, http://documents.jdsupra.com/673d6d07-c6ad-4c11-b85a-2204fd15cfe4.pdf (2011).

Powell R., *Good Faith in Contracts*, 9 C.L.P., 16 (1956).

Poznanski B.G., *The Nature and Extent of an Arbitrator's Powers in International Commercial Arbitration*, 4, J.Int'l Arb., 71 (1987).

Puelinckx A. H., *Frustration, Hardship, Force Majeure, Imprèvision, Wegfall der Geschaftsgrundlage, Unmoglichkeit, Changed Circumstances* 3 J.Int'l Arb., 47 (1986).

Quadri E., *La rettifica del contratto* (Giuffrè 1973).

Ramberg C., *Obligations, Contracts and Sales*, in *Swedish Legal System/Contract Law and Obligations* (M. Bogdan, Norstedts Juridik 2010).

Ramberg C., *Sweden*, 12 ERCL, 506 (2006).

Redfern A. & Hunter M., *International Arbitration* (Oxford University Press 2015).

Renard C., *La théorie de l'imprévision dans les contrats*, II R.D.I.D.C., 17 (1950).

Rivkin D. W., *Lex Mercatoria and Force Majeure*, in *Transnational Rules in International Commercial Arbitration* (E. Gaillard, International Chamber of Commerce 1993).

Roberts P., *Gas Sales and Gas Transportation Agreements* (Sweet&Maxwell 2011).

Roberts P., *Petroleum Contracts - English Law and Practice* (Oxford University Press 2013).

Rosler H., *Hardship in German Codified Private Law - In Comparative Perspective to English, French and International Contract Law*, 3 E.R.P.L. 483 (2007).

Sacco R. & De Nova G., *Il contratto* (UTET 2016).

Sanders P., *Quo Vadis Arbitration?* (Kluwer Law International 1999).

Sanders P., *Arbitration*, in *International Encyclopedia of Comparative Law* vol. XVI, Ch. 12, 70 (Mauro Cappelletti, Mohor Siebeck 1987).

Santoro Passarelli F., *La transazione* (Jovene 1963).

Sarzana S., *The rise of price revision arbitrations*, https://www.cdr-news.com/categories/expert-views/european-energy-disputes:-the-rise-of-price-revision-arbitrations (31 October 2012).

Savatier J., *La théorie de l'imprèvision dans les contrats*, II Études de droit contemporain, 1 (1959).

Schmitthoff C. M., *Hardship and Intervener Clauses*, J.B.L. (1980).

Scott K., *Contract-Repudiation-Performance by Innocent Party*, 1 C.L.J., 12 (1962).

Sekolec J. & Eliasson N., *The UNCITRAL Model Law on Arbitration and the Swedish Arbitration Act: A Comparison*, in *The Swedish Arbitration Act of 1999, Five Years On* (L. Heuman & S. Jarvin, Jurisnet 2006).

Sirianni S. J., *The Developing Law of Contractual Impracticability and Impossibility: Part 1*, 14 U.C.C.L.J., 55 (1981).

Spallon C., *Edison-Gazprom Pricing Dispute at an End*, http://globalarbitrationreview.com/article/1033884/edison-gazprom-pricing-dispute-at-an-end (19 November 2014).

Speidel R. E., *Court Imposed Adjustment Under Long-Term, Supply Contracts*, 76 N.Y.U.L.Rev., 369 (1981).

Stanic A. & Weale G., *Changes in the European Gas Market and Price Review Arbitration*, in 25 J.E.R.L., (2007).

Steiner E., *French Law - A Comparative Approach* (Oxford University Press 2010).

Stern J. P., *European Gas Markets* (The Royal Institute of International Affairs 1990).

Stern J. P., *The Future of Russian Gas and Gazprom* (Oxford University Press 2005).

Stern J. P., *Is There a Rationale for the Continuing Link to Oil Product Prices in Continental European Long-Term Gas Contracts*, https://www.oxfordenergy.org/wpcms/wpcontent/uploads/2010/11/NG19IsThereARationaleFortheContinuingLinkToOilProductPricesinContinentalEuropeanLongTermGasContracts-JonathanStern-2007.pdf, 1 (2007).

Stern J. P., *Continental European Long-Term Gas Contracts: is a transition away from oil product-linked pricing inevitable and imminent?*, https://www.oxfordenergy.org/wpcms/wpcontent/uploads/2010/11/NG34ContinentalEuropeanLongTermGasContractsIsATransitionAwayFromOilProductLinkedPricingInevitableandImminent-JonathanStern-2009.pdf, 1 (2009).

Stern J. P., *The Transition to Hub-Based Gas Pricing in Continental Europe*, https://www.oxfordenergy.org/wpcms/wp-content/uploads/2011/03/NG49.pdf, 1 (2011).

Sutton D. J., Gill J. & Gearing M., *Russell On Arbitration* (Sweet & Maxwell 2007).

Terranova C. G., *L'eccessiva onerosità nei contratti*, in *Il Codice Civile - Commentario* (P. Schlesinger, Giuffrè 1995).

Treitel G. H., *The Law of Contract* (Sweet & Maxwell 2011).

Uribe R. A. M., *The Effect of a Change of Circumstances on the Binding Force of Contracts* (Intersentia 2011).

van den Berg A., *The Application of the New York Convention by the Courts*, in *Improving the Efficiency of Arbitration Agreements and Awards: 40 Years of Application of the New York Convention* (A. van den Berg, ICCA Congress Series n. 9 1999).

van den Berg A., Van Delden R. & Snijders H. J., *Netherlands Arbitration Law* (Kluwer Law and Taxation Publishers 1993).

Van der Bend B., Leijten M. & Ynzonides M., *A Guide to the NAI Arbitration Rules: Including a Commentary on Dutch Arbitration Law* (Kluwer Law International 2009).

van der Hoeven M., Kraven M., van der Leemput B., *The Nehterlands: the energy hub of Europe*, Oil & Gas Financial Journal, 1 (2010).

Veneziano A., *UNIDROIT Principles and CISG: Change of Circumstances and Duty to Renegotiate according to the Belgian Supreme Court*, Revue de Droit Uniforme, 137 (2010).

von Mehren G., *The Arbitrator's Role*, in *Gas Price Arbitration* (M. Levy, Global Law and Business 2014).

Webber C., *The Evolution of the Gas Industry in the UK*, in *International Gas Union Magazine*, April 2010, 198.

White J. J. & Peters D.A., *Essay: A footnote for Jack Dawson*, 100 Mich.L.Rev., 1973 (2002).

Whitford W. C., *Ian Macneil's Contribution to Contracts Scholarship*, Wis.L.Rev., 545 (1985).

Wightman J., *Good Faith and Pluralism in the Law of Contract*, in *Good Faith in Contract* (R. Brownsword, N. J. Hird & G. Howells, Ashgate/Dartmouth 1999).

Williams I., *The Sources of Law in the Swiss Civil Code* (Oxford University Press 1923).

Williams T. I., *A History of the British Gas Industry* (Oxford University Press 1981).

Zaccaria E. C., *L'adattamento dei contratti a lungo termine nell'esperienza giuridica statunitense: aspirazioni teoriche e prassi giurisprudenziale*, 2 Contratto Impresa, 478 (2006).

Zaccaria E. C., *The Effects of Changed Circumstances in International Commercial Trade*, International Trade & Business Law Review, 145 (2005).

Zimmermann R. & Whittaker S., *Good Faith in European Contract Law* (Cambridge University Press 2000).

Conferences, Reports and Studies

American Petroleum Institute, *Understanding Natural Gas Markets*, www.api.org (2014).

Catala P., *Proposal for Reform of the Law of Obligations and the Law of Prescription*, http://www.justice.gouv.fr/art_pix/rapportcatatla0905-anglais.pdf (2005).

DNV KEMA Energy & Sustainability in collaboration with COWI Belgium, *Study on LT-ST Markets in Gas*, www.ec.europa.eu (2013).

GAR News Report, *Gas price reviews: is arbitration the problem*, http://globalarbitrationreview.com/article/1033224/gas-price-reviews-is-arbitration-the-problem (6 March 2014).

ICC Conference on Force Majeure and Hardship (Paris 8 March 2001), 6 Unif.L.Rev., 104 (2001).

ICCA Fifth International Arbitration Congress on Arbitration (New Delhi on 10 January 1975), www.arbitration-icca.org.

International Energy Agency (IEA), *Natural Gas Pricing in Competitive Markets* (IEA 1998).

McNair Chambers, *LNG Price Review Disputes*, http://www.mcnairchambers.com/client/publications/2013/LNG_PRICE_REVIEW_DISPUTES_.pdf (10 December 2013).

Russian Today Report, https://www.rt.com/business/343286-gazprom-europe-supplies-price/ (17 May 2016).

United Nations, *document A/CN.9/264 (Analytical Commentary on Draft Text of a Model Law on International Commercial Arbitration)*, as cited in 1985 XVI UNCITRAL Yearbook Part Two, para. I.B., 125.

Us Energy Information Administration, 2014 Report, www.eia.gov.

Table of Cases

Arbitration Award

Arbitration Tribunal of the Netherlands Oils, Fats and Oilseeds Trade Association, 1977 II YBCA, 156 (10 September 1975), **129**
Atlantic LNG Company of Trinidad and Tobago v. Gas Natural Aprovisionamentos, unpublished (final arbitration award 17th January 2008), **81**
Cosarma v. Agip, I 1974 Giur It, 280 (domestic arbitration award 28 February 1972), **115**
Edison v. Promgaz, unpublished (August 2014), **193**
Edison v. Sonatrach, unpublished (April 2013), **194**
Edison v. Eni, unpublished (October 2012), **194**
Edison v. Rasgas, unpublished (September 2012), **194**
F.R. German v. Polish Buyer, 1987 XII YBCA, 63 (9 September 1983), **100**
Gazprom v. RWE, unpublished (June 2013), **193**
GNA v. Atlantic, www.westlaw.com (S.D.N.Y. 16 September 2008), **175**
ICC case n. 13504/2007, 2009 20 ICC Int'l Ct.Arb.Bull., 93 (2007), **177**
ICC case n. 10351/2001, 2009 20 ICC Int'l Ct.Arb.Bull., 76 (partial award 2001), **162, 169**
ICC case n. 9994/2001, 2005 ICC Int'l Ct.Arb.Bull., 79 (2001), **91**
ICC case n. 9812/1999, 2009 20 ICC Int'l Ct.Arb.Bull., 69 (1999), **81, 82**
ICC case n. 8486/1996, 1999 XXIV YBCA, 162 (1996), **129**
ICC case n. 8420/1996, 2000 XXV YBCA, 330 (partial award 1996), **147**
ICC case n. 6162/1990, 1993 XVII YBCA, 153 (1990), **147**
ICC case n. 6149/1990, 1995 XX YBCA, 41 (1990), **147**
ICC case n. 4972/1989, Collection of ICC Arbitral Awards 1986-1990, 380 (1989), **141**
ICC case n. 5294/1988, 1989 XIV YBCA, 137 (final award 1988), **85**
ICC case n. 5754/1988 (unpublished), as cited in W. L. Craig, W.W. Park &, J.Paulsson, *International Chamber of Commerce Arbitration* vol. 3, 112 (Oceana Publications 1990), **146**
ICC case n. 5505/1987, 1988 XIII YBCA, 110 (preliminary award 1987), **84**
ICC case n. 5485/1987, 1989 XIV YBCA, 156 (final award 1987), **84**
ICC case n. 4761/1987, Collection of ICC Arbitral Awards 1986-1990, 519 (1980), **154**
ICC case n. 4604/1984, 1985 X YBCA, 975 (1984), **147**

Table of Cases

ICC case n. 3267/1984, 1987 YBCA, 87 (final award 1984), **139**
ICC case n. 2708/1976, Collection of ICC Arbitral Awards 1974–1985, 297 (1976), **90**
ICC case n. 2508/1976, Collection of ICC Arbitral Awards 1984–1985, 292 (1976), **102, 163**
ICC case n. 3267/1975, Collection of ICC Arbitral Awards 1974–1985, 76 (partial award 1975), **138**
ICC case n. 2404/1975, Collection of ICC Arbitral Awards 1974–1985, 280 (1975), **139**
ICC case n. 2291/1975, Collection of ICC Arbitral Awards 1974–1985, 274 (1975), **153, 154**
ICC case n. 1512/1971, Collection of ICC Arbitral Awards 1974–1985, 3 (1971), **104, 130, 139**
Quintette Coal v. Japanese Steel Companies, unpublished (28 May 1990), **185**
Wigan Athletic AFC v. Heart of Midlothian 26 ASA Bull., 513 (final award 30 January 2008), **85**

Court Decisions

Australia

Andrews and Others v. Australia and New Zealand Banking Group, http://eresources.hcourt.gov.au/downloadPdf/2012/HCA/30 (HCA 6th September 2012), **61**
Paciocco v. Australia and New Zealand Banking Group Limited, http://eresources.hcourt.gov.au/downloadPdf/2016/HCA/28 (HCA 27 July 2016), **62**

Belgium

Company M v. M SA, 1989 XIV YBCA, 618 (Court of Appeal of Brussels 4 October 1985), **147**
Cour de Cassation 20 April 2006, www.juridat.be., **95**
Cour de Cassation 4 September 2000 www.juridat.be., **95**
Cour de Cassation 14 April 1994, 1994–1995 R. W., 434, **95**
Cour de Cassation,7 February 1994, -1995 in R. W., 121, **95**
Court of Appeal of Antwerp 6 May 1987, 1990 Tijds Belg Burger R, 299, **95**
Court of First Instance of Brussels, 1994 JLMB, 358, **95**
Lorrain Tubes v. Scafom International, as cited in the decision of the *Cour de Cassation* 29 June 2009, http://cisgw3.law.pace.edu/cases/090619b1.html (Court of Appeal of Antwerp 15February 2007), **96**
Matermaco v. PPM Cranes, 2000 XXV YBCA, 673 (Tribunal of Commerce of Brussels 20 September 1999), **147**
Scafom International v. Lorrain Tubes, http://cisgw3.law.pace.edu/cases/090619b1.html (*Cour de Cassation* 29 June 2009), **96**
Scafom International v. Lorrain Tubes, http://cisgw3.law.pace.edu/cases/050125b1.html, 12 (Commercial Court of Torengen 25 January 2005), **96**

Canada

Bashin v. Hrynew, https://scc-csc.lexum.com/scc-csc/scc-csc/en/item/14438/index.do (Supreme Court 13 November 2013), **154**

France

Bacou v. Saint Pé, as cited in H. Beale, B. Fauvarque-Cosson, J. Rutgers, D. Tallon &, S. Vogenauer, *Cases, Materials and Text on Contract Law,* Hart Publishing, 2010, as cited in H. Beale, B. Fauvarque-Cosson, J. Rutgers, D. Tallon &, S. Vogenauer, *Cases, Materials and Text on Contract Law* (Hart Publishing 2010), 1132 (*Cour de Cassation* 6 June 1921), **91**

Case De Gallifet v. Commune de Pélissanne, 1131 (*Cour de Cassation* 6 March 1876), **89**

Case De Gallifet v. Commune de Pélissanne, as cited in H. Beale, B. Fauvarque-Cosson, J. Rutgers, D. Tallon &, S. Vogenauer, Cases, Materials and Text on Contract Law (Hart Publishing 2010), 1131 (Court of Appeal of Aix 31 December 1873), **90**

Compagnie du Gaz de Bordeaux, III Sirey 17 (*Cons. d'État* 20 March 1916), **89**

Cour de Cassation 18 March 2009, RTDCiv, 528, **90**

Cour de Cassation 16 March 2004, D.S., 1757, **91**

Cour de Cassation 24 November 1998, IV Bull.C.C., 232, **91**

Cour de Cassation 30 May 1996, https://www.legifrance.gouv.fr/affichJuriJudi.do?idTexte=JURITEXT000007304993, **90**

Cour de Cassation 18 December 1979, 339 Bull.C.C., **90**

Electricité de France v. Shell France, 1978 J.C.P., 18810 (Paris Court of Appeal 28 September 1976), **92**

Intrafor Cofor v. Gagnant, Revue de l'Arbitrage, 299 (Court of Appeal of Paris 12 March 1985).

Novacarb v. Socoma, 2008 J.C.P., 10091 (Court of Appeal of Nancy 26 September 2007), **92**

Société française des pétroles v. Huard, II 1993 J.C.P., 22614 (*Cour de Cassation* 3 November 1992), **91**

Soffimat v. Sec, https://www.legifrance.gouv.fr/affichJuriJudi.do?idTexte=JURITEXT000022430481 on www.legifrance.gouv.fr.(*Cour de Cassation* 29 June 2010), **91**

Soffimat et Mayennecogen v. Laitière de Mayenne, https://www.legifrance.gouv.fr/affichJuriJudi.do?oldAction=rechJuriJudi&idTexte=JURITEXT000007508427&fastReqId=1786293691&fastPos=1 (*Cour de Cassation* 3 October 2006), **90**

Styrpac v. Gaz de France, (Court of Appeal of Angers, n. 04/01783 15 June 2005), as cited in M. Polkinghorne, *Take-or-pay Conditions in Gas Supply Agreements,* http://www.whitecase.com/sites/whitecase/files/files/download/publications/paris-energy-series-no7_2016.pdf Paris Energy Series No. 7, April (2013), **36**

Table of Cases

Germany

Bundesgerichtshof 8 February 2006, VIII BIZR, 304, **121**
Bundesgerichtshof 14 October 1992, as cited in H. Beale, B. Fauvarque-Cosson, J. Rutgers, D. Tallon &, S. Vogenauer, Cases, Materials and Text on Contract Law, 1144 (Hart Publishing, 2010), **124**
Bundesgerichtshof 16 January 1953, as cited in H. Beale, B. Fauvarque-Cosson, J. Rutgers, D. Tallon & S. Vogenauer, *Cases, Materials and Text on Contract Law*, 1142 (Hart Publishing 2010), **124**
Reichsgericht 27 June 1922, RGZ, 103, **124**
Reichsgericht 3 February 1922, RGZ, 103, **123**
Reichsgericht 21 September 1920, RGZ, 100, **123**
Reichsgericht 15 October 1918, RGZ, 45, **123**

Hong Kong

Philips Hong Kong v. Attorney General of Hong Kong, 61 BLR 49 (JCPC 9 February 1993), **38**

India

National Thermal Power v. The Singer, 1993 XVIII YBCA, 403 (Indian Supreme Court 7 May 1992), **85**

Italy

A.G. et al. v. Renault Italia et al., I Giust.civ., 2671 (*Corte di Cassazione* n. 20106 18 September 2009), **119**
Annoni v. Salvia, I 1985 Giur It, 362 (*Corte di Cassazione* n. 275 13 January 1984), **115**
Caccamo v. Teglia, 3 Obbligazioni e Contratti, 476 (*Corte di Cassazione* n. 8071 28 March 2008), **64**
Corte di Cassazione n. 1067 24 March 1976, I Giust.civ., 1493, **115**
Corte di Cassazione n. 2748 18 September 1972, I Giust.civ., 1886, **115**
Ditta Autocori v. Società Demaca, 2008 XII Giust.civ., 2807 (*Corte di Cassazione* n. 23726 15 November 2007), **119**
Fincantieri v. Ministry of Defence of Iraq, 1996 XXI YBCA, 494 (Court of Appeal of Genoa 7th May 1994), **147**
Helios Technology s.p.a. v. Jiangxi LDK Solar Hi-Tech Co. Ltd, unpublished (16 January 2013 Court of Appeal of Venice), **64**
Officina Meccanica di Crosta Mario v. Tintorie Milano di Cozzi & C., Foro Pad., 80 (Court of Appeal of Milan 4 July 1950), **115**
Moscatiello v. Cerbo, Rep.Foro.It., "Contratto in genere", n. 359 (Corte di Cassazione n. 5922 25 May 1991), **117**
Pagnan v. Butera, 1979 I Giur It, 407 (*Corte di Cassazione* n. 416 18 September 1978), **121**

Pamedil v. Bruno, Giur It, 2279 (Corte di Cassazione n. 46 5 January 2000), **114**
Prisco v. Palumbo, I Giust.civ., 1630 (*Corte di Cassazione* n. 1720 27th February 1985), **118**
Privitera v. Borsato, I 1993 Giur It, 2018 (*Corte di Cassazione* n. 247 11 January 1992), **115**
Rocco v. Federal Commerce and Navigation, 1983 Dir Marit, 774 (Corte di Cassazione n. 6915 15th December 1982), **121**
SEB v. Van Raaij Voertuigen, 1992 Riv Dir Intern Priv & Proc, 574 (Tribunal of Milan 11th November 1991), **121**
Sidoti v. Condominio via Di Castro 25 Roma, I Foro It, 2985 (*Corte di Cassazione* n. 18128 13 September 2005), **64**
Società azionaria per la condotta di acque potabili v. Comune di Torino, I 1960 Foro It, 565 (Corte di Cassazione n. 224, 27th January 1959), **115**
Società immobiliare Bravetta v. Barrese, I 1990 Giur It (Corte di Cassazione n. 4023 11 January 1989), **115**
Tre Monti Residence v. F.M., 3 Obbligazioni e Contratti, 260 (*Corte di Cassazione* n. 21066 28 September 2006), **64**
Valentini v. Mantovani, I Giust.civ., 2564 (*Corte di Cassazione* n. 3347 18th July 1989), **115**
Vettese v. Condominio via Pessina 66, Napoli, I 1987 Foro It, 2177 (*Corte di Cassazione* n. 6584 11 November 1986), **115**

Jamaica

Workers Trust & Merchant Bank v. Dojap Investments, 2 All ER 370 (JCPC 22nd February 1993), **47**

Russia

Supreme Commercial Court of the Russian Federation, Order n. VAS-6632/09, (28 May 2009), as cited in M. Polkinghorne, *Take-or-pay Conditions in Gas Supply Agreements*, in http://www.whitecase.com/sites/whitecase/files/files/download/publications/paris-energy-series-no7_2016.pdf (2013,), **35**

Sweden

Moscow City Golf Club v. Nordea Bank, https://www.arbitration.sccinstitute.com/Views/Pages/GetFile.ashx?portalId=89&cat=79572&docId=1450921&propId=1578, 5–6 (Supreme Court n. T 4982-11 23rd November 2012), **148**

Switzerland

Belgische Sceehpvaartmaatschappij-Compagnie Maritime Belge v. Distrigas, 20 ASA Bull., 493.(Swiss Federal Tribunal 19 December 2001), **102**

Table of Cases

Swiss Federal Tribunal 10 October 1933, as cited in R. Schlesinger, U. Mattei, T. Ruskola &, A. Gidi, *Comparative Law*, 964 (Foundation Press, 2009), **101**

V. v. G., 1993 XVIII YBCA, 143 (Swiss Federal Tribunal 28 April 1992), **147**

The Netherlands

NJA case 1983, as cited in C. Ramberg, *Sweden*, 12 ERCL, 506 (2006) and in B. Lehrberg, *Unexpected Circumstances - National Report from Sweden*, www.unexpected-circumstances.org (2005), **131**

UK

Alder v. Moore, 2 QB, 57 (EWCA Civ 18th November 1960), **46**
AMEV-UDC Finance v. Austin, 162 CLR 170, 193 (HCA 4 November 1986), **38**
Appleby v. Myers, 3 B.& S., 826 (EWHC (QB) 21 June 1867), **103**
Attica Sea Carriers v. Ferrostaal Poseidon Bulk Reederei, The Puerto Buitrago, 1 Lloyd's Rep., 250 (EWCA Civ 1 January 1976), **44**
Azimut-Benetti v. Healey, http://www.bailii.org/ew/cases/EWHC/Comm/2010/2234.html, (EWHC (QB) 3 September 2010), **38**
Beckham v. Drake, 2 Cl.&F. 579, 622 (UKHL 11 July 1849), **41**
Bristol Groundschool v. Intelligent Data Capture, http://www.bailii.org/ew/cases/EWHC/Ch/2014/2145.html (EWHC (Ch) 2 July 2014), **154**
Britishmovietonews v. London and District Cinemas, 1952 AC, 166 (UKHL 26th July 1951), **105**
Campbell Discount v. Bridge, 2 All ER, 97 (EWCA Civ 1 March 1961), **47**
Campbell Discount v. Bridge, 1 All ER 385 (UKHL 25 January 1962), **47**
Cavendish Square Holding BV v. Talal El Makdessi, https://www.supremecourt.uk/cases/uksc-2013-0280.html (UKSC 4 November 2015), **40**
Compagnie Tunisienne de Navigation v. Compagnie d'Armement Maritime, AC, 572 (UKHL 1971), **85**
Coneco v. Foxboro Great Britain, LEXIS (EWCA Civ 24 February 1992), **36**
Davis Contractors v. Fareham Urban DC, 1 AC, 696 (UKHC 19 April 1956), **104**
Dunlop Pneumatic Tyre v. New Garage and Motor, 1915 AC, 79 (UKHL 1st July 1914), **36**
E-Nik v. Department for Communities and Local Government, http://www.bailii.org/ew/cases/EWHC/Comm/2012/3027.html (EWHC (QB) 2 November 2012), **35**
Esso Exploration & Production UK v. Electricity Supply Board, as cited in M. Levy, *Gas Price Arbitration* (Global Law and Business 2014), 157 (EWHC (QB) 31st March 2004), **189**
Export Credits Guarantee Department v. Universal Oil Products, 2 All ER, 205 (UKHL 1983), **46**
Gator Shipping v. Trans-Asiatic Oil, The Odenfeld, 2 Lloyd's Rep., 357 (UKHL 1 January 1978), **44**
General Trading v. Richmond Corporation, 2 Lloyd's Rep., 475 (EWHC (QB) 3 July 2008), **39**

Table of Cases

Hyundai Heavy Industries v. Papadopoulos, 2 All ER, 29 (EWCA Civ 1980), **44**

J. Lauritzen v. Wijsmuller, The Super Servant Two, 1 Lloyd's Rep., 1 (EWCA 12 October 1989), **154**

Jeancharm v. Barnet Football Club, 92 Con LR, 26 (EWCA Civ 16 January 2003), **48**

Jobson v. Johnson, 1 Weekly Law Reports 1026 (EWCA Civ 25 May 1988), **40**

Krell v. Henry, 2 K.B., 740 (EWCA 11 August 1903), **103**

M&J Polymers v. Imerys Minerals, http://www.bailii.org/ew/cases/EWHC/Comm/2008/344.html (EWHC (QB) 29th February 2008), **35**

Mid-Essex Hospital Services NHS Trust v. Compass Group UK and Ireland, http://www.bailii.org/ew/cases/EWCA/Civ/2013/200.html (EWCA 15 March 2013), **154**

Murray v. Leisureplay, http://www.bailii.org/ew/cases/EWCA/Civ/2005/963.html (EWCA Civ 28th July 2005), **38**

Naviera Amazonica Peruana v. Compania Internacional de Seguros del Peru, 1988 1 Lloyd's Rep.,116 (EWCA 10 November 1987), **84**

Paradine v. Jane, Aleyn's Reports, 26 (EWHC (KB) 26 March 1647), **103**

ParkingEye Limited v. Beavis, https://www.supremecourt.uk/cases/uksc-2013-0280.html (UKSC 4 November 2015), **40**

President of India v. Lips Maritime, AC 395 (UKHL 29th July 1987), **43**

Re Park Air Services v. Bairstow, 1 All ER, 673 (UKHL 4 February 1999), **42**

Reichman v. Beveridge, http://www.bailii.org/ew/cases/EWCA/Civ/2006/1659.html, (EWCA Civ 13 December 2006), **45**

Robophone Facilities v. Blank, 1 WLR 1428, 1446–1447 (EWCA Civ 1 January 1966), **39**

Superior Overseas Development v. British Gas, 1982 1 Lloyd's Rep., 262 (EWHC (QB) 27 March 1981), **105**

Tamplin Steamship v. Anglo-Mexican Petroleum, 2 AC, 39 (EWCA 1 January 1916), **104**

Taylor v. Caldwell, 3 B.& S., 826 (EWHC (QB) 6 May 1863), **103**

Tennants (Lancashire) v. C S Wilson & Co, AC, 495 (UKHL 21 July 1917), **105**

Thames Valley Power v. Total Power Gas, 2006 1 Lloyd's Rep. 441, (EWHC (QB) 27 September 2005), **106**

Tullett Prebon Group Ltd. v. Ghaleb El-Hajjali, http://www.bailii.org/ew/cases/EWHC/QB/2008/1924.html (EWHC 31 July 2008), **39**

Yam Seng v. International Trade, 1 Lloyd's Rep., 526 (EWHC (QB) 1 February 2013), **154**

W F Tatem v. Gamboa, 1 K.B., 132 (1939), **104**

White & Carter (Councils) v. McGregor, AC, 413 (UKHL 6 December 1961), **44**

US

Aluminium Company of America v. Essex Group, 499 F.Supp., 53 (W.D. Pa. 1980), **108**

American Diagnostica v. Gradipore, Centerchem, 1999 XXIV YBCA, 574 (NSW Supreme Court 26 March 1998), **85**

Colorado Interstate Gas Company v. Chemco, 854 P.2d, 1232 (Colo. 14 June 1993), **36**

Executone Info. Sys. v. Davis, 26 F.3d,1314 (5th Cir. 12 July 1994), **112**

Florida Power & Light v. Westinghouse Electric, 485 U.S., 1021 (5th Cir. April 1986), **111**

Table of Cases

International Minerals and Chemical v. Llano, 770 F.2d, 879 (10th Cir. 9 August 1985), **33**

Iowa Electric Light & Power v. Atlas, 654 F.2d, 704 (8th Cir. 30 June 1981), **108**

Karaha Bodas v. Perusahaan Pertambangan Minyak Dan Gas Bumi Negara, 364 F.3d., 274 (5th Cir. 23 March 2004), **84**

Lake River v. Carborundum, 769 F.2d 1284 (7th Cir. 9 August 1985), **35**

Louisiana Power & Light v. Allegheny Ludlum Industries, 517 F.Supp., 1319 (E.D. La. 7 July 1981), **107**

McGinnis v. Cayton, 312 S.E.2d, 765 (W. Va. 27 January 1984), **111**

Mineral Park Land v. P.A. Howard, 172 Cal., 289 (Cal. 13 March 1916), **106**

Northern Illinois Gas v. Energy Co-operative, 461 N.E.2d, 1049 (Ill. App. Ct. 27 March 1984), **107**

Phillips Petroleum v. Wisconsin, 347 U.S., 672 (U.S. 7 June 1954), **14**

Prenalta v. Colorado Interstate Gas, 944 F.2d, 677 (10th 4 September 1991), **36**

Roye Realty & Developing v. Arkla, 863 P.2d 1150 (Okla. 13 July 1993), **36**

Steel Corporation of Philippines v. International Steel Services, 354 Federal Appendix, 689 (3d Cir. 19 November 2009), **85**

Timegate Studios v. Gamecock Media Group, http://www.ca5.uscourts.gov/opinions%5Cpub%5C12/12-20256-CV0.wpd.pdf (5th Cir. 9 April 2013), **111**

Unihealth v. US Healthcare, 14 F.Supp.2d, 623 (D.N.J. 10th July 1998), **111**

Universal Resources v. Panhandle Eastern Pipe Line, 813 F.2d 77 (5th 31 March 1987), **36**

W.R. Grace v. Local Union 759, 461 U.S., 1983, 757 (U.S. 31 May 1983), **107**

Index

A

Adaptation and adjustment of the contract, 1, 74, 78, 80, 97, 98, 102, 108, 109, 122, 130, 135–137, 139, 145, 149, 150, 159, 161, 176, 180, 192
Adaptation clause, xi, xii, 26, 32, 71–194
Algeria, 8, 20, 141
American Arbitration Association, 138, 145, 159
Annual contract quantity. *See* Take or pay
Arbitrability, xi, xii, 75, 78, 144–150, 167, 169
Arbitration rules, 137–138, 159, 160, 173, 174, 194
Australia, 61

B

Belgium, 3, 4, 11, 141

C

Carry-forward clauses. *See* Take or pay
CEPANI, 137, 160
Civil law, 35, 41, 62–65, 67, 77, 133, 149
Common law, 35–54, 60–62, 65–67, 77, 78, 102–114, 133, 149, 175, 187, 188

D

Debts and damages. *See* Take or pay

E

Equilibrium, xi, 33, 67, 69–74, 79, 83, 89, 98, 109, 110, 113, 115, 119, 121, 123, 130, 138, 153, 157, 164–166, 168, 169, 183

F

France, 3, 4, 20, 92
Frustration of the contract, 104

G

Gas market, xii, 1–29, 80, 173, 177, 184, 185
Gas sale agreements, xi, xii, 1, 2, 8, 13, 31–33, 35, 48, 53, 54, 56, 58–62, 64, 65, 67, 69–194
Germany, 3, 4, 12, 19, 27, 123–125, 149
Good faith, 70, 72, 73, 81, 83, 91–94, 97, 98, 100, 107, 113, 118–120, 122–127, 131, 133, 135–137, 141–144, 153–159, 163–166, 168, 169, 171–174, 176, 177, 183, 186, 189, 192

H

Hardship, xii, 32, 71, 74, 76, 77, 79–84, 91, 93–99, 102, 105, 106, 109, 114, 118–121, 124, 125, 127–129, 132, 133, 135, 137, 138, 149–151, 154, 155, 165, 167, 170, 175, 186, 187

213

Index

I

Impossibility, 100, 103, 106, 122, 123
Impracticability, 78, 106–109, 149–151, 175, 188
International Chamber of Commerce (ICC), 64, 81, 91, 104, 129, 137–139, 141, 143, 144, 169–172, 177–185, 193
Italy, 3, 20, 64

L

London Court of International Arbitration (LCIA), 144, 145
Long-term, xi, xii, 1–3, 11–13, 15–17, 19–21, 23–28, 31–33, 54, 55, 65–67, 69–194

M

Main obligations. *See* Take or pay
Make-good clauses. *See* Take or pay
Make-up clauses. *See* Take or pay
Minimum Bill Quantity/Take or Pay Quantity. *See* Take or pay
Model Law, 85, 86, 187

N

The Netherlands, 3–5, 27, 149
Norwegian, 3, 11–13, 21

O

Onerousness, 78, 114, 117, 149

P

Penalties. *See* Take or pay
Price review, xii, 7, 20, 26, 32, 74, 79–84, 95, 96, 99, 105, 109, 125, 138, 167, 170, 172, 173, 177–187, 189–191, 193, 194
Principles, xii, 6, 10, 12, 38–40, 46, 49, 50, 53, 54, 61, 62, 67, 70, 72–78, 81, 83–85, 89–99, 101–103, 105–108, 110, 112, 113, 115–120, 122–127, 129–131, 133–144, 146, 150, 152–161, 163–166, 168, 169, 171, 172, 174, 176, 177, 183, 186, 188, 191–193
Principles of European Contract Law (PECL), 83, 84, 165, 166
Procedural law, xi, xii, 1, 75, 76, 78, 84, 85, 88, 89, 122, 132–137, 144, 147, 150, 151, 168, 170, 174, 178, 187

R

Relational contract, 157, 162, 163
Renegotiation of the contract, 80, 98
Russia, 18, 19

S

Scope of arbitration agreement, 144–150, 169, 188, 189
Spot market, xii, 2, 3, 8, 11–13, 16, 17, 19, 21–29, 31, 77
Substantive law, 76, 121, 127–129, 135–137
Sweden, 149
Switzerland, 77, 99–102, 133, 139, 141-143, 148, 149, 170

T

Take or pay, xi, xii, 1, 7, 10, 12, 15–17, 19–21, 23, 27, 28, 31–70, 73, 80, 107, 146, 151, 165, 168, 193
Termination of the contract, 34, 70, 91, 94, 102, 103, 108, 109, 114, 115, 133, 138, 140, 141, 144, 155, 175, 188

U

UNCITRAL, 85, 137, 172–174, 187

Unforeseen and supervening events, xi, 1, 26, 31, 33, 67, 69–74, 77–79, 84, 88, 89, 91–99, 102–109, 111, 113, 114, 116, 120–133, 136, 138–140, 143, 144, 146, 149–152, 155, 157, 162, 165–169, 172, 176, 183

United Kingdom (UK), 2, 3, 8–12, 20, 22, 24, 25, 27, 28, 31, 47, 189, 190

United States (US), xii, 2, 3, 13–17, 20–22, 24, 25, 27, 28, 31, 54, 59, 61, 66, 77, 78, 80, 84, 91, 106, 110, 133, 143, 149, 162, 175, 187

INTERNATIONAL ARBITRATION LAW LIBRARY

1. Moshe Hirsch, *The Arbitration Mechanism of the International Center for the Settlement of Investment Disputes*, 1993 (ISBN 07-923-1993-1).
2. Aida B. Avanessian, *Iran-United States Claims Tribunal in Action*, 1993 (ISBN 18-533-3902-4).
3. Isaak I. Dore, *The UNCITRAL Framework for Arbitration in Contemporary Perspective*, 1993 (ISBN 18-533-3573-8).
4. Vesna Lazić, *Insolvency Proceedings and Commercial Arbitration*, 1998 (ISBN 90-411-1115-8).
5. Joachim Frick, *Arbitration in Complex International Contracts*, 2001 (ISBN 90-411-1662-1).
6. Katherine Lynch, *The Forces of Economic Globalization: Challenges to the Regime of International Commercial Arbitration*, 2003 (ISBN 90-411-1994-9).
7. Christoph Liebscher, *The Healthy Award: Challenge in International Commercial Arbitration*, 2003 (ISBN 90-411-2011-4).
8. Hamid G. Gharavi, *The International Effectiveness of the Annulment of an Arbitral Award*, 2003 (ISBN 90-411-1717-2).
9. Abdulhay Sayed, *Corruption in International Trade and Commercial Arbitration*, 2004 (ISBN 90-411-2236-2).
10. Gabrielle Kaufmann-Kohler & Thomas Schultz, *Online Dispute Resolution: Challenges for Contemporary Justice*, 2004 (ISBN 90-411-2318-0).
11. Christopher R. Drahozal & Richard W. Naimark (eds), *Towards a Science of International Arbitration: Collected Empirical Research*, 2005 (ISBN 90-411-2322-9).
12. Ali Yeilirmak, *Provisional Measures in International Commercial Arbitration*, 2005 (ISBN 90-411-2353-9).
13. Christian Bühring-Uhle, *Arbitration and Mediation in International Business*, second revised edition, 2006 (ISBN 978-9-041-12256-8).
14. Bernard Hanotiau, *Complex Arbitrations: Multiparty, Multicontract, Multiissue and Class Actions*, 2006 (ISBN 978-9-041-12442-5).
15. Loukas A. Mistelis & Julian D.M. Lew (eds), *Pervasive Problems in International Arbitration*, 2006 (ISBN 978-9-041-12450-0).
16. Julian D.M. Lew & Loukas A. Mistelis (eds), *Arbitration Insights – Twenty Years of the Annual Lecture of the School of International Arbitration, Sponsored by Freshfields Bruckhaus Deringer*, 2006 (ISBN 978-9-041-12606-1).
17. Mark Kantor, *Valuation for Arbitration: Compensation Standards, Valuation Methods and Expert Evidence*, 2008 (ISBN 978-9-041-12735-8).
18. Christoph Brunner, *Force Majeure and Hardship under General Contract Principles: Exemption for Non-Performance in International Arbitration*, 2009 (ISBN 978-90-411-2792-1).

19. Loukas A. Mistelis & Stavros L. Brekoulakis (eds), *Arbitrability: International & Comparative Perspectives*, 2009 (ISBN 978-90-411-2730-3).
20. Sam Luttrell, *Bias Challenges in International Commercial Arbitration: The Need for a 'Real Danger' Test*, 2009 (ISBN 978-90-411-3191-1).
21. Monique Sasson, *Substantive Law in Investment Treaty Arbitration: The Unsettled Relationship between International Law and Municipal Law*, 2010 (ISBN 978-90-411-3223-9).
22. Ileana M. Smeureanu, *Confidentiality in International Commercial Arbitration*, 2011 (ISBN 978-90-411-3226-0).
23. Won Kidane, *China-Africa Dispute Settlement: The Law, Economics and Culture of Arbitration*, 2011 (ISBN 978-90-411-3674-9).
24. Karel Daele, *Challenge and Disqualification of Arbitrators in International Arbitration*, 2012 (ISBN 978-90-411-3799-9).
25. Crina Baltag, *The Energy Charter Treaty: The Notion of Investor*, 2012 (ISBN 978-90-411-3428-8).
26. Alexandra Diehl, *The Core Standard of International Investment Protection: Fair and Equitable Treatment*, 2012 (ISBN 978-90-411-3869-9).
27. Manuel Indlekofer, *International Arbitration and the Permanent Court of Arbitration*, 2013 (ISBN 978-90-411-4766-0).
28. Günther J. Horvath & Stephan Wilske (eds), *Guerrilla Tactics in International Arbitration*, 2013 (ISBN 978-90-411-4002-9).
29. Albert Badia, *Piercing the Veil of State Enterprises in International Arbitration*, 2014 (ISBN 978-90-411-5162-9).
30. Nadja Erk, *Parallel Proceedings in International Arbitration: A Comparative European Perspective*, 2014 (ISBN 978-90-411-5264-0).
31. Simon Vorburger, *International Arbitration and Cross-Border Insolvency: Comparative Perspectives*, 2014 (ISBN 978-90-411-5419-4).
32. Ahmad Ali Ghouri, *Interaction and Conflict of Treaties in Investment Arbitration*, 2015 (ISBN 978-90-411-5417-0).
33. Reto Marghitola, *Document Production in International Arbitration*, 2015 (ISBN 978-90-411-5159-9).
34. Alfonso Gómez-Acebo, *Party-Appointed Arbitrators in International Commercial Arbitration*, 2016 (ISBN 978-90-411-6671-5).
35. Jonas von Goeler, *Third-Party Funding in International Arbitration and Its Impact on Procedure*, 2016 (ISBN 978-90-411-5015-8).
36. Dean Lewis, *The Interpretation and Uniformity of the UNCITRAL Model Law on International Commercial Arbitration: Focusing on Australia, Hong Kong and Singapore*, 2016 (ISBN 978-90-411-6700-2).
37. Stavros Brekoulakis, Julian D.M. Lew & Loukas Mistelis (eds), *The Evolution and Future of International Arbitration*, 2016 (ISBN 978-90-411-7004-0).
38. Rémy Gerbay, *The Functions of Arbitral Institutions*, 2016 (ISBN 978-90-411-6217-5).

39. Maximilian Clasmeier, *Arbitral Awards as Investments: Treaty Interpretation and the Dynamics of International Investment Law*, 2017 (ISBN 978-90-411-8357-6).
40. Tony Cole (ed.), *The Roles of Psychology in International Arbitration*, 2017 (ISBN 978-90-411-5921-2).
41. Pietro Ferrario, *The Adaptation of Long-Term Gas Sale Agreements by Arbitrators*, 2017 (ISBN 978-90-411-8232-6).